RUSSIA:

HOPES AND FEARS

*Since Prague, our last year's timid hopes of a liberaliza-
tion of Russia have gone up in smoke, perhaps for a
very long time, while our fears of a return to some
fiendish kind of Stalinism have grown immeasurably.*
—LETTER FROM A YOUNG RUSSIAN
RECEIVED BY THE AUTHOR IN SEPTEMBER 1968

ALEXANDER WERTH

SIMON AND SCHUSTER · NEW YORK

FIRST U.S. PRINTING

SBN 671-20333-9
LIBRARY OF CONGRESS CATALOG CARD NUMBER: 71-79641
DESIGNED BY EVE METZ
MANUFACTURED IN THE UNITED STATES OF AMERICA
BY AMERICAN BOOK–STRATFORD PRESS, N.Y.

*To my children,
Nancy and Nicolas*

CONTENTS

PREFACE

This book had been completed before the invasion of Czechoslovakia and was already at the printer when that tragedy occurred. I have been able to add a few pages at the end, and I have changed the title. Originally the book was called Russia at Peace *(it was intended as a companion volume to my* Russia at War, *first published in 1964). Technically, even after the invasion of Czechoslovakia, Russia was still at peace. No war had been declared on Czechoslovakia. But the very fact that, in August 1968, Russian and Czech blood (however little) was flowing in the streets of Prague made such a title singularly incongruous, if not downright offensive.*

It wasn't easy to choose a new title, but, only a few weeks later, I received a letter from a Russian friend—a young intellectual—which provided, I felt, the perfect one. The quotation from this letter, the basis of the new title, will be found on the title page. In those grim days my young friend was perhaps more pessimistic than I was; his feeling that his hopes, like those of millions of young Russian intellectuals, had been betrayed seemed more than justifiable. But I felt that his fears were exaggerated. I did not believe, nor do I now, that the invasion of Czechoslovakia would intensify in any way a return to Stalinism; this return* had, in various ways, gone on since 1965, the present Soviet leadership, and particularly Leonid Brezhnev, being much more Stalinite in the accepted sense than Nikita Khrushchev was.

When I was in the Soviet Union in 1967, nobody could have foreseen, even in his wildest dreams, a Russian invasion of Czechoslovakia a year later. Under the rule of that perfect old Stalinite Antonín Novotný, Czechoslovakia was regarded as being by far the most loyal and reliable of all the Soviet Union's allies in Eastern Europe. There were a few student disorders, but nothing to compare with those in Poland or Rumania, the former country being chronically unreliable, the latter showing some alarming signs of economic, political and diplomatic independence vis-à-vis the Soviet Union.

---

* A more correct word would be "intensification" or "revival"; Stalinism could not return, since it had never really gone, as I have shown in this book.

9

But what happened in Czechoslovakia in January 1968 was something entirely new: she was the first of Russia's allies to have rebelled ideologically *against Moscow.*

At the first sign of the rebellion, at the end of 1967, Brezhnev paid two lightning visits to Prague in a desperate effort to save Novotny. It was no good. In January Alexander Dubček took over, and when he abolished the censorship one knew that this was the most formidable challenge Russia had ever faced from any ally.

Dubček had committed against Moscow the sin against the Holy Ghost: by abolishing the censorship he was threatening to demolish that absolute conformism, above all of the press, which was the gigantic steel-and-concrete pillar on which the whole Russian bureaucratic system (whether under Stalin, Khrushchev or Brezhnev) rested. And it was clear that the arguments the Russians used to justify their hostility—disagreement with Czech economic policy, the "German menace," etc., were nothing but eyewash, intended to deceive and even scare the Russian people, who are particularly sensitive to any mention of the German menace.

By May, when I wrote to my friends in Russia, the more Stalinite of these said that I severely underrated the "hard ideological struggle" going on in Czechoslovakia, the "only socialist country which had had no emigration to speak of, and whose emigrés had remained inside the country." By August it had become clear that the Kremlin was willing to pay any price for reimposing the censorship and for abolishing all freedom of thought in Czechoslovakia, since the Dubček virus, if not killed, would have spread to the whole of Eastern Europe, and even to Moscow itself.

There has been a war. But it has not been fought over the general issue of liberalization within Communist society. It has been fought almost exclusively over the specific issue of freedom of expression, communication and discussion. And that war, as I found in Russia, is not new. It has been bitterly fought within the Soviet Union for many years.

November 1968   A.W.

Introduction

LESS THAN twenty-five years ago, the Soviet Union had to fight the most terrible war in its existence. One third of the national wealth was destroyed, and twenty million people—one tenth of the population—lost their lives. It was touch and go. Today some Soviet historians argue, without much conviction, it is true, that although in 1941 and even in 1942 the Soviet Union was admittedly in mortal danger, the socialist economy had from the very start laid the foundations of victory; which is one way of saying that if Stalin, for all his errors and crimes, had not industrialized Russia ruthlessly and at top speed in the thirteen years between 1928 and 1941 she would inevitably have been destroyed.

To the Russians today the war of 1941–45 is still a grim reality. The older people remember it only too well. The young people—those in their teens or twenties—have no direct recollection of it; but many lost their fathers and other relatives, and books, papers, magazines, films, the radio and TV never cease reminding them of the fearful years of 1941–45. Nevertheless, time is the great healer, and the young, especially those born since the war, prefer to look optimistically at the present, and into the future.

We hear about all sorts of miraculous recoveries from the war—above all, about the "economic miracle" of West Germany. But this was achieved with Marshall Plan aid and other enormous help from outside. The Soviet Union has restored, and vastly expanded, its economic strength almost without foreign help. In Franklin D. Roosevelt's time, there was much inconclusive talk about an American reconstruction loan of seven billion dollars. But when Truman took over in April 1945 the subject was dropped, though even as late as 1947, in talks with Harold Stassen, Stalin still referred to the desirability of such a loan. But the Cold War was by then in full swing, and certain Americans (and even Englishmen) thought more in terms of dropping an atom bomb on Moscow than of giving Russia seven billion dollars.

It did not come to that, though the "bomb Russia now" group was not negligible, and even Churchill, in his Llandudno speech in 1948, came very close to supporting it.

The Russians in the immediate postwar years did not panic, though they did feel angry; and they took what they thought of as the minimum number of "security" precautions. The Communist *putsch* in Czechoslovakia in February 1948, which turned her into an obedient (if terrorized) satellite and so completed the setting up of an anti-Western *cordon sanitaire* in Central and Eastern Europe, comprising East Germany, Yugoslavia, Poland, Czechoslovakia, Hungary, Rumania and Bulgaria, was one of these. True, in 1948 Yugoslavia detached herself from Stalin's monolithic bloc, but, being on the far fringe, she was expendable, though the subsequent spread of the Titoite heresy in the rest of the bloc was fought with the utmost ruthlessness.

The Berlin blockade of 1948–49 was another attempt to strengthen the *cordon sanitaire*. Thanks to the gigantic airlift organized by the Western Powers—something the Russians had not foreseen—the blockade failed. But by 1949 it no longer mattered desperately. By that year Russia already had her first atom bomb, which made any further talk of "bomb Russia now" particularly foolish. Not only that: 1949, for better or for worse, was marked by the complete triumph of the Communists in China, which at least had the advantage of striking a mighty blow at the prestige of the United States, not to mention her absurd puppet Chiang Kai-shek.

The Russian atom bomb came several years earlier than the American experts had expected. It was a product of that vast reconstruction drive that the Russians initiated, even before the end of the war in May 1945. No help came from the United States. There were some reparations from Germany, especially East Germany; there was some economic exploitation of and, in some cases, reparations from the satellite states and Finland. There was some plain war booty, and there was the usual looting, especially in East Germany. But it was very small stuff compared with what the Soviet Union needed to repair the immense devastation caused by the Germans.

What is remarkable is that, with almost no outside help and despite the fearful drought of 1946 which made 1947 a very hungry year in Russia, industrial production in 1948—three years after the war—was back to its prewar, 1940, level.

In the main, Russia had to depend on her own resources, and on the willingness of a badly underfed and desperately war-weary people to work hard. At the height of the Cold War we heard from our "Russian experts" in the West no end of Russian horror stories (and there were, of course, plenty of horrors of one kind and another—more deportations, more arrests, the Leningrad Affair of 1949, and an obscurantist drive by the Party which wrought havoc not only in art and literature, but even in science); but they overlooked perhaps the most significant fact: that during the last years of a perhaps half-mad Stalin the Soviet Union was making a remarkable recovery. By the time Stalin died, in 1953, not only all the devastated villages but practically all the cities destroyed or partly destroyed in the war had been fully rebuilt.

The rural population was moving fast from the villages to the cities, including vast almost-new cities like Novosibirsk, Omsk and many others in Siberia. By the middle of the 1950s a gigantic housing program was in full swing, not only in the war-stricken cities, but also in old more or less undamaged ones like Moscow and Leningrad. From about 1955 Moscow began to develop like mad in all directions, with thousands of new blocks of four to seven stories all over the city. The same was true in Leningrad and elsewhere. For the first time, Russians were beginning to live the "European" way—in houses which were still too small, but which were clean and hygienic, with central heating and modern plumbing. The picturesque squalor of the *izba,* still often found in the center of Moscow, and the quarrelsome chaos of the "communal flats" (as described by Zoshchenko in the 1920s), were, in the main, becoming things of the past.

In heavy industry much had been achieved under Stalin's Five-Year Plans of 1928–41; but the figures for 1940 (the last prewar year) are still very modest compared with today's: between 1940 and 1967, the production of electric energy rose from 48 billion k.w.h. to 545 billion (an elevenfold increase); steel, from 18 to 100 million tons, almost a sixfold increase; oil, from 31 million tons to 265 million tons, nearly a ninefold increase, and so on.

Various kinds of machinery were being produced in numbers ten or fifteen times higher than in 1940, while things like bulldozers and excavators, which were hardly produced at all in 1940, were now each being turned out at the rate of 20,000 or 25,000 a year. In certain industries, such as steel, the U.S.S.R. was catching up with the United States—100 million tons as against America's 120 million tons.

If Stalin's Five-Year Plans were carried out by people who only a few years before had scarcely been able to read and write, Russian industry today is run by many millions of highly skilled, highly educated people. As I shall try to show in this book, the ordinary Russian of today is not an ideologically fanatical Communist; but he *is* a socialist who is extremely conscious of the fact that *the system works* and has on the whole been an enormous success. What's more, thanks to state control, it works without slumps, economic crises and unemployment.

The Russians had to kill themselves with work during the Five-Year Plans of 1928–41 and then during the war; today they work, in physical terms, much less than they could. The five-day working week has become almost general, and it seldom exceeds forty hours' work. Money is not something to invest, simply something to spend. If people put money into their savings bank, it is simply with the view to spending it—on a car, on new furniture, on a *datcha,* on new clothes, etc.* Russians (except the very poor) spend money readily. But the present machinery of distribution dates back to an era of austerity; and, with consumer goods becoming more and more plentiful, the number of shops, restaurants, etc., has become quite inadequate. So, as many Russians have told me, what Russia now needs is to rid herself of the queuing and the shopping chaos— a "little revolution" which will result in far more shops, restaurants and other eating places and also in an increasing mechanization of the whole system.

Agriculture remains the weakest spot in the Russian economy, and its progress still lags far behind that of Russian industry. It is over agriculture that disputes are sharpest among Russian economists today—disputes with which I deal at some length in this book.

* On the question of money there is a sharp ideological difference between the Russians, on the one hand, and Mao and Castro, who want their people to despise money, on the other.

No doubt, Russia is handicapped by nature. She is at the same latitude as Canada and the United States, but her fertile lands are not vast compared with the total area of the U.S.S.R., and the climatic conditions are often uncertain. Since the war, there have been at least two disastrous droughts—in 1946 and in 1963. Under Premier Alexei Kosygin, especially since the March 1965 Plenum, production has improved; but many economists still hold that the present "reform" amounts only to a half-measure, and that results would be much better if the "socialist sector" were more fully developed. But this is perhaps a pessimistic view. The statistics for 1967 show very remarkable progress, not in the private ("individual plots") sector but in the socialist sector.

As regards the production of food, marketing and distribution, there are still plenty of things to criticize. All the same, compared not only with the Russia of 1913 but also with the Russia of 1940 and even 1950, it is a remarkably efficient country; and the ordinary Russian today is enormously proud of its achievements and is deeply patriotic. The country is, moreover, the greatest welfare state in the world, with 34 million old-age pensioners, a free health service, and a vast free education system.

The Soviet Union today is essentially a "nation state." Its sense of revolutionary mission is very weak—much weaker, indeed, than it was under Khrushchev, with his interest in Latin America (hence his special affection for Castro), his journeys with Bulganin to India, Burma and Afghanistan, his later visit to Indonesia, and the song and dance made over Soviet steel mills in India. Today Indonesia and Latin America, as well as Black Africa, have been as good as written off as areas for intense Russian political or economic activity. Some aid and "technical cooperation" continue to be given to some countries, for instance India, but there are no great illusions about its ultimate effectiveness. It is felt that in a vast country like India there must be major social transformations before the country can really be put on its feet. More interesting to Russia is the Arab world; here it is important for Russia to make friends and influence people, and soon there will be about 100 million Arabs in one of the strategically most important parts of the world, and one, moreover, very close to Russia's own borders.

Russia today is definitely a have, as opposed to a have-not, country. She has suffered for many years from hardships and shortages herself and is not anxious to share what she has with others more than she can help. A close alliance with China would sooner or later have implied lowering the Soviet standard of living in order to raise the Chinese standard. Hence perhaps the seemingly incomprehensible decision in 1960—a decision explained away by all sorts of ideological arguments—to stop help to China. Vietnam *has* to be helped; it would lower Russia's socialist prestige in the world to abandon Vietnam entirely to its fate. In a way, the war in Vietnam suits Russia. It makes the United States disliked in the greater part of the world, including most countries in Europe (in the first place, de Gaulle's France). The United States has become a symbol of war, the Soviet Union a symbol of peace.

It is thought unlikely that, with a gigantic arsenal of nuclear weapons on both sides, it will ever come to a war between the United States and the Soviet Union. China remains unpredictable, and so does West Germany. But West Germany by herself could be easily disposed of. The only problem is whether Germany's *revanche* would be assisted by the United States. If so, then the Third World War would become inevitable. The Russian authorities do not take the possibility of a war with China very seriously so far, even though ordinary people in Russia are extremely China-conscious.

In general, while passionately determined not to become involved in *any* wars, Russia still feels that the international situation is dangerous.

This consciousness of danger perhaps largely explains the con-tinued hardness of the regime, especially in ideological matters. If the Khrushchev years were a strange mixture of Stalinism and liberalism, in which you had on the one hand the ugly Pasternak affair, but on the other periods of liberalization in literature (the (publication of Solzhenitsyn, the heyday of Voznesensky, Akhma-dullina and Yevtushenko, with the latter's devastating poem *The Heirs of Stalin*), today, under the seemingly mild and liberal Kosygin, there is a hardening in the ideological line—witness the Siniavsky-Daniel affair and the other writers' trials, and Brezhnev's ominous threats in March 1968 to those guilty of "ideological immaturity." If science has shaken off the fetters of Lysenkoism, literature and the arts are still dominated by bureaucrats. These, more even than anybody else, are the true "heirs of Stalin."

Who is responsible for this? Somebody on the Politburo—most probably Suslov, the ideological boss—or some of the bureaucrats of the Writers' Union, working together with the censorship and . . . the police? Perhaps the true explanation for the definite hardening of literary policy since Khrushchev is to be found in this: that the liberals, notably Kosygin and his friends, had to throw something to the Stalinists to keep them quiet; and so they abandoned to them literature and the arts, but on condition that they did not interfere in even more vital matters such as Soviet economic affairs and foreign policy.

But whoever is responsible, there can be no doubt, in the light of the conversations with leading writers reported later in this book, that the situation of creative writers is an unhappy and frustrating one and that the short-term prospect for Russian literature is not hopeful.

The struggle between the intellectuals and the bureaucracy continues. It will be a long struggle, and its end is probably not yet in sight, though the recent happenings in Poland, Rumania and especially Czechoslovakia suggest that the intellectuals' victory *may* be nearer than we thought even a few months ago, though the immediate effect of these events in Russia was little short of alarming. Brezhnev in his speech of March 29, 1968, reflecting the Kremlin's alarm over Czechoslovakia, reverted to a virtually Stalinist line, while V. Kochetov, leader of the Stalinist group of writers, sharply condemned Khrushchev for having allowed literature to liberalize itself in the 1950s. This, he said, must stop.

But, as I so often told my friends in Russia, "Look, I have been telling everybody here till I'm blue in the face that if it weren't for cases like Siniavsky's and Daniel's or, worse still, Solzhenitsyn's, and the bureaucrats' constant pressure on literary and artistic thought generally, anti-Soviet propaganda would have mighty little to say. On the other hand, the CIA makes it a full-time job to exploit every little thing in the literary and artistic field, if only to make everybody forget that even worse things are happening in the world—such as the mass murder in Vietnam—than the locking up of a few writers. And don't you realize that you are embarrassing your best friends in the West, even the French and Italian Communists? When even Luis Aragon comes out openly against the Siniavsky-Daniel trial and refuses to come to the Writers' Congress, you should take this very seriously, and not try to dismiss it with cheap cracks to the effect that it's only an election maneuver on Aragon's part—a means of not discouraging French intellectuals against voting Communist in the next general election. To put it in a nutshell, let me ask just one question in conclusion: *Why won't you trust your writers?"*

This book, though much shorter, is a sort of companion volume to *Russia at War.* It is an attempt, after several visits to the Soviet Union and a particularly long one in the jubilee year of 1967, to assess what Russia represents both internally and internationally nearly twenty-five years after the war, and above all to depict the Russian as a human being, able and willing to discuss his country as perceptively and critically as anyone in the rest of the world. For this reason I have reported, verbatim as far as possible, many of the conversations I had during my visit to Russia last year, perhaps at the cost of making the book a little more repetitive and diffuse than it would otherwise have been.

The reader should perhaps be warned here that the first chapter does not fit into this general pattern. It is a summary and close examination of the Central Committee's Fiftieth-Jubilee *Survey,* which is an assessment of the last fifty years and a statement of internal and international policy at the present time and in the near future. This chapter constitutes the backbone of the book, and therefore I feel its length is justified. It gives important indications of the direction in which official policy is heading—witness the attempt to see Trotsky in historical perspective, or the cautious attitude toward the possible eventual transition from socialism to Communism.

An English friend has described this first chapter as "Kremlinological." The charge is unjustified, but it might be worthwhile here to describe briefly the essence of Kremlinology, which is a key word in classifying the attitude of some foreign writers toward Russia. Kremlinology is largely guesswork, and often very wild guesswork, mostly by people who have had no live contact with Russia or Russian life. There has always been a conflict between the Kremlinologist and the bona-fide Moscow correspondent. Both existed before the war, the former perhaps installed in an office in Riga, working laboriously on a jigsaw puzzle of newspaper cuttings, more often than not with half the pieces missing. During the war it was possible for the correspondent on the spot to do a useful job of reporting. Then shortly after the war—especially after 1947—the situation worsened. There were no contacts with any Russians, except on a frigid official level. By 1948 things had become altogether impossible for the genuine reporter, and it was then, of course, that the heyday of the Kremlinologists began. Most of them had little personal knowledge of Russia, but were full-blooded cold-warriors; some advocated, openly or by implication, a preventive war against Russia, one or two persisting in this even as late as 1957, at the time of the first Russian sputnik. The source book for several years was Kravchenko's *I Chose Freedom*, a piece of political gangsterism to be given, before long, academic support by David Dallin and Boris Nicolaevsky in their book *Forced Labor in Russia*, in my opinion one of the greatest frauds of the twentieth century. I shall have more to say about these books in Chapter 3. In 1961— and this was extremely important—censorship of foreign press telegrams and phone calls was lifted, and things got easier for the Moscow correspondent. In addition to the old hands, there has, in recent years, developed a new generation of outstanding Moscow correspondents, such as Kyril Tidmarsh of the London *Times,* Michel Tatu and Henri Pierre of *Le Monde* and Pietro Sormani of *Corriere della sera,* to mention only a few, who have made the London and New York Kremlinologists not only redundant but usually as good as useless.

In conclusion I want to thank all those numerous Russian friends who have talked to me freely for hours and have done so much to help me understand their country's problems, worries and dilemmas. Here in the West, I am particularly grateful to my friends Arthur Crook, editor of the *Times Literary Supplement,* for having allowed me to quote a few passages from that paper (on *Novy Mir,* and Valentin Katayev, and the NTS in particular), and David Gallagher, also of the *TLS,* for supplying me with a valuable memorandum on the origins of the Writers' Union. Many thanks, too, go to my old friend Jean Champenois, leading French authority on Russia, who has now worked in Moscow for over thirty years, for his memorandum on certain aspects of the "Jewish problem" in the Soviet Union—a problem of which he has made a special study. A few passages in the book come from my fiftieth-anniversary articles that appeared last autumn in the *New Statesman* (London), *The Nation* (New York) and *Le Nouvel Observateur* (Paris).

1

Brezhnev and Kosygin Speak: The Fiftieth-Anniversary *Survey*

IN JULY 1967, to mark the Soviet Union's Fiftieth Jubilee, there appeared the Central Committee's *Survey* (*Tesisy*)* of the fifty years since the October Revolution. I had, at first, put the bulky document aside, rather assuming it was one of those dull, pompous, routine documents that the Central Committee produces from time to time. But now I decided to have a closer look at it. Some of it, of course, is dull; it is also pompous in parts. But to say it is routine would be wrong. It is enormously interesting, not so much for what it says as for how it says it, and for the greatly varying degrees of emphasis it places on the different problems it discusses, both internal and international. It is also invaluable as a sort of Brezhnev-Kosygin history of the last fifty years. It thus provides a valuable indication of what Soviet policy, both home and foreign, is likely to be during the next few years, at the beginning of the second half-century of the Soviet regime. The document may be regarded as a compromise between the relatively liberal wing of the Central Committee, as represented by Kosygin, and the conservative wing, as represented by Brezhnev.

---

* Everybody has heard of Lenin's April Theses; the word *Tesisy* was borrowed from the German philosophical jargon so dear to Lenin's heart; and, at a pinch, "Aprelskie Tesisy" could have been translated as "April Theses," but in the case of the fiftieth-anniversary document, *Tesisy* cannot possibly be translated as "theses," which would mean nothing. *Tesisy* means simply a summing up or a survey. I prefer the latter word.

LENIN AND THE REVOLUTION

The *Survey* starts with a theoretical definition of the importance of the October Revolution:

> Half a century ago, our country entered the socialist road of social development. The October Revolution marked the beginning of the liberation of humanity from exploitation and the application to real life of the principles of scientific Communism, and had a profound effect on the subsequent course of world history. It inaugurated the epoch of the universal revolutionary renewal of the world—an epoch marked by the transition from capitalism to socialism.

All this is cautiously worded; it speaks of a transition to socialism, but not yet to Communism. The *Survey* then pays tributes to the Leninist Bolsheviks who prepared and brought about the October Revolution, to the heroes of the civil war and the Second World War, and to those brave men and women who, under the first Five-Year Plans, supplied the Soviet Union with great new industries and with the whole new system of "kolkhozes" and "sovkhozes." In thus increasing the might of the first socialist country in the world, they were also serving the cause of the revolutionary transformation of the world.

In recalling some of the main features of the October Revolution, the *Survey* is careful not to suggest that industrially and economically the new Soviet regime simply had to start from scratch. On the contrary:

> Although Russia was then still a predominantly agricultural country, capitalism had been rapidly developing there, and its industrial production had reached a high degree of concentration. A working class had developed in the country, and its kernel was the industrial proletariat.

The *Survey* speaks of the "cruel exploitation" of this proletariat, of the wretched state of the peasants,* who owned only very little of

---

* The idyllic view of the Russian peasantry is, of course, completely demolished by such sordid descriptions of Russian village life as those found in Chekhov's *The Ravine* and *The Peasants* or in Tolstoy's *Powers of Darkness,* all relating to the 1880s and 1890s.

the land, of the oppression of the national minorities, and of the survival of certain forms of serfdom and feudalism, all of which, together with Russia's dependence on foreign capital, made Russia "both the nodal point of all the contradictions of the imperialist system and, at the same time, the weakest link in this imperialist system."

The Revolution of 1905–7 had shaken the foundations of the tsarist regime and had been a prologue to the great revolutionary upheaval of 1917. There follows a very significant near-admission that but for the First World War events might not have developed in 1917 the way they did:

> The social, economic and political contradictions in Russia assumed a particularly acute form in the conditions of the imperialist world war. For this wholly undermined the economic life of the country and wore out and exasperated both the workers and the peasantry to a quite incredible extent.

The February Revolution of 1917 overthrew the tsarist autocracy; but the bourgeoisie that had come to power neither could nor would satisfy the elementary needs of the workers and peasants. Only the conquest of political power by the proletariat could solve the fundamental social problems. While omitting any mention of the awkward question why the Constituent Assembly of January 1918 (in which the Bolsheviks had only a minority) was brutally dissolved by the Bolsheviks on the very day it first met, the *Survey* significantly stresses the national rather than the international significance of the October Revolution: *"The profound alarm they felt for the destiny of their country* urged Russia's toiling masses to embark on revolutionary changes [my italics]. In 1917 the socialist revolution became an urgent practical task."

After a lengthy tribute to Lenin, "the leader of genius and the uncompromising revolutionary," and to the Bolshevik Party, "which, for the first time in history, succeeded in combining scientific socialism with a mass movement of the working class," the *Survey* stresses that the October Revolution, "though proletarian in content, was at the same time a profoundly people's revolution," since it was marked by the close alliance of the workers and the peasants. Evading the important point made by Isaac Deutscher that the former were carrying out a socialist, and the latter a bourgeois, revolution, the *Survey* goes on:

> The Bolshevik Party . . . was thus able to direct toward the same target all the various revolutionary currents—the socialist movement among the working class aiming to overthrow the bourgeoisie; the revolutionary struggle of the peasantry against the landlords; the national-liberation struggle for national equality [among the ethnic minorities], and the all-people's demand for peace and for the termination of the bloody imperialist war.

In this way, the October socialist revolution was neither a conspiracy nor a palace revolution carried out by a handful of revolutionary activists, but a revolution carried out by millions of people with the working class at its head, the latter itself being guided by the Marxist-Leninist party.

> In 1917 Lenin's party showed a great example of historical initiative and a correct understanding of the balance of class forces, as well as of the concrete peculiarities of a given moment. . . . Very flexible tactics were used, peaceful and unpeaceful, legal and illegal. . . . In this way the Bolsheviks differed in their strategy and tactics from social-democratic reformism, as well as from petty-bourgeois adventurism.

In 1917, the *Survey* continues, the Russian working class struggled for its own liberation from "hired slavery" and became the master of plants and factories. As for the peasantry, the *Survey* significantly stresses that it was "given" the landlords' estates, but that at the same time the Soviet regime nationalized this (and all other) land (which means, in effect, that the poor peasants were given the use, but not the indefinite ownership, of the former estates). Besides nationalizing the land, the Soviet regime nationalized "big industry, the railways and the banks" and established a foreign-trade monopoly. Thus the country's national resources and "the most important means of production" were put in the hands of the people. The decisive economic sectors became the "all-people's property"; and these means of production "in the hands of the people" became the economic base of socialism.

The peoples and nationalities, oppressed under tsarism, were given by the Soviet regime not only equal rights, but also the right of self-determination—a somewhat flexible right, one might observe, which worked (though not without a severe struggle) in the case of the Baltic States and Finland, which broke away from Russia, and did not (within a few years) work at all, for example, in the case of Georgia.

All class divisions and distinctions were abolished, and—a very important point, highly characteristic of the Soviet regime—women were given exactly the same rights as men.

The first thing the newly established Soviet regime did was not to get Russia out of the First World War but to try to stop that war altogether. The very first decree of the Soviet government was the famous Peace Decree. But whether the imperialist countries followed Russia's example or not, Russia at any rate "was saved from a national catastrophe, toward which the ruling classes had been leading her. In the same way, the peoples of Russia were freed from enslavement by foreign capital."

Without, in fact, saying anything about the October Revolution being the beginning of an early world revolution, the *Survey* merely says:

> The October Revolution shook the very foundations of the capitalist world. The world was split into two systems—one socialist, the other capitalist. . . . In terms of world history the October Revolution pointed to the ways and revealed the forms and methods of that revolutionary transformation, which now assumed an international character. The experience of the October Revolution . . . is an inexhaustible treasure house of the theory and practice of revolutionary struggle.

The Soviet regime represented the interests of the masses (as they immediately recognized); the workers in the rest of the world understood this, too. The regime triumphed not only in the capitals (Leningrad and Moscow), but also in the provincial centers. The struggle was, however, far from over; the conquests of the revolution had to be defended; it was now essential to use the dictatorship of the proletariat as the means of achieving "full victory over the exploiting classes" and for "the completion of socialist transformations."

THE CIVIL WAR

But Lenin's creative plans "came up against the class enemy's attempts to destroy the young Soviet state." It was international imperialism which organized the struggle against the Soviet Republic—this imperialism being represented by "the imperialists of Germany, England, France, the United States, Japan, and other countries.*

> Imperialist intervention and the offensive of the White hordes went together with counterrevolutionary conspiracies and rebellions by Social Revolutionaries, Mensheviks and the remnants of the bourgeois parties. . . . All these forces caused incalculable sufferings and hardships to our people. Nevertheless, their attacks were beaten off, and the Revolution won.

Avoiding the old legend of Stalinist historiography that the Red Army had been created on a certain day, on which it immediately stopped the Kaiser's army from advancing any further, the *Survey* much more correctly says that the Red Army of workers and peasants was "born in the course of the battles against the Whites and the interventionists, amidst the flames of the Civil War." And then, to mobilize the whole strength of the country, a workers' and peasants' Defense Council was set up, with Lenin at its head.

This, in fact, is strictly correct; if no specific credit is given to

---

* The *Survey* lumps them all together, without troubling about chronology, or about the degree and nature of the intervention by the different countries. Germany was, of course, at first the chief interventionist, since she occupied the whole Ukraine and other parts of the former Russian Empire until her defeat in the west in November 1918; after that, the others took over, the defeated Germans thereupon playing only a minor part in the Russian Civil War, notably in the Baltic Provinces. The "civil-war aims" of Japan and the U.S. in the Russian Far East were by no means the same; while of Britain and France, both active especially in southern Russia, Britain became more quickly discouraged than France, which continued to support General Wrangel to the bitter end, in November 1920.

Trotsky as the chief organizer of the Red Army, there is no suggestion either—as there used to be in the Stalin days—that his role was
in any way harmful and pernicious.

The *Survey* further gives the greatest credit to the European
working class for the help it gave the Soviet Union with its "Hands
off Russia" campaign. The counterrevolutionary forces are dealt
with so briefly in the *Survey* and with so little venom that the text
almost suggests that even if the Whites were "class enemies" many
among them were still decent Russian patriots, though badly mis-
guided ones. Nevertheless, the civil war had created conditions in
which a Red terror, carried out by the Cheka, was both fully justified and inevitable: "Revolutionary violence against the exploiters
was the people's answer to their own violence." This quotation
significantly avoids any specific mention of either the terror or the
Cheka.

Now comes one of the most interesting parts of the *Survey*—that
on the years immediately following the civil war. No mention
whatsoever is made of Lenin's War Communism—a policy which
enormously contributed to the economic chaos of the country, as
Lenin himself was later to recognize when he introduced the New
Economic Policy in 1921. Instead, the chaos is primarily attributed
to the "imperialists."

> The imperialists failed to destroy the Soviet Republic by armed
> force. But they ruined it to such an extent that, in Lenin's own
> words, they "half solved their problem." We had to start our
> peaceful reconstruction at an unbelievable low level: the output of
> our heavy industry was equal to one seventh of its prewar 1913
> output, and steel production had dropped below five per cent of
> the 1913 output.

As for agriculture, it was now, in 1921, producing less than
half the prewar output. The *Survey* discreetly omits to say that the
Soviet system of food confiscation during the years of War Communism still had something—indeed, a great deal—to do with this
castastrophic drop. The *Survey* then goes on to say that "it was the
great merit of the Communist Party, with Lenin at its head, to have
armed the Soviet people with a scientific plan for the building of
socialism, a plan bearing in mind the economic and social condi-

tions in the country." Lenin aimed at "the industrialization of the country, the application of the cooperative principle to agriculture, and the carrying through of a cultural revolution."

Here there is a clear suggestion that, by and large, all that was to happen later under Stalin and Khrushchev was in conformity with Lenin's blueprint. Lenin's ideas, in short, corresponded to the interest of the people themselves, "who were eager to put an end to economic chaos and backwardness, poverty, obscurantism and illiteracy." In reality Stalin's timetable and order of priorities were to differ enormously from Lenin's.

THE NEP

The New Economic Policy (NEP) adopted at the Tenth Congress of the Party is defined as "an important and indispensable stage on the road to socialism."

> The NEP was calculated to end the economic chaos, to create the foundations of a socialist economy and to develop a large industry; it was intended to create a link between town and country, to strengthen the alliance between the workers and the peasants, to oust and liquidate the capitalist elements and to prepare the victory of socialism. These were the means for achieving this end: the ubiquitous development of the cooperative system, the extensive development of trade, complete with material incentive and "rentability." To speed up the restoration of the economy, permission was given to make use of private capital, provided the high command posts of the economy remained in the hands of the proletarian state.

This passage has a completely modern ring; the liberal school of Russian economists today contend, indeed, that the Lenin-initiated NEP, with its "material incentives and 'rentability,'" had many features which the Soviet economy needs more than ever today; the basic difference between the NEP period and the present is that there is, of course, absolutely no need to revive private capital in any shape or form, and so create a new bourgeoisie, that ephemeral class of "Nepmen" which emerged from the NEP in the 1920s. Important, too, is the reference to the fact that the NEP principles are today "of international significance," since they are

being applied to the building of socialism in other countries—a clear
reference to East Germany, Hungary and Czechoslovakia.

TROTSKY AND STALIN

The subsequent process of building socialism involved a further
struggle not only with the remnants of the "class enemy" but also
with those opportunists who were trying to divert the Party from the
road Lenin had chosen; these included both left and right elements.
In the course of this struggle the political and ideological rout of the
Trotskyites was of the greatest importance; for these *"showed their
disbelief in the strength of the Soviet working class, by maintaining
that, without a victory of the proletarian revolution in the West, a
victory of socialism in Russia was impossible* [my italics]. They
also tried to discourage all hope among our Party and our people of
a successful building of socialism in our country, and denied that it
was of any importance to the world revolutionary movement."

> With the help of leftist and ultrarevolutionary phraseology, the
> Trotskyists aimed at inflicting on the Party an adventurist course,
> which could only have ended in the defeat of socialist construction
> in our country. Their adventurism consisted in artificially egging
> on the revolution in other countries. They also demanded the
> adoption of antidemocratic and militarized methods of guiding the
> masses in our country, thus repudiating the Leninist principle of
> democratic centralism, and insisted on the "freedom" of fractional
> struggle inside the Party, thus slipping down the slope toward
> antisovietism.

Certain Trotskyists or *trotskisants* in the West, as well as some
Chinese ideologists, will no doubt raise numerous objections; but
this passage on Trotskyism in the *Survey* marks an enormous
advance on practically all that was previously written in the Soviet
Union on Trotsky and Trotskyism. Instead of streams of vulgar
abuse and screams of treason, here we have a historical analysis of
Trotskyism which, whether one agrees with it or not, one must
admit to be calm and levelheaded.

By implication, without mentioning him by name, the *Survey* thus
endorses the position adopted in the middle twenties by Stalin, the

principal exponent of "socialism in one country." Altogether, without mentioning him, the *Survey* makes it clear that, as secretary general of the Party, Stalin was doing the right thing during that early post-Lenin period. What it says of the Party's struggle against the "right opportunists" is of course less sound, since Stalin himself, particularly in 1926, closely identified himself with Bukharin—that is, with those elements in the Party who, as the Survey says, "reflected the ideology of the exploiting and kulak (the 'peasant capitalist') strata in the countryside." It was this "rightist" ideology, too, which resisted high tempos in industrialization, as well as rural collectivization and "the liquidation of the kulaks as a class."

THE FIVE-YEAR PLANS

While tending to minimize Lenin's internationalism, the *Survey* makes the most of Lenin's "idea that the building of a socialist society in our country was possible." Starting out from this theory, the Party's Fourteenth Congress declared itself in favor of "industrializing the country and of developing the means of production." There follows a reference to the enormous difficulties under which this new phase of development had to be launched: "This socialist industrialization had to be undertaken in conditions of our country's capitalist encirclement, and of a constant danger of an armed attack by the aggressive power of imperialism." This in itself required that the work should be done within an extremely short time, which meant "an immense concentration of all our strength and of all the economic means at our disposal." Industrialization was carried out without any help from abroad, through internal accumulation together with the most austere economy regime.

If, in saying that this industrialization was carried out "without any help from outside," the *Survey* ignores the enormous quantities of machinery and the numerous engineers and technicians (British, American, German, etc.) brought in from outside, it is for the simple reason that both the machinery and the services had to be heavily paid for in hard cash or on a very short-term credit basis, out of Russia's own extremely meager resources. So the statement that the Soviet Union received no "help" in the real sense from anywhere during that great industrial revolution which began in

October 1928 (the beginning of the first Five-Year Plan) is strictly correct. Even then she was extremely lucky to find some big capitalist such as Henry Ford to whom business was business. It was with the help of Ford technicians and engineers that at Nizhni Novgorod (the future Gorki) the Russians built their first large motor works. The small (by our standards, ludicrously small) beginning of the electrification of Russia had been laid by Lenin's GOELRO (State Plan for the Electrification of Russia); and it was not till the successful completion of the two Five-Year Plans (the third was interrupted by the war in 1941) that the Soviet Union became "a mighty industrial power." Without for a moment denying that there was a substantial industry which had sprung up during the last few decades of the tsarist regime (particularly during Count Witte's "industrial revolution" which began around 1885, though chiefly with the help of foreign investments), the *Survey* notes that during the Five-Year Plans some entirely new industries were created—a car industry, an aircraft industry, and a tanks and tractor industry, besides new branches of the chemical industry. By 1940, the over-all output of Russian industry was nearly eight times that of 1913, while the output of the means of production had increased thirteenfold. What this gigantic effort represented in terms of "blood, sweat and tears" I shall show in a later chapter.

COLLECTIVIZATION

The industrialization of the Soviet Union, which began under the first Five-Year Plan in October 1928, created the "indispensable material base" not only for the economic independence of the Soviet Union and for her vastly increased military power, but also for the socialization of her agriculture. It was a brutal and ruthless undertaking, as we know, and the *Survey* as good as admits it was by saying that socialization of agriculture was *"the most complex and difficult problem of all that the country had had to face since 1917"* (*Survey*'s italics). Millions of small individual peasant holdings took the side of socialism by merging into *kolkhozes*. In the course of the drive to overcome the peasants' resistance to collectivization, an effective compromise was discovered: the agricultural *artel'* (roughly, cooperative), which made it possible to combine the peasants' social and personal interests. In this way the "leftist" attempt to introduce absolute distributionary egalitarianism into the villages was scotched; also an end was put to the practice of ignoring the principle that the peasants' entry into the kolkhozes must be voluntary. This is, of course, a clear reference to the savagery with which Stalin started on his collectivization; not until some months later did he realize that the methods he was using could produce only chaos, if not civil war; hence his famous warning to those collectivizing the villages that they had gone "giddy with success," and must therefore slow down somewhat. This did not, however, mean that mercy had to be shown to the "class enemy," the kulak, numerically "the biggest class enemy of all." The war against the kulaks was an extremely fierce one, as the *Survey* admits, and the kulaks' resistance was finally broken only by the combined efforts of the urban working class and the *bednota* (the poorest peasants), working "in close alliance" with the *sredneye krestyanstvo* (the "medium" peasants). A very important contribution to the socialization of the countryside was made by the creation of sovkhozes (state farms) and the MTS's—the machine and tractor stations— both these and the sovkhozes being state-owned.

Socialist property became the economic base of village life; this eliminated all those factors which had lain at the root of the exploitation of the poor by the rich. Interestingly enough, the *Survey* adds that collectivization proved of the greatest value during the Second World War, with the clear implication that, if there had still been a kulak class in the Russian countryside, this class would gladly have cooperated with the Nazi invaders. This is probably a highly exaggerated claim, since during the Second World War practically every Russian—even countless priests and former tsarist officers—put the country's victory above all class considerations; it might, it is true, have been different in other parts of the country— in the Ukraine, for instance—at least if the Germans had shown a minimum of practical common sense, instead of treating practically everybody in the Soviet Union, including the Ukrainian people, as *Untermenschen.** It seems that the present Kremlin leaders still find

* On the very subtle but, in practice, meaningless differences between the Germans' treatment of Russians and of Ukrainians, see the author's *Russia at War*, particularly Part 6, ch. 2 and 3; and Part 7, ch. 3. See also A. Dallin's *German Rule in Russia*.

it necessary, even if only in retrospect, to find some new justifications for the extreme brutality of the collectivization drive and its (temporarily) disastrous consequences—such as the two years of virtual famine that followed the collectivization of the peasantry, and the fearful shortage of livestock, which continued right up to the war.

The Seventeenth Party Congress of January–February 1934, which met after the successful completion of the first Five-Year Plan during the previous year and the near-completion of collectivization, noted that "the foundation of a socialist economy had been laid." The *Survey* significantly adds that the experience of those two vast reforms was now (in 1967) being "creatively used" by many socialist countries outside Russia, "account, of course, being taken of their own peculiarities and their concrete local conditions"—a very "liberal" and "polycentrist" phrase.

A WHOLLY LITERATE NATION: THE NATIONALITIES PROBLEM

In order to make socialism work effectively, says the *Survey,* it was essential that its building should be closely accompanied by a successful cultural revolution. After quoting Lenin's views on the subject, the *Survey* admits that this cultural revolution was a "complex and lengthy process." Russia was a culturally backward country, with an acute shortage of trained cadres; it was in this country that an entirely new system of popular education, producing within a short time a wholly literate nation, was built up. This system also stimulated the rapid rise of science and culture, and provided for the education of new generations in a spirit of socialism. The "best representatives of the old, pre-Revolution intelligentsia" placed their services at the disposal of the people and greatly helped to train a new intelligentsia that now emerged from the rank and file of the working class and the peasantry.

After the Revolution, an enormous amount was done to solve the nationalities problem, the mutual hostility among the different nations of the old Russian Empire having been one of its ugliest features. In December 1922 numerous nations voluntarily joined in forming the U.S.S.R.; the Soviet Constitution of 1924 consecrated this union.* Thanks to the October Revolution, says the *Survey,* numerous very backward nationalities (notably in the wilds of Siberia) acquired an identity of their own, while some were literally saved from rapid physical extinction. Many of these more-than-backward groups, who had lived under feudal and even patriarchal conditions, rapidly became socialist, without passing through the capitalist stage at all. The leading role in this remarkable metamorphosis was played by the Russian people and the Russian working class.†

There follows an ideological digression: *"The chief weapon in the building of socialism in the U.S.S.R. was the state of the Dictatorship of Proletariat itself"* (*Survey*'s italics). And then comes this definition of the dictatorship of the proletariat: its highest principle is the alliance between the working class and the peasantry, with the leading role being played by the working class. Having made this definition, which was particularly applicable to the 1930s (a somewhat more flexible definition, applicable to the present time, is given later in the *Survey*), it then comes to the grimmest, but also one of the most dazzling and heroic, episodes in the fifty years of the Soviet rule: the great industrialization of the Soviet Union through the Five-Year Plans:

> Our Soviet people spared no effort, consciously accepted all privations and showed countless examples of courage and self-denial in their endeavor to overcome the economic backwardness of the country, and to create in its place a mighty socialist state.

* The wholeheartedness of this "voluntary" adherence to the U.S.S.R. differed, of course, from place to place; it was far from perfect in certain parts of the country, notably Transcaucasia. The *Survey,* in a later passage, also mentions the new members who later "voluntarily" joined the U.S.S.R.—the Baltic States, and the Belorussians, Moldavians and Ukrainians, previously under Polish, Rumanian and Czechoslovak rule.

† There is nothing particularly Russian-nationalist in this assertion; the point is that, of all the peoples of the Soviet Union, the Russians with their large working class, even before the Revolution, were intellectually and politically the most advanced. Nevertheless, even in this *Survey* there are still a few echoes of that immense preference that Stalin openly gave the Russian people over all the other members of the Soviet Union: the Russians were the most loyal, the most genuinely socialist, the most patriotic of all, as, in Stalin's view, the experience of the Second World War had shown. (See *Russia at War,* particularly Part 8, ch. 4, quoting Stalin's "victory speech" of May 24, 1945.)

The building of great new industrial centers like the Magnitka and the Kuzbass, of a railway like the Turksib, of the Dnieper Dam, of a great new industrial city like Komsomolsk-on-the-Amur in the depths of our Far Eastern taiga, and many other new plants, complete with an intensive development of socialist competition and "shock work"—all these illustrate the new, socialist attitude to labor.

The sacrifices as described here, far from being exaggerated, are, if anything, toned down; the *Survey* does not mention, for instance, the hopelessly amateurish but incredibly enthusiastic and foolhardy way in which in the autumn and winter of 1932–33 several thousand Komsomol pioneers began to build the new industrial center of Komsomolsk in the depths of the Far Eastern taiga; during the first winter a large proportion died of hunger and scurvy.

INDUSTRIALIZATION AND THE STALIN TERROR

The *Survey* speaks only briefly of the new December 1936 Constitution of the U.S.S.R., known until not so long ago as the Stalin Constitution. It mentions the important fact that it removed most legal discriminations (against the former bourgeoisie, etc.), as a result of which practically all people had the same voting rights in "direct, equal and secret elections at all levels."

The discretion with which this constitution is treated is no doubt attributable to the fact that in practice it left far too many loopholes for punishing actions which might be regarded as contrary to the interests of the state, and, worse still, for the completely arbitrary police terror which Stalin had already unleashed two years before and which, three months after the adoption of this "superdemocratic" constitution, was for over a year to give rise to the altogether nightmarish wave of terror known as the Yezhovshchina, in honor of the then head of the NKVD, Nikolai Yezhov. If Yezhov's replacement in 1938 by Lavrenty Beria seemed, at least for a time, to slow the terror down, it was because Yezhov too (though acting under Stalin's instructions) had gone giddy with success, to the point of almost wholly disorganizing the country and its industries;

most of the best people were being shot or deported. Some satisfaction was given to the people when on Stalin's instructions Beria proceeded to purge the purgers, having Yezhov himself, and countless NKVD officials who had worked under him, simply shot. Not that the new NKVD generation was to prove much better; but the end of Yezhov meant at least a temporary relaxation of the terror, and a relative return to normal.

THE SECOND WORLD WAR

The prelude to the Second World War is dealt with only very briefly in the *Survey*. The main points it makes are these:

1. The Soviet Union had been developing in an extremely complex international situation, in conditions of a perpetual danger of imperialist aggression. This danger grew enormously when Hitler came to power in Germany and set up there a fascist regime—a blatantly terrorist and chauvinist dictatorship representing all that was most reactionary and aggressive amongst the imperialists. With the help of the American and British monopolies, "which regarded Nazi Germany as the striking force of imperialism," the Nazis rearmed Germany.

2. Aware of the immense dangers threatening it, the Soviet Union proceeded to strengthen the military might of the country, and to put its industries on a war footing after having built many new industries as far away as possible from any potential aggressor.

3. The Soviet government took energetic steps to create a system of collective security in Europe: but these efforts were foiled by the "Munichites" of the Western countries, who hoped to direct Nazi aggression against the Soviet Union and then to ally themselves with Hitler. In these highly complex conditions, the Soviet Union had no alternative to signing her nonaggression pact with Germany. She thus upset the calculations of the imperialists and gained time to strengthen her defense capacity.

4. But conditions were such that it proved impossible to avert a German attack on the Soviet Union. With the connivance of "the ruling quarters of the West," Nazi Germany unleashed the Second

World War and, having captured numerous European countries, then turned against the Soviet Union.

This is no doubt an oversimple account of what happened in 1939–41, and some compliments might perhaps have been paid to Britain, which, in not capitulating to Hitler in 1940, in effect postponed the German attack on Russia by a year; but the true nature of the philosophy is in the main correctly described, as is also Stalin's "counter-Munich" of August 1939.

The war is dealt with very briefly, maybe because most Russians alive today remember it only too well. It was "a war inflicted on the Soviet Union by German fascism and was the greatest military clash yet between socialism and the battle-ram of imperialism. . . . In the Great Patriotic War . . . the Soviet people fought for the freedom and independence of their socialist country, and for socialism." Whether the Soviet people fought more for their "socialist country" or for their country *tout court,* or for socialism, is really left for every reader to decide for himself. On the one hand, the *Survey* avoids the 1941 emphasis on saving Holy Russia, and, on the other, it does not repeat some later post-Stalin assertions that the Russian people were, above all, concerned with saving the Soviet system. The truth is that they wanted to save both; fair enough, and historically almost entirely accurate.

Besides wanting to destroy "the first socialist country in the world," German fascism also "intended to exterminate millions of people, and to enslave the peoples of the Soviet Union and of numerous other countries." All perfectly true. The *Survey* then quite bluntly declares that the Nazis very nearly destroyed the Soviet Union.

> This . . . war was the hardest and most cruel of all the wars in the whole history of our country. . . . The most terrible ordeals were at the beginning of the war. The enormous Nazi army, and the armies of Germany's satellites, all fully mobilized long before the invasion of the Soviet Union, intoxicated by the poison of chauvinism and racism, penetrated deep into our territory. The enemy broke through to the foothills of the Caucasus, to the Lower Volga, blockaded Leningrad, and threatened to capture Moscow. *A deadly danger was suspended over our country.* [My italics.]

After referring to the tremendous experience the Nazis had gained in their recent military campaigns practically all over Europe, to their numerical and qualitative superiority over the Red Army of 1941, and to the fact that they had the economic resources of practically the whole of Western and Central Europe at their disposal, the *Survey* says that the Soviet Union had to cope single-handed with "a military machine of quite colossal power."

There follows a moderately worded but nevertheless quite obvious attack on Stalin, who on June 22, 1941, had been caught napping.

> Serious miscalculations had been made on our side as to the time when Nazi Germany might attack us. No adequate measures had been taken to repel the first blows the Nazis struck at us. Nor did the Soviet troops at the time have the necessary experience for conducting major operations in the conditions of modern warfare.

Yet even then, for the first time on the Continent of Europe, the Germans very soon found that their war would not be a walkover. The rout of the Germans in the Battle of Moscow marked "the beginning of the radical turn in the whole course of the war. It marked the collapse of Hitler's blitzkrieg plan of 1941: and the whole world realized for the first time that the 'invincibility of the German armies' was nothing but a myth."

The entire Soviet people "rose like one man to defend their country, to smash the enemy, to drive him out of our country and to annihilate fascism." The *Survey* recalls that the Party's motto "All for the Front, all for Victory" dominated the whole life of the Soviet people. And then there follows a passage in which, for the first time in the *Survey*, Stalin is mentioned by name.

> A State Defense Committee was set up under the chairmanship of J. V. Stalin. Throughout the country . . . the Party, Soviet, Trade-Union and Komsomol organization did everything to mobilize all the physical and material means for resisting and then smashing the enemy.

Here, significantly, Party and people are put on a par, with a faint suggestion that the people were even more important than the Party, especially during the tragic initial stages of the war: "Our heroic people, under the guidance of the Party, succeeded in overcoming the great difficulties of the earlier stages of the war, and succeeded in 1942–43 at Stalingrad and Kursk in achieving a final turn of the tide."

By 1944 the invaders were finally thrown out of the Soviet Union, and during the last year of the war the Red Army played a "decisive role" in freeing of Nazi occupation the peoples of Austria, Albania, Bulgaria, Hungary, Norway, Poland, Rumania, Czechoslovakia and Yugoslavia, before achieving final victory over Germany. Amusingly, all these liberated countries are given in (Russian) alphabetical order. By including Norway, the *Survey* rather stretches a point, but no doubt the intention is to remind the Norwegians that the first small piece of Norwegian territory to have been liberated from the Germans (it was in the Far North) was liberated, as it happened, by Russian troops.

The defeat of Japan is given only a short paragraph, which includes the statement that "military and political help was given to the revolutionary forces of China and Korea"; whether, at that time, The Kuomintang could still be regarded as "a revolutionary force" is left remarkably vague.

British and American achievements are acknowledged:

> Victory over Nazi Germany was achieved by the combined efforts of numerous nations. In the course of the war there was formed *a mighty anti-Hitler coalition. Serious blows were struck at the enemy by our Western allies,* and the allied troops of Poland, Czechoslovakia and Yugoslavia put up a gallant fight, as well as the members of the various resistance movements. [My italics.]

It is, however, understandable that the *Survey* should stress the fact the brunt of the war was borne by the Soviet Union; she lost "over twenty million people" (this "over" is new)—on the battlefield, under air bombardments and shellings, or else shot by the Nazi gangsters or tortured and starved to death in Nazi camps. (The *Survey* might also have specifically mentioned the million people or more who died of starvation in the blockade of Leningrad—the greatest civilian tragedy in the whole history of wars.)

The familiar figure of the seventy thousand cities, towns and villages laid waste by the Germans is quoted. Then:

The country lost thirty per cent of its national wealth. History does not know anything even approaching such mass barbarism and inhumanity as those displayed by the Nazi invaders. . . . It would be very difficult to find a single family in the Soviet Union which did not lose any relative or very close friend in the war.

Even so, the Soviet Union had won, and its sources of strength had been the Soviet economic system, the political, social and ideological unity of the people, their Soviet patriotism, the friendship among the nations constituting the Soviet Union, and the unexampled heroism and courage of the soldiers.

After a tribute to the guerrillas who fought the Germans in the enemy rear, there is this striking passage on the work in the war industries:

The military victory was also the victory of the workers in our own rear. Our workers, peasants and intellectuals [i.e. "brain workers," technicians, etc.] worked with the greatest self-denial and in appalling conditions. Women and adolescents replaced on the factories and farms those who had gone to the front.

The "appalling" conditions in which the people in the war industries had to work (they were often near to starvation) are described here with less varnish than almost ever before. The main organizing was done by the Party, which carried out such unprecedented feats of organization as the evacuation to the east of no fewer than 1,360 large industrial enterprises.

The bulk of the armaments for the Red Army was produced in the east (Urals, Siberia, Kazakhstan, etc). *In the course of the war, the Soviet Union produced twice as much military equipment as Germany did.* There was also, of course, Lend-Lease.* The Soviet Union received from the United States eleven billion dollars' worth of different goods, which was, of course, of the greatest value; but the fact remains that this represented only three per cent of the total cost of the Second World War to the United States (which, according to President Truman, was 341 billion dollars). It is curious to think that aid to Russia during the Second World War averaged a little under three billion dollars a year, a figure not very

---

* There is a detailed analysis of this question in the author's *Russia at War.*

much larger than that of the present Soviet aid to Vietnam—believed to be about two billion dollars a year (no doubt some allowance must be made in these comparisons for the depreciation of the dollar's purchasing power since the Second World War). Then, in conclusion, this somewhat startling statement, coming as it does on top of all the earlier talk of the mortal danger threatening The Soviet Union in 1941 and, for that matter, in 1942:

> The final results of the Great Patriotic War showed in the most convincing manner that there is no such power in the world as could smash socialism and bring to its knees a nation of people true to the ideals of Marxism-Leninism, devoted to its socialist homeland and rallied round the Leninist Party. The final results of that war are a stern warning to the imperialist aggressors, and a grim and unforgettable lesson in history.

By neglecting this passage on the "final results" of the war, which was meant as a warning to the United States, China and West Germany, and by dwelling instead on Stalin's errors in 1941 and on the "deadly danger" suspended over Russia that year, the young historian A. Nekrich was later to bring down on himself the wrath of those who argued (a little feebly) that since the U.S.S.R. *was* a socialist country she was, as it were, *ipso facto* invincible.

The Soviet victory in the Second World War had created favorable conditions "for the development and the victory of socialist revolutions in the countries of Europe and Asia, and for the creation of a world system of socialism." But the *Survey* does not pursue the point and merely adds that as a result of the war "the international forces of socialism and democracy had grown stronger, and those of imperialism and reaction weaker."

THE MIRACLE OF POSTWAR
RECONSTRUCTION

Significantly, the next theme of the *Survey* is *cultivons notre jardin.* Russia was fearfully devastated by the war, and the first immediate postwar task was to restore the country's economy. How many years would it take—ten, twenty, thirty? Miraculously, the economy was back to its prewar level in *three or four years;* many industries had been rebuilt even while the war was still on; the villages were in the main restored within a few months, and the destroyed cities rebuilt in about six years after the end of the war.

It is very curious that in the *Survey* there should be no reference whatsoever to the extremely dangerous international situation of 1948—the seizure of power by the Communists in Czechoslovakia, the Soviet breach with Yugoslavia and the Berlin blockade. It would seem that, in the eyes of the Party today, the Communist victory in Czechoslovakia was something that "went without saying"; that the quarrel with Tito was an unpleasant matter, for which in the main (though not entirely) Stalin was to blame, and which had therefore better not be mentioned; and that the Berlin blockade was an even greater Russian blunder, also better not mentioned.

Instead, the *Survey* deals at some length with the economic restoration of the Soviet Union during the postwar years, and up to 1960. Perhaps the most remarkable fact mentioned is that *"by 1948, the prewar level of industrial production had largely been attained."* This is indeed a very proud claim; for the first three postwar years, after the appalling destructions caused by the war, had been exceedingly difficult; and the almost unprecedented drought of 1946, in which there were areas where (according to Khrushchev) people literally died of starvation, had made things worse. And yet, within three years, the industrial output was back to the prewar (1940) level. The restoration of industry had, indeed, begun in the liberated areas even while the war was still in progress (as Stalin proudly told de Gaulle in December 1944).* It was during the war, too, that the rebuilding of the wrecked or partly wrecked cities began, among them Stalingrad, Rostov, Kiev, Minsk, Kharkov, Smolensk, Novgorod, Pskov, Vitebsk, Voronezh and Sebastopol.†

Looking ahead to 1960, the *Survey* makes no secret of the fact

---

* See the author's *Russia at War.*

† Of these, Stalingrad, Minsk, Smolensk, Pskov, Voronezh and Sebastopol were completely destroyed, except for a few houses that had survived by accident, as it were. On the other hand, Moscow suffered very little damage from the German blitz of 1941; its antiaircraft defenses were stupendous; in Leningrad, where over a million had died in the blockade of 1941–44, the actual damage to the city through bombing and shelling was relatively unimportant.

that heavy industry continued to have top priority throughout that period (despite Malenkov's short-lived attempt to intensify the production of consumer goods). If, by 1948, industrial production was in the main back to the prewar level, by 1960 the output of steel compared with 1940 had risen from 18.3 million tons to 65 million; oil, from 31.1 million tons to 148 million; gas, from 3.4 billion cubic meters to 47 billion; electric power, from 48.3 billion k.w.h. to 292 billion. There were also numerous new industries of a kind that had not existed before the war, or scarcely—several kinds of new chemical industries, electronics and radioelectronics and a vast new atomic industry. The increases between 1960 and 1967 were even more spectacular. As already mentioned, the Russians had exploded their first atom bomb in 1949, and their first H-bomb in 1953.

The *Survey* also mentions the complex mechanization and automation of production—though these, for "social" reasons much more than for reasons of mechanical incapacity on the part of Russian industry, were never driven to any extremes.

The *Survey* expresses an understandable satisfaction with the immense industrial progress made between the war and 1960, but openly admits that the same could not be said about Soviet agriculture. The villages destroyed in the war were, naturally, rebuilt much more quickly than the towns, and by 1950 over-all agricultural production was back to the 1940 level (two years later than industry). It was, however, during the following years (both before and after Stalin's death in March 1953) that the progress was *not* maintained, with the result that the urban population was worse supplied with food, and especially light industry with raw materials, than in 1949–50. Owing to the extreme postwar shortage of agricultural machinery the progress of agriculture had been slow after the war, and wear and tear on the existing machinery began to make itself seriously felt by 1951. It was not till the Central Committee's Plenum of September 1953 (half a year after Stalin's death) that technical aid to the kolkhozes and sovkhozes was substantially increased; but, much more important still, as the *Survey* readily admits, was the at least partial termination of the ruthless exploitation of the peasantry that had gone on under Stalin, and the creation of "material incentives" for the peasantry. At any rate, this helped to reduce the slowdown that the exasperated peasantry had practiced in the last two or three years of Stalin. Another favorable development in the mid-fifties was the extension of the area under cultivation to the "Virgin Lands" of Siberia and Kazakhstan.

After Stalin's death (I must note, however, that Stalin is mentioned by name in the *Survey* only twice—as head of the Defense Committee during the war and, later, in connection with the Twentieth Congress, which condemned the "Stalin cult"), wages and old-age and war-invalid pensions were increased, and it was in the middle fifties that the Soviet Union embarked on the gigantic housing program which by now has completely changed (much to the distress of tourists and sentimentalists) the traditional Russian urban landscape, and has created for the Russian people a way of life they never knew before—with clean, hygienic houses complete with central heating, modern plumbing, bathrooms, etc.

DE-STALINIZATION

The *Survey* does not explain very clearly why, at the Twentieth Congress, the decision was taken to destroy the Stalin myth and put an end to the Stalin personality cult. Still less does it explain how shortly before this Congress the decision was taken, and to what extent it was a "collective" decision or a sudden brain wave of Khrushchev's—who sprang his report as a surprise on the Congress, during its "secret session" of February 25, 1956.

The whole story is in fact extremely complex. As we know, it was *not* a brain wave of Khrushchev's; in the earlier open sessions of the congress several leaders, notably Mikoyan, already foreshadowed the secret report, while others, especially Molotov and Kaganovich, barely alluded to the cult and were obviously opposed to the whole principle of Khrushchev's secret report. It is also likely that, when it came to the point, Khrushchev laid on the colors even thicker than even his closest supporters had expected him to do, sometimes to the point of absurdity—especially in denouncing Stalin as an utterly incompetent commander in chief who planned his military operations with the help of a school globe!*

* Michel Tatu, the *Le Monde* correspondent, regards Khrushchev's secret report as part of his own buildup, and as a step toward the elimination of all possible rivals. See pp. 143–144.

The *Survey* prefers not to go into any of these details, above all *personal* details. By implication the whole episode is treated as a collective decision by the Party. The Party, says the *Survey,* showed its usual capacity to "put forward the correct political slogans and *to admit and correct past errors"* (my italics). The *Survey* implies the complete unanimity of the Party when it says that at the Twentieth Congress it

> resolutely condemned the Stalin personality cult, a cult which found expression in an exaltation of a single individual—which in itself was wholly alien to the spirit of Marxism-Leninism—as well as in the departure from the Leninist principle of collective leadership, in unjustified repression [a euphemism for wholly arbitrary arrests, deportations and executions] and in other violations of socialist legality, all of which caused considerable harm to our society.

Although the *Survey* does not specifically say so, it should of course be added that the "spirit of the Twentieth Congress" had already found expression several years before, when, immediately after Stalin's death, the forced-labor camps were thrown open, there was talk of a "return to socialist legality," and, in 1954, the famous "thaw" in literature and the arts set in.

There is one curious omission in the *Survey:* there is not a single mention of Beria. Although he was only Stalin's Himmler (and not, as Svetlana absurdly claimed, the ogre who had dominated Stalin), his downfall in 1953 was still a very important landmark in Soviet history. Moreover, there was also a positive side to Beria: though admittedly an odious person, he was a man with a remarkable organizing ability; it was under his general direction that the Russian atom bomb was produced with extraordinary speed—within less than four years of the Hiroshima bomb. But single individuals have very little place in the *Survey.* What, instead, the *Survey* sets out to show is that Stalin did not prove fatal to the Revolution and the regime; the evil things that happened during the Stalin period were "perversions which, for all their gravity, did not alter the nature of socialist society and did not shake the foundations of socialism. The Party and the people profoundly believed in the cause of Communism and worked with enthusiasm,* giving genuine everyday substance to Lenin's ideals and overcoming difficulties and temporary errors and failures." This is a remarkably sober assessment of the stability of the regime and the Revolution, and strikingly free of the woolly verbiage of so much of the earlier official Soviet writing. All this has something of the clarity and precision of Kosygin's own mind, except that it does not dwell sufficiently on the fundamental differences between Lenin's original intention and the lasting effect of what the *Survey* calls Stalin's "perversions."

REVOLUTION WITHOUT A BLUEPRINT

It is in the context of the mid-fifties, marked by de-Stalinization, that the *Survey* speaks of *"the complete and final triumph of socialism in the U.S.S.R.—a triumph achieved by the Soviet people under the leadership of the Communist Party"* (*Survey*'s italics). It then says that the formation of "a world socialist" system and the consolidation of the economic and military might of the Soviet Union altered the balance of power in the world, on a world scale, in favor of socialism, and provided a solid guarantee against the restoration of capitalism in the U.S.S.R.

That it was not easy to achieve this result is readily admitted: "the work of the first pioneers is always the hardest of all." For this "requires constant searching and guessing, the solving of extremely complex problems, and the overcoming of numerous contradictions and obstacles." And then comes one of the very rare quotations from Lenin in the *Survey,* but a particularly remarkable one: "This [Revolution] is something entirely new, totally unknown to history, and about which one can't find anything at all in any books."†

This exactly amounts to what a prominent and liberal Soviet economist told me: "Yes, of course Marx had the profoundest ideas, most of which are applicable even today, after a hundred years or more, but remember that *there is no blueprint in Marx for what is to be done in practice after a successful socialist revolution;*

---

* As was seen above, the *Survey* clearly admitted that there were exceptions—e.g., the peasantry during the last years of Stalin—and not without good reason, too.

† Lenin, Vol. 36, p. 383.

*and the same is absolutely true even of Lenin, till the very day of
the October 1917 Revolution; there was nothing in any book, either
Marx's or his own, on what had to be done once the Revolution had
succeeded;* so in practice, while knowing all about the *theory and
tactics* of revolution, Lenin had, after the Revolution had succeeded, to improvise and grope in the dark—and some of the im-
provisations (such as War Communism) turned out to be very bad
indeed, which, in 1921, Lenin himself readily admitted."

The *Survey* admits that much that the Party did after the Revolution was simply experimental; but the Party went ahead "without
being overawed by the novelty and the gigantic scale of the problems facing it"; for "this experience," as Lenin said, "despite the
extreme difficulties it had to overcome, and its various ups and
downs . . . is an essential new contribution to history, one which
can never be extirpated. . . . It will have provided an invaluable
lesson to the whole revolutionary movement of the world."*

And again the *Survey* sounds the "experiment" theme: "Soviet
society succeeded in showing in practice that the applications of the
scientific theory of Marxism-Leninism to everyday life fully corresponded to the same fundamental interests of the industrial workers, the peasants and all other workers."

There follows a demonstration of the great virtues of the socialist
world, as against the capitalist world:

> Socialism brings the peoples of the world both social and
> national liberation; . . . it does away with exploitation and op-
> pression and creates instead friendships, cooperation and mutual
> aid amongst both classes and nations; instead of an elemental,
> hazardous and chaotic economy, it provides a planned develop-
> ment of the economy. . . . Having radically changed the social
> aim of production, socialism has deprived the worker of all
> anxiety about the next day; Soviet humanity now knows neither
> the fear of unemployment nor the fear of abject poverty. . . .

But this was very far from easy to achieve; for during many years
the Soviet people were virtually without any outside help, facing all
the combined forces of world capitalism, and bearing the brunt of
the struggle against all the powers of reaction. The Soviet people

* *Ibid.*

were faced with the choice of deliberately lowering their standard of living and, by heroic efforts, of creating in the Soviet Union a powerful economic base and of greatly strengthening its military might, or else of being crushed by the united forces of reaction.

Here, if anything, is an implied tribute to Stalinist Russia, which carried out, *within less than thirteen years,* a gigantic industrial revolution, thus rendering Russia's conquest by Germany not inevitable—even in the fearfully unfavorable conditions of 1941, when the greatest disasters could, as the *Survey* says quite correctly, be attributed to Stalin's own blunders and miscalculations. There would have been no such setbacks if the real power of the socialist state had not been concentrated in the hands of a single individual—virtually a despot—whose personal whims had become the iron law of the whole country. We today know how even some of Russia's greatest soldiers were warning Stalin of the absolute imminence of the German invasion of June 22, 1941, and how they had simply to submit (with fury in their hearts) to Stalin's blunt "You are wrong, I know best."

COMMUNISM: KOSYGIN DEPARTS FROM KHRUSHCHEV'S UTOPIANISM

Although on some occasions Khrushchev said that there could be no calendar for Russia's entry into full Communism, on other occasions he spoke of sometime in the 1980s when the Soviet Union would become Communist or prophesied that "our children" would "live under full Communism." Brezhnev and Kosygin are more careful not to say any old thing that happens to come into their heads. They say only that since Russia was enormously successful (despite appalling difficulties and sacrifices) in bringing about her transition from capitalism to socialism, it was normal that this *evolution* should continue, with socialism gradually developing into something even better—that is, Communism. The final achievements of socialism, as seen in Russia today, are enumerated as follows: public ownership of the means of production; immensely powerful productive forces; planned economy; freedom from exploitation; compulsory work for all, but also the state's obligation to provide the work; socialist democracy; the social, political and ideological unity of society; great achievements in science and culture.

All these, says the *Survey,* constitute a sound basis for the building of Communism. However, it hastens to add that Communism "does not emerge in a kind of 'elemental' manner, and can come into being only as a result of the conscious efforts of the entire people and their constant search for the correct solutions of those problems, as created by life itself." In other words, *just as in the case of the 1917 Revolution, when Lenin had no blueprint, and no "books" (not even Marx's and his own) to show him what exactly to do once the Revolution had taken place, so now the same kind of "experimenting" would have to be done before Communism could be successfully achieved.* The great difference between 1917 and now is that the 1917 situation, with the country in a state of economic chaos, called for the most urgent and desperate remedies— or, rather, for an urgent and desperate *search* for such remedies— whereas today the country is in a relatively flourishing state and there is nothing desperate or urgent about finding the "correct solution"; even if it took decades or even centuries to find one, it would involve in the meantime (short, of course, of a nuclear war) neither loss of life nor increased sufferings and hardships. It might also be argued (and many Russians I met did argue that way) that the whole business of the transition to Communism was very largely theoretical, with no immediate practical urgency.

Much of this section of the *Survey* sounds, indeed, like political philosophy rather than practical politics:

> According to Marxism-Leninism, the transition from socialism to Communism will be determined by the existence of an appropriate material and technical base, a great affluence of material and spiritual values, a great increase in the productivity of labor, the final disappearance of the present differences between town and country, between manual and mental labor, and a further strengthening of the scientific concept of Communist morality.

Only if all these conditions are fulfilled can the basic principle of Communism become a living reality: "From everyone according to his abilities; to everyone according to his needs."

Very significantly, the *Survey* then recalls that the Party Program drawn up at the Twenty-second Congress, in the days of Khrushchev, was subsequently, during the post-Khrushchev plenums of the Central Committee, as well as at the Twenty-third Congress, *"examined in concrete terms, full account being taken of the present development of Soviet society, of the actual material, labor and financial resources available, as well as of the international situation"* (my italics). This is a remarkably interesting passage, for it shows that Brezhnev and Kosygin (as distinct from Khrushchev's Party Program of the Twenty-second Congress, which they treat as being largely utopian and unrealistic) expect the transition to Communism to be infinitely more dependent on vital material and even financial possibilities, not to mention the international *konjunktur*. This might, or might not, be favorable to any new attempts to advance several steps from the (highly satisfactory) present socialism to something much better (and "more Communist") still.

As we have seen, an enormous number of conditions (economic, financial and international) must be fulfilled before further progress toward Communism can be undertaken; but, besides these, there are many perhaps even more difficult conditions laid down in the *Survey*. There must be a great intensification of labor; an acceleration of technical and scientific progress; a further improvement in the country's military immunity; some further improvements in the "Communist morality" of the people; an immense further increase in the number of highly trained scientific and technical cadres.

All this sounds perfectly reasonable; and nothing is said any more of creating the *Homo sovieticus,* the kind of perfect human monster which Khrushchev claimed he could produce within a few years, notably by sending children to increasingly compulsory and increasingly standardized boarding schools. The whole superscheme of boarding schools for the creation of Khrushchev's robot had, for lack of popular enthusiasm, to be abandoned, in the main, even while Khrushchev was still in power. When I was in Russia in 1959, with Khrushchev at the height of his popularity, there were a few enthusiasts for the "robot schools"; but nearly everybody considered them as totally unrealistic and at the same time looked at them with some disquiet in case the scheme was persisted in.

Occasionally, the *Survey,* though in the main remarkably well reasoned, lapses into what sounds like pure Utopia. Thus, in describing the fine type of Soviet man who will emerge as a result of his "Communist education," it says: "Such a man will combine, in the most harmonious way, the highest degree of ideological consciousness, a love of work, a high organizing ability, spiritual wealth, moral purity and physical perfection." As a young Russian friend remarked to me about this passage: "Hm, physical perfection—well, yes, but in that case it will be pretty tough under real Communism for anyone to be born, say, a hunchback. What *would* happen to him?" Yes, what indeed?

To sum up, insofar as the complex question of the transition from socialism to Communism can be summed up at all: there is no blueprint for it (any more than there was in 1917); further, even if the perfect blueprint were discovered, the *theoretical* solution of the problem might still meet with serious *practical* objections; there might be international considerations which would make the further progress into Communism undesirable; and there might be both economic and social difficulties which might make it not in the interests of the Soviet Union to intensify this progress. For example, there might not be sufficient *financial* resources for this "acceleration." Although one of the preconditions for the transition to Communism is stated to be greater productivity of labor and more automation, we no longer see at the present stage (as we did in the grim "Iron Age" of the 1930s) the desire to squeeze every ounce of energy out of every worker. There could also be far greater automation than there is; but there is no desire to create an *excess* of automation, for the simple reason that this could only create what would in effect amount to unemployment—which is precisely what the Soviet Union is proud never to have had, at least never since 1928, when the first Five-Year Plan was initiated. The present degree of automation has already resulted in an enormously shortened working week. Although for old time's sake, as it were, there are the same appeals for greater labor productivity and more intensive "socialist competition," the general impression one gets in Russia today is that both the government and the Party, on the one hand, and the industrial workers, on the other, are content with the present state of affairs. Excessive productivity per man might, indeed, result in overproduction, and this would be economically unsound. One of the most significant features of Soviet industry is that both productivity and wages are relatively low—roughly a third of those in the United States. If some extraordinary inter-

national or internal disaster required industry to increase its output
enormously, it could be done; for instance, through the intensification of automation, or simply through the increase of the working
week from the present forty hours to, say, sixty, seventy or eighty—
which is the kind of thing that happened in the war industries during
the Second World War. But today this is unnecessary.

INDUSTRIAL GIANT

It is significant that the Brezhnev-Kosygin *Survey* should suddenly
descend from these lofty heights of Communist theory to the present
material achievements. After a final nod at what constitutes, or,
rather, will constitute, "the material and technical base of Communism through the further development of science and technology,
mechanization, automation and greater labor productivity," the
Survey returns to the present.

What it really boils down to is that if Russia continues to make
such spectacular progress as it has since 1929 (first year of the first
Five-Year Plan), the Soviet Union will someday be rich enough to
effect the transition from socialism to Communism.

How, then, was this progress achieved since 1917, 1928 or 1945?
In themselves the first of the following figures quoted do not mean
much; for the conditions in the different countries mentioned were
not at all the same: the average increase in industrial production
between 1929 and 1966 was 11.1 per cent in the Soviet Union, 4
per cent in the United States and 2.5 per cent in Britain and France.
It was through these enormous tempos that such a rapid and
gigantic industrial development was achieved. "Compared with
1913, the peak year of industrial development under the Old
Regime, *our total industrial output increased sixty-six times—sixty-
six times in fifty-three years.*"

The *Survey* then gives various figures on steel, electric power,
etc., which we can skip; but it adds significantly that, *out of these
sixty-three years, fully twenty years were "wasted" on wars and
postwar restoration;* the three main wars being the First World War,
the Russian Civil War and the Second World War. (Since the wars
occupied about ten years, the remaining ten years had to be devoted
to restoration—a total of twenty years out of fifty.)

Despite all this, the Soviet Union is now the second greatest industrial power in the world, producing in 1967 over 100 million tons of steel, for instance. She now has an immense engineering industry. But it is very interesting that here, instead of enumerating all the various other achievements of industry, the *Survey* turns to what is in fact the main internal problem of the Soviet Union: the weakness of her agriculture.

UNDERSIZED AGRICULTURE

It is thanks to the spectacular growth of industry since the war that agriculture is being more and more mechanized; by the end of 1966 there were 1,660,000 tractors in Soviet agriculture and over half a million combine harvesters; and here there follows an open attack on Khrushchev (though he is not mentioned by name) for what he had done in the realm of agriculture. The "negative results" in agriculture during the last years of Khrushchev had arisen from "the violation of the economic laws of socialist production and of the principle of material incentives, the incorrect combination of the peasantry's social and personal interests, and a subjective handling of the whole problem of agricultural production." Put in simpler terms, this just means that Khrushchev "subjectively" improvised, discovering all the time new panaceas, which in the end all proved unsatisfactory; as regards incentives, Krushchev had done nothing to encourage the peasants to make the most of their private plots (which he had heavily taxed) and had restricted the number of livestock the peasants could privately own. (I remember, for instance, visiting a kolkhoz near Leningrad in 1964, shortly before Khrushchev's fall; the peasants were openly grumbling, one remarking that all he had by way of manure for his private plot was "the manure from two cats and one dog."

All these "Khrushchev" errors were, however, corrected by the March 1965 Plenum, though, as will be seen later, the incentives were still, in the view of a "radical" Soviet economist, the wrong ones, relating much more to the peasant's private plot than to the collective land. This was not quite correct, as is shown by the agricultural production figures for 1967. In any case, in terms of food production, the measures taken in the March 1965 and later plenums had proved good: in 1966 the Soviet Union had a near-record harvest of 171.2 million tons of grain, which was nearly twice the 1940 figure; nearly 11 million tons of meat—2.3 times more than in 1940; and 1.2 million tons of animal fats, or more than three times the 1940 figure. Without claiming to be entirely satisfied with these results, the *Survey* still declared that by the end of the 1966–70 Five-Year Plan agricultural production should greatly improve as a result of the "intensification of crops by means of greater mechanization, more chemical fertilizers, and the more extensive melioration of the soil."

Very interesting, too, is the next claim made by the *Survey:* that the Soviet economy is becoming more and more harmonious and better balanced. Thus, the tempos in the development of consumer goods were approaching those of the means of production. Indeed, a few months after the publication of the *Survey,* the 1968 budget was to show that for the first time in the history of the Soviet Union the production of light industry was greater than that of heavy industry. Thus, the production of consumer goods was for the first time beginning to hold a very important position in the country's economy.

THE ECONOMIC DISPUTE

By far the least lucid passage in the *Survey* relates, in reality, to the present sharp dispute among Soviet economists—at one extreme the conservative Stalinist ultracentralizers and at the other the greater-local-initiative people; it looks as if it were trying to be all things to all men.

> A new system of planning and economic stimulants should be brought coherently into being. This system reflects the altered conditions of socialist management, the greatly increased scale of present-day socialist production, and the qualitative changes in its structure, as well as the new demands of the scientific and technical revolution. . . . This reform implies a new approach to the direction of the economy. In essence it amounts to a great im-

provement in strengthening the economic methods of guidance, a greater perfection in state planning and an extension of the economic independence and initiative of enterprises, and the further adoption and improvement of "profitability" [*khozrash-chet*]. The reform can best succeed if there is a correct combination of centralized guidance with the economic independence of the enterprises, complete with moral and material stimuli, the skillful utilization, on a socialist basis, of money-and-goods relations and the related economic categories—profit, prices, credit, etc.—which, in socialist conditions, acquire a new social content. . . .

The whole passage suggests a kind of compromise between the conservative and liberal elements inside the government and the Party, but with the conservatives still holding very strong positions.

THE WELFARE STATE

The *Survey* then deals specifically with some of the major aspects of what might be called the Soviet welfare state (though the ultradoctrinaires in Russia do not like this phrase, which to them smacks too much of a sort of Anglo-Scandinavian social-democratic paternalism and is also embarrassing in Russian polemics with the Chinese). The principal figures quoted are:

Thirty-four million people on old-age or disability pensions.

Eight million children in kindergartens and other preschool establishments, and corresponding numbers in secondary and higher education.

Totally free medical service, with 578,000 doctors (twenty times more than before the Revolution).

Ten to eleven million people a year move into new or rebuilt houses, and about half the population has moved into such new houses in recent years. (The housing program has been accelerated since 1952, and especially since 1957–58.)

On what is admittedly the weakest spot of all in the Soviet economic system and, indeed, in everyday life, namely, distribution and scarcity and inadequacy of shops, the *Survey* says no more than that *"measures are being taken to improve retail trade and catering establishments."*

On the question of education, the *Survey* stresses that at the present time about fitfy per cent of industrial workers have received full or partial secondary education; and, with technology becoming increasingly complicated, there is much less of a dividing line between engineer, technician and skilled worker. Similarly, with the ever-growing mechanization of agriculture, work in the fields has become more and more like work in the factories; moreover, the sovkhozes (state farms) are based on regular wages, while in the kolkhozes (collective farms) there is now a guaranteed minimum income, not to mention the only recently introduced old-age pensions in the case of the peasantry.

As regards the intellectuals (these, in Soviet terminology, include all types of brain workers, such as technicians, engineers, etc.), their number—notably that of the "technical intelligentsia"—has grown from 200,000 "specialists" in 1913 to nearly 13 million now.

After speaking of the friendship and solidarity uniting all the peoples of the Soviet Union, the *Survey* declares that the CPSU "continues its regular struggle against all manifestations of national narrow-mindedness, any feelings of 'seniority,' nationalism and chauvinism"; there is no contradictions between this and the fact that, amongst all the nations of the Soviet Union, Russian has become a sort of Lingua Franca; but this in turn does not mean that there is any one chosen people in the Soviet Union; on the contrary, all nationalities are given the same opportunity to develop their own national cultures. This passage, though not to be taken entirely literally, still marks a departure from Stalin's eulogies, toward the end of the Second World War, of the Russian people being the "best"—in effect, the chosen people. It does not, however, as much as hint at certain anomalies, such as the continuing tendency in most of the non-Russian republics for many of the most highly responsible posts to be held by Russians; or at the not entirely resolved "Jewish problem," which, though very much less acute than during the last years of Stalin and even under Khrushchev, still presents certain difficulties, especially of a psychological order. This will be dealt with later in the book.

END OF THE "DICTATORSHIP OF THE PROLETARIAT"

Then the *Survey* discusses a question already raised by Khrushchev: Has the notion of the dictatorship of the proletariat withered away? At the present stage, it explains, the role of the socialist state, especially as regards its economic and organizational, cultural and educational functions, is growing increasingly important. Increasingly large sections of the people are drawn into this work.

> *Narodovlastie* [literally, demo-cracy, rule by the people] finds its expression primarily in the soviets, which are organs of popular representation, combining the features of both state and social organizations. This gives the Soviet state a broad social base, and the dictatorship of the proletariat now becomes the political organization of the whole people, under working-class guidance. The present all-people state . . . continues the task of the dictatorship of the proletariat—i.e., on a much wider base than previously, and together with other socialist states; in the international field these conduct a joint class struggle against imperialism.

The *Survey* then adds:

> This further development of the socialist state and of socialist democracy has found concrete expression in such things as the increased role of the soviets of workers' deputies. . . . In the same way the trade unions are playing a wider role as a school of administration and economic management; with eighty million members, they constitute a powerful help to the Party, notably in increasing labor productivity and in accelerating scientific and technical progress. They have the right of legislative initiative, and administer the state's social-insurance system. . . . They also devote much attention to organizing the workers' leisure, holidays, rest homes, sanatoriums, etc.

In reality this passage significantly exaggerates the role of the soviets as something "independent" of the Party machinery. This rosy picture of the "democratization" of the Soviet Union is some-what overdone.*

PARTY AND KOMSOMOL

There follows the usual tribute to the Komsomol: "active helper of the Party, and the reserve of future Party members"; of course, the Young Communist League is no longer, as it was in the early years of the Revolution, a sort of vanguard of young enthusiasts; today it is a huge mass organization comprising no fewer than twenty-three million young men and women, and, since the normal Komsomol age is fourteen to twenty-six, a very high proportion of that age group are Komsomol members. The proportion of Party members in relation to the age groups above the age of twenty-five is, of course, lower. Admission to the Komsomol is almost automatic, but not all Komsomols apply for Party membership, while some, for a variety of reasons, are not admitted. Even so, with nearly thirteen million members in the CPSU in 1967, the membership has more than doubled since the war, representing well over twelve per cent of the population above twenty-five.

What has helped to inflate the Party membership has, of course, been the enormous increase in the number of highly educated people; the *Survey* recalls in this connection that today there are in schools of every kind nearly fifty million pupils (as against under ten million before the Revolution), including over four million in higher education (127,000 under the Tsar); and there are 124,000 public libraries (nine times more than in 1913).

THE OFFICIAL LINE ON THE ARTS

Needless to say, least satisfactory from almost every educated Russian's point of view is the tribute to socialist realism in the arts, which means, among other things, the "inacceptance of any com-promise with bourgeois morality and ideology"; the matter is not made much better by the additional statement that the adherence to

* See p. 145, on the Party bureaucracy.

the fundamental principles of socialist art does not in the least exclude "a progressive forward spirit, a search for new original ways [*novatorstvo*], and a bold artistic pioneering spirit."

All these verbal concessions to the new spirit are hard to take very seriously, and it seems obvious that in the government and Party hierarchy there is still a terrifying hangover from the Stalin days in matters of art and literature; and it is this that sets the tone of all the activities of the Writers' Union and creates the greatest difficulties for young and original writers, and even for some old writers.

The reason why there is no echo of the fundamental struggle between the intellectuals and the bureaucracy in the *Survey* seems, unfortunately, only too simple. Kosygin is primarily concerned with what he considers most important of all—the country's economic development and foreign policy. Literature and the arts are, in the opinion of most liberal elements among writers and artists, simply abandoned to the conservatives, with the provision that they confine their nefarious activities to culture and leave "more important" matters alone. The head of the cultural ultras in the Politburo is believed to be Mikhail A. Suslov, who has the bureaucrats of the Writers' Union (at least in Moscow) completely under his thumb. These, in turn, dominate and bully the entire literary scene—again, above all, in Moscow. The Minister of Culture, Madame Furtseva, is of little importance or influence. What Brezhnev's views on the cultural question are is not entirely certain, but, as distinct from Kosygin, he is believed to incline toward the Stalinite extremists—a view strongly confirmed by the extreme intolerance to "ideological immaturity" and "ideological coexistence" he showed in the spring of 1968, after the great liberalization drive in Czechoslovakia, which was something that most Russian intellectuals have for years been vainly longing for.

THE INTERNATIONAL SITUATION

Particularly important is the *Survey*'s analysis of the present international situation. It starts by setting down the principle that "the October Revolution marked the beginning of the revolutionary transition from capitalism to socialism in the whole world." And in the last fifty years, indeed, more and more countries have been drawn into this process, despite the fierce resistance of the imperialist forces, which at times have succeeded in counterattacking. The experience of the last fifty years, it says, has shown that capitalism, at its present imperialist stage, is marked by its "organic vices" and its "indifference to human life."

> The two world wars unleashed by imperialism have cost mankind sixty million lives; and now it is threatened with an even more murderous Third World War, to be fought with nuclear weapons. Local wars and punitive campaigns—such as that of the American imperialists against the people of Vietnam, and Israel's aggression against the Arab countries—the militarization of the economy and the attempts to set up terrorist fascist regimes (the latest of these is the reactionary *coup d'état* in Greece)—all this demonstrates the true substance of imperialism. It also eloquently demonstrates the correctness of Marxist-Leninist theory, which declares that imperialism acts against the interests of the masses— as, for instance, could be seen from the economic slumps in the capitalist world, particularly in 1929–33. . . . Today, only imperialism, with its terrifying short-sightedness and selfishness, can be blamed for the extreme backwardness of dozens of countries in Asia, Africa and Latin America—a backwardness which is the direct consequence of their being plundered by the imperialist powers, with their policies of colonialism and, now, neocolonialism.

It then says:

> No doubt to prolong its existence, present-day capitalism, which has now predominantly taken the form of state or monopoly capitalism, has had to resort to a variety of new tactics and maneuvers so as to limit the effect of phenomena so dangerous and destructive to itself, such as the anarchy in production, economic crises and mass unemployment.

This is, indeed, a remarkably candid and not wholly incorrect explanation why capitalism has succeeded in prolonging its existence—and for an almost indefinite period, even now, fifty years after the October Revolution. But the *Survey* then says that these temporary cures will not save capitalism forever from grave new difficulties, such as, for example, the enormous growth of automation in recent years.

THE OTHER SOCIALIST COUNTRIES

The *Survey* clearly admits—though not explicitly—that Lenin's earlier dreams of a world revolution failed completely; but, as a result of the Second World War, a number of countries adopted the road shown them by the October Revolution; not only could they rely on the direct aid of the Soviet Union, but they could also benefit from the Russian experience since 1917. And here the *Survey* sounds the "polycentrist" note which was, of course, pure poison to Stalin when he first (more or less forcibly) included the Eastern European countries in his sphere of influence: "While largely following the example of the Soviet Union, each of these countries also contributes much that is peculiar to itself to its own ways and methods of effecting its transition to socialism." The wholehearted acceptance by the Soviet leadership of this polycentrism may, however, be gravely doubted in the light of the attitude in 1968 to both Poland and Czechoslovakia. All the same,

> the new socialist countries now increase their production more rapidly than the capitalist countries. All of them, except East Germany and Czechoslovakia, were economically lamentably backward, but now, taken as a whole, they have an industrial production ten times greater than before the Second World War; as a result, the standard of living in these countries is substantially higher than it was before the war.

And here comes a very curious (veiled) admission: that "the economic reforms now carried out in several of these countries, and intended to increase the effectiveness of socialist production, will . . . create favorable conditions for these socialist countries in their competition with the capitalist countries." What the *Survey* refrains from stressing, however, is that the new methods tried out in Hungary, East Germany and Czechoslovakia are not yet being carried out on the same scale in the Soviet Union, since the latter wants to see first what these as it were NEP–tainted experiments will actually produce, not only economically but also politically.

The *Survey* makes another important admission: that the whole process of establishing friendly and confident relations, on a footing of complete national sovereignty, between the Soviet Union and the new socialist countries of Eastern Europe was not an easy one. There had been, amongst many of them, the fearful heritage of mutual distrust, suspicion and often downright national hatred toward the Soviet Union. . . . This was an appalling problem which the Communist and other progressive parties in these countries had to solve for the first time in their respective histories. Moreover, the economic level in these countries differed greatly, and it was not easy, in respecting each country's sovereignty, to get each one of them to agree to play the most rational role in the common economic cooperation under what became the SEV, or Comecon. All this, in fact, amounts to saying that at the very early stages *immediately after the war there could be no question of absolutely respecting the national sovereignty of a country like Poland,* with its centuries-old anti-Muscovite tradition, or of not exercising considerable pressure on a country like Rumania, which was more eager after the war to industrialize itself than the Russians thought desirable in the general plan of inter-socialist-countries economic cooperation. As for Czechoslovakia, the hard Stalinist regime set up in 1948 continued, under the Novotny dictatorship, longer even than in most of the Eastern European countries. Brezhnev desperately tried to save Novotny, but failed.

CHINA

The *Survey* then turns to China. While, under Comecon and the Warsaw Defense Pact, the Soviet Union and the socialist countries of Eastern Europe showed over the years "a growing sense of mutual trust and solidarity"—rather a sweeping statement—the same, unfortunately, could not be said of China.

> During the first years of the Chinese Revolution, whose victory had been a heavy blow to imperialism, the Chinese people achieved great social, economic and cultural reforms. In achieving these results, China had been greatly helped by the Soviet Union

and the other socialist countries—by their economic, political, military and cultural aid.

But by the end of the 1950s the leadership of the Chinese Communist Party adopted a new line, in both home and foreign policy, which meant a clear departure from the principles of Marxism-Leninism and proletarian internationalism and from the normal building of a socialist society.

The Mao Tse-tung group adopted a line in which were merged petty-bourgeois adventurism and Great-Power chauvinism, all of it covered up by so much "leftist" verbiage. This group thus openly began to undermine the unity of the socialist community of friendship and cooperation, and thus split up the world Communist movement itself.

Mao's course seriously weakened the Chinese Communist Party and the Chinese working class and gave, instead, free rein to the "elemental and anarchist forces of the petty bourgeoisie." But then comes this conciliatory conclusion:

The Soviet people always regarded the great Chinese people as a friend and an ally in its struggle for the revolutionary transformation of society. The complete abandonment by the Chinese CP of the present pernicious policy, the resumption of friendly relations between China, the Soviet Union and the other socialist countries, would be in the interests of the entire Communist movement in the world, and in the very first place in China's own interests.

This is a very mildly worded appeal to China to make friends again, and not to exacerbate the quarrel. The Central Committee's *Survey* refrains from saying anything precise about Mao's "Great-Power chauvinism," which would have meant discussing China's claims on those vast stretches of Soviet territory in Central Asia and the Far East originally "stolen" from China by the various tsars; none of these, except for Port Arthur and Dairen, had the Soviet rulers ever offered to return to China. Nor does the *Survey* make any mention of that other element in Chinese "Great-Power chauvinism"—the Chinese H-bomb.

EX-COLONIES

Turning to the question of the colonial peoples, the *Survey* begins by saying that the October Revolution was soon followed by an effective alliance between the socialist revolution and the national-liberation movements in the colonial territories of the world. Lenin had the tragic fate of the colonial peoples particularly at heart. As a result of the Second World War, the imperialists' hold on their colonial territories was greatly weakened (as we know indeed, particularly from the example of Indochina and, a few years later, from the cases of India, Ceylon, Burma and French North Africa).

The *Survey* makes an interesting point: both in the case of the tsarist "colonial empire" in Central Asia and in that of Outer Mongolia (though nominally part of China, and then an independent country) the Soviet Russians did not pump wealth *out* of them (as real colonialists would have done), they pumped wealth *into* them, a point correctly stressed by Nora Beloff a few years ago in the *Observer* after a visit to Soviet Central Asia. (This is not to say that the Russians did not do a lot of pumping *out* of the Eastern European countries, especially during the years of postwar reconstruction—if only on the ground that the Soviet Union had suffered far greater material damage during the war than most of them—and even more recently, as we see from the virtual Rumanian and then Czechoslovak rebellions against Comecon.)

After saying that in the ex-colonial countries a very sharp struggle was now going on between the "new progressive powers" and those "ready to come to terms with their former colonial [now called neocolonialist] bosses," the *Survey* openly admits that the Soviet Union gives all possible aid to the "progressive powers," even supplying them with "the military means of defending their country"—a clear reference, notably, to Egypt.

WESTERN COMMUNIST PARTIES

In the next section, dealing with the working class in the advanced capitalist countries, the *Survey* is clearly on even less satisfactory ground; but it makes the important point that it was thanks to the October Revolution, which had thrown the capitalist classes into a panic, that they began to make much more generous concessions to their own working classes than before. The *Survey* fails, however, to point to the obvious accompanying phenomenon that these concessions greatly reduced the revolutionary ardor of the Western working classes, and tries to argue that the great success of the Soviet regime continues to be ever present in the minds of the workers of the Western world. Nevertheless the question remains: What about the Communist parties of the West? In fact, only two of them really matter—the French, with a vote of twenty to twenty-five per cent of the poll, and the Italian, with a similar percentage.

On this question, the *Survey* goes a long way back.

> An enormous role in the creation and consolidation of the Communist parties of the world was played by the Comintern [the Third International, created at the beginning of the Bolshevik regime]. This was organized on the initiative of V. I. Lenin. . . . It played a great part in the education of the glorious cohort of outstanding leaders and the most dynamic cadres of the Communist movement. In the last fifty years, the Communist movement has developed into an enormous force.

And then, unbearably stretching a point, it goes on to say that "there are Communist parties practically everywhere where there is a working class." True enough in theory, but nonsense in practice; for if the French and Italian parties are very large political parties, those of, say, Britain and the United States are little more than small political sects, with a negligible membership. While in France nearly one quarter of the population votes Communist and there were, until 1962, seventy-five Communist members in the French National Assembly, there are strictly none in the British House of Commons.

The *Survey* goes on to demonstrate the importance of the harmony and cohesion of the various Communist parties; such meetings as that of the European Communist parties at Karlovy-Vary in 1967 were of the greatest importance. And what were the main subjects discussed at Karlovy-Vary? Significantly, the international situation, and in the first place the danger of West Germany and the war in Vietnam. (The Middle-East war had not started at the time.) In other words, there was common ground on foreign policy, but on little else. The only two major European Communist parties not represented (for diametrically opposite reasons) were the Albanian and the Rumanian.

As for the world Communist movement, the *Survey* recalls the Moscow Conferences of 1957 and 1960, though without mentioning the salient fact that the rot in Soviet-Chinese relations began in a very small way in 1957, and in a very big way in 1960. Nor, of course, does it mention the Chinese—and not only Chinese—suspicion that Moscow's desire to hold the leading role in the world Communist movement is not free of Russian "Great-Power chauvinism."

What follows is very interesting.

> In present-day conditions the greatest importance must be attached to the correct coordination of the national and international tasks facing the world Communist movement. *Outside the struggle for the solution of national problems for the working masses of each particular country there can be no question of fulfilling the Communist movement's international obligation.* [My italics.]

This is, on the face of it, *the Russians' final and entirely unambiguous acceptance of polycentrism.* Each Communist party must, in other words, consider its own *national* interests first. This is a complete departure from Stalinism. Only, is it quite sincere? For, if so, why the great alarm caused in the Kremlin by the liberalization of the Communist Party of Czechoslovakia in 1968? But has not Comecon too been a secret weapon of Russian pressure—and one increasingly resented, notably by Rumania and Czechoslovakia? Under Stalin, Russia simply gave orders to the foreign Communist parties, regardless of the utterly disastrous results these might produce. The most striking example of this was in France at the beginning of the Second World War, when the French Communists were informed that they should treat both Germany and their own country as imperialist powers and therefore do nothing to hinder the Germans. Though they were mobilized into the French Army, and fought as well as anybody, they underwent intense persecution, and many of the leading Communists were arrested and tried as traitors.*

But the Communists of all countries—and here there is no disagreement, except perhaps among those of the "Chinese" variety —are unquestionably agreed on a common policy, which is to be among the chief guardians of world peace. While stressing the immense military power of the socialist countries, the *Survey* still admits that world peace is in danger, as may be seen from the American war in Vietnam, from the "imperialist-inspired aggression of Israel" against the Arab countries, and "the continuous provocations against Cuba." Hence the socialist camp's absolute need for "vigilance and armed preparedness." The socialist countries also feel it a sacred duty to support the national-liberation struggle of oppressed people, and of course to help victims of "imperialist aggression" such as Vietnam and the Arab countries. The ultimate aim of this policy is to save the world from a thermonuclear war.

But, in saying this, the *Survey* does not mention, either here or anywhere else, "peaceful coexistence," a phrase which in the Soviet Union (at least on the official level) has grown thinner and thinner since the war in Vietnam began to assume its murderous 1966–67 proportions.

This *Survey*, which may be regarded as the official Soviet line (and so the voice of Brezhnev and Kosygin), has, as we have seen, its weaknesses; but most Western readers will still find much of it very fundamental and convincing, above all in the antiwar stand taken by the socialist camp, which, unlike the United States, is not today engaged in any major war—apart from supporting, as far as possible, "victims of aggression" like North Vietnam (including the South Vietnam resistance) and Egypt.

* For the story of the tragic dilemma of the French Communists in 1939–40, see the author's *France 1940–1955* (London and New York, 1956), pp. 178–98.

2

The End of Lysenko

MY MOST recent visit to Russia was in the summer of 1967, the year
of the fiftieth anniversary of the Revolution. I had arranged with the
Soviet Embassy in Paris to go not only to Moscow and Leningrad,
but also the wilds of Siberia, especially to Novosibirsk and even
Yakutsk. They had agreed. What interested me in Novosibirsk
above all (though I know very little about science) was the Academgorodok, one of the greatest science centers in the Soviet Union,
over which de Gaulle was particularly rapturous when he visited it a
year or two ago. I wanted to see Yakutsk chiefly for color; also,
newspapers are terribly impressed by datelines like Yakutsk, which
only a few foreigners have ever visited.

I find nothing more boring than long plane flights (and the
Tupolev, flying over Holland, Denmark and a bit of Sweden, took
three and a half hours to get to Moscow). But by an extraordinary
piece of luck the man sitting next to me on the plane was a professor who was working at the Novosibirsk science center. And,
even better still, he was a biologist and geneticist (one of the very
top people in that line in Russia, as I later discovered). In anticipa-
tion of my visit to Novosibirsk, I asked him the one very obvious
question: "Professor S——, can you tell me where you stand over
Lysenko? Until a few years ago, his name kept popping up in the
Soviet press, but I haven't seen it recently."

His reply told me just what I wanted to know: "That charlatan,
who, for years and years, made every Russian scientist's life a
misery, is finished, yes, completely finished. He hasn't been shot, as
he would have been if the Stalin methods were still applied. Though,
by God, he would more than deserve it. It was because of charlatans
like Lysenko that we lost some of our great scientists, such as N. I.

Vavilov, who died in a camp in 1943, and many others. And if you were in the Soviet Union in 1948 you must remember that hideous humiliation we real scientists had to go through to save our lives: we had to cringe and crawl on our bellies to Lysenko (though we knew he was about a hundred per cent wrong) and sing the praises of Stalin and the Central Committee, because they had *decreed* that Lysenko was right and anyone disagreeing with him criminally wrong. We had to cringe and beat our chests; yes, even young Yuri Zhdanov, one of Svetlana Stalina's numerous husbands, incidentally, and a good, though not top, scientist, had to cringe and crawl in a letter of self-criticism in *Pravda*—I think it was in August 1948—shouting *mea culpa, mea maxima culpa.* How could he possibly not have understood that only the Great Stalin and the Central Committee of our Beloved Party could be right?

"You people in the West make a terrible song and dance about Pasternak and all that; but, for God's sake, literature is one thing, and one can have a hundred different opinions about any book; but science—oh, these unspeakable cretins nearly ruined Soviet science between 1948 and Papasha's death. Yes, people in the streets wept when he died; to us scientists it was the happiest day of our life. Great scientists who had been in exile for years were now going to come back, and we could speak freely again about the pros and cons of 'degenerate bourgeois science'—Mendelianism, Morganism and all that—and show Lysenko up as a crook, and even Michurin, who was nothing other than a green-finger gardener and not, as we were told, the greatest scientific genius of all time, next to Stalin, of course."

"Professor, aren't you putting it rather strongly, talking like that about Stalin?"

"No, please don't misunderstand me. Stalin was a horror in lots of ways, but he has two immense achievements to his credit: he industrialized Russia in a big way, and, despite some appalling blunders at the beginning, he did see us through the war to final victory. But when we speak of science, that's quite another matter. Here he was the supreme cretin. If Stalin's treatment of scientists had gone on, today we would be about as backward as the Pauans or the Congolese. Under Stalin—I mean in his last years—we were no longer scientists, but worshipers of totem poles."

I could feel the professor was angry, horribly angry. "Yes," I said, "but Lysenko wasn't liquidated immediately after Stalin's death."

"You're quite right there. But, as in so many other fields, the Stalin hangover took a very, very long time to disappear. Thank God, in science it disappeared almost immediately."

"Yes," I said, "but Lysenko was still around."

"That didn't matter much. He was one scientist, and we were the thousands of others. Now, at last, he was entitled to his idiotic views, but at least *we* were entitled to ours, and the chest-beating was stopped the moment Stalin died. Lysenko kept going, off and on, for a few years longer, and I'll tell you why. Khrushchev fancied himself a tremendous expert on agriculture, although in reality he knew about agriculture about as much as he knew about music and literature. And Lysenko, who had a knack for ingratiating himself with people, kept on promising Khrushchev the moon. So Khrushchev reasoned roughly like this: 'Well, after all, old man Stalin, who was no fool, had a great regard for Lysenko; so the fellow must have some merit.' And he let him go ahead—in a very small way, it's true. And when there happened to be a good harvest—this sometimes happens simply because it rains at the right time— Lysenko claimed the credit for it; and Khrushchev, who was not a bad man, but, as far as science and agriculture were concerned, rather an ass, liked to think that if we had grown ten million tons of grain more than usual Lysenko had, somehow, something to do with it.

"Now Lysenko is, of course, altogether finished. He hasn't been shot; we don't usually use such methods any more. But he's living on quite a fat old-age pension. And good luck to him, the son of a bitch."

And he concluded, "Yes, we Soviet scientists are probably the happiest people in the world today. Do you know who are the most unhappy?"

"Yes," I said: I thought I could guess. "The writers?"

"Yes," said the professor. "This is about the only terrifying thing left in Russia. The Writers' Union is perhaps the last lair of the Stalinist and Zhdanovist bullies. On the surface all goes wonderfully well, but we scientists, we who had to crawl to Lysenko, know what it is like to be a Solzhenitsyn, a Pasternak, an Anna Akhmatova.

I'm not talking about Daniel and Siniavsky. That's a very special case: there was a regular—well, almost a regular—trial, there was such-and-such an article of the Criminal Code, they were able to plead not guilty (which, in itself, is something new in the Soviet Union). They are writers of no great importance. I bought their books in Paris—not bad, but, on the whole, rather third-rate. But the tragedy of great writers like Pasternak and Akhmatova, of Solzhenitsyn, of many, many others like Paustovky, or Ehrenburg or Voznesensky and Yevtushenko, who are just tolerated, but no more —this is where the real tragedy of Soviet literature comes out.

"There was a reason, even an excellent reason, in the early thirties to set up the Writers' Union, so that everybody did his stuff to educate the people, who were then still terribly ignorant; the international situation was appallingly dangerous, and it was no time for art for art's sake and all that kind of thing. Today it is much less sure that there is any need for the Writers' Union— which, unfortunately, gets great encouragement from a few of our Party bosses."

We had talked for over three hours, and for the first time in my life I had not found a plane journey a bore. I had learned quite a few things I had suspected but had never heard stated quite so clearly.

I was met at Sheremetyevo, Moscow's international airport, by my old friend Savva Dangulov, a dark and witty little Caucasian with flashing black eyes and a superb sense of fun and humor, who had gone with me in September 1943 to Leningrad, still blockaded and under constant shellfire. We had remained friends ever since. Savva was then in the Foreign Office press department; after the war, he held diplomatic posts in the Balkans. A few years ago he had returned to Moscow, and he was now assistant editor of the monthly magazine *Foreign Literature*. An excellent war reporter in the early years of the war, he had recently also taken to novel-writing. His best-known novel is called *The Diplomats,* a historical novel of the early years of the Revolution, with Lenin, Krassin, Litvinov and Chicherin as its principal characters. It is a swiftly moving story, the scene shifting from London and Newcastle and Stockholm to Petrograd and Moscow. The characters are well drawn; Savva had, obviously, also rummaged quite a lot in the Soviet Foreign Ministry archives. This is not a genre of Russian novel I particularly like, nor could it make a great appeal in the West, but, as novels of this kind go, it is one of the best. Politically, Savva Dangulov is what I might call mildly conservative or cautiously liberal, a man of the Establishment.

As a Caucasian, partly Georgian, he has, I suspect, a soft spot for Stalin. I once or twice pulled his leg about it: "Savva, why not admit it—you're an old Stalinite at heart, and a bit sentimental still about your fellow Georgian."

He laughed. "No, Georgia is neither here nor there; but you know as well as I do that people of our generation who went through the war of 1941–45 find it hard to dissociate those fearful but still splendid days from the old devil. Let me put it this way: both you and I, without being political Stalinites—that's quite a different thing—are, or at least were, sentimental Stalinites, isn't that true?" I had to admit there was something in it.

It was more difficult to discuss literature with him. Here, I suspect, a kind of defense mechanism came into play; he would not agree with me (whatever he thought in private) about Siniavsky and Daniel; when I regretted that only *Novy Mir* of the three big Moscow monthlies was almost invariably readable, he would try to convince me that there were many good things in *Znamya* and *Oktyabr*.

"Well," I said, *"Znamya* at a pinch—but *Oktyabr!"*

"Oh," said Savva, "it's not so bad. And I strongly suspect you damn *Oktyabr* because it's the right thing to do, without having ever read it."

I said I had tried to read through one number, but it was really quite impossible, even though its editor, Kochetov, wasn't quite as awful a writer as everybody somehow assumed; I had found *The Yershov Brothers* no great shakes as literature, but still of quite considerable interest, what with the "bad" brother, who had served in the Vlasov army, and all that.

"No," said Savva, "you can't judge a magazine merely by reading one issue. You people in the West are more sectarian than any of us; all the names one ever hears in the West are Pasternak and Akhmatova, and more Pasternak, and then Yevtushenko and

Voznesensky, and more Akhmatova. Period. You should read some of the poets *we* like. What about Sofronov and Gribachev?"*

"Savva, you're joking!"

"No, I assure you, I'm not!" But there was a grin on his face; I knew he *was* joking—at least I think so.

* Hack poets, but important as top bureaucrats of the press and the Writers' Union.

3

Unusual Moscow Snapshots: Labor-Camp Bosses and Victims

As A Leningrader, I never very much liked Moscow. I remember the mild antagonism between Glasgow and Edinburgh when I was a Glasgow graduate; but the mutual antipathy between Moscow and Leningrad is very much deeper. Before the Revolution, St. Petersburg tended to look down on Moscow as a great big provincial city or Russia's biggest village. Today it is Leningrad which has become a big provincial city, and since the war, we are told, everything that really matters has moved to Moscow. Leningrad is also sharply conscious of the fact that it suffered infinitely greater hardships during the war than Moscow ever did.

All the same, I have a certain soft spot for the very center of Moscow—for the old Reuter flat in Khokhlovsky Lane where I spent the agonizing summer and autumn months of 1941, or for the old Metropole Hotel, with its Vrubel mosaics, built in the *belle époque* style of 1900, where I lived during the rest of the war and until my virtual expulsion from the Soviet Union in 1948. I also like the first of the great hotels built in Soviet times, the Moskva, where I stayed as an official guest of the Soviet government during the great celebrations in May 1965 which marked the twentieth anniversary of the Allied victory over Germany, when Marshal Sokolovsky himself presented me a war medal.

But Moscow is always overcrowded, especially in summer, and the best that could be found for me was a room on the twenty-third floor of the Hotel Ukraina, one of those "Stalin Gothic" skyscrapers which, it seems, Stalin in his last years ordered to be built in much

74

the same way as the Pharaohs ordered the Pyramids to be built—for their own eternal glory. Among the other famous Stalin skyscrapers are, of course, the university and the present Soviet Ministry of Foreign Affairs. The Ukraina is difficult to get at, with no Metro station within easy reach, and with bus lines which are a little confusing to a newcomer. There are only two lifts available, and one sometimes has to wait five or ten minutes to get up or down.

But the panorama of Moscow from the top of the Ukraina is superb, and it gives one a particularly clear idea of how quickly and enormously Moscow is changing. Apart from the architecturally highly dubious Gorki Street, the new monumental government buildings like the Sovnarkom building, the new Moskva Hotel in the center, and a few new streets on the outskirts of the capital, the Moscow of the war years was not enormously different from pre-Revolution Moscow. There were thousands of wooden houses still, even in the center of the city. It had a drab and down-at-heels look, which contrasted strangely with the incongruous bronze-and-marble palaces, with their crystal chandeliers, of the Metro stations, built only a few years before. But then, after the war, came the Stalin skyscrapers, which already did much to change the familiar Moscow skyline; and now, since the early fifties, more and more houses were being built. The Ukraina Hotel, on the banks of the Moskva River, was now the terminus, as it were, of the vast new Kalinin Avenue, built in the last few years and now, in 1967, being feverishly completed. It had been bulldozed through the picturesque old Moscow quarter of the Arbat and was lined with enormous twelve-story and fourteen-story blocks; and the most spectacular of all, facing the Ukraina, was the "open-book" skyscraper, the new headquarters of SEV, or Comecon, as we call it, the nearest Eastern equivalent of the Common Market.

Unlike Leningrad, Moscow never presented (apart from its churches, many of which had been demolished in the early years of the Revolution) much architectural character, and now since the war, or, rather, since 1950 or so, whole large stretches of "inner" Moscow had been pulled down and replaced by new buildings. The Kremlin no longer dominated the Moscow skyline, and it and the Red Square were no longer even sacrosanct: under Khrushchev a new glass-and-steel Assembly Hall had been built inside the Kremlin, and quite recently a similar glass-and-steel building, the Hotel

Rossiya, had been built right behind St. Basil's Cathedral in the Red Square.

Ranking as an Intourist hotel, the Ukraina provided better service in its restaurants and buffets than did most other places. During my first fortnight there, an international congress of mining engineers was taking place in Moscow, and most of its foreign delegates were living at the Ukraina. Here I had some curious encounters. For instance, I met a German engineer. "East or West?" I asked. No, he had come from West Germany, and said that he was pleasantly surprised by everybody's friendliness and courtesy toward him. And then he said, "Ah, well, it's a long time ago now; perhaps they are beginning to forget the war." I remarked that this was certainly not the case, but that there was no reason why they should have anything against him personally.

I also remember a charming American couple, a mining engineer and his young wife. She was particularly starry-eyed about Moscow. "But," she said, "the food here is *wonderful*. Bill and I thought it would be terrible, and that there wouldn't be enough to eat, so we brought two whole cases of canned food and candy. And not only that," she added, "we thought there was a nine-o'clock curfew in Moscow; but one can go out any time of day or night. And they're such charming people, too!"

"SIBERIA IS LIKE ANYWHERE ELSE"

Despite my conversation with Professor S——on the Paris–Moscow plane, I still had not quite made up my mind, on arriving in Moscow, whether to go to Novosibirsk, Irkutsk and Yakutsk, as originally planned. With an introduction from a friend, I went to see a well-known Siberian writer, Ivan Taurin. I had never met him before, though I had read quite a good regional novel of his. He certainly knew his Siberia. He had started his career many years ago as a chemist, and in 1940, under the labor-conscription law of June 25 that year (enforced in view of the extremely dangerous situation following the fall of France*), he had been sent to Yakutsk.

* See the author's *Russia at War*.

"Ah," he said, "that was still a provincial backwater in those days, and one of the coldest places in the world—this, of course, it still is. It had a population, mostly Yakut natives, of only thirty-five thousand. Today it has grown into a city of over a hundred thousand people; nearly all the newcomers are Russian. People who were sent to those Arctic regions were paid extra bonuses in those days—ten per cent was added to their wages; and people had two months' leave every year and could get a free ticket to anywhere in the Soviet Union; those who stuck it out for three years got six months' leave."

"You mean, of course," I said, "the free, not the forced, labor?"

"Well, yes," Taurin smiled, "the forced labor, that was a *very* different story. I could tell you a few things about the labor camps, too, though I never sat in one myself—but what's the good?"

"How many do you reckon were locked up in those camps?" I ventured.

"Oh, no, let's not talk about that. It's ancient history now. And how many—I've no clear idea, and nobody has. Some say five hundred thousand, others even five million, but never more than five. The usual estimate is two or three million. No, those Arctic bonuses [*severnyie lgoty*] were a good thing. Nobody who can live in Moscow or the Caucasus or on the Don or in the Ukraine would like to live at, say, Yakutsk, or even farther north, where it's dark for nearly nine months in the year, and the temperature, as at Verkhoyansk, sometimes drops to seventy degrees Centigrade below zero. And Khrushchev did an exceedingly stupid thing, which resulted in lots of people flowing back to European Russia—he abolished the Arctic bonuses; and only recently have they been partly restored.*

"The country has its fascination, of course, and many who go there once decide to settle there for good. Thousands of our students from European Russia go to Siberia for three years after graduating, and many stay on. There is, of course, an enormous new population of European scientists, engineers and ordinary workers, what with all the new hydroelectric plants that have been and are being built—the Irkutsk plant built between 1950 and 1958, the gigantic Bratsk plant, and another one, the Ust-Imilevsk plant, some

* They were to be further increased on the eve of the Fiftieth Jubilee in 1967.

two hundred and fifty kilometers farther down the Angara. In Siberia there are quite astronomic quantities of coal and natural gas; all this attracts new prospectors, new engineers, new workers. The gigantic diamond fields north of Yakutsk, richer than anything in South Africa, were only recently discovered. Enormous cities are growing up in Siberia; Novosibirsk alone has 1,200,000 inhabitants now, and near it is the Academgorodok, one of the most famous science centers in the Soviet Union. You should go there, and go to Lake Baikal too, which is of extraordinary beauty. If you go to Irkutsk, you can get to Lake Baikal on a *raketa*—a speedboat—in about an hour and a half.

"But this fantastic industrialization of Siberia isn't all honey; Siberia, with its fabulous rivers, the Ob, the Yenisey, the Irtysh, the Lena, is beginning to have the same troubles as the Volga and the Dnieper. Yes, even Lake Baikal is now being polluted by close-by factories. On some of the rivers where there are hydroelectric plants, the fish are disappearing; there are the so-called *rybohody*—fish corridors—in the dams, but the fish somehow don't usually get through them, and just gradually die off. As I said, even Lake Baikal is being polluted. Though more slowly, you see the same kind of process going on as in most European Russian rivers, and on the Volga the situation is nearly desperate. I shouldn't be surprised," he smiled, "if in, say, ten years' time all the caviar-producing fish became completely extinct. Then there'll be no more *ikra,* no more caviar in the world, except perhaps in a few places like Iran."

"And what do the new Siberian cities look like?"

"Oh, you mean cities like Novosibirsk? Well, they are much the same as any big provincial city in Russia. If you drive up the Leningrad Chaussée in Moscow up to Khimki, it doesn't look all that different from Novosibirsk. Wide avenues, new blocks of flats, the *obkom* building, the theaters, railway stations, cinemas and that sort of thing. Of course, the taiga, the huge primeval forest of Siberia, is something special, and so are the great mountains in eastern Yakutia or in Kamchatka, with its volcanoes."

"And the people?"

"The old type of the *Sibiriak* is becoming increasingly scarce. The *Sibiriak*s have largely become assimilated with the European new-comers—the first- and second-generation Siberians. You still come across the old Siberian types—trappers and the like—but they are becoming pretty rare."

"And the 'natives'?"

"Well, they *look* different from us, of course, all these Eskimo and Mongoloid types; but they also are beginning to conform to Russian ways of thinking and behaving."

"What, then, *is* there to see in Siberia that you can't see here?"

"Lots of things. First of all, the superb scenery, especially in eastern Siberia, the vast expanses of the country; Yakut men, women and children, who are charming, and rather unusual things like reindeer sovkhozes and the like."

Thinking it over, I finally decided against the Siberian trip. I hate very long air flights, and to go to Irkutsk by train would take terribly long. No doubt the Bratsk hydroelectric plant is very super; but I don't know much about these things anyway, and when I'm being taken round I have to pretend to be interested when I'm really not. No doubt it would be interesting to talk to some Yakuts; but it would scarcely be worth all the time and expense of a two-week trip to Yakutia. As for cities like Novosibirsk and Irkutsk, they, as Taurin said, don't look very different from the Leningrad Chaussée in Moscow, and the people are for the most part very like any other people one meets in the rest of Russia. The scenery, yes, but I have always found people more interesting than scenery, no matter how wonderful. I decided I would learn more in an extra fortnight in Moscow than by talking, even for an hour, to the chairman of a reindeer sovkhoz—which I had seen in a splendid Soviet film recently, anyway.

HEAD OF A STALIN "SLAVE CAMP"

I was terribly busy every day, but since my wife and sixteen-year-old son had just joined me in Moscow, I decided to take a Sunday off, and we took the boat down the Moskva River to Kuntsevo, that very Kuntsevo where Stalin had lived in his *datcha* during the last years of his life, and where he had died in March 1953. Oddly enough, although I asked people where Stalin's *datcha* was, nobody seemed to know. So at Kuntsevo we took a rowboat for an hour (it cost only thirty kopecks—thirty cents—an hour) and then walked up the wooded slope to a refreshment pavilion, where beer and ice cream were available, and hung around for the next boat which was to take us back to Moscow. During this return journey, which lasted about an hour, I fell into conversation with a very strange person. Since Nicolas tends to talk French rather than English or Russian, this man knew at once that we were foreigners. He was an elderly man, curiously English to look at, with a toothbrush moustache and fine delicate features, rather unusual in Russia, and the soft, cultured voice of an old-time St. Petersburg intellectual.

"Yes, I like going to Kuntsevo," he said, "because I'm really mad for angling. Not that one often catches anything much in the Moskva River; but it's an old habit I acquired long ago, on the Kolyma."

The Kolyma River, to me, meant one thing, and one thing only: Stalin's forced-labor camps. So I said cautiously, "Kolyma—did you go there, shall we say, voluntarily or involuntarily?"

"Oh, perfectly voluntarily; I was there on government service."

"You mean you were in charge of a camp?"

"No, I wasn't as important as that; I was only a deputy governor."

"But they were frightful places, weren't they? I've just read a most harrowing account by a woman called Evgenia Ginsburg, who was sent to one of the camps in the Kolyma country, somewhere near Magadan, on the Sea of Okhotsk. Have you read her book?"

"No, I haven't, but I have heard a lot about it. And all I can tell you is that she greatly exaggerated the so-called horrors."

"But, listen, she talks of dozens of slave laborers dying of cold and starvation."

"No, that's not quite true. The truth is that those people were quite well fed and dressed, so long as they did their work properly and conscientiously."

"But they were victims of the Stalin-Yezhov purges," I said, "perfectly innocent people."

"Well, that's what people say now," said my friend (he never told me his name); "but in those days we assumed—and often rightly, I'm sure—that if a man had been sent to a camp as an enemy of the people [vrag naroda], or as a close friend or relation of one, there must be some good reason for it. And these people worked, and worked damned hard. We made them work in the goldfields, and the results were excellent. There is also a tremendous road they built with pavingstones, all the way from Magadan to the Arctic Ocean, a matter of twelve hundred kilometers. Oh, I know you call them 'slave laborers.' Well, in a sense they were; we made them work hard; but they were of real economic value, and that was how they were able to atone for their sins to the country."

"But there *weren't* any sins," I said, "at least not in most cases."

"Oh," he said, "that's what they say now, but in those days *we* didn't know; if a man was sentenced to so many years in a camp, it was not *our* business to inquire whether he had been sent there rightly or wrongly."

"And what happened in the end?" I asked.

"Well, as you know, our Party and government began to liquidate the labor camps after Stalin died. I was due for my old-age pension in 1958; however, things got a little unpleasant, and in 1956 I resigned my post in the MVD; that was after the Twentieth Congress, where Khrushchev gave a highly exaggerated picture of what he called Stalin's crimes. So for two years I had to live on my savings. Then, in 1958, when I was sixty, I started getting my old-age pension. Recently my daughter and I got quite a comfortable little flat in a brand-new block. I haven't much to do; but I love coming to Kuntsevo on Sundays to do a little fishing."

I had seldom been so baffled in my life. With his little toothbrush moustache, his gentle voice and manner, this deputy chief of one of Stalin's labor camps looked more like a retired bank clerk on some London surburban train.

There could be no doubt that many horrors had been perpetrated in the Stalin labor camps; everyone knew that, even before Solzhenitsyn's *One Day in the Life of Ivan Denisovich* and Evgenia Ginsburg's book had been published. But it was somehow impossible to imagine that this meek, gentle-spoken elderly man, with his fishing rods, could have tortured or beaten prisoners to death. Or had he?

No, unlike many of Hitler's SS sadists and mass killers, Stalin's "camp criminals" did not suffer much. Like this man, who had somehow found it necessary to resign from the MVD in 1956, they had lived through what must have been some uncomfortable moments. But now, since he had reached the age of sixty, he was living quite comfortably on his pension, like any other Russian of his age. Well, not quite like *any* other Russian. People knew, of course, what he had done in the Stalin days; and people like him were ostracized by their fellow Russians. Not apparently a very severe punishment; and yet perhaps this lifelong ostracism was more fearful than a few years in jail.

Anyway, the *métier* was not entirely extinct. I gathered—though it was difficult to find out anything quite definite—that there are still two "political" camps in the Soviet Union today. Nearly all their inmates are members of religious "anti-state" sects like Baptists and Jehovah's Witnesses. They, and also a few unfortunates like Daniel and Siniavsky.

"THE STALIN PURGES SAVED MY LIFE"

By a curious coincidence, at a friend's house a few days later I met a history teacher who had spent fifteen years in labor camps. Like thousands of others, he had been arrested in 1937, at the height of the Yezhov purges, and had not been released until 1945, when the war was already over. And then, in 1948, during the "second Stalin terror," he was again arrested, and not released till 1955. The reason he was arrested in 1937 was as absurd as the reasons for most other arrests. He had advised one of his students to read a book, a selection of poltical essays, and among these essays was one by Bukharin—a fact my friend had somehow overlooked.

"It was no use pleading not guilty," he said. "I would merely have been tortured or beaten up, and it would not have made the slightest difference to the verdict—or, rather, it might have made it even fiercer. The examining magistrate was quite a decent-looking fellow and merely said, 'Now, you can make your choice: do you want to be sentenced as a German spy, a British spy, or a Japanese spy?' I was then living in Leningrad, and I had several German friends; also, in connection with my work, I kept up a regular correspondence with several English teachers. I had never had anything to do with any Japanese, so I promptly declared myself a Japanese spy. 'Yes, you are probably very wise,' said the examining magistrate, and, patting me on the shoulder, he added, 'Eight years is nothing; you're a young man, they'll pass quickly.' So I was duly released in 1945, and felt I had got off reasonably lightly as a 'Japanese spy.'

"However, at the height of the Cold War I was arrested again—this time, like most people arrested at that time, for 'associating with foreigners.' I had, indeed, made good friends two years before with a Belgian postgraduate student at Moscow University and had also met several other foreigners since 1945. But, for some reason, it was the Belgian on whom they picked. (Fortunately he was back in Belgium by this time.) I confessed that the two of us had been guilty of subversive activities. They didn't even ask for any details, but gave me another ten years. I was let out after Stalin's death, or, rather, in 1955; all these 'rehabilitations' took a long time, often much longer than in my case.' "

It was then that I told him of my strange encounter on the river steamer, referring to my friend as "a little Eichmann."

"No," said the history teacher, "he was no Eichmann. You see, as distinct from the Germans, as a rule we did not go in for mass murder. True, there was Katyn, and I'm told that in 1945 thousands of Japanese collaborators were bumped off when we took over North Korea at the end of the Far-Eastern War. Beatings-up, still less tortures, were very unusual inside the camps; in fact, in my fifteen years' experience I don't remember a single case of torture. The beatings-up and the torture were quite the regular thing in the prisons, with people who were unwilling to confess. And there were some pretty horrible characters among the NKVD officials, though probably very few quite as bestial as so many of the Gestapo and SS men."

"You've read Solzhenitsyn, of course?" I said.

"Yes, and I also recently read Evgenia Ginsburg's book and Chukovskaya's *Deserted House*. Well, let me tell you: the Solzhenitsyn story is the most accurate account I know of life in a camp. That's precisely what my camps were like. The Ginsburg book strikes me as perfectly truthful, though personally I never experienced anything quite so horrible as her journey across Siberia; it's true that both my "excursions" were much shorter: one to Murmansk, the other to the Komi Republic, both inside European Russia."

"But according to Ginsburg," I said, "prisoners were dying of starvation, especially in that horrible camp on the Kolyma she describes."

"Yes, that may be true in that particular instance, but people in

my camp didn't die in large numbers, at least not till the war began
in 1941. As for Chukovskaya's novel, I agree it's a powerfully
written book, and as a work of literature it's admirable; but I think
she lays it on a bit too thick. It was very unusual for one disaster
after another to descend, almost without a day passing, on the same
family, on the same little group of people."

"But those dreadful prison queues? You were in Leningrad at the
time. Didn't things happen just the way Chukovskaya describes
them?"

"Oh, that—yes. But if I'm not quite satisfied with Chukovskaya's
story it's perhaps because she—and her heroine—were a bit too
thin-skinned. Most of us Russians had lived through such dreadfully
hard times that somehow we took even the Yezhov terror in our
stride. I, for one, always liked to see the funny side of things. I am,
as you can see, quite a lively talker, and I never put anybody's back
up; I made good friends with the sentries and guards, and even the
camp officials, who liked me to give them history lessons!"

"But then you said that you began to starve during the war."

"Well, we weren't on a particularly tasty and plentiful diet at the
best of times; the kind of millet soup and other muck we were given
to eat were precisely what Solzhenitsyn describes. But there was
something worse. As in nearly all camps there were two lots of
convicts—the politicals and the common criminals, called *suki*
(bitches), and these were a pretty horrible lot, who went out of
their way not only to victimize the politicals on every possible
occasion, but also to steal from them anything they could lay their
hands on. But, until the war began in 1941, we could still receive
letters and parcels from home in the normal way. For several
months after I got there in 1937, I had to do hard physical labor,
but then, luckily, I was given a job in the camp infirmary. And the
strangest thing during the first few months in a camp was that, for
the first time in years, *you were no longer afraid*. Believe it or not,
when Yezhov was replaced by Beria at the head of the NKVD in
1938, we rejoiced, and were right to do so. Our food rations were
considerably increased, and quite a few people were let out between
1938 and 1941. In short, up to the war, things were no better and
no worse than in *Ivan Denisovich,* icy cell and all. We received
parcels from home, and the postal services were regular. But 1941
and 1942 were the most terrible years. The whole of Russia was
desperately short of food, and the convicts were, naturally, not high

on any priority list. When you think that people in the armaments industries were often literally starving, it's scarcely surprising, and there was no calculated cruelty in that.

"But food was so short that in 1942 people in our camp began to die of hunger; by the end of that year, out of two thousand inmates ten or twenty would die every week; I could hardly move, so badly were my legs and feet swollen with hunger. Only in 1943 did things begin to improve a little bit. We began to get some Lend-Lease calcium and vitamin pills and occasionally even a tin of American Spam, and bread became more plentiful. Then I was let out in 1945 and settled in Moscow, and then, in 1948, as I said, I was picked up again. It may sound absurd, but Stalin and Yezhov saved my life, God bless them! If I hadn't been in a camp in 1941, I would have been called up, and a Russian soldier's chance of surviving till 1945 was practically nil. Or else, if I hadn't been called up at the very beginning of the war, I would almost certainly have died of hunger in the Leningrad blockade. I don't suppose you often hear people say, as I do, 'Thank God for Stalin and Yezhov,' though, in fact, hundreds of thousands of people who were in camps right through the war *were* saved that way. Only the convicts from Leningrad had to be doubly thankful, having thus escaped both the war and the blockade."

I asked my friend how many people he thought there were altogether in labor camps in 1948. "Impossible to give a definite figure, but most people in Russia reckon anything between five hundred thousand and five million." The Stalinist ultras, as a rule, mention a low figure, and the anti-Stalinites a high one—but always between these two extremes. The usual estimate is between two and three million.

During the seven years I had spent in the Soviet Union between 1941 and 1948 I had done my utmost to arrive at an at least approximate estimate of the number of "slave laborers." The figures given me, particularly in 1947–48, by various Russians ranged, as they still do, from under a million to five million. Most estimates were, however, something between two and three million. When I returned to England in 1948, I was therefore surprised to find that the press was speaking in terms of between ten and twenty million, and even more.

I soon discovered that the main source of these impossible figures was a book launched in 1946 by a certain Victor Kravchenko, called *I Chose Freedom*. He had been an official in the Soviet trade delegation in the United States and had deserted from it in 1943. Written partly or wholly by ghost writers, his book was a mixture of the wildest exaggeration with plain straightforward lies. It represented Russia as an enormous concentration camp, where the "slave laborers" were dying like flies, while the rest of the people, except for the members of the NKVD, were living in a state of acute and constant terror, loathing the regime and hoping desperately to be liberated by the "free world."

At first many people in the West, remembering such things as Stalingrad, were rather skeptical, their usual reaction, however, being "Well, if even half of what Kravchenko says is true, it's quite bad enough." Which was no doubt reasonable. But when the Cold War got into its stride in 1947, reaching an almost hysterical climax in 1948–49, the American authorities realized that the book was a most tremendous Cold War weapon in their hands, and hundreds of writers were let loose by their respective editors on an anti-Soviet campaign of unparalleled proportions and viciousness. *I Chose Freedom* became on the official level a book of unchallengeable authority, and many used it as support for their "bomb Russia now" policy—all the more so since, until the middle of 1949, the United States had the monopoly of the atom bomb.

Before long, the same sort of thing began to happen in England, and all kinds of people, most of them knowing little or nothing about Russia, began to blossom out as Russian experts. They appeared in practically every British paper, and the less they knew about Russia the more intolerant they were in their criticisms.*

---

* Even my timid suggestion that the Russian population figures made complete nonsense of these slave-camp figures was disdainfully rejected as propaganda. After all the human losses the Soviet Union had suffered in the war, the country's total population was under 200 million. Male casualties having been much higher than female casualties, there were certainly no more than 70 million males in the country. Since hardly anybody under twenty or over sixty was sent to a camp, the number of men eligible for "slave labor" was, as we know since the 1959 census, exactly 31 million. If the 12-million figure was right, then nearly half of the active male population was in camps and only about 18 million were left for industry, agriculture, transport, the Army, the administration, education, the health service and all the rest. The absurdity of the slave-camp figures was obvious to anyone with even the most elementary knowledge of Russia's population statistics.

Then there occurred a very sinister development. The public still had its doubts about Kravchenko, a man who had betrayed his country in the middle of the most terrible war in her history. But suddenly this shady figure was made "respectable" by the support of two "eminent American scholars," David Dallin and Boris Nicolaevsky, whose book *Forced Labor in Russia,* published at the height of the Cold War, left no doubt in the public mind that what Kravchenko had said was substantially correct. In fact Dallin and Nicolaevsky, with a great display of statistics and apparently serious scholarship, gave slightly more moderate slave-camp "estimates," settling for ten to twelve million. It was one of the greatest frauds of this century. But the "Russian experts," the Kremlinologists, were now sitting pretty, and they continued to do so for several years.

Victor Kravchenko, though very rich, committed suicide a few years ago. He had become so disreputable that even the CIA and his embarrassed friends in the State Department seem to have finally turned their backs on him. Dallin and Nicolaevsky died natural deaths. But Dallin, before he died, published a book on Soviet foreign policy which, though it discussed the internal situation in Russia following Stalin's death, said of the dissolution of the "slave camps" only that there was "a release from prisons of thousands."* No more mention of twelve million! Also, both Dallin and Nicolaevsky were old Mensheviks, with a pathological hatred of Stalin's Russia. The more one thinks about it, the more one is forced to believe that what they, like Kravchenko, were preaching was preventive war—as, indeed, Kingsley Martin pointed out at the time.

Now the whole disgraceful story must be nearly at an end. The "Russian experts" have either admitted their mistakes or fallen silent. And only very, very rarely are the once hallowed names of Kravchenko, Dallin and Nicolaevsky heard. One of the few scholars to take them seriously today is Robert Conquest, who has published a standard book on the Stalin purges in the 1930s in which he demonstrates that twenty million people died. It was lapped up by reviewers—except, of course, those who are serious students of the Soviet Union, such as Iverarh McDonald of the London *Times.*†

* David Dallin, *Soviet Foreign Policy After Stalin* (1961), p. 123.
† Sept. 19, 1963.

4

Population and Sex

POPULATON statistics are not one of the most exciting subjects in this world, but those relating to the Soviet Union are today, fifty years after the Revolution, of the greatest interest. Before the Revolution (1913 figures) the Russian people bred like animals; the situation was not unlike that of underdeveloped countries such as India or the Arab world today: thus, it is reckoned that in twenty years' time, by 1988, the population of Egypt will have risen from 24 million to 60 million—that is, more than doubled.*

In a fundamentally rich and enormous country like Russia, even before the Revolution, there was never such an acute population problem as there is today in the underdeveloped countries; and if, as we shall see, there is considerable reluctance among the Russian people to provide them with very extensive economic help, it is very largely because their problem—to wit, their two billion hungry or undernourished people—is so immense that no amount of conceivable help could make much difference.

In 1913, in the Russian Empire, both the birth rate and the death rate were extremely high. Births were 45.5 per thousand inhabitants†; deaths were 29.1; infant mortality (up to the age of one) was

---

* Hugh Thomas, *Suez* (New York, 1967), p. 26.

† The population figures in this chapter are taken from *SSSR v stifrakh v 1966 godu* (Moscow, 1967), published by the TSSU (the Central Statistical Department of the Council of Ministers of the U.S.S.R.). Highly professional statisticians (even in Poland and Czechoslovakia) have criticized some of the methods used by the Russian official statisticians; but, whatever little holes experts are able to pick in it, the information to be derived from this study for a general book on the U.S.S.R. like the present one, and one not primarily concerned with statistical methods, is not only wholly adequate, but an invaluable mine.

appalling: 269 per thousand. The natural yearly population increase was 16.4 per thousand. What is particularly interesting is that in 1940, on the eve of the German invasion of the U.S.S.R. and twenty-three years after the Revolution, the situation was not greatly different from that of 1913. In 1940, the births had dropped from 45.5 per thousand in 1913 to 31.2, the deaths from 29.9 to 18.0, the natural net increase from 16.4 to 13.2, infant mortality from 269 per thousand to 182 per thousand: an unquestionable progress, but still not sensational.

The population figures since then (per 1,000 population) are worth quoting in detail.

	BIRTHS	DEATHS	NET INCREASE	INFANT MORTALITY
1940	31.2	18.0	13.2	182
1950	26.7	9.7	17.0	81
1958	25.3	7.2	18.1	41
1959	25.0	7.6	17.4	41
1960	24.9	7.1	17.8	35
1961	23.8	7.2	16.6	32
1962	22.4	7.5	14.9	32
1963	21.2	7.2	14.0	31
1964	19.6	6.9	12.7	29
1965	18.4	7.3	11.1	27
1966	18.2	7.3	10.9	26.5

The astonishing thing is that the Soviet population statistics for the last few years are almost the same as in most advanced countries in Western Europe. Thus, taking 1963, the figures for the U.S.S.R. and France are:

	U.S.S.R.	FRANCE
Births	21.2	18
Deaths	7.2	11
Net increase	14.0	7
Infant Mortality	31.0	29.5

Since then, the Soviet trends are very interesting: the death rate has remained stationary at around 7 per thousand; the birth rate has been sharply declining, from 21.2 in 1963 to just over 18 in 1966;

and the net increase from 14 to under 11. Infant mortality has dropped from 31 to 26.5.

If, compared with those for 1913, the figures for 1940 are not spectacular (the infant-mortality rate in the Soviet Union in 1940 was still very high at 182, only one third less than in 1913), those for 1966 are little short of fantastic: the birth rate dropped from 45.5 to 18.2; the death rate, from 29.1 to 7.3; the net increase, from 16.4 to 10.9; infant mortality, from 269 to 26—an *over ninety per cent drop!* The figures are highly revealing; the most spectacular progress was not made during the twenty-three years between the Revolution and the Second World War, but in the twenty-two years between the Second World War and the present day.

A certain confusion arises in the urban and rural population figures. Whereas, in round figures, 45 per cent of the population today is "rural," only 23.6 per cent is described as "kolkhoz peasantry"; it seems, therefore, that the remaining 20-or-so per cent of the rural population belongs, in the main, to "workers and employees"—whose total has sharply risen from 68.3 per cent of the population in 1959 to 76.4 per cent in 1966. This would then mean that, with the transformation of kolkhozes into sovkhozes (state farms, where the peasants rank as "government employees") and the creation of brand-new sovkhozes, notably in the new Virgin Lands, the land is being "industrialized." If in 1940 virtually all the peasantry was included in the 47.2 per cent of the total population and ranked as "kolkhoz population," the actual kolkhoz population is now only 23.6 per cent of the total. This means that little more than half the rural population comes under the kolkhoz category, while the rest (around twenty million) come under sovkhoz and similar "government-employed" categories in the rural areas.

This cutting of the kolkhoz "class" in half since the war is perhaps *the* most important development of the postwar years and, indirectly, a confession of the relative failure of the entire kolkhoz system. The references in the *Survey* to gradually "erasing the differences between town and country" mean precisely that: the continuous transformation of the kolkhozes into state farms, or the independent increases in the number of the latter.*

* The percentages of the postwar urban and rural populations since the war, compared with those of 1913, are:

	URBAN (PER CENT)	RURAL (PER CENT)
1913	18	82
1940	33	67
1959	48	52
1961	50	50
1964	52	48
1965	53	47
1966	54	46
1967	55	45

No specific figures are given in the latest statistical manual comparing the birth, death and infant-mortality rates in the urban and rural areas respectively. Even leaving aside such curious cases as certain districts in mountainous Azerbaijan, which have the highest proportion of people over one hundred (some are even over 120), it seems obvious that the expectation of life in Russian cities is rather lower than in the rural areas. With few exceptions, men holding the highest and most responsible posts in the Party, in the government, in industry, in the administration, etc., usually die at around sixty. Their work involves much nervous strain, and heart diseases ("strokes," "infarcts," etc.) are particularly common among the top-ranking Soviet executives. Many die even before reaching the age of sixty. But, apart from these rather special cases, there does not seem much difference in the expectation of life among Russia's urban and rural populations.

If the peasant has to work harder than the industrial worker, the latter's work is less healthy. With a remarkable health service in both town and country, both the death rate and the infant mortality in both cases appear to be roughly the same. This is very different from tsarist times, when the cities were relatively well provided with hospitals, and the death rate in the cities was consequently much lower than in the villages, which were usually the first to suffer from famines, epidemics, and such "incurable" diseases as tuberculosis and syphilis. Both these diseases have virtually disappeared in today's Russia, and are, in any case, easily curable. On the other hand, as elsewhere in the world, cancer has become more common than it was, and Soviet doctors can no more cope with it effectively than those in other countries.

The enormously improved health services, compared not only with 1913 but also with 1940, account for the "European" death rate in Russia and a "European" life expectancy of around seventy —twice as high as in Egypt.

No recent figures are available on the comparative birth rates in the urban and rural parts of Russia. But it is almost unquestionably lower in the cities than in the countryside. The sharp drop in the birth rate since 1940 (from 31.2 to 18.2 per thousand) is due to several factors: in 1940 abortion had been illegal since 1936; today it is allowed (though not greatly encouraged); but, most important perhaps, especially with immensely improved housing conditions since the war, and (in places like Moscow and Leningrad) especially since 1955, "family planning" is virtually universal in the larger cities. Contraceptives, still limited a few years ago to mechanical devices like condoms, have now been supplemented by contraceptive pills which are not only on sale in every drugstore, but are actually exhibited in its window!

What particularly struck me in cities like Moscow and Leningrad was that young people who had been married for a few years had usually only one child, sometimes two children, but very seldom three or more. This in itself would indicate that the urban population is (except for an influx from the countryside) stationary or even shrinking, and that the rural population has to "work" to maintain the net population increase at around eleven per thousand for the country as a whole. And even this figure is slowly declining. This means, in practice, a population increase of not much more than two million people a year.

How the growth of population has slowed down can be seen from the following figures.

	Total Population in Millions
1959	208.8
1961	216.2
1964	226.4
1965	229.3
1966	231.8
1967 (estimated)	234.4

Roughly, a four-million annual increase between 1959 and 1961*; since then a drop to about three million a year; and finally, in the last year, to two and a half million.

Thus, if the Russia of 1913 was, from the point of view of its population statistics, still largely "Asiatic," she is today entirely "European." Another remarkable fact is the very high proportion of old people; with women receiving their old-age pension at fifty-five, and men at sixty (with further lowering of the pension age during the Jubilee, besides shorter working hours—the almost general application of the five-day week of forty hours—and other concessions), people are *encouraged* to live long. Including some war invalids, etc., old-age pensions are now paid to 34 million persons in the Soviet Union, or over fifteen per cent of the population.

SEX

Outwardly, Soviet life is extremely decorous, almost Victorian. You scarcely ever see any necking or petting or even kissing in Moscow parks or in the Metro; and present-day Russian films and novels

* The statistics for earlier years must be cautiously handled. The territory of tsarist Russia in 1913 was different from that of the Soviet Union in 1921; this, in turn, was different from that of, say, 1940. In 1913, the Russian Empire included a large part of Poland and Bessarabia; in 1921, Soviet territory included neither the Baltic States nor Bessarabia, nor large parts of Belorussia and the Ukraine ceded to Poland; in 1940, it included all these and some more, such as northern Bukovina. These frontiers were restored to the Soviet Union in 1945, with a few "extras," such as the eastern tip of Czechoslovakia, part of East Prussia, southern Sakhalin and the Kurile Islands. The total population given for 1913 (presumably that of the Russian Empire) is 159.2 million, and for 1940 (obviously including eastern Poland, the Baltic-States, Bessarabia, etc.) 194 million. Twenty years later (1959) the Soviet population had increased by only 14 million; here, of course, account must be taken of the 20 million people who died in the war. Stalin's 1944 decree encouraging extra-large families, to make up for the losses in the war, does not appear to have produced results comparable to those produced by "big-family" legislation in France after the Liberation. The reason for this seems to be that during the immediate postwar years life was still extremely hard, and 1947 was a near-famine year. Moreover, the birth rate during the war itself was extremely low and the death rate high; besides deaths caused *directly* by the war, many millions died of overwork and undernourishment, either during the war or soon after.

and plays do not, as a rule, go very deeply into that side of things—though there have latterly been some notable exceptions, such as Galina Nikolaeva's *Battle on the Road.*

No doubt there was in tsarist days plenty of promiscuity, particularly in the villages, while in the cities large-scale prostitution was a widespread phenomenon, complete with licensed brothels; the fact remains, however, that Russians have always tended to be reticent about sex, above all in their writings. It was not till the final years of the tsarist regime (and not without some indirect encouragement from Tolstoy's late writings) that some very bold and near-pornographic novels and stories began to appear, some even dealing with "unheard-of" things like homosexuality (though, in a hush-hush way, this too had existed on a small scale, particularly in the theatrical and musical world, Tchaikovsky being, of course, the most famous case of all—a fact, by the way, never referred to, as far as I know, in any Soviet book on Tchaikovsky).

The Revolution, in the course of which much was made of the emancipation of women, produced a few years of extremely lax morals. This equality of women was interpreted by the young generation as an encouragement to free love, and Madame Kollontai, who later became a leading Soviet diplomat, even wrote novels in favor of this free love as part of the revolutionary spirit. Lenin was, however, wholly in disagreement with this.

What is the position today, fifty years after the Soviet Revolution of 1917? As already said, novels and films provide only few clues; in most of them, everything is highly respectable, and any breach of Communist morality is denounced, as a rule, as being antisocial. No doubt a good deal of "sinning" goes on in Russia, where as a result of the war there are far more women (fifty-four per cent) than men (forty-six per cent). Yet the fact remains that most Russians one meets are respectably married, with a cult of the family and a real devotion to their children. Economic and social conditions have much to do with this: it is easier for a married couple to get a flat than for single persons or "free unions"; also, social pressure plays a considerable part in keeping people "respectable"; in the Party, in the Komsomol, promiscuous living is frowned upon and may even lead to serious trouble if overdone. Since everybody in the Soviet Union has a job, there is no such thing as full-time prostitution. However, in certain places, for example in Ligovka, a part of

Leningrad notorious before the Revolution as the brothel quarter, part-time prostitution continues. In the October Hotel in that very district I received phone calls almost nightly from sweet young things offering to spend a pleasant evening with me.

But, as already said, Russians (though they don't mind, on occasion, telling some very fruity stories) are extremely reticent about sex; one might even say that there is a widespread conspiracy of silence on the whole issue.

That is why a book published in Moscow in 1959 by a prominent medical man, Dr. T. S. Atarov, must be looked upon as something of a major novelty. The book, called *Problems of Sexual Education,* was, as far as I know, the first book of its kind to deal with the problem in popular form. A hundred thousand copies of the book were printed in 1959, and these were sold out within a few days. It has been reprinted several times since.

One of the most important points made by Dr. Atarov was that in the Soviet Union far too many parents and teachers treated sex as a taboo subject, surrounded by what he called a conspiracy of silence, young people being, more often than not, left to find out the facts of life for themselves. More important, he argued that, owing to this conspiracy of silence, no scientific study had ever yet been attempted on the sex life of the Soviet Union.

In Chapter 1, called "Sexual Education and the Schools," the author starts with some general considerations on finding a happy and harmonious solution which would combine "freedom and discipline"—a solution equally as important in sex as in many other matters. Most young Soviet people, having completed their studies in a coeducational school, are then given a job, and "as far as their work is concerned, there are seldom any criticisms we can address to them."

> Yet in their private lives, the shortcomings of our education can often be clearly observed. Things are done which are wholly contrary to Communist morality. . . . There are still people who think nothing of swearing eternal devotion to a young girl and of seducing and then abandoning her; or of getting married and, a year or two later, "getting tired" of their partner, and of abandoning him (or her), as well as the child or children; or, in the case of married people, of having casual affairs on the side. . . . Such immoral behavior is usually practiced by men, but it happens in

the case of women too. Needless to say, in saying all this, we are merely referring to a small minority in our country. . . .

And Dr. Atarov attributes many of these regrettable actions to a tendency on the part of teachers to ignore sex altogether in educating and bringing up children; it is not only a case of teaching young people sex hygiene in a narrow sense, but also of discussing with them the proper relations between men and women in both early and later life. Some parents and teachers are taken by surprise when children ask questions about sex. In fact they should be prepared for these questions, and refer to plants and animals in answering them.

In the 1959 edition of the book, since revised, there is a veiled reference to the housing shortage in Russia, under which whole families live in the same room.

One cannot emphasize too strongly how important it is that the intimate love life of grownups should be concealed from children. Unfortunately many adults forget about this. Sometimes they are too affectionate to each other in the presence of children. Sometimes, in the same or in the next room, they go in for sexual intercourse, believing that the children are sound asleep. They overlook the fact that adolescents often pretend to be asleep. In many children sensuality is prematurely aroused as a result of such careless behavior by their parents. . . . In the presence of their children, parents should also behave with mutual respect, and things like suspicion, jealousy or irritation should not be displayed in front of the children. . . .

Care must be taken not to allow children to read the wrong books, see the wrong plays or films, or take part in the wrong games, all of which might tend to arouse their sensuality. Heavy drinking in the presence of children often leads to disgusting scenes, including fights. Such scenes can only have a disastrous effect on the formative process of a child. "Under the influence of drink, young boys and girls often start an unnecessarily early love life."

Dr. Atarov then deals with what he calls hypocrisy in sex matters.

Sexual relations between very young people, though inadvisable, do not always have to be treated as something fundamentally wicked; such relations often end in marriage. Indeed, when such things do happen among young people who have not reached full maturity, teachers should not be self-righteous about them, but should simply try to see to it that such sex relations do not lead to dissoluteness; they should, in fact, try to persuade those concerned to marry as soon as they have reached the age of marriage.

In short, what's wanted in such cases is the proverbial happy ending.

Dr. Atarov then says that, in the case of young people of eighteen or more, they should be given special talks by the teacher or doctor, each sex being lectured to separately. Similarly, there should be short talks between father and son, mother and daughter.

The next chapter, "Sexual Maturity," stresses the difference between puberty and sexual maturity, which are not the same thing, and deals with the "difficult years" between the two. After a lengthy description of the reproductive process among higher animals, and of the male and female sexual organs, Dr. Atarov discusses the more important first manifestations of puberty, and here we come across some curiously Victorian passages in the midst of much plain common sense.

Pollutions, usually followed by awakening, do not cause any objective or subjective disturbance. But a first pollution may arouse in a boy alarm, astonishment and even fear. Parents should remember this, and if pollutions become frequent, measures should be taken to reduce any outside influence tending to increase sensuality. Some boys have few or no pollutions, but this is nothing to cause alarm. But when pollutions take place during the day, they point to a departure from normal conditions and a doctor should be consulted.

As regards girls, there then follows practical advice on how to deal with menstruation.

Another tricky problem, usually arising during the difficult years, is onanism, or masturbation; boys go in for it more frequently than girls. After enumerating factors which tend to encourage masturbation, and saying again that "the experience of doctors shows that under Soviet conditions masturbation is no longer the mass phenomenon it used to be in the (tsarist) past, though it is not to be entirely excluded even in our conditions," Dr. Atarov emits the somewhat Victorian view that it is a very bad and harmful practice.

> There is not the slightest doubt that masturbation has a bad effect on the nervous system and the adolescent's general condition; he becomes irritable, apathetic, easily tired, and indifferent to both physical and mental labor. If the problem is correctly approached, and the adolescent or youth is properly watched, he usually gets rid of this bad habit, and his health is fully restored.

Having said that, Dr. Atarov, however, admits that Russian scientists are not entirely agreed about the phenomenon.

This is followed by a lot of advice on hygiene.

> The correct organization of daily life is very important, as well as an interest in sports and physical culture. From early childhood children should acquire the habit of washing frequently in cold or cool water. They should keep their bodies clean, take baths regularly, wash their hands after games and work, after going to the lavatory, and before meals. . . . Boys should wash their private parts regularly with soap and water every day, and girls should wash their outer organs with boiled water.* But in washing these parts an excessive amount of rubbing should be avoided.

Also, says Atarov, there are certain trades from which, for sexual and moral reasons, very young people should be debarred.

> Thus, they should not be given jobs as waiters and waitresses in restaurants, cafés or beerhouses. The atmosphere in these places, with their constant coming and going of all kinds of people, has a bad effect on young people working there and tends to encourage them to embark on premarital relations; young unmarried people should not be given jobs in such places.

In Chapter 3, called "The Moral Education of the Young," Dr. Atarov discusses chastity.

---

* "Boiled water" suggests that in some parts of the Soviet Union tap water is still considered unsafe; before the Revolution and for some years after, tap water was undrinkable even in a city like Leningrad, where it was associated with cholera epidemics, etc.

Chastity is completely harmless, not only for young people, but also for adults who, for one reason or another, have temporarily interrupted their sex life; people practicing chastity practically never complain of any ailment arising from it: such is the experience of medical science. On the contrary, such people are full of energy and creative power. On the other hand, sexual promiscuity often leads to premature old age and impotence.

But it is not only, Dr. Atarov argues, the alleged dangers of chastity which make people lead a disorderly sex life. They behave in this undesirable way in virtue of certain ideological survivals.

Some people imagine that in having an affair with somebody they scarcely even know they do nothing wrong, provided there are no serious consequences and everything remains hush-hush. Some such people refuse to realize that, for the sake of getting a momentary physical pleasure, they may have seriously upset the inner world of another human being. Girls are usually the victims of this kind of primitive approach to sex. Thirdly, there are some who think nothing of having a little fun on the side even though they are married.

Such people have no moral sense. To treat sex life as a simple physiological function is contrary to all the moral standards of a socialist society. Under socialist morality, there cannot be any sex life based entirely on the physiological urge and without any spiritual intimacy between the two partners.

. . . And yet there are Soviet citizens who imagine that all this talk about past survivals is a lot of nonsense. "Why," they say, "talk to me about bourgeois survivals when I was born long after the Revolution and have never been in a bourgeois country? The laws of nature *must* be right."

Those who talk like that show that they have been badly brought up.

In Chapter 4 the author deals with a variety of other sex problems, which I shall summarize only briefly. The perfect marriage age is twenty to twenty-four, when young people, as a rule, have completed their education, have got a job, and are in the best possible condition for sexual intercourse, pregnancy and childbirth. True, says Dr. Atarov, touching this time on a very tricky Soviet problem, as a result of the two world wars "there are far more females than males in our country; and this disproportion has led to some disturbances in questions like marriage, the family and sexual relations. But, thanks to the peace policy of the Soviet government, this anomaly will gradually disappear."

There can, says Dr. Atarov, be no successful and happy marriage unless the feelings of devotion, attachment, attraction and love between the two are mutual; incompatibility may also arise from a very different upbringing, very different levels of culture, etc. Some marriages also break down because they have been entered into, by one side or both, for some sordid material reasons.

> When a young person thinks of getting married, parents should not remain completely neutral. In the U.S.S.R. marriage is not merely a personal matter; it is connected with the interests of society and the state. Parents should, therefore, take a discreet but genuine interest in the prospective marriage of their children, so as to prevent bad marriages, as far as possible.
>
> People who look upon marriage as a temporary amusement, who lightly break up a home and abandon husband or wife (and a child) are committing a crime against socialist morality.

The section on birth control starts with a description of a common practice, the *coitus interruptus;* but this may lead to nervous upsets among both men and women; and it is better to resort to contraceptives, of which the condom is the best; there are also other devices used by women.

Concerning abortion Dr. Atarov writes:

> Today in our country [as distinct from a long period which began in 1936] women are able to decide themselves about effecting an abortion. Every provision has been made for performing these by qualified medical personnel. At the same time, both the state and public opinion condemn a frivolous attitude toward abortions—i.e., those carried out without some very good reason of a personal or social nature. Some women resort to abortion for purely selfish motives. Even more serious is when husbands urge their wives, for purely selfish motives, to have an abortion performed; such an attitude should be sharply condemned.

A clear distinction appears to be made here between married women and unmarried prospective mothers. In the case of the latter, abortion is more justifiable.

> Women should also remember that abortions are not completely harmless, especially when frequently practiced. They may lead to sterility and premature old age, as well as to various nervous and gynecological complications.

In cases of sterility which medical science is unable to remedy, provided husband and wife, anxious to have a child, get on well together, the best solution for them is to adopt a child from an institution.

After a section on V.D.—"against which gigantic progress has been made in our country," but which still, unfortunately, exists, despite such measures as compulsory treatment and compulsory examination—the author deals with sexual morality.

What, in the author's view, are breaches of sexual morality in a socialist society?

Premarital relations; these, however, are not necessarily wicked, especially if they end in marriage.

Marital infidelity—very bad.

Bad, too, is getting married for mercenary reasons, without any mutual affection and love uniting the two partners.

So also is seeking a divorce without some very strong reason, and, of course, abandoning a family without divorce.

On divorce Dr. Atarov says:

> Divorce is allowed in the U.S.S.R., but it is a right which should not be abused. Often frivolous reasons are given for a divorce petition, such as "incompatibility of character," cooling-off of love, sexual frustration, etc. In reality, these are sometimes mere excuses in an attempt to contract a more advantageous marriage. Under our laws, the main condition in granting a divorce is that the children's interests be respected.

Actually, the divorce procedure in Russia today is extremely unwieldy; there continues to be much controversy in the press in favor of easing up divorce; present difficulties in obtaining a divorce no doubt largely account for what the author indignantly describes as *"de facto* divorces," when husband (or sometimes wife) sets up a home on the side. "Usually such 'divorces' are due to dissolute sexual behavior, drunkenness or, in a few cases, unwarranted jealousy." From such situations, children suffer, of course, most of all.

The book ends with a rather lofty discussion on two "painful situations"—first, when a married person falls genuinely in love with a third party (in this case, he demonstrates that it is best if "duty is made to triumph over passion"), and second, what happens in cases of unrequited love.

> Unrequited love sometimes causes deep emotional and mental disturbances, especially in the case of very young people. Sometimes only a great effort of will power and time can cure the sufferer. But such unrequited love should not be looked upon as a final failure and as a great tragedy. Under socialist society, in which public service is the main thing, and provided the sufferer has enough inner discipline, he should get over his troubles. Work and the moral support of his comrades should be of the greatest help.

There can be no doubt that this kind of puritanical approach to sex is very much part of Soviet upbringing; that, for a large number of reasons—such as the advantages of an "orderly" existence, and also because of the housing problem—a very considerable proportion of the young generation, especially in the cities, adhere to these rules. This seems particularly true of the young technical elite, who are interested, above all, in their work and in getting on, and who are aware of the fact that "scandalous" behavior can be damaging to their careers.

No doubt Dr. Atarov overstates many of his points; love and marriage are, to him, so much a matter of social significance that one would think people made love not for pleasure, but merely as a social duty. The sexual act is also reduced by Dr. Atarov to its simplest and most primitive form, without any refinements of any kind, whereas "dreadful" things like homosexuality* are not men-

---

* In the standard textbook on psychiatry, *Uchebnik Psychiatriyi,* by O. V. Kerbikov and others (Moscow, 1958), p. 313, we find the following on this point: "Why are sexual perversions so unusual in our country? Because phe-

tioned at all, as if they just did not exist. Similarly, there is no mention of complex psychological problems, partly on the ground that Freud has always been treated in the Soviet Union as something of a charlatan,* as he is, indeed, according to the Russians, by serious scientists in the West as well.

The final section of the book deals with illegitimacy. Although fatherless children are given the fullest protection by the law, a stigma still attaches to children who are described in the official school list as "So-and-so, father ———," that is, no father's name is given. Such children are often nicknamed (schoolchildren being cruel the world over) "Father-Blank." Dr. Atarov argues for a radical change in the present law.

---

nomena like homosexuality (which are acquired and not innate) have nothing in our environment to encourage them. . . . In the capitalist world, with its sadistic films and books, there is a good deal of sadism. In prewar Berlin there were numerous papers for homosexuals, and 120 widely advertised clubs, beside numerous cafés where people sharing this tendency met. The healthy atmosphere in which Soviet youth is brought up provides no conditions which would encourage the development of such perversions; and these are very unusual in our country. Under our law (Article 154-a of the Criminal Code of the RSFSR), homosexual practices between males are punishable; and although homosexuality is a morbid phenomenon, persons guilty of such practices are considered responsible for their actions and cannot plead irresponsibility."

* From the very start, at the beginning of this century, leading psychiatrists refused to treat psychoanalysis as anything other than a sectarian current. Freudianism is of no scientific value. Its popularity must be sought in its ideological significance: it is highly profitable to the ruling classes, since, instead of dwelling on the hardships brought to the masses by the capitalist system, it dwells on the alleged psychological chasms of human nature, on its unconscious urges and instincts. People with only a superficial understanding of clinical psychiatry are taken in by it. As W. Mayer-Gross, E. Slater and M. Roth say in their study *Clinical Psychiatry* (London, 1954), p. 20, it is "popular only amongst half-baked amateur psychologists, journalists, writers and critics, and is much disliked by neurologists and psychiatrists with long clinical experience."

5

Religion in Decline

"WELL, let me put it this way," said Albert, a twenty-four-year-old, during an evening I spent at his house. "All right, there is Lenin and there's Jesus Christ. I doubt whether a lot of you people in the West really believe very firmly in Jesus Christ. But we *do* believe in Lenin. Directly or indirectly we really owe everything to Lenin. Oh, I admit I haven't read more than perhaps a quarter of all the fifty-five volumes; his polemics with renegade Kautsky and much else are old hat, I admit; and there are many things he didn't foresee—the *embourgeoisement* of the working class in most countries in Western Europe, or fascism, or still less the atom bomb and the H-bomb. But look, for instance, at what he has to say about the shocking condition of education and of the medical services in tsarist days— and look at them now. Also, what he thought of the world in the year 1919 went all wrong, but what he has to say on imperialism, though in a different context, is still largely valid, or on the oppression and exploitation of the colonial peoples. No doubt in "independent" countries like India and Ceylon this exploitation has taken on different forms, but substantially it amounts to pretty much the same thing—not quite so blatant and brutal, but bad enough. Seventy per cent of the tea plantations, for instance, are still in the hands of British capitalists, isn't that right?"

"Yes, I suppose so," I said, "though I don't remember the exact figures offhand. But then," I said, "we hear about the final aim, which is complete Communism. Do you really believe in it?"

Albert laughed. "Yes," he said, "that *is* the final aim; and that idiot Khrushchev told us some years ago that it was just round the corner. Well, that's just where he was wrong. He said our children would live under complete Communism and once or twice even mentioned some precise date—wasn't it 1980?

"One can't really remember *everything* that Khrushchev said, but by getting himself sacked in 1964 he saved us from a real national disaster. Had he stayed, he would have insisted that all his speeches be published; that would have made sets of about five hundred volumes. No, as regards complete Communism, it isn't as simple as that. Today the Party is much less definite in its prophecies; in the Fiftieth Jubilee *Survey* you won't find any kind of timetable saying *when* exactly we'll attain a state of complete Communism. To put it crudely, we believe in complete Communism pretty much the way you people—or some of you—still believe in the Kingdom of Heaven, or in the next world; in both cases, I should say, it may come off or it mayn't come off. Nor do we really know, if it does come off, whether it will be complete Communism in the whole world or only in the Soviet Union—'Communism in one country,' as Stalin said."

"Now, Albert, you treat God, and Jesus, and the Kingdom of Heaven, and the next world rather as a joke. Aren't there still quite a lot of people in the Soviet Union who believe in God? After all, in both Moscow and Leningrad there are still quite a number of churches going strong."

"Yes, there are still quite a lot of people in our country who believe in God, but they are mostly old, usually very old. In another generation or two the churches will have gone completely out of business. Now, take my family. Neither my father, now about sixty, nor my mother believes in God. In the early years of the Revolution my father, who was a young worker at the Kirov works—it was then still called the Putilov works—was in the Komsomol and was tremendously active in the Godless League, doing antireligious propaganda. It was crude and by our standards pretty offensive stuff; but then Lenin did loathe the Orthodox Church and the priests as the backbone of the tsarist regime and as the most obscurantist and reactionary influence among the Russian people, including the working class. Our workers were still rotten with religion as late as 1905 when, egged on by Father Gapon, they went to present their petition to Nicholas II on Bloody Sunday, carrying God knows how many ikons and portraits of the Tsar, the Little Father. The massacre on that Bloody Sunday did knock their faith in the Little

Father on the head, but it still didn't knock religion quite out of them.

"My grandfather, also an old Putilov worker, who's now about eighty, did lose faith in God—let alone the Tsar—after that Sunday; but my grandmother, now seventy-five, still slinks away to church from time to time, and especially during the greater church holidays. And she insisted that even I, her grandson, should be christened by a *batyushka,* and she has made us all firmly promise that after her death she would be given a proper church funeral. My parents weren't at all keen on the christening; but the old lady was so hurt when they refused that they finally gave way. As for her own funeral—well, a promise is a promise, and we'll have to go through all the mumbo-jumbo when the time comes. Not that I really mind, and there is, in fact, something rather beautiful about the Orthodox funeral service and the Eternal Memory, the *vechnaya pamyat'* chant, at the end of the service.*

"To me all that sort of thing has a kind of historical value. A lot of genuine Communists still like the Orthodox Church for that reason: for the beauty of the singing and the ikons and incense and all that. Not that they believe, even a tiny bit, in God. But the church has become respectable as a kind of museum piece to us Communists and Komsomols. Have you noticed that though in the early years of the Revolution some of the most beautiful churches— real works of art of the fifteenth, sixteenth, seventeenth and eighteenth centuries—were ruthlessly demolished, especially in Moscow, now all the churches of any historical value that are still left, most of which were literally failling to pieces, are being thoroughly restored, in Moscow, in Leningrad and everywhere? Take that eighteenth-century church, built in the reign of the fabulously dissolute Empress Anna Ivannovna, at the corner of the Mokhovaya—where you say you lived before the Revolution—and the Semyonovskaya: it was a ruin until last year; now it's a perfect beauty. And then there are those three or four little churches or chapels just off the Red Square in Moscow, near St. Basil's and the new Rossiya Hotel. Those charming little churches were a complete mess, fit, one would

* The Orthodox Church, though disapproved of in principle, like all churches, has been more or less tolerated as part of the Soviet Establishment, following the "concordat" of 1943. Less tolerance is shown for the Roman Catholic Church, while certain Protestant sects are actively persecuted.

have thought, only for demolition. But not a bit of it. They have now been turned into one of the most delightful sights of Moscow.

"It just shows we are no longer *scared* of the church. None of these restored churches will be used as places of worship, but they are beautiful and are, after all, part of our national heritage. But, as I said before, in twenty or, let's say, fifty years there will be no religion left in Russia; in the past people used to go to church to beg God for this, that and the next thing; now they get practically everything from our socialist state, and our people now realize that if a man is seriously ill a doctor and a bottle of antibiotic pills are much more likely to save him than God. Yes, these fifty years of the Soviet regime have been pretty hard, as I, and even more so my father, could tell you; but things are really getting on very nicely in Russia now. Just look at this new flat, into which we moved two years ago. Did Russians—except, of course, the very rich before the Revolution—ever live as comfortably as we do now?"

6

The World's Greatest Welfare State

THE Soviet Union, with 236 million inhabitants, is today the world's greatest welfare state. There are, as I have already said, 34 million old-age pensioners, including, since a few years ago, peasants and peasant women. In the cities the old-age pensions (which begin at fifty-five for women and at sixty for men) range roughly from thirty rubles (thirty dollars) a month to one hundred rubles or occasionally more, while in the countryside they are much lower—usually fifteen or twenty rubles. But even this is a departure from the old Russian tradition of keeping Grandfather and Grandmother, and of making Babushka do a little housework and look after the grandchildren while her health lasts. To old peasant women the pension is merely money for jam—a little extra to make the old woman happy and grateful to "our Soviet state." It creates great good will among the *kolkhozniki,* and is really a drop in the huge bucket of the state budget. A moon rocket probably costs more than a whole year of peasants' old-age pensions put together.

The two other main elements of the welfare state are education and the health service.

As regards the statistics of education in the Soviet Union, so much has been written that I need deal with the matter only briefly. But its social and psychological side is quite a different matter: it is education above all which has made the Russian people of today an entirely different nation from what they were not only before the Revolution but even before the Second World War. *Taken as a whole,* they are, as I hope to show later, probably the most civilized and cultured nation in the world today.

The number of persons with higher and secondary (complete and

incomplete) education per thousand inhabitants is shown in the
following table.

	Per 1,000 persons of the total population			Per 1,000 persons of the working population (engaged in the national economy)		
	1939	1959	1967	1939	1959	1967
Complete higher education	6	18	27	13	33	49
Incomplete higher education and complete or incomplete secondary education	77	263	333	110	400	515
Total	83	281	360	123	433	564

Whereas the total number of students in the United States was
still higher than in the Soviet Union in 1965–66 (212 per 10,000
population in the U.S. and 167 in the U.S.S.R.), with a slightly
larger total population in the latter, Russian books of statistics
explain why the two figures are far from relating to exactly the same
kinds of students. It is, indeed, difficult to get a general over-all
comparison, the standard and quality of the students in question
being in some cases higher in the U.S. than in the U.S.S.R., and vice
versa. It is clear, however, that the Russian statisticians are not too
happy that the total proportion of students in higher education in
the United States should still be substantially higher than in the
Soviet Union, though the latter is streets ahead of other "civilized"
countries. The following list gives the number of students receiving
higher education for every 10,000 of the population in various
countries.

No figure is given for Egypt, but it is somewhere between those
given for Pakistan and Iran, while that for Israel more or less con-
forms to the Western-European level.

If the Russians have given up all idea of a world revolution
(except in theory), the intense education drive in all the socialist
countries except for war-ravaged North Vietnam is remarkably

Socialist Countries

Bulgaria	84
Cuba	31
Czechoslovakia	98
East Germany	64
Hungary	100
North Korea	155
North Vietnam	15
Outer Mongolia	104*
Poland	86
Rumania	69
U.S.S.R.	167
Yugoslavia	94

Capitalist Countries

France	71
Great Britain	58
Italy	47
Japan	84
United States	212
West Germany	45

Underdeveloped Countries

India	24
Iran	10
Pakistan	18
Turkey	28

* Including those studying abroad, mostly in the Soviet Union.

significant. The education figures coming closest to that of the U.S.S.R. are, significantly, those of two of the most "backward" socialist countries, Outer Mongolia (104) and North Korea (155). Cuba, at a still early stage of socialist development, is, of course, still low on the list, with only 31 per 10,000.

The table Russians find even more satisfactory is that showing comparative annual output of engineers in the U.S.S.R. and the U.S. and reflecting the former's immense technological progress since 1950.

	1950	1960	1965	1966
U.S.S.R.	37,000	120,000	170,000	179,000
U.S.	61,000	43,000	41,000	43,000 (est.)

Even allowing for all kinds of differences in quality and standard (one way or the other), it is clear that the output of engineers in the U.S. in the last fifteen years has been relatively stable, whereas in the U.S.S.R. there is an enormous yearly increase in the number of engineering graduates. The number of diplomaed engineers employed in the national economies follows the same trend.

	1940	1950	1960	1965	1966
U.S.S.R.	295,000	400,000	1,135,000	1,631,000	1,789,000
U.S.	170,000	310,000	590,000	725,000	750,000

Apart from the fact that the output of engineering graduates and their employment in the national economy is progressively greater in the Soviet Union* than in the United States, all these figures tend to show that the general level of education in the Soviet Union has also made remarkable strides. If in 1939 only 12.3 per cent of the population could be considered properly educated, now the proportion had risen to some 56.4 per cent. In the case of the urban population the percentage is of course much higher, in that of the rural population correspondingly lower.

To the Russians, education is immensely important in both national and international terms; as we shall see later, the catastrophic rout of Egypt by Israel in June 1967 was very largely attributed to the simple fact that whereas the Israelis were all highly educated the great majority of Egyptian soldiers were scarcely literate, while some were entirely illiterate.

During my two-month stay in the Soviet Union in the Fiftieth-Jubilee summer of 1967 nothing impressed me more than almost everybody's passion for education and "culture." If at Le Bugue, for instance, the Dordogne village where I have an ancient tumbeldown country house, the uneducated are wholly resigned to being uneducated (it is amazing what a very small proportion of the French rural population can write the simplest letter without making count-

---

* In recent years there has been a new phenomenon in the Soviet Union— a frequent *overproduction* of engineers; young graduates often have nothing better to take than skilled-worker jobs until a vacancy becomes available. Such young graduates, like their counterparts in Western Europe, are often extremely dissatisfied.

less spelling mistakes), spelling mistakes in Russia are something very unusual today.

It is not true that there is a classless society in the Soviet Union. But classes can be divided according to two entirely different criteria: money and education. There are very rich people in Russia, and there are very poor people: those at the top end of the scale include members of the government, top industrial executives, top people in science, engineering and medicine, active or retired marshals and generals, outstanding theatrical or cinema actors, and the composers of famous song hits (who get a rake-off every time their song is performed not only on the radio, but even in a dance hall). Many of these people have, even by American standards, enormous incomes, and can afford full-time "servants" and a private car complete with chauffeur.

The purchase of cars is not encouraged; a small Russian car selling abroad for eight hundred dollars costs five times that amount inside Russia. Four thousand rubles is a lot of money. Perhaps the principal reason for discouraging the purchase of countless cars is the ghastly example of places like New York and Paris, where the whole traffic problem is becoming increasingly insoluble every year.

A few yeas ago, Khrushchev declared that (apart from official government cars and the like) no private cars in a place like Moscow were necessary at all; if there were, say, five thousand or ten thousand taxis for the whole of Moscow, this was quite sufficient. In other words, unless you had some heavy luggage to carry, there was no reason why you shouldn't use the (very cheap) public transport—the Metro, buses, trollybuses, or even trams, still to be seen on the outskirts of Moscow. Today the "Khrushchev rule" has been somewhat relaxed; there are far more private cars in Moscow than there were, say, five years ago, and as a result of the purchase by the Soviet Union of a new motorcar plant from Fiat in 1966, Moscow may someday become a traffic hell like New York or Paris; but the prospect is still very remote, and with state planning the danger can if necessary be averted.

At the other end of the financial scale are the street cleaners, unskilled laborers, and the like, earning sixty, seventy, or eighty rubles a month (female buffet attendants, for instance, earn usually between seventy and eighty rubles a month), and the old-age pensioners, who might receive as little as thirty rubles a month (in the cities).

But money is not the only class criterion; and, by and large, people accept the great financial difference between rich and poor in terms of merit and value to the state. If a retired marshal of the Soviet Union receives a remarkably fat pension, it is because he was, in his time, of great value to the country. The attitude is less tolerant, though, to certain literary hacks with a lot of money.

Among the proudest Russians are the young technical and engineering elite, and next to them (under present technology, there is not such a great difference between an engineer and a highly skilled worker) is the industrial working class as a whole. The industrial worker (not to mention the engineer and the technician) regards himself very much a first-class Soviet citizen. In this there is something almost instinctive.

I remember a very curious episode at a Leningrad railway station. I was suddenly accosted by a drunk who demanded "a smoke." I thought he meant a match. With drunken aggressiveness he explained he didn't want a match, but a cigarette. I rather reluctantly parted with one of my two remaining cigarettes and no doubt looked at him with a certain expression which he apparently interpreted as one of annoyance, if not downright contempt and disgust (I don't much like drunks accosting me in the street). "Now," he suddenly said, "don't you look at me like that! What do you think I am? A hooligan? A tramp? No, comrade, I am a *rabochi* [an industrial worker]—a better Soviet citizen than most!" And then came this parting shot: "Oh, you f——g intellectuals! The country wouldn't get very far if it had to depend entirely on people like you!" And, puffing at my cigarette, he staggered away, bumping into other passengers.

If the Russian industrial worker is a very proud individual, people in "trade" are rather ashamed of doing nothing better. They attribute their lowly condition, very significantly, to lack of education. Very many do their utmost to get out of it, by taking evening classes or correspondence courses. The feeling of being second-class citizens, and of belonging to the most inefficient part of the national economy—which retail trade certainly is—may largely account for the proverbial boorishness and couldn't-care-less inefficiency of, say, most shop assistants.

The Soviet citizens who feel worst of all, however, are waiters, who are deeply ashamed of having a "lackey occupation" (*lakeiskaya dolzhnost*). Gone are the days when there were wonderfully efficient and courteous waiters in Russia. I knew a few during the war. They were all very old men. Old Suvorov, of the Metropole in Moscow, was proud of having been a waiter under two Tsars, and then during twenty-five years of the Revolution—"but that hardly counts." But he would tell, with a kind of nostalgia, of the tremendous feeding orgies the rich Moscow merchants would go in for before the Revolution, and he talked about a club where he worked at one time. "All the famous people I served, you would hardly believe it: Fyodor Ivanovich Chaliapin, and Leonid Andreyev, and Sergei Vasilievich Rachmaninov, and Alexander Nikolaevich Skriabin and Maxim Gorki. Yes, I heard Chaliapin sing, and Sergei Vasilievich play the piano—it was unforgettable!" But then he would add, "Only they ate far, far too much, really ruined their insides. And some also drank rather more than was good for them. When Fyodor Ivanovich Chaliapin really got drunk, he was quite frightening!" Old Suvorov was so efficient at his job, even though he was by then nearly eighty, that he was made top waiter at the Teheran and Yalta conferences. I have a photo of him serving a lip-smacking Churchill a huge crystal bowl of caviar.

But this species is now completely extinct. There are some professional full-time waitresses; but if they are that, it is usually because they have a large family and no education. The men waiters are nearly all part-time. I had a long talk with one of them, that very Albert Ivanovich whom we met in the last chapter, at the October Hotel in Leningrad. He was a young fellow of twenty-four with a wife and two children. As a waiter he was quite useless, but then he was proud of *not* being a waiter. He was a student at an engineering college and was adding to his student's grant of only thirty rubles by earning an extra eighty or ninety rubles a month as a waiter. But he hated it. And he was a good example of how democratic Russians are today; there may be not enough *liberté* in Russia, and no *égalité*, but there is *fraternité*. When I ran into him in the third-floor buffet of the hotel, not only did he treat me to a glass of cognac and then offer me a Havana cigar (one of those millions of unwanted Havana cigars Castro dumps on Russia), but he invited me home for supper the next evening. In what other country would that have happened?

He had a nice three-room flat in a new block beyond Chernaya Rechka, on the northern outskirts of Leningrad, complete with bathroom, fridge, TV and so on. His young wife, an elementary-school teacher, and his two small children were charming, and I spent a delightful evening with them. After supper, he turned on his tape recorder and played me a whole program of pop music, English, French and American—Johnny Halliday, and Aznavour, and the Beatles, and many more; he had picked them all up from foreign radio programs. He seemed to like the Beatles best.

"I am, naturally, a Komsomol," he said, "and I hope in a year or two to be admitted to the Party. But I can tell you, every Komsomol simply adores this kind of foreign pop music. At first some of the old Party fogeys—I mean ideological fossils like Suslov—frowned upon our enthusiasm. But it was no good, nothing would discourage us from recording and playing them. So some clever chap in the Party found a wonderful way out: after all, he said, this is *narod-noye tvorchestvo,* the creative art of the people—the people of France, America and England. And, indeed," Albert Ivanovich laughed, "isn't it perfectly true that our greatest favorites, the Beatles, for instance, are the purest Liverpool proletarians?" However, having exhausted the Aznavour and Beatles program, he turned on his record player and played me the Gillels record of the Emperor Concerto.

No, unlike the Russians in the Stalin days, or even in the Khrushchev days, the present-day Russian has no blinkers on. The real *Homo sovieticus* of today is not the ghastly monster of Mr. Khrushchev's and his agitprop chief Ilyichev's imagination, but just the kind of fellow Albert was—the intensely patriotic Russian, the very civilized human being, mad for culture and education, with much inner discipline injected into him by the Komsomol, but also with a remarkably nonsectarian view of the world. Or, shall we say, a man who adores, each in its own way, both the Beatles and the Emperor Concerto. No, the Russian today has no blinkers on. He usually finds the Soviet papers a bore; and to add to his understanding of what goes on in the world, he turns on the BBC or the Voice of America. (Most Russians I met prefer the BBC, which they find more objective and less cantankerous.) Sometimes they also turn on Radio Peking, but only for fun, to hear the elaborate obscenities with which the Chinese treat the Soviet leaders! (I am told that high up among the Party ideologists, some worry and concern are caused by all those Chinese charges of anti-Marxism, anti-Leninism, *embourgeoisement* and revisionism, but I have never met a single Russian of today who was in the least worried by that; and even if the Chinese *had* an ideological case against Russia, well, so what? For nearly fifty years Russia had little to feed on except ideology; it was high time the Russian people got a little bread and butter and cheese and *kotletki* for a change. Now, for the first time in fifty years, the Russian people were, at long last, living in the present, living for their own happiness, and not living in the dim future, slaving away for the happiness of future generations.)

I don't know how much the BBC is listened to in the Russian villages, but in the larger cities thousands listen to it. (It was even a little embarrassing to find on my arrival in Moscow that *everybody* seemed to have read in *The London Magazine,* the small-circulation monthly, a rather poisonous article I had written on Mikhail Sholokhov; I then discovered that it had simply been broadcast by the Russian service of the BBC!) The BBC also informs Russians of such things as the Solzhenitsyn letter to the Fourth Writers' Congress,* of further developments in the Siniavsky-Daniel affair, and, of course, of Svetlana Stalina Alliluyeva. The attitude to Stalin's daughter was very typical: she was a twerp, totally unpatriotic; when you are the daughter of Stalin, you ought to have a little more dignity; if not a great man, Stalin was a big man, after all, and he held an enormous place in his country's history; *noblesse oblige.* And she was a liar too, saying that Stalin had fallen under the evil influence of Beria; all the horrors of the Yezhovshchina had started long before Beria had become head of the NKVD in Moscow. As for her ill-earned millions of dollars, the least she could do was to hand them over to North Vietnam; she might then recover a little of all the respect she had lost in her own country.†

---

* See page 278 *ff.*

† The man I knew who was best acquainted with Svetlana was Serge Mikoyan, son of *the* Mikoyan. He had been a childhood friend of Svetlana's. He couldn't make head or tail of Svetlana's motives and behavior. "It's so much out of character," he said. "She is, and always was, a very nice person. We always thought until now that what she loved most in the world were her two children." One theory current in Russia is that it was the ultra-Stalinites who smuggled her out, so as to give the Western world a more favorable idea of Stalin.

Culture is dirt cheap. Books cost next to nothing. A cinema seat costs ten or twelve kopecks. The most glorious gramophone records can be bought for about fifty kopecks, with the best performers, nearly all of them Soviet Russian—Richter, Gillels, Sofronitsky, the two Oistrakhs, Rostropovich.

One of the few friendly and helpful shop assistants I met in Russia was the young girl in the record shop in the Gostiny Dvor in Leningrad. I had long talks with her, and asked what kinds of records were best sellers and worst sellers. Well, there was quite a market for the latest song hits, usually by somebody like Solovyov-Sedoi; also there was a market for Russian folk songs, Russian choirs, etc. Many still loved re-recordings, however bad, of great singers of the past like Chaliapin, Sobinov, Caruso. Opera albums were in great demand—especially Tchaikovsky's *Eugene Onegin* and *The Queen of Spades,* Mussorgsky's *Boris Godunov* and *Khovanshchina,* and some of Rimsky-Korsakov's.

But the greatest demand was for classical orchestral or chamber music and also for piano music. Altogether, I doubt whether the average Russian music lover's tastes are in the least different from those of his English opposite number. The two top best sellers are Tchaikovsky's Piano Concerto No. 1, and Rachmaninov's No. 2, closely followed by the Beethoven piano concertos. Piano music (especially when played by Richter) is in huge demand, whether Chopin, Liszt, Mozart or Beethoven. So are Sofronitsky's Skriabin records. There is a steady but not enormous demand for Mozart, except that one of the best sellers is Mozart's *Requiem;* and Bach is becoming more and more popular—the Feinberg album of the forty-eight preludes and fugues is in constant demand. Increasingly popular is Brahms—all the four symphonies, and practically everything else, his chamber music especially; the Beethoven symphonies are also in constant demand; Schubert and Schumann are slightly declining; but Dvořák is increasingly popular, and so is Mahler. On the other hand, there continues to be a kind of instinctive dislike of Wagner.

It is only the very sophisticated who buy modern music records. There is a considerable demand for Prokofiev, but very little for Shostakovich; a fair demand for Debussy and Ravel; also for Stravinsky; only in the last few years has there been something of a demand for Bartók, Hindemith and Benjamin Britten. There are very few records in existence of young Soviet composers, except Shchedrin and Sviridov, and the demand is "not overwhelming." Of Soviet composers scarcely known in the West, the late Nikolai Miaskovsky (d. 1951) had a small but quite appreciable public of his own, especially among professional Russian musicians, who considered him a great symphonist in the great Russian tradition, but he is still much underrated in his own country and almost unknown abroad.

There is something to be said for dull newspapers and magazines, for these help the Russians to be the greatest readers of books in the world. They know the best Soviet books, but above all they know their classics inside out—Pushkin, Lermontov, Gogol, Turgenev, Dostoevsky, Tolstoy, Chekhov and so on. On the *Estonia,* which at the end of August brought me from Leningrad to Le Havre (a delightful journey I can strongly recommend to tourists), I talked to a young seaman of eighteen or nineteen. He said, "Can you explain this to me? It's very puzzling. I, and *all* of us, know not only our classics, Gogol, Pushkin, Tolstoy and the rest, but we also know some of the great writers of the West—Shakespeare, and Balzac, Dickens, Stendhal, Hemingway and Knut Hamsun, for instance. In the West they don't seem to know anything! I asked some dockers at Tilbury which Shakespeare plays they liked best, and they said, 'Shakespeare—oh, the bloke who wrote plays. Never read any of them.' And then I said, 'And Byron, do you like him?' 'Byron, who's he?' And the only books they had read were by somebody called James Bond."

Yes, such is the culture, the people's culture that the Soviet educational system has produced in Russia. In their secondary schools the proletariat are not only taught both math and physics, they are also taught to read—and love—both Shakespeare and Mayakovsky.

So much for the Soviet education system.

I need not say much about housing; I have already often referred to it. As we have seen, it was not during the first twenty-three years of the Soviet regime, but during the last twenty years, since the end of the Second World War, that the entire urban scene of Russia has changed entirely. Every other person one meets has moved into a new or modernized house in the last few years. Probably the only urban territory which has scarcely changed at all since the Revolution is the old center of Leningrad. Here everything looks just the same as it looked fifty and even a hundred years ago—the same Winter Palace and the Neva quays, the Summer Garden, the Nevsky Prospekt and even the Sennaya (the Haymarket) of Dostoevsky's *Crime and Punishment*—minus all the stinks and noises of 1860. Nothing in Leningrad is being pulled down; if new houses are needed, they are simply built in the form of new suburbs. It is the "eternity" of Leningrad that constitutes its unequaled charm, but also makes it suspect in the eyes of the Soviet regime. All the old charm and splendor of Imperial Russia are now to be found in only a few square miles of Leningrad—nowhere else in the Soviet Union.* A million people died of hunger in the Leningrad blockade, but Leningrad, except for a few scars, survived. Today, after the tragedy of the war, very few real Leningraders are left in the city. But the newcomers—from Moscow, from Siberia, from the Ukraine, from anywhere—though they haven't a drop of "Leningrad blood" in their veins, become Leningraders within a very short time, and begin to look at Moscow down their noses.

The third great element of the welfare state is the health service. I do not know enough about the health service in highly civilized countries like Switzerland, Sweden or Denmark to say that the Russian health service is better or worse. But it is better than in either France or England, and the complete opposite of medical services in the United States, where, unless a patient is heavily insured, a serious illness lasting several weeks is the most appalling disaster to all except the millionaire.

There is, of course, nothing to prevent a fussy patient from going to see a doctor of his or her own, and paying him a reasonable fee. But, in general, the medical service in the Soviet Union is completely free to all, and everything tends to show that today the country is healthier than it has ever been.

Not counting the medical personnel of the armed forces, there were, in 1966, 580,000 doctors "of all specialties" (that is, includ-

---

* There are a few minor exceptions, such as the ancient "church-and-monastery" towns like Suzdal, Rostov the Great near Moscow, and Odessa, which, though damaged in the war, has preserved its general pre-1917 appearance.

ing also G.P.s and dentists of "high qualification")—or nearly twenty-five per 10,000 population; this compares with an average of about seventeen in the people's democracies, fifteen to eighteen in Western Europe and the United States, two in India and less than one in Pakistan. Japan, with 14.3, is a "Western" country in this respect. As in all countries, so also in Russia, there are good, bad and indifferent doctors, just as there are also certain eminent and very highly paid specialists in all branches of medicine. (The finest specialists are, of course, to be found in the principal hospitals.) Most Russian doctors are women. It is generally admitted that they, like most teachers, are poorly paid; but both professions are so honorable that there has never been any shortage of young people anxious to enter either teachers' training colleges or the medical faculties.

7

The Great Economic Dispute

So far, so good. But it would be a mistake to imagine that everybody is satisfied with the present economic system in the Soviet Union. In recent years, there has been not much more than a tentative and experimental departure from Stalinist overcentralization.

All recent writing, especially outside Russia, on the stimulation of the profit motive and the like has usually been associated with the economic theories of Professor E. Liberman, of Kharkov University. In a very cautious analysis of the "innovations" in Soviet economy in recent years*—an analysis written for foreign consumption, since it was published in *New Times,* a Moscow weekly printed in several languages—Professor Liberman starts with some general considerations on the superiority of the socialist system over the capitalist system; thus, he says that

> the national income of the Soviet Union . . . increased by 264 per cent between 1950 and 1965; that of the United States, by only 66 per cent. But this criterion, too, has been questioned. The absolute growth of national income, it is said, must be translated into relative, per capita terms. . . . But if we do that, we shall still see that, during those 15 years, per capita national income in the U.S.S.R. went up 185 per cent, in the U.S.A. only 30 per cent.

He then answers another Western argument, that "the growth of national income as a whole is no indication of the effectiveness of production; this income should be channeled in optimal proportions to consumption and accumulation," by saying that in recent years

* "The Soviet Economy Forges Ahead," *New Times,* 1967, No. 29.

seventy-two to seventy-five per cent of the national income of the
U.S.S.R. has gone for consumption, leaving the rest for investment.
"On this score some Western sociologists . . . claim to have dis-
covered the secret of the high growth rate in the U.S.S.R. The
U.S.S.R., they say, has gone in for restricted consumption and
excessive accumulation."

But this, says Liberman, is an open secret. The whole history of
the last fifty years shows that the Soviet people "spared no effort
and consciously denied themselves essentials in order to overcome
the country's economic lag." He says that, instead of sneering,
Western critics of the Soviet Union should remember that it was
thanks to the extremely hard Russian industrialization effort of the
1930s that the Soviet Union was at all able to fight the German
invaders and bear the brunt of the Second World War, thus saving
the Western Allies unspeakable hardships and disasters. But despite
this guns-instead-of-butter rule which had become imperative for
Russia in the 1930s if she was to survive at all, and then the fearful
ordeal of the war and immediate postwar years, what had been
achieved since the war was altogether remarkable.

Liberman admits, however, that there are some "difficulties of
growth still to be overcome."

Very cautiously, he says "the economic reform now under way"
was "not prompted by any 'failure' of planned economy." On the
contrary, *it is because of the expansion and growing complexity of
our economy that the old methods, necessary though they were at
the time, are no longer adequate."* He goes on:

> The U.S.S.R. had not yet attained the average consumption
> level of the more developed capitalist countries, notably the
> U.S.A. Its productivity of labor is, too, accordingly lower. Hence
> the emphasis on ensuring a great improvement in the living
> standard. . . . The prerequisites for this have been created. . . .
> The living standard is decisive in our economic competition with
> the West.

Once the Soviet living standard has risen to the American level,
the peoples of the world will no longer question the effectiveness of
the socialist system. (This, apparently, applies in the first place to
the underdeveloped countries, many of which are still hesitating
between the Soviet way and the capitalist way.)

Speaking of the present tentative economic reforms, Liberman then says that these are "designed to increase returns from production."

> Added incentives to better performance are being provided in both the country and the cities. . . . State purchasing prices for farm produce have been increased. . . . Incomes are increasing in conformity with the growth of labor productivity and *the profitability of enterprises* [my italics]. Inflationary tendencies are thus ruled out.

Liberman proposes this combination of "state planning" and "greater economic stimuli to the enterprises" and "encouragement of initiative and independence" which still more "progressive" economists than he consider an impossibility. However, he persists in saying that "there is no contradiction between being guided primarily by plan and taking account of consumer demand and technological progress. This does not imply any weakening or 'dismantling' of the system of planned guidance."

> Since it is in the interests of the enterprises to make the most effective use of their plant, there is no need to prod them to undertake a capacity load. This is shown by the experience gained in applying the new system to 704 enterprises in 1966. . . . [In short] the centralized plan provides the over-all guideposts, while the market "tunes" the plan to the required degree of precision.
>
> [But] there can be no question of any return to spontaneous regulation through the market mechanism alone. The market without a plan will lead to anarchy, . . . depressions and unemployment. On the other hand, a plan which ignores the organized market stands in danger of becoming bogged down in red tape. . . .

As for various innuendoes in the Western press to the effect that the Soviet Union is returning to capitalism, Liberman tries to deal with these too. He quotes one French economist as asking "why such bourgeois levers as money, prices, etc., have not only been retained, but are now playing an increasing role in the Soviet economy." All this, the same French economist said, seemed to him incompatible with "the Marxist thesis of abolishing commodity fetishism." Liberman replies:

Nobody in the U.S.S.R. is rejecting the Marxist thesis of abolishing commodity fetishism. Inasmuch as the means of production have been removed from private ownership, each factory and office worker . . . knows that he is not working for the shareholders of his firm . . . but for their own common cause. . . . The moral sublimation of a man who has accomplished something, however modest his place in production, is a far cry from the fetishization which disguises the production relations of people as relations between things.

As for what I have called the Soviet welfare state, Liberman ridicules those Western critics who say that "with rising of the living standard in the socialist countries, socialism itself is degenerating and drifting towards capitalism." And then comes this parting shot: "The Chinese pseudo-theorists say the same, thereby coming round to the position of the bourgeois critics of Marxism."

This Liberman article, written for foreign consumption, is very cautiously worded. While in Moscow I had the opportunity of meeting a very eminent Soviet economist (whom I shall call Professor X) who thought Liberman overcautious and not nearly progressive or radical enough to bring about any major changes in the Soviet economy—especially with his rather pathetic attempt to combine what this radical called "the economic method" and the old Stalinite "administrative method." There is a sharp conflict in Russia between such radical economists and the conservatives, or Stalinites; and the influence of these is still so strong that the radicals have the greatest difficulty in getting their own writings published.

What Professor X said during a two-hour conversation can be summarized as follows:

"There are several economic schools in the Soviet Union now; but at the two extremes, as it were, are the administrative economists and the radical economists. The administrative economists do not particularly believe in managing the country's economy with the help of economic levers; they prefer to enforce their decisions by means of administrative measures. The radicals, on the other hand, hold that economic levers must be used, but hold that the different levers must not conflict with each other. The administrative economists, or 'centralizers,' took up a dominant position in Russia in the late 1920s. Their theory was: 'We don't need economic laws; we can go faster if we make decisions regardless of what the cost data show.' Thus, there is no harm in the money reckoning being independent of the physical units. This approach made *money* a measure of only secondary importance, since what really mattered was the *physical units* produced. If you set up a plant, you did not really have to bother about its financial aspects; you simply did not have to count in money terms; instead you counted in terms of units of timber, cement and the number of men employed. This was all right so long as there was an *extensive* development of the economy, and when great resources were wasted, but it was essential to build economic projects—as was the case under the Stalin Five-Year Plans.

"All this made it impossible to *count* in the Soviet economy; and Soviet planners, indeed, lost the habit (if they ever had it) of counting and comparing, or of calculating what was more expensive or less expensive; they did not count in financial terms, only in physical terms. Money was, to them, no yardstick. With this method continuing after the war, some economists grew alarmed; they pointed to the wastefulness of the method, and to the mistakes which had now become quite apparent. Those of the administrative or Stalinist school do not realize it yet; and among the progressives or radicals not all fully realize it, either.

"This economic argument," Professor X said, "went in fact a long way back. Thus, even before the war, Oscar Lange, then a professor at Chicago, who later returned to his native Poland, disagreed with those Western economists, who said that because the socialism of those days had no yardstick it would never be capable of being more efficient than capitalism.

"Lange pointed out that a socialist economy was in fact as perfectly able to aim at an optimum as capitalist economy was. In capitalist economy, he said, it was the market which set the prices, and the price was determined by supply and demand. Lange's line was that the same could be done in a socialist economy; all that state enterprises had to do was to balance supply and demand, and, since they had all industry at their disposal and could manipulate prices, they could also set prices in such a way as to control consumption. But once a price has been set, socialist industry must satisfy the demand at that price.

"Unfortunately," said Professor X, "our economists scarcely know Lange's book, *The Economic Theory of Socialism,* first published in 1938 in the United States and recently reprinted there; it has not been translated into Russian.

"The kind of planning which uses these ecoomic levers and the supply-and-demand forces is quite different from our present Soviet planning, which, until recently at any rate, was still entirely laid down in terms of physical units and disregarded the monetary aspect altogether. It did not, and often still does not, bother if this method is profitable or not to a particular factory.

"What generally happened was this: A socialist enterprise, whether farm or factory, was given a plan in physical units, and this it had to fulfill, whether it was profitable to it or not. But at the same time the government demanded that the enterprise also show a profit in actual money terms. Thus, every such enterprise had two contradictory orders given it. On the one hand, the prices were set by the government, regardless of whether certain products were more profitable to this particular enterprise than others; on the other hand, there were the physical units that had to be produced under the plan.

"Now, particularly in agriculture, there are some products more profitable to produce than others, but the farm still has to produce what it has been ordered by the state plan to produce. Thus, every time it fulfills the state plan it reduces the profits it *could* have made if it had followed its own initiative. What we radicals say is this: Why give a farm two contradictory orders? The state, we say, can give only one order; but give this order in economic (money) terms—if the state wants more of this product; the alternative is to set a relatively higher price for the product.

"Now, if a farm produces milk under the plan but finds it unprofitable, then the more milk it produces the bigger is its loss. What we say is that, through the manipulation of prices, we must get the interests of every enterprise to coincide with the interests of society as a whole. The manipulation of prices can be very usefully done: if a farm finds the production of sunflower oil enormously profitable but that of milk unprofitable, the government can always restrain the sunflower-oil production by lowering the price in favor of milk. This system whereby farms produce unprofitable crops is particularly felt on the kolkhozes, where each individual member gets part of his pay from the net income of the kolkhoz. (On the sovkhozes—state farms—where the workers are wage earners, the situation is, of course, different.)

"No, the trouble with our conservative economists is that they still refuse to recognize what Western economists have achieved by way of developing methods in calculating the optimum. Our conservatives refuse to accept either Western methods or Western theories; whereas we so-called radicals are convinced that the mathematical method can be more effectively used in a socialist economy than in a capitalist economy.

"In order to be able to do this, we must have the money yardstick, and prices will have to be set according to the laws of supply and demand. . . . Altogether, it is very important to get away from 1930 ways of thinking. The so-called reform worked out at the September 1965 Plenum of the Central Committee (less than a year after the fall of Khrushchev) is being carried out only very slowly. There are really no proper theoretical guiding principles, and those carrying out the "reform" have no clear conception of what must be done; so far, only small changes have been made here and there. The new system has never really been applied, all the more so as there is no end of resistance and interference from the old fogeys. You can't have one part of the economy applying the new system and the other part sticking to the old.

"In short," he continued, "there has been no over-all change since the 1965 Plenum, and there is even some pulling back by those who are terrified by the idea that the new methods savor too much of capitalism. What we propose, for instance," said Professor X, "is that the workers should get a percentage of the profits of the enterprise; this would be a real incentive. I daresay the piecework system in our factories is all right, but where there is mass production no individual initiative is needed. But the same does not apply to our farms. There *can* be individual initiative here. We've got to do something which we are not doing at present, which is to interest the members of a kolkhoz in the farm's end results.

"At the March 1965 Plenum (barely six months after Khrushchev went) the enormous encouragement given to the peasants to intensify the cultivation of their private plots was, in fact, a confession of failure to get appreciably better results than before from the *socialist* part of the farm. To reduce taxes on the private plots and to allow the peasants to have as much livestock on these private plots as they can accommodate has, in a sense, produced good results: the kolkhoz markets are crammed with chickens and geese and vegetables; but all this has nothing to do with the socialist part of the kolkhozes. This is, of course, a bit of an oversimplification; through the manipulation of prices, some incentives were given to get better results than before from the actual kolkhoz lands, but not nearly enough.

"The truth is, you can't run the economy as you run an army; yet at present what is used is still the Army method, not the economic method. What we radicals want is a real change. At one time, we had hopes; but, as it turned out, Khrushchev didn't really understand anything. Instead he went in for pure demagogy, inventing new panaceas every year or every six months.

"No doubt there have been some improvements. As I've already said, more food is produced on the private plots than before 1965, and the rise in prices on stuff produced by the collective land has had some effect. But still not enough has been done; the real economic incentive in agriculture is to make the farms produce what is most profitable *to them*. By all means, make the farms produce what the country needs, but don't do your planning in *physical* terms. Farms, in fact, should be allowed to decide for themselves what to produce by basing themselves on the prices set by the government. Instead of which, prices are set, but at the same time there are also compulsory quotas of *what* the farms are to sell, quite regardless of the profitability to the farm itself.

"Our conservatives have a pet argument: they accuse us of wanting to follow in the footsteps of Yugoslavia. But this is totally irrelevant. Yugoslavia largely lives on foreign investments, and here in the Soviet Union the question obviously does not arise. Much better examples are Czechoslovakia, Hungary and East Germany, where there are no foreign investments. We very much hope our conservatives or reactionaries (yes, I don't mind calling them even that) will eventually abandon their resistance when they see that these 'elemental' or 'chaotic' methods—I mean planning in monetary terms—are *not* dangerous to socialism. They accuse us radicals of believing in the virtues of elemental methods; we simply say that their methods are so wasteful that they literally undermine the true principles of socialism. I am now speaking in international terms. We could be ahead of other countries; instead, we are still lagging behind, especially as regards the productivity of labor. What we propose, for instance, is that we adopt the methods already adopted in agriculture in a country like Czechoslovakia.

"We want our economy to adopt the truly Leninist idea of a cooperative system, under which every kolkhoz and sovkhoz becomes a real cooperative, for greater initiative means greater development. The point is that the old administrative method is based primarily on extensive development; what we advocate is intensive development, with far greater productivity.

"The administrative kind of socialism is not the only one; it is, in fact, bad and backward. *Our* modern kind of socialism would be a step forward, so much so that the West would be impressed; now the West is pooh-poohing our methods, and not without some reason. For before our country becomes a real model for other countries we must develop a more efficient kind of socialism. Thus, we want the developing countries to adopt the socialist way, the United States wants them to go the capitalist way, and, so long as things are no better here than there, the developing countries can't make up their minds. As things are at present, America still has certain serious advantages over us as regards the backward countries. Socially, we are progressive, but our economic mechanism is still conservative and inefficient.

"Now, Marx never really visualized how socialist economy was to be run; his line was, 'When we come to it, we'll see.' And, indeed, when the Bolsheviks under Lenin took over, they did not really know *how* to run the country. So there were 'experiments' like War Communism, on the principle that you could exchange goods without money coming into it; it didn't work. To save the situation, the NEP had to be introduced. Now, as we see it, there were two sides to the NEP. On the one side there were private retail trade and small-scale production in private hands; this cannot be repeated. But the other side of the NEP is of some real interest even now: the running of socialist industry with the help of economic levers and incentives; this is one of the major arguments of an economist like Lisichkin, nicknamed by his conservative opponents a 'nepman.' No, the NEP was Lenin's idea; and there are certain elements in the NEP which we ought to study more carefully than we do.

"The trouble is that the foreign Communist parties in the West, whether the French or the Italian (these are the only two that really matter), have learned nothing so far; they are still thinking, where economics is concerned, in Stalinist terms of overcentralization.

"Unfortunately, here too the conservatives or Stalinites are still dominating economic thinking, and we radicals are having a very steep uphill fight, and having great difficulty in getting our writings published. My view is that we ought to experiment ourselves, instead of using Hungary, East Germany and Czechoslovakia as if they were our guinea pigs; but the conservative argument is, 'Well, let's see; if they succeed without sinking back into capitalism, well and good, and if they do succeed we may perhaps adopt the same methods, but not before.' All this is, of course, wrong. At the very top of the Party and the government there are people who more or less hold our views, but for the present they are greatly outnumbered by the Stalinite conservatives. We have in the Soviet Union an immense labor force, and labor reserves are being built up all the time. Only, too many are today employed in industry; productivity is low, and everybody seems quite happy to work much less than he might. But this too is wrong. If we intensified production (which we could easily do) we could supply the developing countries much more successfully than the United States does.

"True, there is this infernal problem to which we have not yet found an answer: How would the developing countries pay? They have no hard cash; although we are developing our trade with them, they haven't many things to sell us which we really need. So the tendency is, obviously, for our industry not to overproduce but to underproduce—that is, to produce well below its capacity. If we had enormous food surpluses, it would make our economic position in the world much stronger, but for the present we haven't got them. That is why we radical economists are so anxious to concentrate on bigger incentives in our *rural* areas. In industry we have made spectacular progress ever since 1928, and especially since the war, but not in agriculture."

But if the radicals are still dissatisfied with progress in agriculture since 1965 and claim that the good results (more food) were achieved the wrong way, the more conservative people strongly protest against such assertions. Thus, after I had described, in an article published in the West, the radical economists' criticisms of the "wrong way" and of the halfheartedness with which the 1965 "reform" was being carried out, I received a rather irate letter from my friend Yuri Zhukov, of *Pravda*:

> You seem to have become a victim of the legend being built up by Western correspondents about an alleged conflict between "radicals" and "Stalinist centralizers." You should know better than most people how our society is organized; you should also know that when our Party makes a decision of principle, then it applies it in actual practice—firmly, consistently and without hesitation. This applied in particular to our present economic reform. It would be naïve to talk, as you do, of "the strong resistance of the conservatives" and suggest that our leaders have, in these conditions, to maneuver and make some sort of concessions to somebody.
>
> I know you did not go so far as to say that the reform represented a restoration of capitalism, but the Chinese in Peking do talk like that. Here in the Soviet Union we do not take this kind of talk seriously.
>
> On the other hand, it is quite untrue that, as you claim, we are waiting to see what the "Czechoslovak and Hungarian guinea pigs" will produce in the end, before *we* take any clear decision as regards the Soviet Union. We have, in reality, taken a firm decision, and are going along our own way.
>
> As for agriculture, you make an even bigger mistake when you say that, although the food situation in Russia since 1965 is much better, the reform resulting in greater production from the peasants' private plots did not prove a success as regards *socialist* agriculture. Now, let me say this: I often visit my kolkhoz constituents, and with the utmost responsibility I can assure you that it is precisely the *socialist* part of our agriculture, following the decisions of the March 1965 Plenum, which is developing *incomparably faster* than the private plots. It is, indeed, socialist agriculture and not private plots which is providing our shops with the abundance of food that can now be observed in the Soviet Union.

So the economic debate continues. The radical economists claim that the March 1965 reform isn't producing nearly as much as it could have done; the conservatives, reflecting the government's view (or part of the government's view), maintain that the policy is being applied and will be more and more applied, and that the Soviet

Union will be increasingly prosperous with every year, without the need to scrap any of the centralist principles altogether; make them subtler, but don't scrap them.

Since Yuri Zhukov's rather angry letter of November 1967, the official statistics for industrial and agricultural production for 1967 were published in the Soviet press on 25 January 1968. And here I am ready to admit that much of what Zhukov said is largely borne out by the figures, above all his assertion that the great increase in the production of food came principally *not* from the peasants' private plots, but from the "socialist sector," from the kolkhoz and sovkhoz lands proper.

The weather in 1967 had not been good at all, and the production of wheat and other cereals was much lower than it had been in the record year of 1966. The 1967 harvest was average, totaling only 147 million tons, as against 171 million tons in 1966. (The figure for the "drought" year of 1963 had been 107 million tons.)

But what strongly supported Zhukov's contention was notably the figures for sugar beet. The average annual output of this had been only 59 million tons in 1961–65; in 1966 it had risen to 74 million, and in 1967 to 86 million. Quite obviously, since sugar beet is not grown on tiny private plots but on the socialist land, these figures were indeed a remarkable illustration of the rapidly growing success of the 1965 agricultural reform, with its new incentives to the peasantry to concentrate their energies on the socialist sector.

This, of course, does not mean that the radical economists are entirely satisfied and are ready to capitulate; what they claim is that, while the progress made since 1965 is undeniable, even better results could be achieved if certain of their principles were adopted.

8

Liberals and Stalinites

THE conservatives, or Stalinites, as they have come to be called, are very angry when one suggests that in nearly every field in the Soviet Union there is a conflict between left and right: between liberals or radicals on the one hand and Stalinite conservatives on the other; between fanatics of socialist realism and those who try to get away from those socialist-realist literary canons laid down at the height of the Stalin regime, from 1932 to 1934. But in fact there is only one field where the domination by the Stalinites, the right, or, for that matter, simply the state, has ceased, and that is science. Gone, thank God, are the days of bourgeois science and Soviet science, bourgeois genetics and Soviet genetics, even of bourgeois mathematics and Soviet mathematics!

I still have some good friends among the old Stalinite guard; they are not all bad people, simply wrongheaded; and they can never get away from the idea that but for Stalin, whatever his foul methods, Russia would not have been industrialized in time and would therefore inevitably have been conquered by the Germans or somebody else. When I told one of these old Stalinites about my conversation with Professor S——on the Paris–Moscow plane on June 29, and particularly his remark that the scientists were the happiest people in Russia because they did not have to worship at the Lysenko shrine or any other shrine, he said, "Yes, I suppose it was inevitable in the case of science. But we do not much like it, for science has become a state within the state." And he suggested that this could not be helped, but that neither literature nor economics nor anything else would be allowed to become a "state within the state."

THE RELATIVE LIBERALIZATION OF
HISTORY

In history too the supremacy of the historians *tout court,* as against the Stalinist historians, has made remarkable progress by Soviet standards since the Twentieth (de-Stalinization) Congress of 1956. I am not speaking here of the history of the Soviet Communist Party; this is still a kind of reserved domain of the Central Committee, and so long as Trotsky, Kamenev, Zinoviev, Bukharin, Radek, etc., have not been officially rehabilitated they will not figure to any extent in histories of the October 1917 Revolution or subsequent years. Even so, it is a sign of progress that in the Brezhnev-Kosygin *Survey,* as we have seen above, Trotsky, for instance, should no longer be treated as either an "imperialist agent" or simply a "hyena," but merely as a man who was wrong and who misunderstood both the internal and the international situations in the middle of the 1920s, whereas Stalin, for all his faults and subsequent crimes, happened to be right.

But, even so, the histories of the Party published after Stalin's death are not half as crazy as the *Short History of the Party,* first published in 1938, of which Stalin wrote one (theoretical) chapter, but for the whole of which he later claimed the authorship. The book is a falsification from beginning to end; thus, Stalin is represented as Lenin's sole right-hand man even in October 1917, and there is no mention at all of Trotsky except to abuse him. The history of Russia too has been rewritten over and over again; there was a time, at the beginning of the Revolution, when Ivan the Terrible figured as a monster; but later, in the 1930s, he became one of Russia's great state builders who, together with Peter the Great, was an obvious forerunner of Stalin. (Hence the joke about Soviet historians: "We never can tell what will happen yesterday.") Alexei Tolstoy's play on Ivan the Terrible and his novel on Peter the Great (or, rather, Peter I), and Eisenstein's famous film on Ivan the Terrible, were in fact intended as glorifications of Stalin's forerunners and consequently of Stalin himself. Ivan the Terrible's *oprichniki,* the special anti-boyar and anti-sedition force, were made to look like the noble forerunners of Stalin's equally noble NKVD. All these naïve *images d'Épinal* are now being repainted by serious Soviet historians.

But the changes in the writing of history have been most remarkable of all in respect of the Second World War. With rare exceptions, histories or monographs written before Stalin's death, or even before the Twentieth Congress of 1956, were falsifications of history. The three-year period between Stalin's death and the De-Stalinization Congress was neither one thing nor the other; literature, with Ehrenburg's *The Thaw* and literary almanacs like *Literaturnaya Moskva,* showed new signs of vitality; but Stalin, as war leader, still remained something of a sacred cow, and his explanation that the Russian disasters of 1941 were due to two things, the unequaled perfidy of Hitler and the absolute unexpectedness of the German invasion, were still accepted.

Luckily, after the 1956 Congress historians were liberated from these myths (which very few people found possible to believe, anyway). The Department of the History of the War in the Marx-Lenin Institute embarked on the enormous task of writing the official history of the war—the six-volume *Istoria Velikoi Otechestvennoi Voiny Sovietskogo Soyuza* (commonly known as *IVOVSS*), which is of immense historical value. No doubt holes can still be picked in it. It is long-winded; it is too detailed; it evades a detailed discussion of the number of Russian prisoners taken by the Germans in 1941 and during subsequent years; it speaks of the "unanimous heroism" of the people of Moscow in October 1941, when in reality there was a panicky flight to the east of about half the population; it still attaches more importance to the Russian rout of the Japanese Kwantung Army in Manchuria and the capitulation of Japan than to the two atom bombs dropped on Hiroshima and Nagasaki. Published in the early sixties (except Volume Six, which did not appear till 1965), it attaches far greater importance to the role played in the war by Khrushchev than he deserves. (In Volume Six there is hardly a single mention of Khrushchev!)

But, these flaws apart (and other Russian publications have corrected many of them), *IVOVSS* still contains an enormous amount of factual material; and nothing is discussed more convincingly, and in greater detail, than the reasons why on June 22, 1941, the Soviet Union was unprepared to meet the Nazi invasion. The book does not pull any punches about the wholly inadequate frontier defenses;

or Stalin's orders that Germany should on no account be provoked; or his credulity about Hitler's good intentions; or his neglect of warnings of the German invasion of June 22, coming not only from "suspect" British and American sources, but even from his own generals and his own intelligence, including a master spy like Richard Sorge, who enjoyed the full confidence of Ott, the German ambassador in Tokyo; or the total inadequacy of the equipment produced by Russia during the Soviet–German Pact period of 1939–41; or the disastrous effect on the Army of the purges among its officers and generals in 1937–39, and even later; or the myth of invincibility that Stalin and the whole of Soviet propaganda tried (mostly successfully) to spread throughout the country during that period, by such means as the inane but highly popular film *If War Comes Tomorrow,* in which a German attempt to attack the Soviet Union is scotched by a rebellion, in the German rear, of the German proletariat, and so on, and so on.

For all its shortcomings, *IVOVSS* marks a gigantic advance on Stalinite historiography as regards accuracy and truthfulness, and it uses sources otherwise found only in remote archives—for instance, those concerning the transfer of the war industries to the east, and the appallingly hard conditions in which equipment was produced to make the victory of Stalingrad possible at the end of 1942.

Many of the gaps in *IVOVSS* have been filled by special studies written by military experts on this or that battle; by detailed monographs on such aspects of the war as the partisan war behind the enemy lines; by numerous memoirs by generals and others; or even by extracts from novels, such as Konstantin Simonov's *The Living and the Dead,* telling the real facts of the Moscow panic of October 16, 1941.

A particularly lurid episode, the Dunkirk of Tallinn, when a large naval force and several troop transports were forced to escape under enemy bombing and shellfire through the German mine fields to Leningrad after the German capture of Tallinn, is described in all its unvarnished detail in an article in *Voenno-Istoricheski Zhurnal* in 1966. *IVOVSS* still tends to describe this Dunkirk as a fairly successful evacuation; the author of the article in the *V-I Zhurnal* reveals that, even if most of the warships got away to Leningrad, most of the wholly defenseless troop transports had to be abandoned and were then sunk by the Germans. In short, it was all much more horrible and tragic than even *IVOVSS* made out.

Not at once, but gradually, the whole truth about the Second World War is being published. Unless there is a sharp Stalinite reaction (never something to be entirely ruled out, especially in today's tense international situation) I should not be surprised if in five years' time, if only for the benefit of students of history, the complete works of, say, Bukharin or Trotsky were published. There are also some excellent monographs on foreign countries by serious Soviet historians, such as Professor V. G. Trukhanovsky's very valuable *British Foreign Policy During World War II*.

More evidence of this liberalization process of Russian history is provided by the story of how my thousand-page book *Russia at War* was published in Russian. I had written other books on Russia, notably during the war, and these were in many ways more pro-Soviet than *Russia at War* (which reveals a good many warts on the face of Stalinite wartime Russia). But, although I had a polite notice in *Izvestia* about my book *Leningrad* (1944), the question of *publishing* any foreign book on the war in Russia simply did not arise, not even in the case of *Leningrad,* though it was the first eyewitness account to appear abroad on the ghastly tragedy of the city.

When, in 1946, my large book *The Year of Stalingrad* appeared, I had a typical Soviet reaction (of those days) from Leonid Sobelev, very much at the top of the Soviet literary Establishment: "I think that's the way books on the war in the Soviet Union should be written: ninety-five per cent gold and five per cent shit; but this five per cent damns the book in *our* eyes in advance, and there is no hope in hell of its ever being published here. I wish *we* could write like that; perhaps someday we will, but now it's absolutely impossible. We can't even be five per cent wrong, still less our beloved Stalin."

After the Twentieth Congress, things began to change very rapidly. In 1964 I published *Russia at War* in England and the United States. Soon after that it was scheduled for publication in about fifteen other countries. In December 1964 *Pravda* gave it a long favorable review, though naturally with some reservations. But what was a little odd was that it was written not by a staff correspondent of *Pravda* but by an American lady, an occasional contributor to the paper, living in New York.

When I went to Moscow in May 1965 for the celebrations marking the twentieth anniversary of the victory over Germany, I found that all the important people had read my book—in a for-private-circulation, wholly unexpurgated Russian translation of perhaps a thousand copies. But most people still doubted whether it would be published, either abridged or unabridged, for the general public in Russia.

It was not till a year later, after various preliminary letters, that the Progress publishing house cabled me to say that the translation had been finished and to ask if I would come to Moscow to "approve" the cuts and changes. They suggested that I myself should rewrite the first part—on the 1939 period—since it contained some wholly "inacceptable" passages, such as Molotov's speech of October 31, 1939, saying that the French and the British, not the Germans, were now the aggressors, the story of the Finnish puppet government under Otto Kuusinen, etc.

The "editor" of the book was my old friend Professor and Major General E. A. Boltin. On arriving in Moscow, I was presented a mountain of typescript—the "abridged" Russian version. Most of it was genuinely abridged—it was a very long book—but some had been censored. In fact there were only three major changes. First, the story of the Soviet–German Pact, which I myself had condensed (I preferred this to leaving it to some overcautious local hack). I had given a fairly full account of the story, including certain things not to be found in Soviet history books—for example, the consternation caused in Russia by the rapid collapse of France, and the genuine sympathy felt in Russia, especially by the intellectuals, for Britain during the Battle of Britain and the blitz winter in London. It also gave a fairly full summary of what I had to say about Molotov's famous visit to Berlin in November 1940.

The second cut, which I had foreseen, was, to my surprise, not as complete as I had expected—I mean the story of Katyn Forest. Here the "editor" enumerated the bits of evidence favorable to the Russians, but still let me say that "the case had been presented by the Russians (the NKVD) in a most clumsy and unconvincing manner," and that this had "placed the foreign correspondents in a very embarrassing, indeed impossible, position" if they did not want to play into the hands of the Germans. On the face of it, it was difficult to make head or tail of the Russian version of my Katyn story; but quite enough was left of it to enable an even mildly intelligent Russian reader to read between the lines—which has become second nature with him—and to draw precisely the same conclusions as myself: that the evidence was overwhelmingly against the NKVD.

Thirdly, the "editor" left out the chapter on Stalin and the church. There were also some smaller cuts which were to be foreseen.

When, after three agonizing days spent in my hotel room wading through the typescript, I was summoned to an editorial conference, the head of Progress, Mr. I. K. Zamchevsky, and his second in command, G. G. Lensky, said they would like their version to be authorized by me. I raised a number of objections. I had a few passages on the Soviet–German Pact restored; as regards the "Stalin and the Church" chapter, they argued that it was of no interest today. I did not feel very strongly about it, and let it go. I did not argue about Katyn; I felt it was an absolute maximum they would publish in Russia. (It was, in fact, a wonder that they should have devoted even two pages to it; nobody had ever been allowed to mention it except as a "monstrous German crime," and more recently there was a kind of conspiracy of silence on the whole subject.)

After extracting quite a few other, though minor, concessions, I finally "authorized" the translation. The way I reasoned was this: the very fact that today, in 1966, they were publishing even a shortened version of the book was a sign that things were rapidly changing for the better. I also felt that if things went on like this there was no reason why a wholly unabridged version should not be published in a few years' time. Also, the book was full of personal reminiscences, reflections and conversations which it would be enormously interesting for the Russian public to read. Should I deprive them of the book because Molotov's compliments to Ribbentrop had been cut out, or because the story of Katyn had been given in a garbled, though still reasonably intelligible, version? After all, to well-informed Russians Katyn was by now an open secret; as one leading Russian writer said to me in 1965, "It's one of those sore pimples we don't like to touch." It had also great scarcity value as the very first big book on the Soviet–German war by a non-Communist Western author to be published in the Soviet Union. In short, it was better for me to "authorize" the book than to let them do precisely as they liked: the effect might have been disastrous from my point of view.

Although there was no big song and dance about it in the press when it was first published, in June 1967, the book aroused enormous interest; Russian readers described it to me as the first proper "human history" of the war, and several women readers told me that the Leningrad chapter had made them weep. There was much in it that Russians, except possibly specialists, had not read before: all the hanky-panky about the Arctic convoys, the two Churchill visits to Moscow, the funny business that had gone on at Potsdam between Churchill, Truman and Stalin about the newly exploded atom bomb, and much else. The stories of Leningrad and Stalingrad were told not so much in military as in human terms. The first twenty-five thousand copies were sold out in two days; then there was a long gap; the next fifty thousand were not put on sale till shortly before the Fiftieth Jubilee in November, and were also sold out in a few days; and the black-market price was now twenty rubles (twenty dollars), against the published price of 2.79 rubles!

In December 1967, now that the "Jubilee rush," with its frightful consumption of paper, was over, I was told that another edition of 100,000 copies would "shortly" be printed—though "shortly" is a very elastic term, especially in the U.S.S.R.

My "editor," Major General Boltin, was, on the whole, Stalinite rather than anti-Stalinite, and, although it was mostly a question of faint nuances, his Russian version of my book was slightly more Stalinite than my English original—a point significantly raised by a five-page review of the book in *Novy Mir* of March 1968.

Not that Boltin, to be entirely fair to him, omitted any of my major criticisms of Stalin—for example the fearful damage he did to the Army by having Tukhachevsky and hundreds of other officers and generals shot in the purges, but a few others he did leave out.

Altogether, a balanced view of the last fifty years is given in most of the literature published in Russia today. Take, for example, even a book by a very hard ex-Stalinite, and, I imagine, crypto-Stalinite to this day, like my old friend Yuri Zhukov, the top commentator on international affairs in *Pravda,* who for several years after the war was Paris correspondent of the paper. He had presented me a copy of *Ludi 30kh Godov* (*People of the 1930s*) when I went to have a long talk with him at his office in the *Pravda* building. I found it fascinating as history—it would have been inconceivable under Stalin. I was glad to see a long review of it in the *Times Literary Supplement* of November 2, 1967.

People of the 1930s is a remarkable book in that it catches the true spirit of what has been called Russia's Iron Age—the years when the Dnieper Dam was completed, when hundreds of factories were springing up all over the country, among them the Kharkov and Stalingrad tractor plants and the great new industrial centers like Magnitogorsk, Chelisbinsk, etc. It is an account of the heroic mass effort made by the Russian working class to industrialize the country and of the often appalling conditions in which the work had to be carried out. Zhukov stresses that all this was done under the leadership of Stalin, but he does not disguise first the bewilderment and then the horror caused by Stalin's purges.

This is, in a sense, still a typically Stalinite book; it does not deny the horror and iniquity of the purges; but it shows not only what enormous sacrifices the Russian people made to bring about their industrial revolution of the 1930s, without which they would unquestionably have been crushed by the Nazis, but also that Stalin was, after all, the great mastermind who started this industrialization in 1928. This, on the credit side (for such is the book's implication) is much bigger, after all, than what one finds on Stalin's debit side—the purges themselves, and the blunders he made just before the war and at its very beginning.

It is over the errors, crimes and achievement of Stalin that Russian historians are still divided into Stalinites and anti-Stalinites. Thus, as already mentioned, there appeared in 1965 a small book by a young historian, A. M. Nekrich, called *1941: June 22.* Not a very important book in itself, it nevertheless aroused some angry exchanges amongst historians who had come to discuss it under the chairmanship of Major General Boltin. The opponents of Nekrich describe it as a "bourgeois concoction" in which practically all the misfortunes were attributed to Stalin himself, who, among other things, had failed to take any notice of the warnings about an imminent German invasion in June 1941 from either British or American sources, let alone Russian intelligence agents.

This, the Stalinites argued, was un-Marxist and unscientific. The important thing which Nekrich had overlooked, they said, was the fact that in the end the Soviet Union did win the war—which means that from the very outset the Soviet state had laid the foundations for victory. The fact that, through Stalin's faults and blunders, Russia had very nearly *lost* the war was somehow "disproved" by the final result.

It was, apparently, a very nasty row among the historians; in the end Nekrich was expelled from the Party—not, though, because he held the "wrong" views, but because he and/or his friends had sent abroad what was declared to be a falsified report of the discussion over his book, a report that was to be published by *Der Spiegel* and other magazines.

DIVISIONS ON TOP?

There is, as we have seen, a left and a right among writers, among economists, and—though less obviously, except during a big rumpus like that over the Nekrich book—among historians. There is also undoubtedly a left and a right in the Soviet government itself, and even on the Central Committee, though these divisions are objects of rumor, and there are few hard facts to go by. There is little or no evidence of there being a pro-Chinese wing anywhere, though the degree of hostility to China (as also to America) may not be the same with all members of the government or all members of the Politburo.

In ideological matters there are also strong differences. Suslov is firmly believed to be one of the most orthodox members of the Politburo, and to be mainly responsible for the hard ideological line applied to literature and the arts.

Kosygin is widely considered the liberal—a man who, in foreign affairs, is anxious not to burn any bridges anywhere, and who, it is said, opposed the trial of Siniavsky and Daniel and favored their amnesty during the Jubilee. He is also said to have favored the publication of the two confiscated Solzhenitsyn novels, as well as that of *Dr. Zhivago,* but to have met with uncompromising opposition from Suslov and his friends, whoever they are. More recently still he is believed to have successfully supported an anti-hysterical line on Czechoslovakia. Nevertheless, a Stalinist secrecy continues to surround the actions of the government and the top echelons of the Party, and some of their "unanimous" actions are very hard to explain.

The same was true under Khrushchev, in relation to literature in particular, as we shall see in Chapter 18. One day he would allow Solzhenitsyn's *Ivan Denisovich* to be published; the next day he would make those incredibly gross and asinine remarks on painting during his visit to the Manège in January 1963.

As regards Khrushchev, there may be a great deal in the theory expounded by Michel Tatu in his outstanding book on the Khrushchev period, *Le Pouvoir en URSS*. What it amounts to is briefly this: Khrushchev was primarily interested in one thing only—his personal power. Even as late as 1955 he had never said anything to suggest that he was an anti-Stalinite. There was no political purpose at the time in taking an anti-Stalin line. On art and literature he had no ideas or feelings of his own; he was scarcely literate in these matters. If there was a "thaw" in literature a year after Stalin's death, it left him indifferent; it was all to the good to give the country the impression that the government had become more tolerant.

Then came the Twentieth Congress. According to Tatu, the main purpose of the "secret report" on "Stalin's crimes" was to undermine the position of such powerful rivals as Malenkov, Molotov and Kaganovich. After the "October Revolution" in Poland and the Budapest rising soon after, Khrushchev looked for scapegoats inside Russia and promptly pounced on the writers and other intellectuals, whom he declared to be accomplices of the Hungarian "counter-revolutionaries," such as the Hungarian intellectuals of the Petöfi Club, who had many friends among the progressive Russian writers. Having already undermined his principal rivals at the Twentieth Congress, Khrushchev went one step further and in 1957 excommunicated them as being members of what he called "the anti-Party group," and he proceeded to discredit them more and more by associating them with "Stalin's crimes," though he himself, as the dictator of the Ukraine, had a record no better than theirs and possibly worse. In literary matters he blew hot and cold, and in

1957, so soon after the events in Poland and Hungary, his utterances were little different from Zhdanov's in 1946 and 1948. However, soon after, he found it was in his own interest to make himself popular with the intelligentsia, and the period of 1958 to 1962 was among the most liberal in the arts. At the Twenty-second Congress it was expedient to him to knock another nail in the coffin of Stalinism and openly to brand the "anti-Party group" as accomplices in the worst crimes of Stalin, whereupon he had Stalin's remains removed from the Lenin Mausoleum.

Now the foundation had clearly been laid for a Khrushchev personality cult; to discredit his other rivals, all more or less associated with Stalin, he started building up a party machinery of devoted Khrushchevites; and nothing served his purpose better than to discredit the Stalin regime still further by not merely allowing but instructing *Pravda,* in October 1962, to publish Yevtushenko's poem *The Heirs of Stalin,* and *Novy Mir* to publish Solzhenitsyn's famous labor-camp story. And then—then came the Cuban crisis, which seriously weakened Khrushchev's position in the Party; he had to look for support among the Stalinites, and the rest of his reign was marked by a deep literary and cultural freeze, complete with his incredible performance at the art exhibition in January 1963 and his savage offensive against Ehrenburg, Paustovsky, Yevtushenko and the other liberals. But on top of the Cuban fiasco, which had made Khrushchev extremely unpopular in the country, there came the disastrous drought of 1963.

So, according to Tatu, there were many long-term reasons for Khrushchev's downfall, but the immediate reason was his decision to call a meeting of the Central Committee in November 1964, at which, it seems, he was preparing to denounce a new "anti-Party group," one including all his new rivals, among them Mikoyan, Suslov, Brezhnev and Kosygin. After the elimination of these, the Khrushchev cult could have been developed through all the familiar artifices of Soviet propaganda.

In short, in cultural and literary matters, which did not interest him in the least, Khrushchev was neither liberal nor anti-liberal; he could be either, if it happened to suit his personal promotion toward a position comparable to Stalin's. All the same, apart from the Pasternak case, there was nothing under Khrushchev like the Siniavsky-Daniel affair, the Solzhenitsyn "scandal" and all the various more recent trials.

So, although there is a constant struggle between left and right, with a fair chance of the left winning when an entirely new generation takes over, the gradual softening of the regime is by no means automatic. What is ominous is that it was not the old people but relatively young people like Semichastny who launched the crudest, most violent and most offensive attacks on Pasternak in 1958.

THE STALINIST PATTERN CONTINUES

But there are quite a few Party people who, while rejecting the left-versus-right pattern, have lately contrasted Stalinism with Leninism. They say that all this cult of Lenin is all very well, but in reality it is Stalinism and not Leninism that characterizes the style of government in Russia. Leninism, they say, had certain democratic elements which were totally discarded under Stalin.

I remember a long conversation with a prominent professor of philosophy, who had some strong feelings about it, but in spite of them, or perhaps because of them, did not want to be quoted by name. Probably *because* of them, since, almost at the beginning of our talk, he said, "We still have some very powerful Stalinite bureaucrats, who are highly vigilant and, on occasion, very spiteful and vindictive."

The truth was, he said, that if there was a cult of Lenin today it was because, after fifty years, things had turned out reasonably well in Russia. There was a welfare state—the finest and most effective in the world, perhaps—and materially people were living better and better every year. In ten years' time they might well reach the Western-European standard of living, but without the danger of slumps and depressions and the constant fear of unemployment. The means of production had been nationalized. The country could, in this respect, be regarded as socialist in the best sense.

But the welfare state in Russia was not what Lenin had dreamed of in the first place. For a long time, at least up to the end of 1920, he did not visualize the Revolution being limited to Russia; he still imagined that it must spread to Western Europe, in the first place to Germany. There had been no blueprint for a *Russian* revolution only, and if the Russian Revolution spread at all, it spread to Asia (in the first place, China), but not to Europe. But even as late as 1920 Lenin wrote a preface to the French edition of his book *Imperialism: The Highest Stage of Capitalism* in which he said that the Russian Revolution was merely the forerunner of the socialist proletarian revolution in the West. But nothing of the sort happened, either then or during the next fifty years.

What Lenin then imagined was that by carrying out some kind of cultural revolution in a backward and almost illiterate country he could win over to socialism both the working class and the peasantry. But, as we have seen, what happened on the land was a sort of peasant-bourgeois revolution, with the peasants simply grabbing the land for their own uses. The "socialist" label attached to this process did not alter the matter. No doubt it was essential for the working class and the peasantry to be united against the Whites; but they were united for different reasons: the peasants represented a bourgeois revolution, the working class a proletarian revolution.

Hence the latent conflict between the two, and the failure of War Communism—which simply could not work, because urban Russia was not producing the commodities with which to pay for the food rural Russia was producing. Lenin's idealistic view was that the country could be run by the same kind of "primitive democratism" embodied in the soviets. But the soviets themselves soon began to rule by proxy. They began to set up *ispolkom*s (executive committees), working under the guidance of Party administrators with definite political functions. The congresses of the soviets created a central government, complete with commissars, the beginnings of a bureaucratic machinery—besides the Cheka, an organ of police terror, which was intended to protect the new order not only against the counterrevolution but against *all* opposition. The existence of a new bureaucracy was already consecrated at the Tenth Congress of the Party in May 1921. Lenin's view was that this bureaucracy was an inevitable but temporary evil; in his opinion the Party would absorb the "vanguard of the proletariat" and the trade unions would constitute the link between the Party and the masses. However, over a period of fifteen to twenty years, the trade unions, representing the masses, would gradually take over the management of the economy.

At this Tenth Congress there were three tendencies: the anarchosyndicalist, represented, in Lenin's view, by Trotsky and Bukharin;

the Party-plus-trade-union tendency, which would finally result in what Lenin regarded as the best thing, a kind of democratic centralism; and, finally, the Party-plus-bureaucracy tendency, which placed the powers of the state *above society and above the workers.* Officially, the middle course, that of Party plus trade unions, with its democratic centralism, was adopted as *the* correct policy. It implied an ever-growing activization of the masses as they became more and more educated, and an increasingly widespread discussion of public affairs both at the highest level (Party congresses, etc.) and at the local level. But already Lenin realized that the conditions for this kind of democratic socialism simply did not exist in Russia; already he spoke of "the bureaucratic corruption of the workers' state," and soon after the Tenth Congress he found it necessary to limit the powers of the trade unions in favor of the "economic organs"—that is, simply in favor of the bureaucrats of industry.

In the case of the peasantry, which had in fact carried out a bourgeois revolution, a *modus vivendi* had to be established after the failure of the "socialist" experiment of War Communism. This took the form of the NEP. Under this, the urban bourgeoisie was able to revive some forms of light industry and trade, and this eased the altogether catastrophic food situation in Russia in 1920–21. Lenin's idea now was to turn a NEP Russia into a socialist Russia through the development of "cooperation" among the peasantry and a thorough cultural revolution which would give the peasantry a proper "socialist consciousness." In Lenin's view, this would take a good long time to achieve—perhaps twenty years, or perhaps as much as fifty. But violent collectivization, as carried out under Stalin, did not enter into Lenin's plans for the future.

Lenin regarded the bureaucracy as a *temporary* evil and thought that in twenty or thirty years the trade unions could take over the administration of the national economy, while during the same period the peasantry would have accepted cooperation and have gone by then through a cultural revolution.

"There was, I must admit," said my friend, "something slightly utopian about these ideas of Lenin after the failure—at least provisional failure—of his hopes of a proletarian revolution in Western Europe. When Stalin took over, he promptly put an end to all democratic discussion at *all* levels. 'Socialism in one country,' the first shoots of which could already be detected in Lenin's time, albeit on a purely temporary basis, became the official dogma. It is unpleasant to admit it, but the truth is that during the last years of his life Lenin was being unrealistic and was not taking nearly sufficient account of the capitalist encirclement of the Soviet Union. He made no provision for a possible, or even probable, invasion of Russia, somehow assuming, no doubt, that the proletariat of the Western countries would never allow it.

"Lenin did not make any far-reaching plans for creating a heavy industry in Russia; his GOELRO electrification scheme was child's play. By 1928 Stalin firmly decided to industrialize Russia in a big way; and, indeed, within thirteen years he turned her into a major industrial country. This involved a vast expenditure of human energy and the creation of a powerful executive bureaucracy. Especially under the second Five-Year Plan the most dubious and revolting methods were used (including the creation of a large slave-labor force) to squeeze every ounce of energy out of the country; hundreds of thousands of people were falsely accused and driven into labor camps. It may be a horrible thing to admit, but, regardless of all these more than questionable methods, Stalin did succeed in building a heavy industry which was quite indispensable if Russia was to be saved from foreign conquest.

"There was much opposition to Stalin from Trotsky and Zinoviev, who did not believe in 'socialism in one country,' and this leftist opposition was virtually liquidated in 1927 at the Fifteenth Party Congress. The right opposition, represented by Bukharin, Rykov and Tomsky, claimed to represent the true Leninist tradition, complete with the transformation of the peasantry—through the NEP, combined with the cultural revolution—into a socialist force; they were expelled from the Party in 1929. But both the left and the right oppositions to Stalin continued to be fairly active.

"I do not exclude the possibility of there having been an anti-Stalin underground in Russia; Stalin, at any rate, was certain there was. Hence the purge trials, the killing off of the Old Bolsheviks. Free democratic discussion at any level became entirely taboo. It was replaced by the unquestioned authority of the Party hierarchy, with Stalin at its head. It was in this way that the Stalin personality cult developed. Although lip service continued to be paid to Lenin and his democratic centralism, what took place was something entirely different. Men like Kuibyshev, Orjonikidze and Kirov who still represented the Leninist, 'democratic' style of leadership were, in one way or another, eliminated.*

"Stalin now reigned supreme, depending on a vast and powerful bureaucracy and especially on the NKVD. By the middle of the 1930s the Party, in the Leninist sense, ceased to exist; it became the Party apparatus wholly subservient to Stalin. There was no Party congress between 1939 and 1952, and Stalin did not deem it necessary to render account of his actions to his 'comrades.' The trade unions, which, according to Lenin, were to start running the economy in fifteen or twenty years' time, were reduced to nothing but an organ which as far as possible looked only after welfare matters; it also became bureaucratized to a large extent and avoided any conflicts between the workers' interests and those of the state. Instead, the Party bureaucracy developed rapidly at all levels; there was the Central Committee of the Party in Moscow; there were the local central committees, the territorial *obkom*s, *raikom*s, etc., and the *mestcom*s in individual enterprises and offices.

"One must also distinguish," my friend said, "between, on the one hand, Party members and also non–Party members who enjoyed real authority, and, on the other, those—whether Party or non-Party—who did not. This distinction arose from an important measure taken in the 1930s by the Party hierarchy—that is, by Stalin himself—which was to draw up a 'nomenclature,' or a list of persons, Party and even non-Party, who could be absolutely trusted. It was these 'nomenclature' officials who were given the most responsible jobs in industry, administration, etc. These people were highly paid, lived in relative luxury and worked without being subjected to any kind of democratic control.

"Stalin's line was that such a ruthless bureaucracy must be ordered to run the country, since Lenin's 'soft' and 'democratic' ways were totally unsuitable in a world in which Russia was threatened with extinction by capitalist encirclement, particularly by the rising power of Nazi Germany. Russia could get no foreign loans and had to depend entirely on her own still largely untapped resources; the Marxist surplus value from industry did not go into the pockets of the workers, but into those of the state, including the

---

* Kirov was, I was told, a great philanderer and was shot by a jealous husband; but the indications are that the latter was given surprisingly free access by the NKVD to Kirov's office, where he shot him.

bureaucratic hierarchy; nearly all of it was, nevertheless, plowed back into industry. This surplus value was achieved through the payment of low wages to the workers and the regulation of prices in state shops. In the countryside, after the ruthless collectivization of agriculture, the kolkhozes were mercilessly exploited, and those in north and central Russia lived, indeed, very poorly; only in some parts of the south—the Don country, certain parts of the Ukraine and the Kuban—did the kolkhozes manage to become reasonably rich.

"There were no open discussions on economic problems at any level after 1930 or so. The Soviet people were shown the 'achievements'—new factories, new mines, new power plants; but how all this had been achieved was shrouded in mystery. Secrecy [zasekrechivanie] became the general rule in the Party's economic planning— and in all else. Hidebound bureaucrats, enjoying absolute authority, were often guilty of incompetence, of lack of initiative, of freezing new scientific inventions, and of a kind of fetishism—as in the case of the Lysenko dictatorship in biology—which hampered scientific progress. The bureaucracy certainly failed miserably to make full use of the 'two years of peace' gained by the Soviet–German Pact to prepare Russia adequately for the imminent German invasion; official optimism, self-confidence, and 'Stalin can't be wrong' became the rule of the day.

"In the 1930s the dictatorship of the proletariat had developed into the dictatorship of the Party hierarchy, and 'soviet power' became a meaningless phrase. For it was the hierarchy which ruled, *not* through the soviets, but through the Party organizations—the Central Committee, the *obkom*s, etc., as well as through the Council of Ministers and the various government departments. And the deputies 'elected' by the people to the Supreme Soviet and other soviets had all been vetted in advance by the Party hierarchy, or by local Party cliques. 'Soviet power,' therefore, existed, especially in the Stalin days, only in the sense that the Party hierarchy ruled through the deputies they had themselves chosen."

I asked my friend whether things had not greatly improved and changed since the Stalin days.

"Yes," he answered, "there has been a definite change for the better. Under Stalin a terrible lot of thugs got the most highly paid jobs, and not only in the NKVD—though this was genuinely a state within the state—but also in all other fields. Now the level of culture and education among our bureaucrats is infinitely higher. Party congresses have been resumed at regular intervals since Stalin's death. True, there is no democracy in the Leninist sense; but where, I ask you, is there real democracy? Not in France, where everything is decided by de Gaulle and his ministers; not in England, where Parliament is only a façade, except for things like capital punishment or divorce bills, and the real decisions on anything truly important are taken at 10 Downing Street. To run a big modern state is much too complicated a matter to be entrusted to Leninist or any other kind of 'pure' democracy, in which the ordinary citizen has much say. Whether the people vote Democrat or Republican, Conservative or Labour, is ultimately of very little importance. Has the ordinary citizen much say in the decisions of the White House? In Russia, as elsewhere, the machinery of the state is infinitely complex.

"Since Stalin's death, there have been definite improvements: the powers of the NKVD have been drastically curtailed; police inquisition, though it still exists, is more discreet than it used to be. A man like Khrushchev, though a fool in many ways, was more democratically minded than Stalin; and Kosygin is better still. But there has been no proper return to Leninist democratic centralism. Secrecy still applies to many fields of activity. It is strongest of all in the field of ideology. The Politburo, or some of its leaders, have their liberal moments; but frequently they also have extremely reactionary, near-Stalinist moments. Nobody knows exactly how the machinery functions: why certain articles are allowed or are not allowed to appear in the press; why certain books have to wait for years before they are released for publication, or why they are buried alive. Who exactly decides, to take a small example, that Bulat Okudjava's songs are not to be released in the form of gramophone records? Who decides that Solzhenitsyn's novels are to be confiscated by the police? Who decides that there is, or is not, to be a trial like that of Siniavsky and Daniel?

"The common belief is that the great watchdog of ideological purity is a man like Suslov; but no one, except those in the very closed and secret inner circle, knows who takes such decisions. *Zasekrechivanie,* the secrecy rule dating back to the Stalin days, is still very strong. The pompous and thoroughly dictatorial style of the Stalinist bureaucrat has largely disappeared; our captains of industry are men of the highest education and culture; the thug, the proverbial biblical Ham—which a Stalinist bureaucrat, with unlimited personal powers, almost invariably was—has, more or less, vanished.

"After all, those who turned Russia since the war into a flourishing country in less than twenty-five years are (with few exceptions) men of the greatest technical and administrative competence. The Party, under Brezhnev and especially Kosygin (for whom there is everywhere the greatest personal respect), is not, at least on the face of it, blatantly dictatorial. But the ordinary citizen has very little say in running the country, and people on the whole *trust* the Party and the leadership. But when they stop trusting the top leader (as in the case of Khrushchev in 1964) there do happen palace revolutions in the Kremlin, and therefore public opinion is still of some importance. With the welfare state developing in the most spectacular manner, people are on the whole satisfied and do not demand that they be given democracy of a kind associated with the name of Lenin. People like you seem to have an obsession with freedom in literary and other matters, but our ordinary people are far more interested in the *material* improvements in their everyday life. One reason why the rules of secrecy are still observed, and why the Stalin type of authoritarian bureaucrat is still unwilling to change his ways, is that ever since the end of the war the Soviet government's greatest worry has been rearmament, and this calls for both secrecy and a strong authoritarian manner—though, outwardly, it is more civilized and less brutal than it used to be in the Stalin days. This rearmament business is one reason why open and Leninist discussion is discouraged.

"The people who feel the heavy weight of the Party most of all are not the workers, who live more and more comfortably, but certain intellectual groups, and above all the writers. They are still in the position in which the scientists were in the days of the Stalin-Lysenko dictatorship. The triple pressure of the Central Committee itself, Glavlit (the censorship) and the bonzes of the Writers' Union, often simply carrying out the instructions of somebody on the Central Committee or the Politburo (most people believe it is Suslov, others speak of Suslov plus Brezhnev), is most strongly felt in the field of culture, and especially literature. Here you have on the one hand one of the worst survivals of Stalinism and on the other something amounting to open grumbling, defiance and even rebellion. This defiance takes the form of a whole vast clandestine literature, hidden in bottom drawers or circulated in typescript. What is needed at the head of cultural affairs is a man of real culture—somebody like Lunacharsky in the 1920s, whom Lenin chose and Stalin finally sacked. While he lasted, we had a varied and brilliant literature. Katya Furtseva, our Minister of Culture, may be a charming woman, but she has very little culture herself—mighty little, at any rate, for a Minister of Culture."*

* This analysis of the bureaucratization of the Soviet Union has many points in common with Isaac Deutscher's *The Unfinished Revolution,* that brilliant essay published shortly before his death in 1967, but with one essential difference, that whereas my "nationalist" friend reluctantly admitted that Stalin's "socialism in one country" had *saved* Russia, to internationalist Deutscher it was the source of all evils and misfortunes.

9

The Copyright Business

WHEN I arrived in Moscow at the end of June 1967, I was already a bit of a celebrity. The Russian translation of my *Russia at War* had been published a fortnight before; there had been a few short but complimentary notices in the press, and the first five or six hundred copies that had been sent to the bigger Moscow bookshops had been snatched up in a couple of days. I. K. Zamchevsky, the head of the Progress publishing house, a tough Party man who had been one of the top Party people in Leningrad during the war, was a little on the close-fisted side, and when I called on him at his office in the Zubovsky Boulevard, he gave me only four author's copies. True, he was very affable, and a bottle of white Yugoslav Riesling, a chocolate tart and some red-cheeked apples from his own *datcha* had been spread out on his office desk. With him were the deputy director, the much jollier G. G. Lensky, and some other members of the staff.

"There is a balance of about twelve hundred rubles [$1,200] in your favor," he said. "You can have half of it transferred to France or England, if you like. Or do you want the money paid into your *sberkassa* in Moscow?"

I said that since I was going to stay in the Soviet Union two or three months he might as well pay the money into the *sberkassa* (savings-bank account). Living in tourist hotels in Moscow was rather on the expensive side; a single room cost about ten rubles. Also, I might perhaps go to Siberia, and I would also need the money for the return tickets by sea from Leningrad. As my wife and son were soon coming to Moscow, too, twelve hundred rubles wasn't exactly a huge fortune.

The Soviet Union is not a signatory to the Berne Copyright

Convention, and, strictly speaking, Progress did not have to pay anything; but in recent years a kind of gentlemen's agreement has been arrived at between Western and Soviet publishing houses under which Western authors receive royalties (of sorts) for their books published in Russia, and vice versa. Some Western publishers ignore the agreement, but this has become unusual. For one thing, Western publishers don't like complete anarchy in these matters. For instance, two publishers may, unknown to each other, translate the same book, in which case the slower of the two loses his money. So, before translation is undertaken, the publisher usually makes an agreement with the Russian author himself or through the Soviet international publishing agency, Mezhdunarodnaya Kniga. The Soviet author in fact loathes Mezhdunarodnaya Kniga; it pockets the dollars, pounds and francs and pays him (with rare exceptions) in rubles. If he deals direct with a Western publisher, he has some foreign currency put aside for him abroad and can go for a holiday to Paris, London or New York.

On the whole, Soviet publishers are very conscientious in these matters, though they make a curious exception: if for any reason they publish a foreign book which is violently hostile to the Soviet Union, the author gets nothing. Thus, as Mr. Zamchevsky told me, several books by German generals who had fought the Russians in the Second World War were published in Russian, for the benefit of Russian historians of that war; but "you don't really imagine we are going to pay out money to General Guderian or Field Marshal Manstein?" Russian publishers can do this kind of "pirating" more safely than can Western publishers, since they do not compete with each other and they coordinate their publishing plans every year. And anyway, nearly all foreign books—except highly scientific works, which are usually dealt with by the Soviet Academy of Sciences—are published by Progress, which used to be called IIL, the "Publishing House of Foreign Books."

If I wanted copies of my book in addition to the four author's ones, I had to pay cash for them, at two rubles and seventy-nine kopecks (nearly three dollars), and by the time I was finished with my Russian trip I had had to buy thirty or forty copies to give away to friends and even casual acquaintances, since the book was virtually unobtainable. While in Moscow, I bought straight from the publisher some twenty-five copies; the rest I bought in Leningrad, but the chief bookshop there sold them to me only as a special favor. Zamchevsky said that out of a planned 75,000 copies only 25,000 had so far been printed. About six hundred had been sent to Moscow shops, the others to the rest of the country, "and it's a pretty big country, you know, and a hard-reading one." In Leningrad, I discovered, only three hundred copies had been sent to a population of four million; but a few people called on me, both in Moscow and in Leningrad, to get their copies autographed; one had bought his copy at Tbilisi, the other at Sebastopol. Later I learned that the remaining fifty thousand had not been printed till shortly before the November Jubilee, and a Dutch friend who had gone to Moscow for the Jubilee wrote that in a huge new bookshop opened in the new Kalinin Avenue it had been selling *comme des petits pains* for three days, after which the stock was exhausted.

In paying royalties to foreign authors, there is a certain system of discrimination among Russian publishers; as I have said, very "anti" authors are paid nothing. One hundred per cent "pro" authors, if important, like Aragon, are fully paid in foreign currency, if they want it; second-rate "pro" authors, like Aragon's wife, Elsa Triolet, have to content themelves with rubles; I found myself in a sort of 1(b) category, insofar as Mr. Zamchevsky offered to pay me six hundred dollars in foreign currency; but I rather think it was just a friendly gesture and no more; he knew I needed a good deal of money in Russia, so there was not much point in sending the money abroad and then asking the bank in Paris to sent it back to Moscow.

As far as I know, the ruble accounts are the most common practice; I may be wrong, but am told that best-selling foreign authors, such as C. P. Snow, J. B. Priestley and especially one of the great new favorites of the last few years, Heinrich Böll, the German novelist, have some pretty fat savings-bank accounts in Moscow. (I had quite a nice balance of nearly three thousand rubles, too, for, apart from *Russia at War,* in 1958 the Russians had also published my big book on France, *France 1940–1955,* and some of *that* money was still left over. However, a holiday of over two months in the U.S.S.R. for three people costs a great deal, and there are now only a few hundred rubles left in my *sberkassa.*)

In this connection, Soviet income tax on book royalties is something our Inland Revenue might copy, for the good of culture and literature; the Soviet tax is only about five per cent!

I rather think that in the case of foreign authors' heirs Soviet publishers feel under no great moral obligation to pay them large sums, or anything, in either rubles or foreign currency. Thus, Conan Doyle's Sherlock Holmes books had been sold in huge quantities in Russia for years, but after Conan Doyle's death his heirs asked to be paid Russian royalties and the answer, I believe, was to the effect that the author was one thing, but the heirs (particularly of an enormously rich man like Conan Doyle) were something different; and the Russians paid them nothing.

It sometimes also happens that some of the foreign authors published in Russia (they are seldom informed or consulted in advance) have to ask for their Russian royalties before they get paid—if they do get paid. Erich Maria Remarque, for instance, who is very popular in Russia, appears to feel very strongly about this high-handed treatment, and he also objects to payment in rubles, which he does not particularly want. Others would still get nothing however hard they tried; all the telegrams and registered letters in the world from, say, General Guderian would not bring him in any money—all the more so since it is more than doubtful whether the author of *Panzer Leader* would be much interested in having a ruble account in a Moscow *sberkassa,* where, moreover, he would have to collect the money in person!

In fact the amount of royalties collected by foreign authors has nothing to do with the number of copies of the book sold. (In the case of Russian writers who are members of the Writers' Union it is quite different.) Foreign authors are not paid so much per copy, but so much per sheet (sixteen pages). The rate varies from forty to ninety rubles per sheet; Mr. Zamchevsky offered me sixty rubles; however, with the help of Mr. Lensky, he relented and finally agreed to eighty rubles, which was reasonably near the maximum. And, since the book had some six hundred pages (about forty sheets), it made quite a nice little sum. But, on the other hand, it made no difference to me financially whether he printed two thousand or two million copies.

Both Russian authors and Russian publishers are very divided on the question whether the Soviet Union should sign the Berne Copyright Convention; there have been endless discussions about it for years. So far nothing seems to have been settled, though the adherence of Russia last year to some similar international patents convention is regarded by many as a promising precedent. There is, as we know, pirating on both sides—though rather less than there used to be—and my guess is that within a few year the Russians *will* sign the Berne Copyright Convention, or at any rate enter into bilateral agreements with the numerous countries in whose literature they are interested. Something along those lines is already being done in the case of France and the Soviet Union. If only the Soviet Writers' Union and the censorship did not prevent so many first-class Russian books from being published, Russian adherence to the Berne Convention could bring into Russia an enormous amount of foreign currency. It is the tough men of the Politburo, working hand in glove with the Writers' Union bureaucrats and the censorship, who have made minor Russian writers like Siniavsky and Daniel into world celebrities.

10

The Eighteen-Year-Old Who Doesn't
Remember Stalin

A FEW days after my arrival in Moscow, I had a phone call from
the Moscow evening paper, *Vecherniaya Moskva,* asking me to give
their reporter an interview. "We have just received a copy of your
book, and we'd like you to say something about your wartime
experiences in the Soviet Union. Will it be all right if our Comrade
M—— calls on you at ten o'clock on Sunday morning?" I said I'd
be delighted to see him.

Comrade M—— was a rosy-cheeked youngster of eighteen.
"What's your *imya-otchestvo* [name and patronymic]?" I asked.

He laughed. *"Imya-otchestvo?* Nobody calls me by that. Just call
me Sasha!"

It was in fact not an interview at all. We talked for nearly an
hour, and a few days later there appeared in *VM* quite a biggish
article, which had, however, very little to do with what we had
talked about, except that it did refer to some of the things I had said
about life in Moscow during the war.

During that long talk with Sasha I had the unpleasant feeling of
being horribly old. Sasha, indeed, had been born in 1949. To him,
the Russian Revolution of 1917 was just about as remote as the
French Revolution was to me. The Second World War had ended
long before he was born, and he was only three and a half when
Stalin died.

"Now, Sasha," I said, "I can tell you all you want to know about
myself in five minutes, so if you have any time to spare, do you
mind if I interview *you,* and not the other way round?" He beamed.

Young people of eighteen are very vain. "Now tell me: what do you know about the purges and the slave camps? Did you like Khrushchev? What kind of house do you live in? Well, that'll do to go on with. And just another point: how much do you earn?"

"Well," said Sasha, "I'll answer the last and the simplest question first. As a mere beginner, all I get so far is fifty rubles a month. As for the Revolution, of course, I don't remember it. Even my father doesn't remember it, for he was born in 1926. I know about the Revolution only from history books. I know there was a kind of half-capitalist, half-feudal system under the tsars; then there was the bourgeois revolution in February 1917 and then, under the leadership of Lenin, there was the Bolshevik Revolution in October. I have seen films about October—the storming of the Winter Palace, the cruiser *Aurora,* and all that."

"Have you read any Lenin?"

"No, not very much," he said apologetically. "But at our Komsomol meetings we've had people talk about Lenin, and I've also gone to a few lectures on Marxism-Leninism."

"Did you find them interesting?"

He hesitated. "Well, yes, I suppose so, but a lot of things aren't quite clear to me yet. Perhaps *you* could explain to me what exactly 'dialectical materialism' means."

Though not being, to tell the truth, absolutely clear about it myself, I made a feeble effort to explain its meaning.

He listened carefully and then said, "Yes, I think you explained it better than the comrade who came last week to our Komsomol meeting; but I am still not quite clear about it." And then he grinned. "Now do you mind if I ask you a question?"

"Go ahead, Sasha!"

"You're old enough to be my grandfather, so you must have learned an awful lot in your lifetime, but have you ever studied Marxism-Leninism *very* thoroughly?"

I had to confess that I hadn't really, though I had read most of Lenin's principal works. As for Marx's *Capital,* I found it pretty heavy going.

"You're telling me!" he exclaimed. "I've tried to read Marx, and also found him rather above my head." And then he suddenly added, lowering his voice, "But soon after the war my dad bought a complete set of Stalin's works—you know, those dark-purple bindings—in thirteen volumes. I'm told they are almost impossible to get now. I find Stalin much easier to read. At least he's brief and to the point, and you can get through a volume in an afternoon. And also Stalin's wartime speeches are pretty magnificent! You were lucky to have lived through those glorious times of our Great Patriotic War. My father was too young to be called up, since he was born at the end of 1926. But the greatest pride in our family is Uncle Petya, my father's elder brother. He was a Hero of the Soviet Union and was finally killed, toward the very end of the war, in the fighting round Königsberg—what we now call Kaliningrad."

"Sasha, do you know anything about the purges?"

"No, not really, except that I have met one or two people—quite old people, about fifty—who had been deported in 1937 and had worked in camps and hadn't been allowed to come back till they were rehabilitated, in 1958 or 1959. As for the purge trials, I still used to be told when I was a very small boy at school that Bukharin and Rykov were Trotskyite hyenas, and we even nicknamed one boy 'Trotskyite hyena'—which made him absolutely furious, and even made him cry. Now I think there's a more historical approach to all those things."

"What do you remember about Stalin, Sasha?"

"Well, really not very much," he grinned, "except, as I told you, I like to read his books. After all, I was only three and a half years old when he died. We were living in Moscow, and I remember the funeral, though only very vaguely. But we had a big portrait of Stalin in our house, and both my father and my mother cried at his death; I had never seen my father cry before. And, of course, I cried too. Ever since I remember myself, I had been told that Stalin—we called him Papa Stalin—was the wisest and kindest man in the world, and that our country owed everything to him. He had made our country great and had won the war for us, and so on."

"You bring to mind, Sasha, my journey to Voronezh in 1943, just after it had been liberated from the Germans. The whole city was in ruins, but one building had somehow been patched up and turned into a kindergarten. There was a tiny girl of two or three there, and the schoolmistress said to her, pointing at me, 'Ninochka, do you know who this comrade is?' And Ninochka looked at me and then suddenly said, 'Why, is it Papa Stalin?' The schoolmistress was truly scandalized. 'But, darling, look at him, and look at Papa Stalin's

picture! Papa Stalin has a moustache, and this comrade hasn't.'
Ninochka slunk away in confusion."

Sasha laughed. "Well, yes, that's quite true, that's just the way all
we kids felt about Papa Stalin."

"And have you still got that Stalin portrait on the wall?"

"No. You see, what happened was this. We lived in a pretty dingy
old house in the Zamoskvorechie till the end of 1961, and then we
got a beautiful modern three-room flat not far from the present
university. By this time I was already twelve. After the Twentieth
Congress of 1956, which terribly upset my father, who has been a
Party member since 1952, he did not take Stalin's portrait down.
Only when we moved into the new flat he did not put it up again.
But then that was after the Twenty-second Congress, after which
Stalin's body was thrown out of the Lenin Mausoleum. I think my
father was still very upset about it, but he said nothing. Instead of
the portrait we now have an enlarged photograph of Uncle Petya."

"So you've had a pretty peaceful life, Sasha," I said. "Do you
realize how lucky you are to belong to the first generation of
Russians since the Revolution not to have *suffered* from anything?
No wars, no famines, no epidemics, no NKVD visits at three o'clock
in the morning—nothing! Have you ever suffered?"

"No, not much. The dark basement where I lived till I was twelve
was pretty awful, all the same; however, as I said, we got a nice new
flat in 1961. Actually, I did suffer last year. I was in love. But she
went and married someone else."

"But you must remember Khrushchev. What about him?"

"Oh, he amused us at first, he made funny speeches, but then we
got a bit tired of the same old buffoonery. And we did not like it
when he took off his shoe at the U.N. and started banging his desk
with it. It was not in the papers, but we heard about it. The head of
the CPSU and the head of the Soviet government really mustn't
behave like that. Of course, we had good moments under Khrushchev. I remember the first sputnik; I was only eight then, but the
excitement at our school was terrific. But then in 1962—and this I
remember very clearly, for I was nearly fourteen—there was a real
scare in Moscow, when we thought the American atom bomb would
be dropped on it because of Khrushchev's row with America over
Cuba. I didn't know exactly whether he or Kennedy was right; but
the very fact that he had very nearly brought us to the brink of a

nuclear war was something we never quite forgave him. And when he was thrown out two years later, nobody was sorry."

"And Kosygin and Brezhnev?"

"We don't really know much about them. But they are quiet people. When they make speeches, they talk sense. It isn't all the fun and nonsense we had with Khrushchev, but after a few years we had really had enough of him. Especially after the Cuban affair."

My interview with Sasha had lasted about an hour; then came his "interview" with me. I told him a few things I remembered about the Second World War, the first bombings of Moscow, the visit I had paid to the ZIS motor works, which the German radio claimed had been "Coventrated."

"You know, Sasha, what 'Coventrated' meant?"

"No, what's that?"

And I had to explain all about Coventry. He hadn't heard about it.

My meeting with Sasha M——, born in 1949, was perhaps my most interesting meeting of all: a Russian who, ever since he remembered himself, had lived a quiet life, had never known war or hunger or police persecution. This was Russia's New Generation, which had made its very first appearance in Soviet history in the last few years. And what a glimpse into the future he provided! There was only one thing in the world that really worried him: the possibility of a nuclear war; and that was why he was glad to see the last of Khrushchev.

As for literary quarrels, he was too young to have any definite opinions about them; but he had read most of the Russian classics, and his only comment was that very few new books "half as good" were published now.

My general impression was that he was not wildly interested in ideology, but was very proud of living relatively prosperously in a well-run country that took such good care of all its citizens.

11

An Old Man Looks at the Past

A FEW days later, I took a car to see my old friend Professor and Major General E. A. Boltin, out at his *datcha* near Dimitrovo, about thirty miles north of Moscow. Since the war he had worked at the Marx-Lenin Institute, in the department dealing with the history of the Second World War.

A few months after I had met him to discuss the cutting of *Russia at War,* he had fallen seriously ill. He had had coronary thrombosis and had remained in the hospital for three months. Now he was convalescing at his *datcha,* in the midst of birches and pine trees, and with the typical Russian flower beds of sweet-smelling tobacco flowers and phlox. With him was his charming wife, Galina Georgievna, much younger than himself. In their sixties, hard-working Soviet citizens like Boltin often develop serious heart trouble. It seems a kind of occupational disease of administrators, scholars and professors; ordinary people who are pensioned off at sixty usually live another ten or twenty years. The Major General was living well; it was a charming *datcha,* and there was the usual round of *zakuski,* complete with vodka, and then a couple of bottles of Yugoslav Riesling.

"Have you met any interesting people since you got to Moscow?" he asked.

"Oh yes, Evgeni Arsenyevich, lots. I mean lots of my old friends—Polevoi, and Ehrenburg, and Surkov, and some of the younger writers I hadn't met before. Trifonov, who wrote that astonishing book about his own father, a hero of the 1905 Revolution and then of the 1917 Revolution who, in the end, perished in the 1937 purges. But, to tell you the truth, my most exciting encounter was with a youngster called Sasha, a reporter from *Vechernaya Moskva.*" And I told the Major General about him.

"Yes," he said, "that is a far more useful experience than reminiscing about the war with old friends like Surkov or Polevoi. People of our age, I'm afraid, tend to live in the past—especially we Russians, for these last fifty years have been wonderful in many ways, but terribly, terribly hard.

"What we are apt to forget is that over eighty per cent of the Soviet population was born after the Revolution. They know about capitalism only from their history books. Now, what is the real significance of the last fifty years? It is that there have been the most tremendous social changes. In 1913, the last 'normal' year under the tsarist regime, workers and employees, as we now call them, constituted only seventeen per cent of the population; now workers and employees account for seventy-six per cent of the population. The whole class structure of Russia has radically changed. In 1917 the bourgeoisie, the merchant class, the landowners represented seventeen per cent of the population; now there are no such classes. Now, fifty years after the Revolution, our people are used to living without capitalists. As I said before, our young generation knows about capitalists only from books. Its whole way of thinking and reacting is entirely different from the Western way.

"Take for instance, our attitude to a simple thing like money. Like everybody else, our people *like* money. But still, money means to us something different from what it means to you people in the West. To us, the accumulation of money is not a means of radically changing one's way of life. It would never occur to a Soviet citizen to save a lot of money to buy, say, a shop, or to become a partner in a firm. If people put money into their savings bank it is simply in order to acquire objects—buy clothes, furniture, a car, maybe even two cars, a *datcha* and so on. That is why we never worry about how much we spend. Nobody really saves on food, for instance; if anything in a shop takes your fancy, you don't really worry whether you can 'afford' it or not. Incomes, of course, vary a great deal, and in the very lowest income groups—pensioners with thirty or forty rubles a month, for instance—people have to choose between a good meal and a new pair of shoes, but such dilemmas are becoming more and more unusual. And the ease with which our people, except the very poorest, spend money is extraordinary; and that's why, with every year, the demand for consumer goods grows to a quite fantastic extent—and also shows up the utter inadequacy of our distribution system. There are still not enough refrigerators in Russia, but now nearly everybody who has moved into a new flat is pining to buy a refrigerator. Hence the chaos you see in the shops: everybody wants to buy something! Distribution needs top-priority reform—a bloodless revolution, in fact, which need last only a year or two. Our shops were adequate in a world of austerity, rationing and fearful shortages, but now there are not nearly enough. Our restaurants and even cafés are really bad. Our imitations of Western self-service places are still completely useless."

"Yes," I said, "but what I found was that Soviet people in trade are *ashamed* of doing nothing better, and want to get out of it by taking evening classes and what have you. Who's going to serve in shops and restaurants?"

"Yes," said Evgeni Arsenyevich, "that *is* a psychological problem. But there will be two ways of overcoming it: first, by convincing people that there is nothing shameful in working in a shop or café; and, second, by mechanizing both shopping and catering to the utmost. If you think of the 1930s you'll remember that we've carried out an immensely greater industrial revolution; to reorganize shops and cafés is mere chicken feed in comparison.

"That's in the future—the almost immediate future," he continued. "But now let's turn to the past. You and I belong to a different generation; we keep on arguing how good or how bad Stalin was, and so on. To young people, as you discovered from your talk with Sasha, the beginning of the first Five-Year Plan, or the Stalin purges of 1937, are perhaps even more ancient history than Ivan the Terrible is to us. Naturally, nearly every family in our country has taken part in the industrial revolution of the 1930s, or has lost a large part of its friends and relatives in the war. But for nearly half our population today even the Second World War is little more than history! Therefore, when people of forty or fifty compare the present and the past (and by 'past' I mean the war and the immediate postwar period) they feel good, for the Russia of today gives them an enormous sense of achievement.

"And when they look at our new towns—the hundreds of square miles of the new parts of Moscow, for instance—they see what an entirely different country Russia has become! People abroad still

think Russians sit round their tea or supper-cum-vodka tables discussing the pros and cons of Stalin. No, to most of them Stalin has
become a dim historical figure. What is much more important is that
the urban population since the Revolution has increased by a
hundred million people! And just as the Holy Russia of your
childhood has become a thing of the distant historical past, so Stalin
is rapidly receding into the past, too; it is only people of our
generation who still feel strongly about Stalin, one way or another.
Even our rural population is developing an urban mentality. I don't
think in twenty years' time there will be many kolkhozes left, and
the rural population may be down to twenty per cent of the total."

I then told Evgeni Arsenyevich what Sasha had told me about
Khrushchev.

"Yes," he said, "that's a very common attitude. Those who
suffered in the purges will never forget that Khrushchev (though not
he alone—another Western myth) threw open the camps; and they
are grateful to him. But to younger people the purges and the camps
are ancient history now; what they do remember, though, is his
brinkmanship over Cuba, and *that* they will never forgive him."

"Just one point," I said. "You say that Stalin is becoming a dim
figure of the past. Personally, I don't believe that. There are hang-
overs of Stalinism in lots and lots of things."

"That's another matter," he said. "What I mean is that to the
young generation Stalin is no longer a subject of violent controversy.
They agree, by and large, that he had his good points and his bad
points, and they leave it at that. It's only to people of our generation
that Stalin continues to be something of an emotional problem. And
to us historians the weighing up of the pros and cons of Stalin in our
country's history will be a full-time job for a long time yet."

12

Two Touching Fan Letters

Soon after the publication of *Russia at War* in Russian, I received about a dozen fan letters, some after my departure from the Soviet Union. Most of them were conventional, but these two seem to me, each in its own way, striking enough human documents.

The first was from a woman of thirty whom we had met, together with her ten-year-old son, Sashenka, while visiting the famous churches of Novgorod. We had fallen into conversation with her; she was fascinated to meet "real foreigners"—she had apparently never met any before. She held a small municipal post and was a Party member, and her husband was a foreman in the local brewery. The boy was a charming fair, blue-eyed kid. A few months later I received the following letter.

> May I, with all my heart, send you all our very best wishes for 1968, for good health and happiness. You have probably forgotten your momentary friends in the Novgorod kremlin, Sasha and his mother. But we haven't forgotten you, and we expected to hear from you all these months. Dear Alexander Alexandrovich, I have now read your book *Russia at War*. It is quite a titanic achievement, and I should like to congratulate you on your clever and kind book.
>
> And let me tell you this. Although you live in so beautiful a country as France, I feel your heart longs for your native land. I can read that between the lines. The whole book shows that you are a good and kind man, and Alina Ivanovnna and Kolya must be proud of you. Your life and work are very interesting, and may they be useful to good and honest people!
>
> Here the winter is in full swing. If you were here, you'd just love it. Twenty-five degrees of frost, the trees covered with hoar-

frost, everything whiter than white. All are preparing for the New Year, buying fir trees and decorations. Enormous New Year trees have been put up in all the main squares. This is the loveliest holiday in the year. And do you remember how we sat on the little bench on the steep bank and looked at Lake Ilmen? It was sunny and warm then, but now the lake is frozen, and the amateur anglers go off for the whole of Sunday to fish in holes in the ice. Yes, our Russian winter has a great charm.

And Sashenka is now in the sixth year, a good lad, always near the top of the class, and like all boys he does a lot of skiing and skating . . .

Goodbye, and with all best wishes,

M. B.

P.S. I hope you've got the 1968 calendar we gave you that day. The Russian–English dictionary you bought Sasha and the French and English coins you gave him we are keeping as souvenirs. He is starting English at school next year.

A much more unusual letter came from an analytical chemist of twenty-nine somewhere in Siberia.

DEAR ALEXANDER ALEXANDROVICH,

I have just read your remarkable book *Russia at War.* (By the way, was not its title inspired by H. G. Wells's *Russia in the Shadows?*)

I am twenty-nine years old. I first went to school during the first year of peace, in September 1945. During the war I had not yet learned to read, but would fall asleep, not to a lullaby, but to the sound of Levitan's voice reading the war communiqués; in Novosibirsk, to which we had been evacuated, the communiqués reached us only very late at night, owing to the difference in time. I also clearly remember my return to Moscow on the night of the great salvo to mark the final liquidation of the Leningrad blockade—that was on January 27, 1944. And then I heard many other victory salvos in Moscow, and finally that of Victory Day, on May 9, 1945. I hardly remember my father, who was killed on the Kalinin front in 1942. I know my mother only as a gray-haired woman. Being Jewish, she lost all her family at Mariupo [in the Ukraine] when the Nazis came.

I knew your name even before your present book. In his *Memoirs* Ehrenburg (dead, alas!) wrote very warmly of you. I

remember your bitter joke when, frightened of the earlier bombings of Moscow, Ehrenburg's Scotch terrier began to howl during
a victory salvo. And you then said, "I see this is a really British
dog; he's a bit scared of Russian victories." I got to like you right
away. Vera Ketlinskaya recently recalled your visit to Leningrad
during the blockade, and she was greatly moved by the question
you then put to her: "Why and how could Leningrad take it—all
this?" In the book by Yeremeyev, published by the Academy of
Science and called *Through Friend and Enemy Eyes* (quotations
from British, American and also German writings about us during
the war), there are also numerous quotations from you.

I don't know what struck me most in your book. It may be that
one can read between the lines of your seemingly calmly told story
an undisguised hatred of our common enemies, the German
fascists. You call them (as we used to call them) simply "German," but during the war, and long after, we called them fascists;
only lately has the word "German" come into its own again. It is
also clear from your book that you admired not only our soldiers
but also the workers in our industry—women and adolescents
mostly, who suffered fearful privations, often much worse than
our soldiers at the front, but who did everything that was possible
and impossible in the name of victory. And it is clear from your
book that the victory of our people in the Great War was not
simply the victory of our armaments over what Pasternak called
"the naked power of evil," but also the moral victory of our Soviet
people over the bestial ethics of the *Übermenschen*. I am proud to
think that, in spite of everything, our people have no hatred for
the Germans as a nation. But I can only agree with you that it
took more than a handful of "bad Germans" to murder six million
Jews. And it is also easy to understand why the appeal by the
"Free Germany" committee to create an opposition to Hitler
before Germany's final defeat should have met with no support
inside Germany—not even as late as May 1945. I rather think that
the healthier elements among the German people had emigrated,
just to get away from the Nazi regime; plus the physical extermination of the best people who had stayed on, and a kind of
conspiracy of guilt which created an insoluble link between the SS
Gruppenführer and the Frau Müller who had as an unpaid
servant a Ukrainian girl slave. Those orders that were sent to the
"Chopin Warehouse" of the Maidanek Extermination Camp for
things taken off the victims of the gas chambers show up the
absurd theory that "ordinary Germans" knew nothing about the

death factories. The revolting orders sent to this "warehouse" by the Hitler Jugend show up the nature of that organization, though its very name is sufficiently indicative. But even more fearful and more cynical is a German mother's request to the Maidanek warehouse to send a complete layette and a pram for her newborn child. Now that I have written this, I feel literally sick. What could have come of such a child, with such a mother? Will this woman at least feel ashamed if she reads your book?

I know, of course, that there are some decent people among the Germans—people who were ashamed of the atrocities the Nazis committed in their treatment of our war prisoners and the millions of slave deportees. I have read of isolated acts of opposition to the Nazi regime even in 1942—such as Hans Fallada's novel *Every Man Dies Alone*—not to mention 1945; nevertheless it makes me feel bitter that the German people should have had neither the will nor the guts to overthrow this regime even as late as May 7, 1945—i.e., a day before Germany's capitulation.

I am glad your book has also been published in West Germany. Maybe some of the "refugees" from the east will understand (I am not closing my eyes, I can assure you, to the personal tragedies of ordinary people driven from their homes) that all these misfortunes are not the fault of the Russians or the Poles, but of the Nazis themselves. Their expulsion from eastern Germany was not an act of petty revenge on our part, but a fully justified measure against another world war.

From a purely informative point of view, I found of the greatest interest your chapter on the Polish problem and its effect on the relations between the U.S.S.R. and her Western allies. Much of what you say in these chapters is entirely new to me. . . . It seems to me that even if you do not wholly approve of our policy on this question, you are still fully aware of the Soviet Union's desire to help to create a new Poland which would be our reliable friend and ally.

You seem to write with particular emotion (and this makes this chapter perhaps the most moving of all in your book) about the Leningrad epic, which will live eternally in the hearts of the whole of humanity. Maybe someday there will be a new Homer who will write a new *Iliad* on the Leningrad blockade. I am sure your book would inform and inspire him; for you make no secret of your admiration for the unequaled valor and spirit of self-sacrifice of the people of Leningrad. In me your chapter on Leningrad has produced both unbearable pain and the greatest pride. I have not read the book by Léon Goure to which you refer, but, as you say, there was nothing in the struggle and martyrdom of the people of Leningrad resembling the self-sacrifice of the early Christian martyrs; our Leningrad people simply knew what would happen to them and their beloved city if they capitulated. I don't know how many people would have perished at the hands of the Nazis if the city had surrendered, and how many of its great historical buildings and art treasures would have been reduced to dust; but judging from the grim fate of so many of our other cities conquered by the Germans, the losses would have been enormous. That is why the people of Leningrad grumbled and cursed their fate, but still preferred to die a martyr's death in their unconquered city. It will remain an eternal shame of the Wehrmacht that, after its troops had failed to take Leningrad by storm, it should have made peaceful civilians in the city pay for the Germans' rage and disappointment. There can be no forgiveness for murderers who, having lost all hope of capturing Leningrad, proceeded to kill its civilians with their bombs and shells. There was absolutely no military purpose in this; it was simply an act of spiteful, vile and helpless rage.

I have never written to an author before. Maybe my letter is a little muddled. But in conclusion I should like to say how happy I am that our country should have some wonderful friends like you. And I should like to conclude with these lines from Alexander Tvardovsky:

> *Yes, Russia's great and holy labors,*
> *Her patient, silent torments,*
> *Our grandchildren will piously*
> *Exalt and glorify.*
> *And they will say, in paying*
> *Full tribute to our valor,*
> *And full of admiration*
> *For all that old and bygone tale,*
> *"What times those were,*
> *What men those were!"* . . .

With gratitude and admiration,

A. V., RESEARCH CHEMIST

These two letters—one from a woman of thirty in a small provincial town, who now lives a perfectly normal, peaceful life with her husband and little boy fifty years after the Revolution and nearly twenty-five years after the war, and the other from a young scientist of twenty-nine who today has no material troubles, but who, having lost most of his family in the war, still largely lives in the past—are to me like the voice of the Russian people today. Uncensored and un-self-conscious, they are truer, more genuine, more spontaneous than anything I have read for months or years in any of the Soviet "fat" monthlies.

13

The Ex-Stalin Motor Works

AFTER my interview had appeared in *Vecherniaya Moskva* I had a phone call from a Comrade Fedorov, the assistant director of the ZIL, the Zavod imeni Likhacheva (the former ZIS, the Stalin motor works), in Moscow.

"This is Fedorov, the assistant director of the ZIL. We read what you had to say about your visit to the ZIL—then the ZIS—in 1941 and we should be glad if you could come and see us again. There have been enormous changes since 1941." We made an appointment for the next afternoon.

I remembered the grim summer of 1941. The antiaircraft defenses of Moscow were stupendous—infinitely superior to those of London during the blitz winter of 1940–41; all the same, out of some two hundred German bombers ten or twelve usually broke through the gigantic barrage surrounding Moscow. As I have already said, the German radio had boasted of having "Coventrated" the ZIS motor plant. So a number of correspondents were taken to the ZIS to see that only minor damage had been caused. I remember the remark of poor Philip Jordan of the *News Chronicle* (he died soon after the war, after he had worked for a few months as Mr. Attlee's press officer at 10 Downing Street—he can't have been more than forty or forty-five) on the way to the ZIS. He said, "Alex, to tell you the truth, I'm not really interested, and never have been interested, in ironmongery."

The ZIS was then, as now, turning out trucks (which were badly needed in the Soviet Union, as we know from the fact that during the Second World War the United States had to deliver hearly half a million trucks and jeeps to the Red Army), as well as the super-limousines specially designed for Stalin, Voroshilov, other members of the Politburo, ambassadors, etc.

I was no more interested in "ironmongery" than Philip Jordan had been. Nevertheless, it was interesting now, in 1967, to talk to one of the top Russian excutives of the Russian motor industry and with some of the other people of the ZIL. Assembled in his office, with lemonade bottles and biscuits on his desk, were, apart from Nikolai Alexandrovich Fedorov—a dapper man of not much more than forty—the deputy chief engineer, the chairman of the local Party organization, and the chairman of the trade-union organization of the ZIL. Comrade Fedorov said he was too young to have been here in 1941, but said he had a rough idea of what it (or rather ZIS) had been in those days: a much, much smaller plant than the present one. Now it extended over 250 hectares, nearly 450 acres. The ZIL was employing no fewer than 60,000 persons, including 24,000 women; of all these, ninety-eight per cent were members of the trade union (the remaining two per cent were too young). The ZIL had subsidiary plants at Ryazan and near Smolensk. Its chief output was that of three-axle and two-axle four-ton and five-ton trucks; the production of three-ton trucks had been discontinued some years ago. Five hundred a day were being produced, and this fully met the needs of the Soviet Union; moreover, ZIL trucks, about one third of them, were being exported to forty-one countries, among them Vietnam, Kuwait, Ceylon and Indonesia. Exports to Vietnam had lately become particularly large.

Altogether, the Soviet Union was now producing 550,000 cars (of all kinds) a year, and by the end of the present Five-Year Plan the total production would be around 1,200,000. As regards foreign markets, there was no Russian dumping. The prices of Russian trucks were, roughly, world prices. But in the event of a crisis like that of 1929–35 in the capitalist world, dumping might become a formidable political weapon compared with which dumping in the 1930s would be child's play.

The VIP limousines for ambassadors and the like were only a small sideline in the ZIL's output; a very important new line was that of refrigerators, 143,000 of which had been produced in the last year; but this figure would rise to an annual one million within a few years. Five years ago there were still long waiting lists, but now these refrigerators were freely sold in shops; all the same, the demand for these was constantly growing as more and more new houses were built.

Among the sixty thousand workers employed at the ZIL the average wage was 142 rubles, with a minimum of 80 or 90 and a maximum of 250 rubles. The salaries of the directors and chief engineers were, of course, much higher; some earned as much as eight hundred to a thousand rubles a month.

Attached to the ZIL were several significant organizations. There was the VTUZ (Vyssheye Teknicheskoie Uchebnoye Zavedenie pri Zavode), a higher technical college with students who were also part-time workers; this also provided "quick" courses for workers— eight thousand of them—who were thus receiving a "higher qualification"; there was at the plant, moreover, a general school, as well as two technical colleges. Compared with 1941, there were now incomparably more polyclinics attached to the plant, with a medical staff of six hundred and over a hundred doctors of all specialties. In the factory there was a hospital with 140 beds, and in the workshops twenty-three "health points" and a first-aid post. One of the great principles of these medical services was to practice prophylactic medicine. Belonging to the plant were sanatoria and four rest homes—the Maurice Thorez Home at Yalta in the Crimea, another at Yessentuki in the Caucasus, and two outside Moscow—where three thousand people could live. Annual leave varied from fifteen to thirty-two days; forty per cent had around twenty days, the rest fifteen or sixteen days. There were twenty canteens at the plant, and a three-course meal cost fifty kopecks. No vodka was sold there.

For the workers' small children there were thirty-five kindergartens inside or near the factory, with 120 to 180 children in each. In summer (as now) practically all the children were in children's colonies or camps. The parents paid for their keep according to their own earnings; an engineer paid twelve or thirteen rubles a month for both the kindergarten and the holiday camp; lower-paid workers paid five to seven rubles; the lowest grade paid nothing.

Comrade Fedorov said that enormous progress had been made in the mechanization of the plant; if in 1941 there were only two assembly lines, now there were 240. He then took me round the various workshops; here were the usual bodies of trucks suspended in midair and moving along an overhead cable; there were mountains of wheels and tires; since I was not well versed in ironmongery, it did not mean much to me. But there were two important things I noticed: whereas in 1941 men and women looked grim beyond words (the Germans had just captured Smolensk, Moscow was being bombed, and they themselves were exhausted by fire watching at night), they now all looked cheerful and healthy; and their work seemed neither very intensive nor supermechanized. Many of the jobs (like loading spare parts into tip trucks) were done by hand, and I could well believe that the productivity of labor in a place like the ZIL was one third that of a similar plant in, say, the U.S. The wages were accordingly much lower, too. But the workers looked quite contented. They worked, on the whole, only five days a week, and not usually more than seven hours a day.

There are, as we have seen, disputes among Soviet economists on whether this system is right or wrong; some say that if productivity in Soviet industry were greatly intensified, Russia would be in a better position than she is to send ample industrial supplies to the underdeveloped countries; but there is the eternal question, how would these countries pay for the Russian supplies? Egypt pays in cotton, which Russia scarcely needs; Cuba pays in cigars, which nobody wants, and in sugar, most of which the Russians resell. Tea, coffee, oranges, bananas, peanut oil, are among the few things the ex-colonial countries can usefully supply to the Soviet Union. Vegetable and animal fats, butter, meat, etc., which the Soviet Union is still relatively short of, are precisely the kind of products which most of the underdeveloped countries are scarcely in a position to export. Much more important is the trade with the countries of the socialist bloc (East Germany, Czechoslovakia, Poland, Hungary, Rumania, Bulgaria, Yugoslavia), all of whom have something to sell to the Soviet Union; indeed, seventy per cent of the Soviet Union's foreign trade is with these; the rest is with the capitalist countries and the underdeveloped countries.

After the inspection of the ZIL plant, Fedorov and his colleagues took me to a political lecture attended by some two hundred workers. Here a tough Party man, a Comrade Sergeiev, gave about half an hour's talk on the Middle-East crisis. He declared that by herself Israel could not have attacked the Arab countries; but she had been encouraged by the forces of American and, to a lesser extent, British imperialism, which were trying to seize control of the Suez Canal and overthrow the progressive governments of Syria and

Egypt to please Aramco. At the same time, he spoke with some disdain of the Egyptian Army, whose soldiers were illiterate and whose officers and generals belonged to the "old feudal gang." Like the Soviet press, he invariably referred to the Israelis as Israelis, never as Jews, but said that people like Moshe Dayan were the hawks of Israel, who were on the best of terms with fascists like "Marshal" Ky of South Vietnam and the extremists of the Pentagon.

I made a short speech, in which I spoke in general terms of the Middle-East crisis and also recalled my last visit to the ZIL plant, back in 1941. One old worker came up to talk to me after the lecture and said he remembered the "fearful days of 1941"; he said that part of the plant was afterward (in October 1941) evacuated to the east, and that he had stayed there till the end of the war. "We worked there in appalling conditions, with hardly anywhere to live and with hardly anything to eat. And if today we work a five-day week and an average of seven hours a day, we then worked thirteen or fourteen hours on empty stomachs."

The ZIL today produces five hundred trucks a day; I asked Fedorov if, in an emergency, they could produce, say, twice as many.

"Yes, of course."

I said, "Three times as many?"

"Yes, probably."

"Four times as many?"

"That would be more difficult and would require a few weeks' reorganization."

"Then why do you produce five hundred now?"

"It's quite simple. Our country at present doesn't need any more, and, as I told you, we shall about double our production by 1970. At present we don't need so many, and our export market is limited. To produce three times as many overnight as we are producing now, we should have, in the first place, greatly to increase the number of working hours—make our people work as they worked during the war, twelve to fifteen hours a day. This is quite unnecessary."

On the following Sunday we went by bus and tram to the old sixteenth-century village of Kolomenskoye, with its churches and its old wooden house of Peter the Great, transported here from Archangel. We got out of the bus and took the tram somewhere near the

ZIL works. There were lots of drunks around; some of them were ZIL workers. One of the minor (or major) curses of the Soviet Union is drunkenness; if nobody appears ever to be drunk while at work, the Russian workingman tends to make up for it during the weekend. The vodka bottle interferes quite a lot with the additional culture which workers are supposed to acquire during their days off.

14

Farewell to Ilya Ehrenburg

A FEW days after my arrival in Moscow, I received a phone call which made me very happy. It was from Lyubov Mikhailovna Ehrenburg, saying that she and Ilya Grigoryevich would like me to come to lunch two days later.

I was all the happier as my last meeting with Ehrenburg, in 1965, at the time of the twentieth-anniversary-of-victory celebrations, had left me with a confused and rather unpleasant impression. Before that, I had not seen Ehrenburg since the Partisans of Peace Congress in Paris in 1949, and I reminded him of how he had scarcely said hello to me, though we had been very good friends during the war. He explained, "Well, you see, those were very, very difficult times," and left it at that.

I had also dropped a terrible brick during that earlier lunch. When asked what kind of journalism I was now doing, I said, among other things, "I am also in a very profitable little racket—writing obits for a Western paper."

"What's that?"

I explained that a lot of the bigger papers had in reserve biographical notices of more or less famous men, which went straight into the paper the day after the person's death. Thus, I had recently written long obituaries on Marshals Konev, Zhukov and Malinovsky. Then, jokingly, I added, "A year or two ago I also wrote a longish piece on you, Ilya Grigoryevich."

I don't suppose either Ilya Grigoryevich or Lyubov Mikhailovna was superstitious, but my flippant remark had obviously made a disastrously bad impression. "And how much did you get paid for writing this notice?" Lyubov Mikhailovna remarked acidly. I said I didn't remember, but probably twenty or twenty-five dollars. I hastened to change the subject, but the chilly atmosphere continued. I was happy to feel that they must have forgotten about the unfortunate incident. Also, I had heard that Lyubov Mikhailovna had been seriously ill recently and had had two heart attacks. Now, over the phone, she seemed as bright and cheerful as ever. Lyubov Mikhailovna, who had lived for many years in Paris and was a remarkably good painter, though totally un-Soviet in her manner of painting, must have been a very beautiful woman in her day (she still was, though she was now well over sixty), and she shared her husband's likes and dislikes as regards Soviet painters, poets and writers.

Flat 48 at 8 Gorki Street was not so much a flat as a museum, worth probably a million pounds or more. Here were early Chagalls, several Modiglianis, three or four Légers, a couple of Matisse drawings, several Falks, one or two Saryans, but above all half a dozen superb Picassos of different periods. All these had been given to Ehrenburg as souvenirs by the painters themselves—in the old Montparnasse days before and during the First World War in the case of Modigliani, during later periods by the others. Matisse, whom Ehrenburg had not known before and had first met in Paris shortly before the artist's death, had given him the two line drawings only a few years before. The Picassos were particularly wonderful; among them was the "classical" pencil portrait of Ehrenburg, inscribed *"Pour toi, mon ami."* Picasso had drawn it in 1948 at the time of the Wroclaw Peace Congress in Poland. The atmosphere at that congress had been particularly unpleasant; the Cold War was at its height; the Russian hacks at that congress denounced in the most virulent terms all that a man like Picasso stood for; nevertheless, Picasso was officially a member of the French Communist Party and tried to regard these scarcely veiled attacks on him as a temporary aberration. Ehrenburg had tried to persuade him (though he scarcely believed it himself) that "these people's" bark was worse than their bite.

I found Lyubov Mikhailovna bright and cheerful, and she seemed to have completely recovered from her heart attacks. This time Ilya was friendly, and as bright, witty and outrageous as ever; only he looked physically terribly enfeebled and spoke in a faint, scarcely audible voice. The lunch was, as usual, very French; I forget now exactly what we ate, but I remember the excellent bottle of real iced

Chablis and the blue packets of Gauloises. In this connection, Ilya told me a very funny story. Being very fond of Camembert, he had wanted it to be produced in Russia, and he went specially to Normandy to find out how exactly it was made. On his return, he took the recipe to a cheese dairy near Moscow, which produced an excellent imitation of the French product, and several hundred Camemberts were sent to Moscow shops. The effect was disastrous. The newspapers were flooded with letters from people complaining of the "stinking filth" that had been sold to them under the guise of cheese. And that was the end of Soviet Camembert.

In 1965 it had been obvious that Ehrenburg was an unhappy man. Khrushchev and his propaganda chief Leonid Ilyichev had been particularly offensive to him with their anti-Semitic innuendoes, and he was not at all sure what "these new people" (Brezhnev and Kosygin) were going to do to him. But this time he was in a talkative mood. For one thing, he was now working again (he seemed at a dead end in 1965); he said he was continuing his autobiography, and this last volume would deal with the Khrushchev period.

"I suppose you'll make it pretty hot for Nikita Sergeievich," I suggested.

"Well," said Ilya Grigoryevich, "Khrushchev wasn't really a bad man, and he will always have to his credit the fact that he (though not only he) had a good deal to do with throwing open Stalin's labor camps. But God only knows why our so-called statesmen have to stick their necks out and lay down the law on what kind of books we are to write and what kind of pictures we are to paint. In this respect, Khrushchev was particularly absurd, and he behaved with the greatest arrogance too, pretending he knew what he was talking about. Also, he had lived for too long in my—though not his— native Ukraine and had been infected by the kind of visceral anti-Semitism that is still very far from having been stamped out there. It has practically disappeared in a place like Moscow, but you still get a lot of it in Kiev. As for Ilyichev, he was a typical old-regime *zhidomor* [Jew-baiter], though a member of our Central Committee and what have you.

"But even the Ukraine is changing today in a quite extraordinary way. In the past, there used to be all these Petlyura and, later, Bandera nationalists who loathed practically everybody—the Russians, the Poles and, of course, the Jews. These they simply massacred. The only people they really admired were Hitler's Nazis. Today there is a very strange new kind of Ukrainian nationalism. These people (it's never happened in the Ukraine before) deplore the old Ukrainian anti-Semitism, and those new Ukrainian nationalists are liberals—yes, liberals, who look upon the Great Russians, above all in Moscow, as reactionary and anti-Semitic. Their sympathies lie with Western culture. They feel that that Great-Russian nationalism, which Stalin, though a Georgian himself, represented so well (and so aggressively toward the end of the war), is still continuing to weigh heavily on the cultural life of every part of the Soviet Union."

This kind of nationalism, Ehrenburg said, was taking on all kinds of strange forms in various parts of the country. Thus, when he recently went to Ufa, the capital of Bashkiria, formerly a Moslem country, he found that if a few years ago only two or three very old men went to the mosque on Fridays, now nearly everybody went—not out of religious feeling, but as a kind of nationalist demonstration, to show, as it were, that "we Bashkirs are not the same as the Russians."

"Surely," I said, "this is an extraordinarily characteristic phenomenon of our epoch. On the one hand you have the 'polycentrism' of the foreign Communist parties—the Italian, and latterly even the French, who are becoming more and more independent of Moscow. You have the Poles, the Hungarians, the Czechs and, especially, the Rumanians, who are behaving more and more independently. You have, thanks to de Gaulle, the breakup of NATO. Just as the 'monolithic' Stalin bloc 'from the Elbe to the China sea' has become a loose-knit federation, with some big and small members (China and Albania) dropping out altogether, and with Rumania perhaps on the way out, too, so the Soviet Union itself, it would seem, is becoming increasingly loose-knit, with the Ukrainians and even the Bashkirs now wanting a national identity of their own, instead of being almost anonymous members of a thoroughly *gleichgeschaltet* Soviet Union. The concept of the nation is becoming stronger and stronger every year; just as the Rumanians feel increasingly independent of Moscow, so do also the Ukrainians, the Bashkirs, and no doubt the Armenians and Georgians."

Ehrenburg laughed. "Yes, that's quite true. The whole world is growing Gaullist. The Russians are Russian Gaullists, with a sense of their own superiority, but there are also the Ukrainian Gaullists in the Ukraine, who now begin to contest the national superiority of the Russians and even the supreme authority of Moscow. For economic, military and other practical reasons, the Soviet Union will stick together, no doubt, though I should not be absolutely sure that in, say, a hundred years a large and rich country like the Ukraine, with now over forty million people, will necessarily remain part of the Soviet Union. Anyway, under our constitution the Ukraine may declare herself independent and cease to be a member of the Soviet Union. The present line is, of course, 'Just you try!'; but how do we know what will happen in a hundred or even fifty years? A lot of Ukrainians feel, of course, that although they are heavily represented in the Supreme Soviet and on the Central Committee, the tone everywhere is still set by the Russians, at least in most cases."

I began to think about the Ukraine. Surely, I felt, it has a culture of its own, a history of its own, a national identity of its own. I was told that there was a remarkable Ukrainian literature; I had never seen much of it; most books ostensibly translated from the Ukrainian had the same old Soviet pattern, even more conformist, if anything. Was it not also strange that for many years the top rulers of the Ukraine should not have been Ukrainians, but Khrushchev, a Russian, and Kaganovich, a Jew? And even if at the Supreme Soviet the Ukrainian spokesman was usually somebody like Korniets, with his long, "typically Ukrainian" moustache, this was not much more than so much window dressing.

To please the Ukrainians, the Russians were making a frightful fuss over their "national poet," Taras Shevchenko; it is quite common to hear Russians say that Shevchenko is as great a poet as Pushkin. It all reminds me a little of the English raptures over Scotland's "national poet," Robert Burns. (On the quiet, of course, I have heard many an Englishman say that if Burns hadn't written in Scottish dialect and had been born in England, he would merely rank as one of the minor poets of the eighteenth century.) To say that Shevchenko is the equal of Pushkin is like saying that Burns the Scot was the equal of Shakespeare the Englishman. In reality, the Ukraine has only one writer of genius, Gogol; but he wrote in Russian—just as Scott, of Edinburgh, wrote in English! And I very much doubt whether, even if the Ukraine loosens its bonds with Moscow (a typical present-day phenomenon), the Ukrainian language will ever become *the* language of the country, any more than Gaelic is *the* language of an independent Ireland. I even doubt that much of the present make-believe such as the publication of newspapers in Ukrainian (when practically everybody finds it easier to read precisely the same thing in Russian) will be kept up.

But to return to the Ehrenburg lunch. He thought things in art and literature were still far from satisfactory in the Soviet Union. There were modern painters of real talent, and even genius, he said—Weisberg, and the two Nikanovs, and Birger, and Andronov and his wife Yegorishina, and Mikhail Ivanov—but they were not being officially recognized. On the quiet, people bought their pictures—even some officials, like the same Leonid Ilyichev who publicly thundered against "decadent art." The Russian people were becoming more and more civilized and sophisticated. Falk was a major "Cézannesque" painter, though he had not been recognized; but to show what the true taste of Russian art lovers was, it was enough to say that when for a short time a Falk exhibition was held in Moscow, no fewer than 300,000 people went to it. At a recent exhibition of Picasso drawings in Moscow, there had nearly been a riot, so many thousands wanted to get in.

"I don't know," said Ehrenburg. "We're told that there's a more liberal atmosphere in Moscow today. I'm not at all sure. This month it may be more liberal, next month it may be less liberal. We've had all sorts of beastly things happening in the literary field in the last few years; and the Siniavsky-Daniel affair is not the worst. After all, they had a trial of sorts, they were sentenced under some article of the Criminal Code. They could even plead not guilty. There *is* here a difference between a trial, even a trial of sorts, and the Stalin method Sholokhov advocated in the case of Siniavsky and Daniel—standing them up against the wall and just bumping them off."

"Speaking of Sholokhov," I said, "what did you think of that last attack he made on you at the Writers' Congress?"

"That doesn't worry me," said Ehrenburg. "That sort of thing has happened too often before. Besides, he made an ass of himself; he suggested that I had deliberately gone abroad so as not to be present at the Writers' Congress in May, and that I preferred to go to the Stendhal Congress in Italy, 'warming my old bones in the Mediterranean sun,' and that sort of thing. But in fact I had gone to the Stendhal Congress by arrangement with the Writers' Union." He laughed. "The trouble is that we've got only one Party, so everybody gets in, even a fascist like Sholokhov!

"A more liberal atmosphere in Moscow today," Ehrenburg repeated. "Yes, this month; but what about next month? They say now that Solzhenitsyn's two novels confiscated by the police (he explained all this in his memorandum to the Writers' Congress, which, of course, refused to discuss it) will be published in a few months. They also say that Pasternak's *Doctor Zhivago* will be published in Moscow this year. Well, perhaps. They also say there's going to be an amnesty in favor of Siniavsky and Daniel when the Fiftieth Jubilee comes. Well, let's wait and see.*

"Our literature is in a very strange conditon," said Ehrenburg. "Except very occasionally by chance, nothing worthwhile ever gets into our principal magazines. Tvardovsky, the most courageous of our editors, the editor of *Novy Mir,* is feeling discouraged. And yet—and the Party bosses know it—the country is teeming with literary talent. But rather than wait for twenty years, till the present hacks have died off—the ones who control our magazines—our young writers get themselves published by *samizdat;* that's to say, they get their poems, novels, short stories typed or multigraphed; and these then circulate all over Moscow. And our bureaucrats have to turn a blind eye to *samizdat;* only very seldom does a *samizdat* writer get locked up, and then only if he writes something really viciously anti-Soviet. There are *samizdats* in other towns too, in Leningrad and Kiev and Odessa and practically everywhere. It doesn't even cost an awful lot to be published by *samizdat,* though naturally it doesn't bring in any income."

"How much does it cost to type a longish novel, for instance?"

"Well, the typist charges twelve kopecks a page,† that means twelve rubles for a hundred pages. *Samizdat* doesn't, of course,

---

* Ehrenburg's doubts were more than justified. There was to be no amnesty for Siniavsky and Daniel; and neither the Solzhenitsyn novels nor *Zhivago* were to be published.

† Solzhenitsyn alleged in his letter that it was a criminal offense to type or copy an uncensored manuscript; but he was almost certainly wrong there, except perhaps insofar as such a "law" was applied to him.

publish novels the length of *War and Peace;* but you could get, say, something the length of an average Turgeniev novel into three hundred typed pages. Well, that's thirty-six rubles; of course, you'd have to pay extra for the carbon copies. Or you could get the thing multigraphed, which is cheaper still, though some think it a bit risky. And there are lots of people with money who gladly help young writers to pay their typing bills, so you get some *samizdat* works printed in several dozens or even hundreds of copies."

"Ilya Grigoryevich," I said, "you mentioned twenty years . . ."

"Yes, quite right. I shall not live to see it, but I firmly believe that in twenty years' time our country will start producing a great literature, yes, something of the Tolstoy-Dostoevsky class. Here we have, on the one hand, the immense literary genius of the Russian people and, on the other, a hideous bureaucratic machine which continues to encourage the mediocrities by printing them in our 'best' magazines, while the others—well, the others have to depend on *samizdat.* But it can't go on forever. The terrible thing is that the Writers' Union, founded in 1934, was a Stalinist institution for the regimentation of thought. Perhaps it was necessary in those days, with the industrial revolution of the 1930s at its height and Hitler on our doorstep. Nobody wants it any longer now, except the Writers' Union profiteers—those who hold the fat jobs in the union itself or in their editorial chairs, and the small hacks who live on the union's charity and get themselves published in preference to real writers."

"But," I said, "there are the middle-of-the-road people—not writers of outstanding genius, but all the same good writers, very readable and above all wonderfully nice people."

"Who, for instance?" he said.

"Well, Simonov, Surkov, Boris Polevoi, Savva Dangulov, Victor Nekrasov, to mention just my close personal friends; they are nice, human people. I think the fact that they, or most of them, were soldiers or war correspondents in the last war has much to do with it."

"Yes, that may be so," Ehrenburg said, "though there are some you mentioned I don't like personally." I knew roughly whom he liked and whom he didn't. "These people still write reasonably good stuff and even get it published; it's because they write about the war.

That is always an acceptable subject.* But many of our young people were born after the war; and Russia can't go on writing about the war forever. Our young writers, those who publish their works by the *samizdat* process, want to write about their inner world, about delicate and controversial subjects. They want new writing; they want satire; and this has very little to do with either the war or the latest computer invented by a Russian engineer of genius."

We had gone on talking for a couple of hours. I felt that Ehrenburg was feeling very tired. I remember his last, optimistic remark: "I keep talking about twenty years; but things move so fast in the world today that we may have a great Russian literature in even ten years' time. And perhaps even I shall live long enough to see it." And he wrote down my Paris phone number (which is more than he did in 1965), saying he would come to Paris in the autumn.

This chapter has a sad and also sordid epilogue.

I arrived in Paris on August 26 and remembered my promise to send Ehrenburg a copy of the French edition of *Russia at War,* since he found English hard to read, while the Russian edition was somewhat "abridged." I sent off the registered parcel. Then one morning a few days later, while I was staying at my house in the Dordogne, I went as usual to Madame Hascoët's paper shop, and there was *Le Monde* with a large headline: "ILYA EHRENBURG EST MORT."

I was genuinely upset, and sent a cable to Lyubov Mikhailovna to Moscow—one of those dreary *condoléances* cables which all look alike and never really reflect the sender's feelings. Then, on the Monday, came a further shock. The postman brought the London *Times* and the *Observer*. The *Times* had an admirable two-column obituary on Ehrenburg. The author of the article knew the subject and had probably known Ehrenburg personally. He had studied his writing, discussed intelligently Ehrenburg's problem of "surviving" under Stalin, paid tribute to his immensely important work as a propagandist during the war and so on. It was not an uncritical article, but was intelligent, well-informed, fair-minded. The *Ob-*

---

* Even some war novels, however, have lately been violently attacked for showing up disastrous blunders made by the NKVD within the Army, or collaborationist or defeatist tendencies.

server, on the other hand, had an article by Edward Crankshaw, under the title "The Unhappy Villain." I found it profoundly shocking. It stated that Ehrenburg had "actively joined in the witch hunt" against Soviet Jewish writers around 1950 and, though a "cosmopolitan" himself, had "assisted Zhdanov in the hounding of 'rootless cosmopolitans' "—that is, all Russians who showed an interest in foreign ideas. Both charges were equally grotesque. Ehrenburg's alleged anti-Semitism never amounted to more than his statement that, although he was a Jew, he was anti-Zionist; as for Zhdanov's purge in the arts and literature, it is enough to say that the art dictator's principal victims were among Ehrenburg's closest personal friends—Akhmatova and Pasternak, Russia's two greatest poets, and Shostakovich and Prokofiev, Russia's two greatest composers.

I must admit that I lost my temper, and, although I had not intended to write any Ehrenburg obituary myself, I wrote a sort of reply to Crankshaw's *Observer* article in *The Nation,* in which I said, among other things:

> I had known Ehrenburg for years, and although I had my ups and downs with him, I never found anything sinister or evil about him; on the contrary, he was a man of great goodness. Thus, he was immensely helpful to any young writers of talent he discovered, such as the soldier-poet, Simeon Gudzenko, and many others. . . . After Stalin's death, he became the greatest and most effective liberal influence in Russia, even at a time when nobody else yet dared to speak up against either Zhdanov or Stalin. . . . He had the courage to defend Pasternak in 1958 and to protest violently against the Siniavsky-Daniel trial. . . .
>
> No, he was neither a "villain" nor "unhappy." The thought that he had done, and was doing, so much to liberate Russian literature made him very happy indeed.

In the September issue of *Novy Mir* were two touching tributes to Ehrenburg—one by Boris Polevoi, who recalled the enormous popularity of his writings with the Red Army during the Second World War, the other by Alexander Tvardovsky, who treated him as one of the noblest and most youthful influences in Soviet literature.

At the end of October, I received in Paris a visit from a very old Moscow friend, Jean Champenois, the former Agence France-

Presse correspondent. (Like all the best correspondents, he was, of course, sacked in 1948, at the height of the Cold War.) He told me the mournful story of Ehrenburg's funeral, to which he had gone. Ehrenburg loved France and the French, and he and Champenois had been very old friends.

"It was all rather dreadful," said Jean. "Lyuba was so grief-stricken that I can hardly bear to think of her. There were a lot of people at the funeral, but hardly a single official personage.* If there *was* anybody official there, it was somebody very third-rate, whom nobody knew. I felt it was shameful that no official token of gratitude should have been brought to one who, especially during the war years, had served Russia so well. Even Stalin once said, 'Ehrenburg, with his propaganda, is worth twenty or thirty divisions to us.'

"But there was one redeeming feature about that dismal funeral: there were hundreds—several hundreds—of young people, boys and girls of sixteen, seventeen, twenty, and most of them were in tears. To them Ehrenburg meant the future—a better and happier future for Russia in art and literature."

* I was later told that at the Writers' House there had been an official farewell ceremony of sorts. But the Soviet daily press was worse than perfunctory in its obituary notices of Ehrenburg.

15

Comecon and the
Developing Countries

SEV (Soviet Ekonomicheskoi Vzaimopomoshchi—Council of Economic Mutual Assistance), or Comecon, as we call it—is popularly described as the Eastern-European equivalent of the West's Common Market, but it has only a few features in common with it. My conversations with the SEV people, and later with those of the Soviet government department dealing with the underdeveloped countries (or "developing" countries, as they were officially—and more politely—called), were among the more "official" interviews I had in Moscow and were consequently rather less interesting than the others. Nevertheless, much was of considerable significance, particularly the contrast between the general desire to help the developing countries and the considerable skepticism in the face of the gigantic problem of the world's two billion hungry or undernourished people.

The U.S.S.R., Poland, Czechoslovakia, Rumania, Hungary, Bulgaria, the German Democratic Republic (East Germany) and Outer Mongolia constitute the Council of the SEV. Juridically Albania could be a member, but in June 1962 she declared that she did not wish to participate, and she has not since then paid her fees to it. Yugoslavia can be regarded as a *de facto* member. The whole staff consists of about seven hundred persons.

The SEV's chief function is to coordinate the national economic plans (Five-Year Plans, etc.) of the member countries as far as possible. Some plans such as health and finance do not come into it. Nor do *all* the national plans—only those which call for cooperation among the various countries. Each country works out its own plans;

the SEV does not draw up any general ones. It does, however, act as a corrective. Thus, in 1962 one member was proposing to build a soda plant; SEV advised this country against it, since in the general economy of the member states it would be redundant.

An important task of the SEV, I was told, was to coordinate plans which then became the basis of bilateral and multilateral trade agreements. The SEV made numerous recommendations, but there was absolutely nothing supranational, as there was in the Common Market. With some irony Mr. Ptichkin, an official I talked with at the SEV, remarked that it was, indeed, easier for the Common Market to function than it was for the SEV. In the Common Market, decisions were not always determined by the national interest of the country concerned. There were certain capitalist monopolies which could act quite independently of any national interests.

"Thus, if an Italian firm wants to build a plant in France," another SEV official said, "it can do so without bothering about the national interest of either country. The SEV, on the other hand, has to coordinate the national and international interests of the member states, and sovereignty must be absolutely respected. The kind of situation that arose in 1948 when Yugoslavia rebelled against the Soviet Union because she was being treated as a satellite is quite inconceivable now. We in the Soviet Union sometimes send our so-called satellites certain goods of which *we* are short, but which they need even more. Or to take another example, we send these countries crude oil; we could, of course, send them refined petrol, but we don't want them not to have their own oil refineries.

"Every country has its own economic plans; but when we think they need correcting in terms of the general economy of the SEV, then we try to use persuasion. The principle underlying our work is the division of labor, with each country gaining from it. Among the members of the SEV we have preferential prices, free exchange of scientific and technical information, and the exchange of specialists."

For all the socialist countries, he then said, it was essential to have some *valuta* (foreign exchange—e.g., dollars, pounds, francs), since there were certain kinds of machinery which had to be imported from the West; here there was "a certain amount of pooling" of *valuta* resources.

Important features of SEV activity are such international ventures as the "Friendship Pipeline" supplying Hungary, East Germany, Poland and Czechoslovakia with Russian oil. It was fairly clear from several officials' remarks that they were not entirely happy about Rumania and probably attributed her excessive independence, and her insufficient interest in the common interest of all the SEV countries, to her oil, which she could export to the West and so had a bigger flow of *valuta* than most members of the SEV. Altogether, the Rumanians had lately tended to shirk their "moral responsibilities" to other member states, and to not take part in any SEV discussions which did not interest them directly. The SEV officials also spoke a great deal of the coordinated efforts made by the SEV countries to help the developing countries. In particular, they referred to the arms supplied to the Arab countries, and especially Egypt, by both the Soviet Union and Czechoslovakia.

The cooperation among SEV countries often took the form of exchanges between a highly industrialized country like Czechoslovakia and an underdeveloped country like Bulgaria. Bulgaria, of course, wanted her own industry, but the question of redundancy was inevitably the object of certain SEV "recommendations," even though in principle each country's sovereignty was sacrosanct.

An important aspect of the SEV is the fact that it constitutes a fairly coherent economic whole, comprising a population of over 300 million people, with, on the average, seventy per cent of the countries' foreign trade taking place within the SEV framework and only thirty per cent with the outer world (capitalist or underdeveloped). Nevertheless, the latter is increasing. Between 1960 and 1965 trade between the SEV countries and the "advanced" capitalist countries increased 4.2 times, while that with the developing countries increased 9.5 times.

All this SEV activity, I was assured, makes sense. Its members include predominantly industrial countries like Czechoslovakia, the G.D.R and the Soviet Union itself; predominantly rural but increasingly industrial countries like Hungary and Poland; relatively underdeveloped countries like Bulgaria in Europe and Outer Mongolia in Asia. Rumania, a country of great natural wealth (in both agriculture and oil), sees less advantage than the other SEV countries in belonging to the organization in much more than a purely formal way; there are also political and psychological reasons for this. Rumania was heavily exploited by the Soviet Union in the immediate postwar years, especially as regards her principal exportable wealth, oil; and although, in settling the frontier between Rumania and Hungary, Stalin was more generous to the former, a certain air of contemptuous condescension always characterized the Russians' attitude to the Rumanians—an attitude which differed from their attitude to, for instance, Czechoslovakia and even Hungary, both of which were regarded as serious and hard-working countries. (Despite many mental reservations, the Russians also showed much respect for the efficiency of East Germany.) Rumania was never really treated by the Russians as a serious country; she was regarded in much the same way as was France by Victorian England. There are other reasons for Rumania's antipathy for the Russians: she has an intelligentsia which is much more pro-Western than any other in Eastern Europe, except perhaps those of Czechoslovakia and Poland; and there is a growing Rumanian grievance against the reannexation by Russia of Bessarabia. (It had been annexed first from Turkey in 1812, lost at the end of the First World War, but reannexed in 1940 and again in 1945.) Bessarabia's Moldavian population is, in fact, very like the Rumanians, speaking practically the same language—which, since 1945 or 1946, is no longer printed in Latin but in Russian characters; this is regarded as an additional affront by the Rumanians.

No doubt the majority of the Rumanian people are living better than they did under the feudal order of prewar Rumania, with better housing, a better health service, a much fairer distribution of wealth, etc., but they want their socialism to be as un-Russian and as Rumanian as possible. They also differ from, say, Poland and Czechoslovakia in that they do not share these countries' understandable obsession with the "German menace"—a menace which does so much to create solidarity between the Soviet Union, Czechoslovakia and Poland (despite the Poles' own traditional dislike of the Russians, a dislike which, as Stalin said in 1945, "will disappear only in a couple of generations"). The Rumanian attitude to Russia is, in some respects, not unlike that of Yugoslavia, which, significantly, is not a member of the SEV, though it takes part in its discussions whenever its own national interests are affected.

Bulgaria, the most underdeveloped of the Eastern-European countries, is more wholeheartedly a member of the SEV, since she is most likely to benefit from it; moreover, there is a traditional feeling of sympathy between the Bulgarian and Russian peoples; their languages are very similar (much more than Russian is to Polish, Czech or Serbo-Croat), and the fact that Bulgaria was "freed from the Turks" by the troops of the Tsar Alexander II is still remembered in Bulgaria. Significantly, even though the Bulgarian government was a satellite of Hitler, the Soviet Union did not declare war on Bulgaria during the Second World War except after the rout of Rumania, in August 1944, after which, in the course of a bloodless "two-day war," the Russian troops under Marshal Tolbukhin occupied Bulgaria and were enthusiastically welcomed as "liberators from the German yoke and from Hitler's Bulgarian flunkies" by the greater part of the people.* These "flunkies" were soon to be exterminated in large numbers in the best Bulgarian tradition.

But when we are told that the Comecon organization makes sense, it does not follow at all that it works particularly smoothly and is not often faced with considerable difficulties, not least from the Soviet point of view. The façade of perfect harmony is maintained, but this is somewhat deceptive. In connection with Comecon moving into its new quarters, the "open-book" skyscraper in Kalinin Avenue in December 1967, Pietro Sormani, the excellent correspondent of the *Corriere della sera,* gave an admirable summary in the December 29, 1967, issue of the paper of the highly complex problems confronting the organization. In describing its new headquarters, Sormani said that this represented the "unity of all the member countries": the cement used for building was Soviet, the glass Czechoslovak, the telephones East German, the furniture Rumanian, etc.; but this external harmony could not camouflage effectively the disputes and dissensions going on inside the building. Thus, a few days before, Sormani said, Mr. Ceausescu, the Rumanian Communist leader, had denounced the countries which "didn't stick to their agreements"; by these he meant, in the first place, the Soviet Union. And then Sormani asked:

Will the new Comecon palace be like the Commonwealth Palace inaugurated in London four years ago just as the Commonwealth was on the point of breaking up? Probably not; because the parallel between the two does not apply, since the relationship among the member states of the two organizations is by no means the same.

* See *Russia at War.*

The position of the Soviet Union is so predominant that the Comecon will probably last as long as Moscow needs it. The Soviet Union's interest in Comecon is political, though she also derives certain economic benefits from it; but for these she has to pay a heavy price. If the Russians are willing to pay this price, it is because Comecon enables them to exercise pressure on Eastern Europe. But for that, the centrifugal movement would be much stronger.

As for the Eastern-European countries:

These undoubtedly have a strong economic interest in Comecon. Even those like Rumania, which has tried to divert as much as fifty per cent of her trade to the West, are still dependent on the Soviet Union for the supply of raw materials. And although Ceausescu angrily complained, just the other day, about the delays in supplying steel to Rumania, which she badly needed for the new engineering works at Galatz, there is really no alternative, for the present, to Comecon.

What was really happening, he said, was this: nobody wanted to dissolve Comecon, but practically all the member states wanted to change the present system in one way or another. Meantime exchanges between the member states had been increasing much more slowly since 1955; during the 1950–55 period the exchanges were showing an average yearly increase of 13.6 per cent; since then the rate of increase had been only 8.8 per cent. This drop reflected the drop in the rate of increase in industrial production; during the same period this had dropped from 9.5 per cent to 5.8 per cent. (In Czechoslovakia in 1963 it had dropped to less than zero.)

This was partly due to the increase in the "economic maturity" of the system; but the main reason was in the difficulty of integrating countries all at different levels of economic and technical development. Thus there is a striking contrast between Czechoslovakia and Bulgaria, the former's per-capita income being three and a half times greater than that of the latter.

Other problems, he continued, derived from the very structure of Comecon, above all that of price-fixing. These, by and large, were the main exchanges inside Comecon: the Soviet Union exported raw materials and imported finished and semifinished articles. The prices were based on international prices, and the present trouble was that the world prices of raw materials had dropped and those on manufactured goods had increased; this, obviously placed the Soviet Union at a disadvantage. Hence her request for an increase in the price of raw materials and of agricultural products. Moscow had even gone so far as to threaten to block its own exports. As against this:

> Other Comecon countries, notably Czechoslovakia and Hungary, accuse the Soviet Union of selling raw materials such as oil to other countries at prices below those ruling inside Comecon; the Russians' reply to this is that the prices of manufactured goods they import from Comecon countries are also above world prices. The Russians have even asked the other Comecon countries to give them credits so that they (the Russians) could improve their plants, and especially their transport (above all, the extremely long railway lines from the Urals and Siberia), and so reduce costs. All the Comecon countries except Rumania have indeed made loans to the Soviet Union in recent years at very low interest rates and repayable in kind.

As Sormani then says, the fixing of prices is one of the most crucial problems, the present system of enforced prices satisfying nobody—neither the economists, who have to make empirical calculations for adapting capitalist prices to Comecon conditions, nor the ideological purists, who hate to admit that the socialist camp is incapable of working out its own price system.

> In 1959, Academician Ostrovitianov suggested the adoption of "socialist prices," but gave no indication of how these were to be calculated. The idea has been taken up again in recent years and is, apparently, going to be adopted in future—but only to agricultural products and to certain specialized industrial goods, or to goods assigned to the production of single countries. But it is still uncertain how these socialist prices will be fixed. A Western economist remarked that the Comecon countries would have to fix their prices with reference to world prices, adding jokingly that if, one day, socialism managed to take over the whole world, *one* country with a capitalist regime would have to be kept, so that the actual level of prices could be known!

Is there, then, a solution? In reality, even inside the Soviet Union there is no precise rational criterion for fixing prices. So now some of the other Comecon countries, notably Czechoslovakia and Hungary, argue that the only way out is to adopt the market economy, complete with a reform of internal prices. Sormani believes that this course will sooner or later have to be adopted by the Soviet Union—sooner, indeed, than many people expect.

And his conclusion is worth quoting in full:

> The fate of Comecon is linked with the success of the economic reforms now being introduced in Rumania and other countries, and soon to be introduced by the rest. The great question is whether this will operate for or against integration amongst the Comecon countries. Is it not possible that the increased autonomy of industries and their dependence on the profit motive may lead them to seek more profitable outlets, either outside the Comecon or inside it, *but not in accordance with the directives received from above* [my italics]? Another possibility is that the freeing of prices will show up the backwardness of certain Comecon countries in relation to others, and of the community as a whole in relation to the Western world.
>
> It is hoped that, with the effects of these reforms beginning to become evident, the integration of Comecon will have advanced so far that there will be no turning back. . . . And this explains the feverish activity that has been going on in Comecon in the last few years regarding industrial specialization, coordination of plans, etc. This coordination did not exist before 1960; now, on the contrary, under Comecon's present Five-Year Plan, this coordination has become very comprehensive, going down to the first details.
>
> But, despite all this activity, with meetings, consultations, etc., there are still some unresolved questions, and the official inauguration of the Comecon headquarters will take place in an atmosphere of uncertainty.

There are two possibilities, Sormani says: Comecon will become either the live center of a dynamic community or else "the useless brain of a disintegrating body." That would be "an ironic fate for one of the newest and finest buildings in all Moscow."

The Comecon officials, with whom I raised some of these questions, tried not to sound as skeptical as the Italian correspondent, but admitted, all the same, that any precise and long-term prophecies about Comecon's future were not easy to make, and that there *was* the problem of prices and the exchange rate of the ruble.

The Czechoslovak "revolution" of 1968 was not unconnected with the Czechs' dissatisfaction with Comecon. They felt that, with the complicity of Novotny, they had been exploited for years by the organization. They had had to make loans to Russia to build pipelines and to improve railway transport for Russian shipments to Czechoslovakia; Russia was selling her oil to them in unconvertible currency for twice the price the Italians paid for it in convertible currencies; above all, Comecon was the chief obstacle to Czechoslovakia's currency becoming convertible, which would enormously facilitate that country's trade with the West. Also, Russia had been constantly forcing Czechoslovakia to provide commodities, within the unprofitable Comecon framework, to the underdeveloped countries. The Czech protests, following those of Rumania and Yugoslavia, rocked the Comecon skyscraper.

Apart from SEV, which is the main economic organism for economic cooperation among the socialist countries of Europe (and more recently also with those of Asia—though so far only Outer Mongolia is a full SEV member), there is also, in a large building on the Moskva River, a Soviet government department called GKES (Gosudarstvennyi Komitet Ekonomicheskovo Sotrudnichestva— (State Committee for Economic Cooperation). I had a meeting there, also on a very official level.

Characteristically, after the usual greetings and the pouring out of drinks (here, apart from lemonade, quite substantial glasses of cognac were also filled), the meeting began with somebody reading out a quotation from Lenin. His prophetic words, this official said, words he had uttered even before the Revolution, were now coming true:

> We shall make every effort to come nearer to, and merge with, the Mongols, Persians, Indians and Egyptians; we feel that it is both our duty and in our interests to do so. . . . We shall try to give these peoples, even more oppressed and backward than we are, all the disinterested cultural help we can give them. . . . We must help them to learn to use machinery, to make their work

easier; we must help them along the road of democracy and socialism.*

There were, I learned, thirty-five developing countries with which the Soviet Union had agreements for economic and technical co-operation. There were sixteen countries in Asia—Afghanistan, Burma, India, Indonesia, Iran, Iraq, Yemen, Cambodia, Kuwait, Laos, Nepal, Pakistan, Syria, Turkey, Ceylon and Singapore; seventeen countries in Africa—Algeria, Ghana, Guinea, Cameroon, Kenya, Congo (Brazzaville), Mali, the United Arab Republic, Senegal, Somalia, Sudan, Tanzania, Tunisia, Uganda, Ethiopia, Morocco and Zambia; and two in Latin America—Chile and Brazil.

When I asked about Cuba, I was told that it was not a developing country, but a socialist country, not at all the same thing, and it did not come under the GKES.

This kind of aid to economically backward countries, I was told, had already begun before the war, but only on a very small scale; some technical help had been given to Turkey (in the days of Kemal Pasha, when Turkish-Soviet relations were good), and also to Afghanistan, whose King Amanullah was one of the first Asian potentates to recognize the potential economic importance to his country of the Soviet Union. (He even paid a visit to Moscow, much to the annoyance of the British in India, who did not like to see Afghanistan behave in so independent a way and promptly got him overthrown by a rival clique.) But this aid to underdeveloped countries was interrupted by the war and was not resumed until the middle fifties. An important landmark was the Khrushchev-Bulganin visit to India, Afghanistan and Burma in 1955. This was to be followed by several similar visits, including a long visit by Khrushchev to Indonesia in 1960.

At present, according to official Soviet sources, six hundred "objectives" had been built or were in the process of being built in the "developing" countries with Soviet aid. They included forty-three machine-building plants, twenty chemical or oil-refining plants, twenty combines, plants or workshops for ferrous and nonferrous metallurgy, thirty power stations, seventy enterprises of light or food industry, one hundred agricultural "objectives," sixty

* The quotation, I was told, came from Lenin's *Complete Works*, Vol. 23, p. 55.

transport and communications "objectives" and one hundred educational establishments. A number of enterprises for manufacturing medical instruments and pharmaceutical products were being set up or had been set up with Soviet help. Other objectives were roads, railways, airfields, bridges, harbors, irrigation canals, dams, hospitals, blocks of flats, etc.

The results of all this Soviet aid (or, officially, "cooperation") would, according to the same source, bring about annual increases of 7 million tons of steel, 4.9 million tons of iron ore and 8.5 million tons of refined petrol. There would also be "substantial" increases in electric power (about 6 million kw.), in the number of port installations, etc.

At the GKES the officials stressed the following points: "Our help is based on the needs of the country—that is, the state sector of the national economy; in other words, there is no question of the Soviet Union subsidizing private firms, no matter how useful or deserving. We do not do the building itself; this is done by the developing countries; but we give them technical help. What we say to them is this: 'You do the building, but when you find you lack experience, you come to us, and we shall help you with our advice.' Our geologists and other prospectors have been of great help. Thus, when India said she wanted her own oil, the West said, 'You are wasting your time,' but in 1956 we sent a small team of specialists, and in a few months they did find oil in India; thanks to us, India is now producing three and a half million tons of oil, and will be producing six and a half million tons by 1970.

"In the same way, we helped Syria to find oil, Afghanistan to find natural gas, Iraq to find sulphur, Guinea to find diamonds. A part of the gas we found in Afghanistan we now buy from that country.

"As little hard cash as possible comes into our dealings with the developing countries; what we normally get in return for the industrial equipment and so on that we send them are such things as tea, mineral oils, ground nuts, bananas and other kinds of fruit. One of the great advantages these countries have in the trading with us is that we provide them with a solid, reliable and lasting market for these exports."

This point is well illustrated by Anthony Nutting, Prime Minister Eden's Secretary of State at the British Foreign Office, who resigned in 1956 at the height of the Suez crisis in protest against Eden's maniacal anti-Nasser policy. Speaking on the BBC ten years later, Nutting said:

> Never mind what the Russians do with the Egyptian cotton crop; they can put it at the bottom of the Black Sea; but the important thing is that they buy it—and they usually leave it to the last minute, when the Egyptians are literally on their knees. . . . Then they come and bail them out. This is the sort of thing that makes friends and influences people.*

The idea of making friends and influencing people had, of course, much to do with the Soviet Union's aid to, or "cooperation" with, the underdeveloped countries. Trade with a country like India was rapidly growing; it had multiplied more than tenfold between 1955 and now, and this trade would be even more considerable if India had not had three disastrous harvests in succession, which left her no rice surplus for export. In principle, trade between the Soviet Union and the "developing" countries was well balanced; in their trade with the United States these countries always had an unfavorable trade balance.

Today the trade between the Soviet Union and the "developing" countries amounted to 1.7 billion rubles, which was six times more than in 1957. The Russians were expecting that the present trade would increase sixfold in the next fifteen years, which would mean about ten billion rubles.

The GKES officials attached particular importance to the Aswan Dam in Egypt, reckoning that when finally completed it would increase the prerevolutionary national income of Egypt by about one half and represent an annual saving of 100 million Egyptian pounds in terms of foreign currency.

Plans had also been drawn up for building, with Russian help, a Euphrates dam in Iraq, and an agreement had already been signed. This hydroelectric plant would be of the greatest value to Iraq's economy.

The largest Soviet contribution to India's industrial development was the iron and steel works of Bhilai; Russia had paid about eighty-five per cent of its initial cost. Now some 150,000 to 200,000

* *Ten Years After,* edited by Anthony Moncrieff, BBC Third Programme Series, p. 87.

people were employed there. As a result of this help, Bhilai alone was now producing two and one half million tons of steel, and the whole of India seven million tons—not a spectacular figure, but far more than she had ten years ago. As a result of this Soviet help, more and more people in India were being drawn into industry. All this was, in the long run, of enormous educative value.

A very important point was made in this connection, or, rather, in connection with the Aswan Dam in Egypt (but the same also applies to the new steel mills in India), by an American professor, W. R. Polk, in the BBC discussion already mentioned:

> The real importance of the Dam, I suspect, is symbolic. It is a symbol of the regime, and on this the Egyptian government simply had to continue, no matter where it got its aid from. . . . I am sure the Egyptians are very grateful indeed to the Soviet Union. . . . *But, most important of all, perhaps, is this: the High Dam was the school, above all other schools, in which the new kind of Egyptian was trained—the engineer, the technician, the foreman are all graduates of the High Dam.* [My italics.]*

The Russian officials seemed to attach particular importance to the help the Soviet Union had given India† and Egypt, and to the feelings of friendship she had aroused in both countries and in the Arab world generally. An important contribution to the economy of Ceylon was the tire plant the Soviet Union had helped to build there; in the past, Ceylon used to export rubber and then buy tires made abroad; now, with her own rubber, she made practically all the tires she needed. Meantime, seventy per cent of all Ceylon's tea plantations were still in British hands. This last remark seemed somewhat irrelevant, but it was no doubt meant to stress the fact that the Russians are not taken in by the nominal independence of a country like Ceylon, where colonialism had simply been replaced by neocolonialism.

Altogether, the GKES officials said, it was more profitable for the "developing" countries to trade with the Soviet Union than with the

* *Ibid.,* p. 89.
† As distinct from them, other Russians, as we shall see, are extremely skeptical about India.

capitalist countries of the West. In trading with the Soviet Union, not only did they not suffer from adverse trade balances, but, in the case of credits, Russian interest rates (two per cent) were more favorable than Western interest rates (usually five and a half per cent), and the payments to the U.S.S.R. were made in goods.

But while they had much to say on the successful and expanding trade with certain countries, such as Egypt, India and Afghanistan, they had relatively little to say about Africa, even though they had cooperation agreements with no fewer than seventeen African countries. True, an oil refinery producing 500,000 tons of petrol had been set up in Ethiopia with Russian help, and numerous African students came to the Soviet Union to study industrial methods in Soviet factories. "All this kind of help we give these people simply cannot be measured in ordinary dollar terms." In Algeria, the Russians had helped to build a metallurgical plant; had helped with the irrigation system; had sent specialists to de-mine the country after the end of the war with France; and had helped to set up some special schools, one dealing with oil problems, another with geology and prospection. President Houari Boumédienne had paid a special tribute to the Russians who had de-mined Algeria. Other African leaders had expressed their gratitude to the Soviet Union. Kenya's President Kenyatta had said, "Help came to us from the Soviet Union when we needed it most"; King Hassan of Morocco had spoken warmly of the geological work done by the Russians in his country, and of the help they had given Morocco in training medical personnel; and Mali and the Congo (Brazzaville) had also thanked the Soviet Union for various forms of help.

The strong impression I had, all the same, was that Black Africa did not particularly interest the Russians. A serious attempt in the past to help Patrice Lumumba in the Congo had ended in a fiasco for them and in tragedy for Lumumba himself. There were few, if any, Black African leaders for whom they had any respect; most of them, in the Russian view, belonged to a plutocracy and were very corrupt and corruptible, and seldom capable of resisting bribes from the United States. "We are not rich enough to compete with the CIA in subsidizing those Black African presidents, most of whom are plain crooks," was a common attitude.

Since the Chinese had also completely failed to make any impression in Black Africa, there was no longer any problem of competing with the Chinese there. India was another matter; India had, in some measure, to be protected against China.

What, then, was the general purpose of this "cooperation" with the "developing" countries? There was, on the one hand, the ideological basis of "disinterested" help to peoples "even poorer than ourselves," of whom Lenin had spoken; on the other, there was that desire to make friends and influence people, especially those who, like the Arabs, had acutely suffered from colonial exploitation and were still, in a more camouflaged way, continuing to do so.

Looking far ahead, many Russians today feel that in the balance-of-power game the friendship of so vast a population bloc as the Arab countries is not to be neglected. (Not that there are no very strong charity-begins-at-home moods in Russia, especially among the general public; but with this psychological problem I shall deal later.)

Of all the Arab statesmen, Nasser is the one who enjoys the Russians' greatest respect, and there are also special psychological reasons why Russia should, already for a long time now, have felt obliged to take Egypt (and, to a lesser extent, Syria) under her protection.

16

The Middle-East Crisis

IN December 1943, soon after the Teheran Conference, and while nothing very important was happening on the Russo-German front, I had the opportunity of getting a free ride in an American Embassy plane from Moscow to Teheran, and then to Cairo. (For correspondents in wartime such free rides were the regular thing.) Cairo was then under British occupation; King Farouk, who had behaved somewhat obstreperously during the previous year, when it seemed uncertain whether the British could hold Cairo against the advancing Germans and Italians, had now been browbeaten into obedient silence, after a strong British military demonstration, tanks and all, outside his palace. The atmosphere in Egypt was unpleasant. The British never referred to the Egyptians as anything other than "wogs." Later I was to see something of the same kind in Algeria, where most of the French referred to the Algerians as *bicots* and the like.

This contempt shown to the Egyptians on every occasion deeply offended them, and the Russians were fully aware of it. I remember calling on the newly appointed Soviet minister, Mr. N. Novikov, in Cairo. A few days later he invited me to lunch, and here were several Egyptian guests; and I was struck by the extreme courtesy and friendliness with which the Soviet minister treated them. And then, during the same week, he was received in audience by King Farouk. It is extremely doubtful whether the Russians had any particular liking for King Farouk, then little more than a very lascivious fat boy; but, on coming out of the palace after his meeting with King Farouk, Mr. Novikov declared to the crowd of Egyptian reporters who had gathered at the gates that he had had a most satisfactory meeting with His Majesty, and that, in his view, Farouk was a "very great king." The evening papers in Cairo, including those printed in French, appeared with enormous banner headlines: " 'LE ROI FAROUK EST UN TRÈS GRAND ROI,' DÉCLARE M. NOVIKOV, MINISTRE DE L'URSS EN ÉGYPTE."

Among Egyptians this made a tremendous impression. To them, King Farouk, whether they liked him or not, was at the time a kind of symbol of national Egyptian resistance to the British occupation authorities. Mr. Novikov had taken a clear anticolonialist stand. The Egyptian people fully understood it, their feelings toward Stalin's Russia warmed accordingly, and at the British Embassy in Cairo they were of course furious with the Soviet minister.

For a variety of reasons, this budding wartime friendship between Russia and Egypt did not burst into flower after the war. The Russians had an endless number of other problems on their hands, including all the immensely complex problems that had arisen from President Truman's policy of hostility. Stalin did not entirely lose sight of the Moslem world but, obsessed as he was with Russian security, he was more interested in territories much closer than Egypt to the Soviet border, primarily (apart from Eastern Europe) Iran and Turkey. But both Stalin's move to secure a sphere of influence (complete with oil concessions) in northern Iran and his attempt to force Turkey to share control of the Black Sea Straits, with the help of a Russian air and naval base on the Bosporus, came to nothing. Truman was bellicose on these points, and the Russians, having no atom bomb at the time, did not persist. But, despite Truman's sharp intervention in favor of Iran and Turkey, to the Russians the main villains in the Middle East were then still the British rather than the Americans. Although the wartime flirtation between Russia and Egypt had helped to produce some strong progressive and even Socialist and near-Communist movements in the Arab countries, and particularly in Egypt, Stalin decided to concentrate on weakening the British hold on the Middle East in the manner least likely to please the Arabs—by making Russia the first power to extend *de jure* recognition to Israel. In June 1947, at the United Nations, the Russians had proposed the creation of a Jewish-Arab state in Palestine as being the only fair solution to both peoples; but in November 1947 Gromyko suddenly accepted the partition plan and the creation of a Jewish state. When, in May 1948, David Ben-Gurion proclaimed the state of Israel, Russia hastened to give it *de jure* recognition, while even the United States was still at the *de facto* stage.

The Russian Communists, starting with Lenin himself, had always been hostile to Zionism; if Stalin now overcame these prejudices, it was because he saw in the Jews of Palestine the most determined enemies of British imperialism. The new state of Israel, with its wealth of talent, technical skill and dynamism, was also more likely than any other country in the Middle East to develop something in the nature of a "progressive" and "socialist" state. The Arabs, on the other hand, seemed to the Russians still under the powerful influence of the British warlords and of the American oil corporations. Stalin saw to it that the Haganah was well provided with arms, principally from Czechoslovakia. This Soviet patronage of Israel had, of course, a disastrous effect on the Egyptian "progressives" and Communists, who were subjected to the most violent persecution between 1948 and 1950. Since many of the Egyptian Communists were of Jewish origin, they were described as a "Jewish fifth column" and massacred. Paradoxically, this wholehearted Russian support of the new state of Israel coincided, in Russia, with the beginnings of the ferocious anti-Semitic drive that marked the last years of Stalin. But the two policies were kept more or less distinct; help to Israel was intended to create great difficulties for British imperialism; the anti-Jewish, and particulary anti-Yiddish and anti-Zionist, campaign in Russia was one aspect of Stalin's struggle for monolithic conformism, not only inside the Soviet Union but, especially after the defection of Yugoslavia, inside the entire socialist bloc.

Then, in the early fifties, the attitudes began to change. Israel became more and more identified in Russian eyes not with British but with American imperialism, and all dreams of Israel as an outpost of socialism in the Middle East were gradually abandoned. At the Prague trial of Rudolf Slansky in 1952, American and British imperialism and Zionism were all three denounced in the same breath, and the most damaging conclusions were drawn from Slansky's contacts (no doubt authorized by Stalin at the time of the arms shipments to Palestine in 1948–49) with the Israeli Zionists.

What brought about a sudden new *rapprochement* between Russia and Egypt was the Anglo-Franco-American declaration of 1950 for the preservation of the status quo in the Middle East. The Arabs saw in this an attempt to consolidate Israel within its new, 1949 frontiers, while the Russians resented being left out of this agreement among Washington, London and Paris. Egypt was then fighting the British on the Suez Canal, and in December 1951 she began negotiations for Russian arms. The overthrow of Farouk and the seizure of power by the officers under Naguib and Nasser interrupted these talks, the Russians strongly suspecting at first that the new Egyptian rulers were American stooges.

The Russians, however, embraced Nasser when, following the Baghdad Pact (from which Egypt was excluded and which made Iraq—dangerously close to Russia—the real center of Anglo-American strategy in the Arab world) the new Egyptian leader attended the Bandung Conference. By doing so, Nasser openly declared himself an anticolonialist, which also greatly raised his stock in Egypt itself. In July 1955 Nasser received a visit from Dimitri Shepilov, the future Russian Foreign Minister; and that same month Mr. Solod, the Soviet ambassador, casually informed him that Czechoslovakia would sell him arms. Soon afterward, Nasser made a dramatic announcement to that effect.

Needless to say, the mad Anglo-French Suez adventure a year later played into the hands of the Russians. Even if Nasser attributed the collapse of the adventure largely to Eisenhower, the view among the Arab masses, according to Jean Lacouture, the leading French authority on Egypt, was that the Khrushchev-Bulganin threat to obliterate London and Paris had been decisive.

But in 1958 new complications arose between Egypt and Russia over the *Anschluss* of Syria, one of its purposes having been to stop the rapid progress of the Syrian Communists. This "union" of the two countries was followed by fierce persecution of the Communists in both Egypt and Syria. The Syrian Communist leader, Khaled Bagdash, fled to Russia, where he undertook a violent campaign against Nasser, whom he pictured as a militarist and chauvinist. Relations were for a time extremely strained between Cairo and Moscow; and yet in 1960, and despite continued persecution of the Communists in both Syria and Egypt, the Russians availed themselves of the undreamed-of opportunity, given them by the American refusal to cooperate, of subsidizing the Aswan High Dam in a grand manner. Khrushchev paid a triumphant visit to Egypt in 1964, when he conferred on Nasser and Amer the title of Hero of the Soviet Union—much to the dissatisfaction of his colleagues at home. There was much speculation at the time as to just why Khrushchev was making all these desperate attempts to please the Egyptians. To create a Cuba in the Middle East? To eliminate the danger of Anglo-American bases being set up in the Arab world? To control the Middle-East oil supplies in emergencies? Or simply to make friends and influence people? All of these motives played their parts, but most important perhaps was the value of the Aswan Dam as propaganda for Soviet technology among the developing countries, and the creation of a whole new class of Egyptian engineers, technicians and skilled workers in connection with the dam.

The Castro–Nasser parallel scarcely holds water, since Castro is a real revolutionary and Nasser is not. Nevertheless, Khrushchev, departing from Stalin's stay-at-home caution, still liked to think he was pursing a Leninist policy; at least, he did until he burned his fingers on Cuba. Significantly, Khrushchev's successors are today more interested in Nasser than in Cuba. Cuba is dangerous, and Castro now reproaches the Russians for not being revolutionary enough, and for signing trade agreements with reactionary regimes in Latin America. The Arab world attracts them for the reasons mentioned above, and also for the very specific mission of protecting the hungry Arab masses from Chinese influence.

A special place in this strange tangle is held by Syria. Both Moscow and Cairo were somewhat alarmed by the left adventurism of her leaders; nevertheless, both capitals felt that it was impossible to abandon Syria to Israeli aggression. When, on April 7, 1967, the Israelis attacked Syria, destroying six MIGs in the process, Moscow sharply warned Israel to forgo any further moves against that country. Since more attacks on Syria were nevertheless expected, Nasser closed the Gulf of Aqaba and demanded the withdrawal of UN troops from the Sinai Desert, both steps being taken without consulting the Russians. Without having taken these moves as seriously as they ought to have done, they grew extremely alarmed on June 2, and one of their diplomats rushed to see Nasser at 3 A.M. on June 3 to warn him against going through with an Egyptian attack which, the Russians had learned, was to be launched against Israel that very day. A similar warning had been given to Israel by de Gaulle only a few hours earlier.

Since both the Egyptian Air Force and, in effect, the Egyptian

Army were knocked out by the Israelis in the Six-Day War which followed, in practice there was very little that the Russians could do immediately to restore the balance in the Arab countries' favor. Hence the surprising weakness and meekness with which they accepted a United Nations cease-fire resolution which did not provide for the withdrawal of the Israelis from the Egyptian, Jordanian and Syrian territories they had conquered within a few days.

True, they branded Israel's knockout blow against the Egyptian Air Force on June 5 as a blatant act of aggression; and when, after the official cease-fire, Israeli troops continued to advance into Egyptian, Jordanian and Syrian territory, they broke off diplomatic relations with Israel and gave her a stern warning that if she occupied Damascus, let alone Cairo, the Soviet armed forces would intervene "in one way or another"—which probably meant one of two things or both: the dispatch of Russian airborne "volunteers" to Syria or the dispatch of a strong bomber force over Israel. If the Israelis had indeed occupied Damascus, there is no doubt that the Russians would have done something. Not that they had any desire to intervene militarily in the Middle-East war if it could possibly be helped. Although they doubted whether the United States was prepared to take on another war, with the war in Vietnam already on her hands, the danger of a major showdown with America in the Middle East (and, before long, Heaven knows where else) could not be entirely ruled out.

Besides, what was the hurry? In the long run, Israel, with her tiny population of less than three million people, would have to agree to some kind of settlement with her Arab neighbors. Not only was it doubted that the United States was prepared to fight a major war over Israel, but it was known in Moscow that the British government was greatly divided in its sympathies, many of its members being "traditionally" pro-Arab and only a few all-out pro-Israel; while in France General de Gaulle had openly condemned Israel's attack on Egypt on June 5, even though a kind of anti-Arab and pro-Israel hysteria was being worked up in France by a large part of the press—some of it Jewish-controlled, like M. Pierre Lazareff's *France-Soir,* some of it violently anti-Arab, in the old *"Algérie française"* tradition. But the fact remained that if the Russians warned Nasser in the first days of June against attacking Israel, so the French government had officially declared, as early as May 24, that it would "put in the wrong" any of the sides that would be the first to be guilty of an "armed action," and then, on June 2, de Gaulle himself had strongly repeated this warning to Mr. Eban, the Israeli Foreign Minister, during the latter's visit to Paris.

The official Russian line was, of course, that Israel was *the* aggressor, though everybody suspected that things were not quite as simple as they looked. During a long conversation with a high official of the Soviet Foreign Ministry, I was told that the Israelis had of course been guilty of the grossest act of aggression on June 5. Nevertheless, he admitted that the withdrawal of the UN forces and the closing of the Gulf of Aqaba—steps taken without consultation with the Russians—had been a sort of provocation. And although Nasser was a genuine statesman, perhaps the only real statesman in the whole Arab world, there were, the Russian official said, a good many irresponsible people in Egypt and in the other Arab countries—people who talked not only of wiping out the state of Israel but even of exterminating, in Hitler fashion, every man, woman and child in Israel. Particularly guilty of this kind of murderous talk was Choukeiri, one of the heads of the Palestinian Arabs. No doubt he had bitter and even legitimate grievances against the Israelis, who had been quite ruthless in their treatment of the Arab refugees, but it was this kind of talk which had caused an understandable panic among the Israeli population (many of whom remember Hitler's extermination of six million Jews during the Second World War only too well) and so played into the hands of Israeli hawks like General Dayan—"a real fascist type," as he was often described in the Soviet press. (Much was also made of the visit he had recently paid to "Marshal" Ky of South Vietnam, and of his great friendship with the hawks at the Pentagon.)

When I asked the same official at the Foreign Ministry what the repercussions of the Israel–Arab war was on the Jews in the Soviet Union, he said, "There's no connection at all. Our Jews are loyal Soviet citizens, and if during the last years of Stalin and even under Khrushchev—who was pretty anti-Semitic—there were many Soviet Jews who wanted to get away to Israel (or anywhere else, for that matter) and not stay in the Soviet Union, the same is no longer true. There may still be a few sentimental Zionists among the Jews in Russia, but even if there are they can be only a very, very small minority." But we shall return to the question of the Jews' position in Russia in the next chapter.

What was highly significant in the weeks immediately following the outbreak of the war in the Middle East was the extreme tact and caution with which the Soviet press (with a few exceptions) dealt with the matter. The Israelis were always referred to as Israelis, never as Jews, the clear implication being that the state of Israel had absolutely no connection with Soviet Jewry. Jews, in short, were one thing, and Israel and Zionism were something entirely different.

If the Soviet press was, on the whole, remarkably free of anti-Semitism, it did, however, launch occasional (though not very frequent) attacks on Zionism, particularly "international Zionism." The most vitriolic article of this kind appeared in *Izvestia* on July 2, 1967, and was called "Whom Do They Serve?," with the subtitle "The True Face of Israel's Ruling Group."

It started with a description of the funeral in April 1967 of that "patriarch of neo-Nazism, Konrad Adenauer." Here, among the mourners, were that "British agent" Abba Eban; "the man of the American monopolies," Nahum Goldmann; and "that socialist" Ben-Gurion. And all three of them, according to Yuri Ivanov, the author of the article, remembered Kaiser Wilhelm II's talk with Herzl, the father of Zionism. In the course of this conversation Herzl had spoken with joy of the day when the Jews in Germany would regain their own identity and become free citizens of Zion. But between Wilhelm II and Adenauer there was a missing link, and that was Adolf Hitler. Mr. Ivanov quoted *Der Spiegel* of December 19, 1966:

> The victory of the German anti-Semites and Hitler's appointment to the post of Reich Chancellor filled the Zionists with indescribable joy. Here at last was the smashing defeat of civilized Western Jewry, which did not give a hang for Zionism, but preferred to become members of the national community amongst whom they were living. And since the Zionists and the Nazis knew nothing more important than the concepts of "race" and "nation," there was, obviously, a clear link between them.

Whether *Der Spiegel* is correctly quoted or not, it is quite clear that Mr. Ivanov tried to demonstrate that the Nazis and the Zionists had one thing in common: just as the Nazis regarded the Germans as the *Herrenvolk,* as the chosen people, so the Zionists also considered the Jews the chosen people, superior to all others. The article continues with the story of "connivance" between the Nazis and the Zionist leaders, especially in the Kastner case. In 1953 the Hungarian Zionist Kastner had to admit that during the war he had negotiated with the Nazi chiefs in Budapest. "Although Kastner knew that the Nazis were liquidating half a million Hungarian Jews, he kept completely silent, gave the prospective victims of the Auschwitz gas chambers no warning whatsoever, and preferred it that way"—for this was how he managed to save the lives of a certain number of Zionist activists.

This sinister story of the *Judenräte,* sufficiently familiar to readers of Hannah Arendt's famous book, seems to have been related in the article—for the first time in the Soviet press—as a demonstration of "the complete cynicism and ruthlessness" of "Israel's present rulers." There followed a long list of charges against Israel's territorial expansionism, and these sinister activities were then linked with—the United States.

> The top leadership of Israel, whom we must on no account identify with the people of that country, preaches Zionism and is part of that Zionist international organization, with headquarters in New York, and working under the control of the United States. . . . In this organization the senior partners are the Rockefellers, Oppenheimers and Rothschilds; the junior partners, the Ben-Gurions, Dayans, Eshkols, Ebans, etc.

Mr. Ivanov then relates how these Zionist leaders threw Israel open to two hundred firms from West Germany and other countries which in a few years poured no less than seven billion dollars into the country—above all, into its armaments expenditure. The "ordinary people" of Israel got very little of this money. Israel was, in fact, the scene of an increasingly sharp class struggle: in 1964, there were 43,000 strikers; in 1965, 93,000; in 1966, over 100,000. The aggression of June 5, 1967, was unleashed partly in order to get Israel out of her economic impasse.

The *Izvestia* article went out of its way to distinguish between the Zionist leadership, on the one hand, and the ordinary people of

Israel and her Communists, such as the deputy Wilner, on the other. But in the end all the people of Israel would have to suffer for the folly of her leaders, for their attempt to overthrow the "progressive" governments of Arab countries like Syria and Egypt.

There is an interesting reference in the article to the fact that Herzl, the father of Zionism, advocated that the Jewish National Home be set up in Uganda and not in Palestine—which is like saying that the establishment of the state of Israel in the midst of a hostile Arab world was a fatal mistake from the start, even though the Soviet Union *was* the first country to give it *de jure* recognition.

Although, with the Egyptian Army and Air Force smashed in the Six-Day War, the Russians were in no position to make any immediate demands on Israel, the Soviet Foreign Ministry official I spoke to said it would be a great mistake to regard it as a small localized war; the defeated Arabs, though smarting under the humiliation of June 5, would never accept the permanent occupation by Israel of all the Arab areas she had grabbed from Syria, Jordan and Egypt. The Arabs' sheer weight in numbers would prove fatal to Israel sooner or later if no international settlement were reached. The Israelis' best hope to survive at all lay in the UN controlling the frontiers and other strategic points. It would be best, of course, he said, if Egypt and Syria and the other Arab countries recognized the existence of the state of Israel and sat down with the Israelis at a conference table; but "we Russians cannot compel the Arab countries to recognize Israel if they don't want to."

At that time, as we have already seen, the Russians, short of going to war themselves, could not force Israel to withdraw from the occupied territories. But in Moscow it was already clear even a month after the Egyptian debacle at the beginning of June that the Arab countries, and particularly Egypt, were beginning to be supplied with new armaments from Russia. People who had come that month, from Odessa were saying that masses of tanks and other military equipment were being shipped from there to Egypt. So it was only a question of waiting for Egypt to be strong enough to bring sufficient pressure to bear on Israel to abandon the occupied territories. One thing was also certain: the Russians, having lost a billion dollars' worth of equipment that had been given to Egypt, would not allow the Israelis to repeat their easy victory of June 5.

There had been not only an unpardonable lack of vigilance on the part of the Egyptians but, very probably, plain treason.

During my meeting with Marshal Zakharov, Soviet Chief of Staff, at the Soviet Embassy in Paris in October 1967, he recalled his own visit and that of Mr. Podgorny, the President of the Presidium of the Supreme Soviet, to the Arab countries after the debacle. Zakharov had gone there, as he now freely admitted, to get Nasser to purge the Egyptian Army and Air Force. The Marshal had two important things to say—one about the Egyptian soldiers, the other about the Egyptian officers.

For modern warfare, he said, the Egyptian soldiers were practically useless. Most of them were simply illiterate, and it was not with soldiers like these that one could wage a modern war; they hadn't the slightest idea of how to deal with complicated modern equipment such as tanks, rockets and planes. The Israelis, on the other hand, were highly accomplished soldiers, and their airmen (most of them flying French Mystères and other supersonic machines) were first-rate. The Egyptian Air Force personnel was of very doubtful quality, and there could be some truth in the story that they had all gone off for their morning coffee at eight-ten and that it was during the next five minutes that the Israeli planes, flying in from the northwest (where no one had expected them to come from), virtually wiped out the entire Egyptian Air Force. There could also be no doubt that the Israelis' intelligence was first-rate and that of the Egyptians altogether useless.

As regards the Egyptian officers and generals, Marshal Zakharov said that they were nearly all the wrong kind of people: they belonged to the feudal class of Egyptian landlords, a class wholly out of sympathy with Nasser and socialism or anything like that. He thought it highly probable that certain of them were working hand in glove with the CIA, and that their greatest ambition of all was to overthrow Nasser—even at the cost of humiliating defeat at the hands of the despised Israelis. Zakharov had got Nasser to purge the Army of six hundred to seven hundred generals and officers. The Russians also made it plain to him that if Egypt was to be rearmed the Russians themselves would keep a close watch on the Egyptian Army and Air Force.

By the end of 1967, there were already three thousand "advisers" in Egypt and three thousand more in the other Arab countries. The country had in fact two rulers: Nasser himself, whom the Russians regard as remarkably able and by far the most progressive states-man of the Arab world, and one who *will* turn Egypt into a properly progressive and perhaps even socialist country; and Mr. Sergei Vinogradov, the most brilliant of all the Soviet diplomats and a man of outstanding cunning and intelligence.

Vinogradov was Soviet ambassador at Ankara—one of the trick-iest places to be in—during the Second World War; and it was largely he who got the Soviet government to recognize de Gaulle almost immediately after the German invasion of Russia, at a time when no other government was willing to take de Gaulle seriously. He also played a leading part in the disintegration of Hitler's grand alliance, by preparing the ground for countries like Rumania, Bulgaria and even Hungary getting out of the war. Later Vino-gradov was for many years Soviet ambassador in Paris, and he showed the greatest political lucidity in maintaining close personal contacts with General de Gaulle even during the 1953–58 period, when practically everybody assumed that de Gaulle was finished; Vinogradov, on the contrary, knew (or at any rate guessed, with an extraordinary flair) that de Gaulle would inevitably return to power.

It was one of Vinogradov's tasks to "save" Nasser. To the Russians, Nasser has one great advantage over all the other Arab leaders: he has immense popular support from the people of Egypt; without this support, which "forced" him to withdraw his resigna-tion in June, he would have been finished. Unlike so many other Arab and especially African leaders, Nasser is totally incorruptible and believes in a "progressive" Egypt; and only the Russians can help him, with armaments or hard cash, to turn Egypt into such a "progressive" country. Nasser's two chief enemies are the "Moslem brethren" and the CIA; and nothing would please the United States more than the elimination of Nasser—through assassination, if necessary. Not that the CIA can find its task in Egypt very easy since the closing of the American Embassy soon after the events of June 1967; since then the red-and-yellow flag of Franco Spain has been flying from the U.S. Embassy, Spain being the country to "protect American interests" in Egypt.

Besides the dispatch of hundreds of Soviet experts to supervise the creation of a new Egyptian Army and Air Force, several hundred young Egyptians are now being trained in Soviet military and Air Force schools—officers of a type very different from those who so shamefully lost the Six-Day War.

Today Egypt is becoming a much more formidable fighting force than it could ever have been before June 1967, with its illiterate soldiers and its feudal officers. But in the summer of 1967, a month or two after the Egyptian debacle, the Russians showed nothing but contempt for the Egyptians as soldiers. They felt extreme exasperation over the way the Egyptians had allowed themselves to be beaten, despite all the splendid armaments Russia had given them.

What, on the other hand, was the attitude to Israel? She was *the* aggressor, though it was admitted even in official quarters, as we have seen, that the aggression was "not entirely unprovoked"— there had been withdrawal of the UN troops and the closing of the Gulf of Aqaba, and there had been the Hitlerlike threats from Choukeiri and other Arab leaders to wipe out not only the state of Israel but also all its Jewish inhabitants. But what was constantly stressed was, of course, the fact that by herself Israel would never have dared attack either Syria or Egypt. It was firmly believed, for instance, that the Israelis would never have dared deliver their knockout blow on June 5 without the certainty that the American Sixth Fleet would protect Tel Aviv and other cities of Israel against a possible Arab counterblow, should the attack on the Egyptian airfields not have proved as successful as it turned out to be.

Secondly, as already said, the Israelis were always referred to as Israelis, never as Jews; in other words, all Soviet Jews were supposed to follow the line that their one and only country was the Soviet Union and nothing else. The only man who openly declared that there was something to be said for the Israeli victory was the irrepressible Ilya Ehrenburg: "Well, it's just as well they didn't allow themselves to be exterminated by the Arabs, as they were in the Hitler days. Although there were plenty of excellent Jewish soldiers in the Red Army, and many of them were even made Heroes of the Soviet Union, there is still this unpleasant feeling that it's 'natural' for Jews to be massacred. If, following in Hitler's footsteps, the Arabs had started massacring all the Jews in Israel, the infection would have spread: we would have had here a wave of anti-Semitism. Now, for once, the Jews have shown that *they* can also kick you hard in the teeth; so there is now a certain respect for the Jews as soldiers. . . . And in Russia we always have a great respect for highly efficient soldiers and airmen, which the Jews—sorry, I mean the Israelis—certainly proved to be."

Although it was assumed that the Soviet Jews regarded the Israelis as simply aggressors, there was nevertheless at least a slight suspicion that there existed in the country a certain sympathy and admiration for the Israeli Army and Air Force, especially among the Soviet Jews, and that the latter were generally sensitive to this whole Middle-East crisis. But, unlike the Poles, the Russians did not throw people out of the Party and professorial chairs merely because they were Jews.

There are now some thirty Soviet warships in the eastern Mediterranean, and, according to French intelligence reports, some of these ships are equipped to carry substantial numbers of Russian marines. The Russians are also building aircraft carriers, which are expected soon to enter the Mediterranean. They believe that the presence of their Navy is calculated to reassure the Arabs. (There is nothing new about this; the tsars maintained Russian naval forces in the Mediterranean, and until their breach with Albania the Russians had a submarine base there.)

On the face of it, the situation looks dangerous, with the Russians rearming Egypt, and the United States, after the Eshkol visit to President Johnson, intensifying the rearmament of Israel. But there is good reason to suppose that the Russians feel in a sense that they, not Israel, are the real victors of the short war in June 1967. They disappointed the Egyptians by not intervening militarily, but, since the Western powers broke off relations with Egypt and most other Arab countries, these countries feel that Russia is their only friend. Vinogradov, by all reliable accounts, is not grooming Egypt for a resounding *revanche,* but is, on the contrary, trying to soften Egyptian susceptibilities to the point where the Arabs (or, at any rate, the Egyptians) will agree to a realistic peace settlement. Special importance is attached by qualified observers to the particularly warm reception given in Moscow to Hussein, the "little feudal King of Jordan," of all people. The explanation is quite simple: Hussein stands for a realistic settlement of the Palestine problem. This would mean that Arabs and Jews would sit down and talk. One thing to which the Russians will not agree is the annexation by Israel of the occupied territories—unless any transfer of territories is made part of a political settlement which might ultimately result in the de-Zionization of Israel and the setting up of a larger multi-national Palestine where the different races and religions would live peacefully together, as they do in Lebanon.* The Russians do not want to risk a nuclear war over Egypt any more than they want one over Vietnam. The rearmament of Egypt, the Russian Navy in the Mediterranean, etc., are no more than weapons in a diplomatic game, the final purpose of which—in the Russian view—is a realistic settlement, after which Russia may expect to find that Egypt, and some of the other Arab countries, will still see Moscow as their best friend and benefactor. The Egyptian intelligentsia is well aware of this. When John Foster Dulles handed the Aswan Dam over to Russia, he did not know that he was taking the first step toward turning a large part of the Arab world into a Russian sphere of influence, with Egypt as Russia's great show window of benevolence toward the Third World. As one Egyptian intellectual said, "We prefer the Aswan Dam treatment to the napalm treatment that the Vietnamese people are getting."

Not that the Russians have any revolutionary ambitions. Kosygin is not carried away by any revolutionary Leninism. He distrusts the firebrands in Syria, but he likes to deal with a "reasonable guy" like Nasser. It is by working through such reasonable guys that Russia helps to maintain "progressive" (though not Communist) regimes in the developing countries. It can do this more easily every year as bigger and bigger export surpluses accumulate from its spectacular industrial development. Nevertheless, Russia does not like to give away too much for nothing—or for little. That is why a limited objective like Egypt is preferable to, say, India, where (it is argued in Moscow) nothing much can be done to establish a reasonable standard of living until some far-reaching transformations are made in the whole fabric of the society. In Egypt much bigger results can be achieved at much smaller cost.

* On de-Zionization, apparently favored by the Russians, see also the arguments for it by Walter Laquer in *The Road to War, 1967,* and by C. Douglas Home in *The Arabs and Israel* (both London, 1968).

17

The "Jewish Problem"

I WOULD not deal with the "Jewish problem" at any length were it not for the fact that any suggestion one makes in the press that there is no longer in Russia a tragic or very serious Jewish problem invariably provokes violent protests from Zionist (and even non-Zionist) Jews, as well as non-Jewish anti-Soviet organizations, to the effect that things are infinitely worse in reality and that the persecution continues. Thus, in a letter to *Le Nouvel Observateur* a reader suggested that I was wrong to minimize the "Jewish problem" there. He stressed three points: every Soviet Jew has "Jew" marked in his passport; the Soviet Jews have the greatest difficulty in leaving the country or even in going temporarily abroad; there is a real *numerus clausus* against Jews in the majority of Soviet universities.

Let us look some years back. When, in 1917, the "pale of settlement" was liquidated (under which Jews of Jewish religion were allowed to live only in certain parts of Russia—notably Poland, Belorussia and parts of the Ukraine), many Jews flocked to the big towns like Petrograd and Moscow. Those who did were predominantly literate and educated Jews with a mighty grievance against the tsarist regime (which was guilty of pogroms and acute discrimination) and men of revolutionary temperament.

Secondly, there were many Jews in the "first" emigration, and Lenin was "surrounded by Jews"—Trotsky, Kamenev, Zinoviev, Radek, etc.; and later, under the Litvinov regime, the Soviet Foreign Office was nicknamed "the synagogue," some of the principal Soviet ambassadors being Jews—Suritz, Rosenberg, Umansky and Litvinov himself. Jews were also prominent in the Cheka. Most of these Jews were internationalist in temperament, and all of them were unreligious or antireligious. Many, like Manuilsky and Zinoviev himself, played an important role in the Comintern.

The years between 1917 and about 1930 were exceptionally good years for the Jews in Russia. In the 1930s they were, so to speak, on a par with Russians, who were rapidly becoming educated. During the war their role was a little more ambiguous: on the one hand, there were 500,000 Jewish soldiers in the Red Army, and at least one third were decorated for military valor, among them 114 Heroes of the Soviet Union; but, on the other hand, there were nasty jokes ("a gallant Jewish division has victoriously captured the city of Tashkent"), and, with wartime and postwar shortages, Jews played a prominent role in the black market. I discovered that there were even food speculators in famine-stricken Leningrad, and among them some Jews; thus, a concert grand was exchanged for half a pound of butter. Jewish—though not only Jewish—black-marketing continued during the hard postwar years. Both Lenin and Stalin, without being anti-Semitic (at least as far as the former was concerned), had a strong prejudice against Yiddish "bourgeois nationalism" as exemplified by the Bund, particularly when the latter insisted that the members of this party and its affiliated trade-union organization should be allowed to celebrate Jewish religious festivals and to not work on the Jewish Sabbath.

Although a Jew (Lazar Kaganovich) was one of his right-hand men, Stalin, with his ultra-Russian nationalism (the fact that he was a Georgian made it even stronger), did not like Jews on the whole. Thus, during the war, he eliminated practically all Jews from the Soviet Foreign Ministry, and with the Cold War in full swing in 1947–48, something of an anti-Semitic campaign began. The Jews were suspected of being more pro-Western than the Russians (many, indeed, had relatives in the United States and other places), but, above all, Yiddish culture was considered a manifestation of a narrow Jewish kind of nationalism, fundamentally alien to all that was Russian and Soviet. Although during the war the Jewish Anti-Fascist Committee had played a prominent part in appealing for help to Russia among the Jews in the United States, and the Yiddish actor Solomon Mikhoels, famous for such parts as King Lear, was sent specially to the United States to raise funds and create goodwill there, especially among the American Jews, this hobnobbing with the Americans was now held against Mikhoels and other members of the committee. In January 1948 Mikhoels was mysteriously murdered, together with another Jew, the ballet critic Golubov, during a visit to Minsk. It was said officially that they had been murdered by "pro-Nazi bandits," but it was fairly obvious that they had both been knifed and razor-slashed by the NKVD. Sergei Eisenstein, the greatest genius of the Russian cinema, though not a Jew by religion and of only partly Jewish origin, had his life made such a misery in 1947–48 by Stalin's veto on the second part of his film *Ivan the Terrible,* on which he had worked for years, that he developed a heart disease and died of a heart attack at the early age of forty-nine.

But worse was to come. When Golda Meir, the first Israeli ambassador, arrived in Moscow in the summer of 1948, several hundred orthodox Jews staged a demonstration in her honor. This was regarded by Stalin and the authorities as a Zionist demonstration, and Zionism implied, in their eyes, divided loyalties, if not downright disloyalty to the Soviet Union. The imputation of a combination of pro-Zionism with pro-Westernism produced a wave of anti-Semitism in Russia, and a new phrase, "rootless cosmopolitan," probably coined by Stalin himself, appeared. All that was Yiddish came to be considered un-Soviet, something belonging to the medieval, ghetto phase in the history of the Jews, and therefore totally unacceptable to the Soviet Union. The Yiddish Theater (the head of which had been Mikhoels) was closed. So, one by one, were Yiddish newspapers and publishing houses. There followed a holocaust among Yiddish writers and among former members of the Jewish Anti-Fascist Committee; one to be shot was Solomon Lozovsky, an old man who had been an Old Bolshevik and a friend of Lenin's in the emigré days, and later deputy foreign minister and a deputy head of Sovinformbureau, who also gave press conferences in the early days of the war; in 1952 twenty-four Yiddish writers were shot, among them Bergelson, Markisch and Feffer. Although there were no victims among Russian writers of Jewish origin, they had an uncomfortable time.

So long as a Soviet Jew was neither "Zionist" nor "Yiddish" he was reasonably safe, except during the last months of Stalin's life, when the by now half-insane dictator is said to have played with the idea of deporting, if not exterminating, all Jews in the Soviet Union. Shortly before his death, there had taken place in Prague the famous

Slansky trial, in which nearly all the accused, most of them Jews, were hanged, convicted of being either British intelligence agents or Zionist agents, or both. (The fact that Slansky, as we have seen, had—at Stalin's behest—had armaments sent to Israel in its struggle against the British was now treated as evidence of his collusion with Zionism.)

The Jews, like many others, heaved a sigh of relief when Stalin died; shortly before his death there had been the famous "Doctors' Plot"—and most of the doctors implicated were Jews. It was generally thought that Stalin had thought up the plot himself, as a prelude to drastic action against Soviet Jews generally. A few weeks later the doctors were declared innocent and released, though one or two had died in the NKVD's torture chambers. The woman doctor who had been awarded the Order of Lenin for her "vigilance" in discovering the doctors' "crimes"* and for denouncing them was deprived of her decoration—though no doubt the poor woman had herself been bullied and blackmailed into making her "revelations," just as Robert Magidoff's secretary, Cecilia Nelson, back in 1948, had been bullied by the NKVD into denouncing him as an American spy. In 1948 and the subsequent years, *any* correspondent who paid occasional calls at his own embassy could, *ipso facto,* be treated as a spy.

After Stalin's death came first the Malenkov-Khrushchev period, and then the Khrushchev period *tout court.* There is, of course, an old anti-Semitic tradition in Russia (as there is in most countries). Khrushchev himself was not free of an anti-Semitic complex. Though not a Ukrainian but a Russian by birth, he had spent many years in the Ukraine, notorious for its strong anti-Semitic traditions. When, in 1956, he went to Warsaw to deal drastically with the "rebellious" Poles, who had staged their own "October revolution" mainly directed against Russian domination, he not only called Marshal Rokossovsky, the Russian-appointed Polish Minister of

---

* They were charged with having caused, by "medical" means, the deaths of several prominent members of the Soviet hierarchy, among them Shcherbakov and Zhdanov, who had died, respectively, in 1945 and 1948. In reality both had suffered from serious heart trouble, and Shcherbakov, in particular, was enormously and unhealthily fat. It was also alleged that the doctors were preparing to murder several prominent Russian generals, and perhaps Stalin himself.

Defense, a *zhopa,* a horse's ass (*"ty zhopa a ne Marshal"*), but commented angrily on the fact that there were, in the Polish Party and government, too many Abramovitzes and Rabinovitzes who had given themselves Polish names ending in *-ski.* Later, together with his propaganda chief, Leonid Ilyichev, he viciously attacked Ilya Ehrenburg, and these attacks were full of "rootless cosmopolitan" and plainly anti-Semitic innuendoes.

Today, since the fall of Khrushchev, there is a marked improvement in the position of the Russian Jews. No doubt there are minor forms of discrimination still; there are only four Jewish deputies in the Supreme Soviet, and only two or three Jewish members of the Central Committee; but in the government there is one important minister who is Jewish, as is the Vice-Premier, Veniamin Dymshitz. There is one field from which Jews are virtually excluded: the Foreign Ministry and the diplomatic service; but this is substantially also true of Britain, France and many other countries. This is in sharp contrast with the early days of the Revolution, or with the Litvinov regime at the Commissariat for Foreign Affairs.

On the other hand, Jews are very prominent in the Academy of Science, in scientific research, notably in nuclear physics, in engineering, in the administration, in medicine, in journalism, in literature, history, the cinema and music, and even in the Army, which has several Jewish generals. One of the three greatest pianists (the other two are Richter and Sofronitsky), Emil Gillels, is a Jew; apart from these giants, Lev Ginsburg is one of the greatest Chopin and Liszt pianists and Samuel Feinberg the finest Bach performer; all the three greatest Soviet violinists, David Oistrakh, Igor Oistrakh and Leonid Kogan, are Jews; most of the best-known film directors—Heifetz, Mikhail Romm, Mark Donskoy, Sergei Butkevich, Roman Karmen and Alexei Kapler (of Svetlana fame) among them—are also Jews.

There have been social transformations among the Jews, as among all other Soviet nationalities. A high proportion of them are technicians, engineers and ordinary industrial workers, and no longer shopkeepers; of the few hundred "Heroes of Socialist Labor" (the highest industrial distinction) fifty-five are Jews. There is a high proportion of Jews among journalists, though many of them write under "Russian" pseudonyms like Mikhailov, Mayevsky, etc.

Some are among the most violent denunciators of the "Israeli aggressors."

Since ninety-six per cent of the Jews in the Soviet Union live in the cities, there is among them a higher proportion of students than among the population as a whole—315 per 10,000 persons, as against 166 per 10,000 for the whole population of the U.S.S.R. Similarly, out of three million Jews nearly half a million have "higher or specialized secondary education"—fifteen per cent, as against a national average of about five per cent.

As regards religion, this is just as much in decline in the greater part of the Soviet Union among Jews as it is among Russians— probably even more so, since many Russians still have a sentimental attachment to the church and like, at any rate, to be given a church funeral. There is only one large synagogue in Moscow, and there are only two or three small ones in the neighborhood of Moscow; but there are still some forty active churches in Moscow itself, and lots of unreligious people go there for old times' sake or out of curiosity during great church festivals, such as Easter Night, or for the pleasure of hearing the church choirs or of watching the picturesque services.

The Jews, on the other hand, are becoming more and more assimilated, largely through mixed marriages. Once married to a Russian (or a Ukrainian or an Armenian), the Jewish partner almost automatically breaks with any Jewish tradition, religious or otherwise. In 1959 only twenty per cent of the Soviet Jews regarded Yiddish as their mother tongue; the proportion is now estimated to have dropped to not more than ten per cent. In cities like Leningrad and Moscow the Jews (about five per cent of the population) are nearly all "assimilated"*; they are much less so at Kishinev and Czernowitzy (twenty per cent of the population); it is these former parts of Rumania (where the Rumanian government succeeded in saving most of the Jews from Nazi extermination) that one finds the last strongholds of both the Yiddish language and the Jewish religion. Because during the war a large number of Jews were evacuated who have since returned, there is still a ten to fifteen per cent Jewish population in Kiev, Vinnitsa and Odessa in the Ukraine, and in one or two places, such as Gomel, in Belorussia. It is precisely

* Lenin, and even more so Trotsky, regarded assimilation as the best solution of the "Jewish Problem."

in places like Kiev that anti-Semitism is still strongest, this being in the "good old Ukrainian" tradition.

As we have already seen, there is in Russia generally and not only in places like Kiev an anti-Semitic tradition of long standing, though, as my friend Jean Champenois jokingly remarked, "Russian anti-Semitism my foot! The Russians are not only anti-Semites, but also anti-Georgians, anti-Armenians, anti-Ukrainians, anti–all foreigners, of course—in fact, anti-everybody!" It is possible, and indeed probable, that there is here and there some unofficial discrimination against persons of Jewish origin. Thus, it is persistently rumored that, although there is no official *numerus clausus* against Jews anywhere, those responsible for Moscow University, for instance, prefer not to have too high a proportion of Jewish students; if there are five per cent Jews in the population of Moscow, then the tendency is not to allow more than five per cent of Jewish students to enter Moscow University. That such discrimination exists in certain particularly famous universities is suggested by an extensive migration of Jewish students, engineers and scientists to Siberia; thus, in a new city like Yakutsk, which in the last thirty years has grown from 30,000 to 100,000, the proportion of Jews among the teachers and scientists is much higher than, say, in Moscow or Leningrad.

It has also been alleged that in the Academy of Sciences certain Jewish scientists are slower to be appointed to the very top jobs than, say, Russians or Ukrainians. This again is highly probable, but does not some similar discrimination or prejudice exist in most other European countries? Even the presence of Jewish cabinet ministers in the British government sometimes leads to some unpleasantness—take the case of Hore-Belisha, for instance; and if Pierre Mendès-France were called Dupont, would he not, with his extraordinary ability, have made a much more dazzling political career than he actually did?

In short, whatever happened under Stalin and under Khrushchev, I think it may be said that there is no more discrimination against Jews in Russia—except in some parts of the Ukraine—than there is in most other "civilized" countries. And it is becoming less and less of a problem as the assimilation of Jews progresses still further. (The same, unfortunately, cannot be said of Poland, which has a much stronger anti-Semitic tradition than Russia. Its pernicious effect could be observed in 1968, even at the top echelons of Mr. Gomulka's party and, even more so, among General Moczar's "Partisans.")

And this brings us to the notorious question of passports. One would think, listening to some critics of Russia, that the inscription of "Jew" in a Soviet passport was equivalent to Hitler's yellow star, which every Jew had to wear on his sleeve. This is completely wrong. There are two things that must be distinguished: citizenship and nationality. Everybody in the Soviet Union, except, of course, a foreigner, is a Soviet citizen. As Jean Champenois, the former Agence France-Presse correspondent, who has lived in Moscow for over thirty years and has made a special study of the problem, writes:

> *The Soviet citizen is of the nationality to which he declares himself to belong* when, at the age of sixteen,* he has his personal passport delivered to him. The official at the registry office (ZAGS) simply registers the nationality as declared by the person in question. Such an official has no right to verify, dispute or contest the nationality the person wishes to show in his passport. In other words, if you want your passport to say that you are Russian, even if you are an Uzbek, a Ukrainian, a Jew or a Tatar, "Russian" has to be entered. Even if you have the odd fancy to declare yourself Japanese or French you still have the legal right to have your nationality in the Soviet passport marked as Japanese or French; that does not alter the fact that you remain, in any case, a Soviet citizen.
>
> Under the law you also have the right, at any time after reaching the age of sixteen, *to change your nationality;* thus, any Jew can say that he wishes the nationality in his passport to be changed from Jewish to Russian (and even vice versa!). If this is not usually done, it is because it is of no practical importance; nor are such changes encouraged by the Registry Office officials, who have more important things to do. However, if you insist, they would have to accede to your demand.
>
> When a child is born, it is inscribed in its parents' passports, and the parents decide of what nationality the child is to be; thus,

* Under the 1932 passport law, passports are delivered at the age of sixteen. At eighteen, Soviet citizens come of age; at twenty and at forty they have to have their passports re-registered, but after that nothing more has to be done, though nationality can still be changed at any time.

a Tatar couple need not necessarily declare the child Tatar, but, say, Russian or Armenian. At sixteen the person receives his or her own passport and then decides of what nationality he or she is to be. The notion of nationality has nothing to do with either race or religion; no religion is mentioned in any Soviet passport, not even in the Central-Asian republics where the older people, at any rate, do not call themselves Uzbeks or Tadjiks, but simply Moslems. The main purpose of "nationality" is simply statistical.

For some time now there has been talk of abolishing the "nationality" entry in all Soviet passports, so that everybody should be simply a Soviet citizen and nothing else.

And Champenois adds:

It is also perfectly true that Soviet Jews have great difficulty in obtaining an exit visa for going abroad, either temporarily or forever. But then the same is precisely true of *all* Soviet citizens, and not only of Jews. And there are many anti-Semitic Russians (and there are, unfortunately, still plenty of them!) who would be delighted if the Jews could leave the country for good and the frontiers were thrown wide open to them!

Such is the legal position: you choose your own nationality at sixteen. It is certain that the words "Jewish nationality" in your passport represented no handicap until about 1947–48, when Stalin started on his anti-Semitic campaign. After that, Jews found it awkward to change their nationality to, say, Russian; either this change was not taken seriously by the Jew-baiters or it was plainly ridiculous, if the man happened to be called Finkelstein or Rabinovich. To change one's name legally (not merely by adopting a pseudonym) is, however, a lengthy procedure, as it is indeed in many other countries; the reluctance to allow anyone to change his name arises from the suspicion that the person is trying to dodge his creditors or to avoid paying alimony to an ex-wife, etc.

So the Rabinoviches seldom ask for their nationality to be changed, though some do; hence the story of a man applying for a job. "What's your name?" "Rabinovich." "Oh, a Jew!" "No, a Russian." "Well," says the boss, "if we *must* have a Rabinovich, we'd sooner have a Jewish Rabinovich!"

It is the children of Jews with less characteristically Jewish names who find it easiest, at sixteen, to declare themselves Russian or Latvian, etc. I have also known of some peculiar cases of persons of remote Jewish origin whose grandparents were Russian Orthodox and who, when given a passport with "Nationality: Jewish" inscribed, did not protest and demand that it be changed to "Russian." Thus, the wife of a Leningrad writer who had this happen to her simply said, "I did not like them to change 'Jewish' to 'Russian' in case they [the Registry Office people] thought me anti-Semitic." The anti-Semites prefer Jews to preserve their identity; but those indifferent to Jews or friendly toward them consider that as a nationality the Jews should gradually disappear through intermarriage and assimilation. Only ten per cent are now reckoned to be Jewish by language; all the others are already more or less assimilated, and those who are Jewish by religion are, in the main, to be found in a few places like Kishinev and Czernowitz. As a territorial entity, the Jews scarcely exist; the attempt to set up an "autonomous Jewish territory" has proved a failure; in Birobidjan, with its 162,000 inhabitants, only eight per cent today are Jews. Champenois remarks that people are in future to be simply called Soviet citizens, without any nationality being mentioned. This is all the more logical since a high proportion of the national groups no longer coincide with any particular territory. Thus, of the Tatars of the Autonomous Tatar Republic (round Kazan on the Volga) only about one third actually live there; the rest, in the process of industrialization and urbanization, have moved to the Russian Republic, the Ukrainian S.S.R. or other parts of the Soviet Union. Similarly, only fifty-six per cent of Armenians actually live in Armenia; the rest live in other parts of the Soviet Union; while twenty per cent of Russians live outside Russia proper.

In short, there has been so much intermarriage, not only between Jews and non-Jews but amongst all the numerous nationalities of the Soviet Union, that "nationality" often no longer makes any sense. The move to do away with nationality other than Soviet nationality might also be intended to combat those peculiar local nationalisms and those polycentrist tendencies of which Ehrenburg spoke in connection with both the Ukraine and Bashkiria.

So one observes two opposite currents: on the one hand, assimilation and intermarriage and an obvious attempt by the present Soviet rulers to reduce all national particularisms (including those of the Jews); on the other, the revival of essentially anti-Moscow nationalisms, with many nationalities trying to reassert their national identity. Assimilationism would seem the simplest solution for the Jews, with no religious, linguistic or territorial attachment; but if there are to be strong anti-assimilationist (in effect anti-Russian) currents not only in Georgia, Armenia or the Ukraine but even amongst people so little nation-conscious hitherto as certain small nationalities like the Bashkirs and the Kazakhs, will not this, in itself, slow down the assimilation of the Jews and even make them revert to a nationalism of their own? One thing, however, is certain: in Russian eyes Zionism is no solution; the very geography and demography of the Middle East showed up, during the 1967 crisis, the ultimate weakness of Israel; for the alternatives to a very small Israel, able to contain only two or three million people, are either a dangerous kind of expansionism, which can only lead, sooner or later, to a lethal clash with the surrounding hostile Arab world, or de-Zionization.*

If there were any Zionists in Russia before June 1967, there can scarcely be any now. In the long run, it will still be safer and quieter to live in Moscow, or Kiev, or Minsk, or, better still, in Novosibirsk or Yakutsk, than in Jerusalem or Tel Aviv! Or, to put it another way, there is far more room in the vast expanses of the Soviet Union for many more Jews than there is in the tiny Israel enclave. The drift of so many tens of thousands of Jews to the vast, scarcely explored expanses of Siberia is highly characteristic. At Yakutsk there is no local anti-Semitism as there is, say, in Kiev, or even in Moscow. This migration of the Jews to Asiatic Russia is perhaps one of the most significant phenomena in recent years—and, both geographically and psychologically, the very opposite to Zionism, with its oppressive togetherness and exclusiveness.†

* See pp. 219–220.
† It is noteworthy that on this "Jewish question" conclusions very similar to mine were reached by Peter Grose in his contribution, "The Kremlin and the Jews," in *The Anatomy of the Soviet Union* (New York, 1968), an outstanding series of essays by staff members of the New York *Times* (a paper owned by the Jewish families of Ochs and Sulzberger, and with a New York readership at least half of which must be Jewish). The volume is edited by Harrison E. Salisbury, who himself contributes three admirable essays—a survey of Russian history since the 1917 Revolution, a piece on the tragic plight of Soviet literature, and one on Soviet foreign policy.

18

Foreign Friends and
Foreign Enemies

IN the summer of 1967, the Russians were generally exasperated with the Egyptians for having wasted a billion dollars' worth of equipment and for having been so stupidly caught with their pants down.

"What's the good of wasting money on these people?" was a common reaction. Charity-begins-at-home moods are strong in Russia, and perhaps understandably so. Since the Revolution, Russia has had a very hard life; it was not until the last few years that life in Russia could be considered at all normal, and now she has a fair prospect of approaching the Western-European standard of living within the next ten or fifteen years. I was unable to get any comprehensive statistics on what exactly Russia was giving away to the "developing" countries, or to Cuba, or even to Vietnam. According to UN figures, France spends over two per cent of her national income on underdeveloped countries, Britain and the United States about one per cent, and the Soviet Union no more than 0.5 per cent. There are various arguments against spending too much on these countries; India, for example, with her caste system and her sacred cows, is too enormous a country to be helped effectively; she needs some fundamental social changes before she can ever become a modern industrial state. The rulers of the African countries are mostly corrupt, and any help given them usually ends up in a very, very small number of pockets. To win over the Arab world, and particularly Egypt, is much more important; a man like Nasser can be trusted.

CUBA

Cuba now tends to be regarded in the Soviet Union as rather an invention of Khrushchev's, and the memory of the Cuban crisis of October 1962 is an extremely unpleasant one. Because of Cuba— though it was scarcely Cuba's fault—the Soviet Union was very nearly engulfed in a nuclear cataclysm. By 1966 Castro seemed highly conscious of the cooling off of Russia's friendship for him. In the past, Cuban slogans were all to the effect that Cuba was not alone, Cuba could depend on the protection of the mighty Soviet Union. More recently all these slogans gave way to others which say that "we have only ourselves to depend on."* Khrushchev had fancied himself as something of a great revolutionary, but his illusions that Castroism would spread right through Latin America were not taken seriously by his successors. For one thing, since 1966 they had drawn the unpleasant conclusion from the war in Vietnam that the Americans were absolutely ruthless, and that any revolutionary movement in Latin America would be stamped out with napalm, gas, "lazy dogs" and the other fiendish weapons of mass destruction which the American Air Force has been using against the Vietnamese, and which the United States is no doubt still developing.

What, then, are Soviet-Cuban relations in 1968? In the popular view in Russia, Cuba costs us a lot. This is, in reality, not quite right. According to Castro himself, it is untrue that Cuba now has a "subsidized socialism"—subsidized, above all, by the Soviet Union. In his *New Statesman* statement he asserted that the only thing he got free from Russia was armaments; for everything else he had to pay—in cash or, more commonly, in kind. Now, here is one of the difficulties: two of the most important Cuban exports to the Soviet Union are, of course, sugar and cigars. Russia scarcely needs the Cuban sugar, and she resells most of it in the world market—at a profit. Cigars are a different matter. Cuba's greatest market for cigars used to be the United States. Now most of these cigars go to the Soviet Union, who cannot resell them to, say, Western Europe,

* See Castro's statement to K. S. Karol in the *New Statesman* of September 27, 1967.

which can buy them direct from Cuba, nor does she need them herself; the Russian is not a cigar smoker, and very few seem to have taken to Havana cigars. So they are either totally wasted or are bought only as a birthday or New Year present for Father-in-law. Thousands of cigars in Russia simply lie in the shops till they dry up completely and have to be thrown away.

This is, of course, a relatively minor problem. More important is the rapid deterioration in Soviet-Cuban relations, especially during the second half of 1967 and the early months of 1968. The disagreements are of various sorts. Some are ideological; thus, Castro's idea that under real socialism people should be taught to despise money is clearly a Maoist and not a Soviet concept; more important still, the Soviet Union, unlike Cuba, is totally uninterested in fomenting revolutions and guerrilla wars in Latin America, especially since the tragic failure of the Bolivian guerrillas and the death of Che Guevara.

By the time of the Fiftieth Jubilee celebrations in Moscow, it was amply clear how seriously relations with Cuba had deteriorated; neither Castro nor the President of Cuba came to Moscow; only a minor member of the Cuban government represented her, and he scarcely said anything. Worse was still to come. Castro protested to the Russians about their maintaining and developing trade and diplomatic relations with the reactionary "anti-people" governments in Latin America; the Russians rejected these protests. At the beginning of 1968 a "microfaction" inside the Cuban Communist Party was exposed as being "pro-Soviet"; some of its members were tried and sentenced to long terms of imprisonment, its leader, Anibal Escalante, being given fifteen years' imprisonment. A confused and rather unconvincing explanation was offered to the effect that this trial should not be regarded as an anti-Soviet move. The best one can say is that Castro decided to go it alone and to adhere neither to Moscow nor to Peking. And it was largely in order not to offend Peking that he refused to send any Cuban representative to the Communist Budapest Conference at the end of February 1968.

Today one thing seems certain; Castro has no illusions on the subject. His slogan now is "We are alone"; this means in effect that the Cubans are no longer sure that Russia would go to war with the United States even if the latter invaded Cuba. Obviously, the Russians could not intervene directly in Cuba; but would they even occupy, say, West Berlin as a retort to an American attack on Cuba? This might well start some very dangerous chain reaction in the countries of Europe, who, in many—probably most—Russians' view, had better stick to their present status quo; it has, after all, lasted without many disturbances for the last twenty-five years.

"NO WAR WITH THE U.S.A."

There is a sort of fundamental belief that, whatever else the United States does, it will not embark on a nuclear war against the Soviet Union, because even if such a war did not mean the total destruction of both countries, but only a "partial" destruction, the only beneficiary would then be China. That is why there is a deep conviction that nothing would please China better than a war between the U.S.A. and the U.S.S.R. This alleged Chinese ambition is openly discussed. Chinese industrial production is still negligible by Russian and American standards; but if the U.S.A. and the U.S.S.R. were industrially half destroyed, China would very rapidly catch up with what would be left of the Russian and American economies. Hence the alleged attempts to provoke a clash between the two: for instance, the Chinese reluctance to allow anything beyond a bare minimum of Russian supplies for Vietnam to be transported by rail through China, so that the Russians are forced to send most of them by sea from Vladivostock to Haiphong—with a fair prospect of a naval incident between Russia and America, to be followed, with luck, by an all-out war between the two.

RUSSIA AND VIETNAM

A question often asked is whether the Russians would, in any circumstances, go to war with America over Vietnam. When I discussed the matter with Yuri Zhukov, top commentator on international affairs of *Pravda,* in the summer of 1967, he drew attention to one fact which he thought significant. He had said three times in recent weeks in his paper that if the Americans landed land forces in North Vietnam, Russia would have no choice but to intervene, either directly or by sending to North Vietnam airborne "volunteers"; and not a single American paper had, as far as he knew, ever reproduced this warning.

Not that direct Russian intervention in Vietnam would be popular. Today the Russians are sitting pretty. Unlike the United States, Russia is not waging any war anywhere and is proud of being the greatest "peace force" in the world; moreover, there was a strong hope, if not a conviction, in 1967 that sooner or later American public opinion would turn against Johnson and force him to accept some kind of face-saving settlement. The growing unpopularity of the war in Vietnam, especially among the young people in the United States, was closely watched. It had been foreseen by the Russians for a long time. If there was much admiration for de Gaulle's definite stand against the war, there were disgust and anger with Britain's "feebleness"; for if France by herself could not stop the war, Britain plus France, it was believed, certainly could. When, in November 1967, the pound was devalued, it was felt that this disposed of the one solid argument Harold Wilson had for not coming out openly against the war in Vietnam.

There was, of course, much sympathy for (to use the usual Russian newspaper cliché) "the heroic and long-suffering people of Vietnam"—both the people of the North and the guerrillas of the South. In 1967 there was felt to be an incredible cynicism on the part of the United States to pursue what is, in reality, a quite senseless war. It is doubtful whether if it came to the point the Russians would insist on the immediate evacuation of all American troops before any negotiations could be begun. It is even possible that the Russians might accept something on the lines of the statement made to Harrison Salisbury of the New York *Times,* during his visit to Hanoi in January 1967, by a leader of the Vietcong to the effect that the Vietcong might well consider at least the temporary division of the country in two, the North remaining a "socialist" country and the South a "democratic" country, its "democratic" government excluding, however, such an archfascist as "What-we-need-is-a-Hitler" Marshal Ky. The fact that the Russians are chary of going all-out in their anti-Americanism in relation to the war may be seen from their refusal to send any representatives to the Bertrand Russell War Crimes Tribunal which, in the end, convicted the United States as being guilty of genocide.

RUSSIA'S ARAB FRIENDS

In a sense, the war in Vietnam is playing into the Russians' hands; it makes them out to be the great peace factor in the world, and the United States the great war factor; it raises their prestige in the eyes of the Third World and makes the American hawks, with their napalm and "lazy dogs" and the other wonders of American military technology for killing hundreds of thousands, perhaps millions, of innocent Vietnamese, particularly odious. It is true that these "genocide" tactics in Vietnam are having a discouraging effect in Latin America and Black Africa; if, as a result of the Israel–Arab war, the Russians have spread their sphere of influence to the grateful Arab world, it is a very substantial gain—and at relatively very little cost. Moreover, the Arab world is very close to the borders of the Soviet Union, and indirectly all sorts of gains may be made in supporting the Arabs against Israel and her American patrons (without whom Israel would of course be "nothing"). I have already referred to the Suez Canal; sooner or later, the canal will have to be reopened to shipping, and the Russians, with Nasser's support, might well make a bid for a new regime for international waterways generally—in particular, one affecting the Black Sea Straits.

VIETNAM AND CHINA

Yes, there is much sympathy for the "heroic and long-suffering people of Vietnam"; and yet Vietnam too is a long way away, and between Vietnam and Russia there is the vast and unpredictable physical, moral and political barrier of China. Some Russians I talked to wondered whether the Vietnamese, being "much more like the Chinese than like us to look at," were not more pro-Chinese than pro-Russian; when I replied that, having studied the history of Vietnam, I was certain that the Vietnamese were at heart only one thing, pro-Vietnamese, with a long and traditional dislike of China —who had always tried to dominate and conquer them—they were not entirely convinced. There were also some Russians who were taking a sort of humanitarian, if not downright defeatist, line to the effect that it was all very well for Ho Chi Minh and Pham Van Dong and the rest of the Vietnamese leaders, "sitting safely inside their antinuclear shelters," to expect the Vietnamese people to sacrifice themselves like this day after day, instead of getting at least the best possible terms from the Americans. And also young people in Russia, happy to be out of it all, were to a certain extent indifferent to a war that was being waged a long way away and, above all, were rather tired of all the blah in the press about it. Ehrenburg told me that when he declared to an audience of mostly young people at a Soviet–Vietnam friendship meeting that he had not brought (or written) any poem on Vietnam, there were loud cheers and much laughter.

THE U.S.A. AND GERMANY: WHO IS ENEMY NUMBER ONE?

Not that Ehrenburg was particularly pleased with this reaction. He thought the young people of Russia were much too interested in their own welfare to care about anybody; things were very different in the days of the Spanish Civil War, when millions in Russia (and not only in Russia) felt very strongly about helping the Spanish republicans against the Nazi and Italian Fascist interventionists. But there was this difference, of course: Nazi Germany was (already very obviously) the Soviet Union's enemy number one. With America one was not sure of that at all; whatever the Americans did (unless they went completely crazy and suicidal), they would not attack Russia. America was a "major nuisance" rather than a direct menace: but for her, Russia would not have to spend a vast proportion of her national income on armaments and would be infinitely more prosperous than she was. What is more, Russia would be a freer country; the armaments race was tending to maintain in Russia a hard regime, with the Stalinist bureaucracy still very reluctant to abandon its command posts and to allow the country to return to something like the ideal democratic centralism of Lenin, with free discussion and a direct participation of the people in the running of the economy and of public affairs generally.

And then also Vietnam was costing Russia a lot of money,

probably about two billion dollars a year, or nearly as much as the United States had spent, on the yearly average, on Lend-Lease to Russia during the Second World War. But it was not possible for Russia to abandon North Vietnam, a friendly socialist country, to her fate, still less abandon her to the tender mercies of China, with the Chinese getting all the credit in the Third World for being alone in helping Vietnam.

In theory, the United States is Russia's enemy number one. But only in theory. The nuclear "balance of terror," if nothing else, makes a Soviet-American war very unlikely; moreover, there has never been a war between Russia and America, and there is no area in the world today where American and Russian interests clash in any violent way. If the Americans strongly felt that it was their duty to the "free world" to destroy Communism, they would—and should—have started long ago on destroying Russia (rather than little Vietnam); but, as de Gaulle said, there were at least a dozen different Communisms, and the Russian variety has become one of the most innocuous, with the concept of the nation state strongly predominating over that of revolutionary mission in the world.

No, the United States is not enemy number one, but only enemy number three. Enemy number one—at least in Russian popular imagination—is China; and enemy number two is West Germany. The young generation of Russians, those born during or since the war, have no direct experience of the Nazi invasion, but they are constantly reminded of it in books, on radio and TV, and in films. One of the best things to have happened after the war, in the Russian view, was the division of Germany into two states; at least one third of Germany is free of the Nazi poison and of dreams of revenge. Even if there are some secret Nazis in East Germany, they at least keep very quiet about it. At heart, most Russians distrust *all* Germans, whether East or West; all the same, they are conscious of the fact that, economically, the German Democratic Republic, after several very hard years of reconstruction and near-famine, is proving a major success; and it is hoped that at least the young generation of East Germans are beginning to accept the socialist way of life. One great thing plays in favor of this. Whether she deserved it or not, Germany suffered in the war, too, and not least East Germany. The ruthless (and unnecessary) destruction of Dresden in East Germany by the RAF toward the very end of the war, with

135,000 people being killed in one night, is something of which the
East-German government never ceases to remind its citizens.

West Germany is a very different matter. In August 1967, one of
Mr. Gromyko's right-hand men, speaking of Kosygin's meeting with
President Johnson in Glassboro, told me that there were two main
reasons why, in spite of everything, the Soviet Premier still decided
to meet Lyndon Johnson: to get a move-on with the nonprolifera-
tion treaty, to which the Russians attach the greatest importance,
and secondly (and this was even more important) to warn the
President that if the West Germans were to get atomic or nuclear
weapons "in any shape or form" the Russians would not hesitate to
take the law into their own hands. There was one thing on which
they were prepared to take the gravest risks, even the risk of another
world war, and that was a renewed threat of a German invasion of
Russia.

Whether, in the event of the West Germans being armed with
nuclear weapons, the Russians would occupy the country or simply
drop a few H-bombs on it Kosygin did not say to Johnson, but the
Foreign Office official "fervently hoped" that the West Germans
would draw the necessary conclusions from the very severe warning
given them via the American President; if, in their anger, they were
now turning to neo-Nazism, it couldn't be helped. What Kosygin
meant to convey was that even if, in the process of a third world
war again unleashed by the Germans, America and Russia more or
less destroyed each other, West Germany would certainly be the first
to be wholly exterminated.

It is hoped in Russia that even the neo-Nazis are fully conscious
of this fact and will be extremely careful not to do anything foolish.

IS CHINA ENEMY NUMBER ONE?

Quite a different matter is China. Either top Russian officials do not
take the military power of China terribly seriously or else they say
that for all their bluster and screaming the Chinese are in reality
extremely cautious people, carefully calculating every step in their
foreign policy. If they were as fanatical as they like to sound, would
they allow Hong Kong to go on existing as it does? If they were all
that fanatical, would they not have intervened in the Vietnam War

long ago? On the contrary, *they* are anxious to avoid a war with the United States; but nothing would please them better than a war between Russia and America.

The Russians, of course, do not say this; but at heart no doubt some of them would welcome the destruction by the Americans not of China generally, but of China's nuclear industries. For the Chinese H-bomb, not to mention the apparently already quite considerable number of Chinese A-bombs, presents one of the great unpredictables in the world today. Top Russian officials take the line that the Chinese will use these bombs as a bargaining counter, even as a piece of blackmail, but will never dare start an atomic war against either Russia or America; they also doubt that any Chinese is insane enough genuinely to believe that there will always be enough Chinese left to carry on, therefore China can afford to embark on a nuclear war. On the contrary, they say, China is much more vulnerable than either America or Russia; most of the population is concentrated in a relatively small area.

Mr. Sergei Lapin, until the end of 1966 Soviet ambassador in China, was not taking an unduly serious view of the "Chinese menace"; no doubt, he said, the Chinese would love Russia to get into a war with America, but "they could just wait." He did not take the Cultural Revolution very seriously, either; China's economy was still so primitive that it did not even interfere very much with it. He thought certain sectors of the economy were undoubtedly under full government control, for the Chinese would never otherwise have managed to produce their H-bomb. Asked why he had been withdrawn from Peking, he jokingly remarked, "Well, if the Soviet ambassador is beaten up, that's a major diplomatic incident; if the chargé d'affaires is beaten up, it's only a minor one." And he thought that in the end China and the Soviet Union would restore what he called "reasonably friendly relations."

But this kind of relative optimism is shared neither by the Soviet press nor, still less, by the ordinary public in Russia. For one thing, it is clear to the latter, at any rate, that the real quarrel with China is not over ideology, that it is, in reality, a quarrel between two nation states; that the Chinese, already 700 or 800 million strong, will soon have a billion people, and that their population cauldron may well explode some day, and that there is something particularly sinister in the frequent incidents on the Chinese–Soviet border, and in the territorial claims made on various Russian territories in Central Asia and the Far East allegedly stolen from China by the Russian tsars.

MAO'S CULTURAL REVOLUTION

We cannot here examine Soviet–Chinese relations during the last fifty years or so; but it is enough to say that relations between Stalin and the Chinese Communists under Mao Tse-tung were, to say the least, ambiguous. Always putting "Russian security" first, Stalin was not at all helpful to the Chinese Communists. He failed to help them in 1927 when the urban Communists in Shanghai were ruthlessly exterminated by the thousand by Chiang Kai-shek. When the war with Germany was nearing its end, Stalin, in speaking to the Americans, whom he wished not to offend, treated the Chinese Communists as not real and not serious Communists, and he kept on urging the latter to come to terms with the Kuomintang. Even as late as 1948, with the Kuomintang in complete decay, Stalin continued to press on Mao the necessity for the Chinese Communists to "cooperate" with the Kuomintang and Chiang Kai-shek. In the Far East after the Second World War, just as in Europe before it, Stalin was anxious to preserve the status quo, so as not to allow Russia to become involved in any major crisis. In China in 1948 Stalin still dreaded to provoke the Americans by backing Mao against Chiang Kai-shek. When Mao won his dazzling victory in 1949 without Russia, and even despite Russia, there was little choice for Stalin but to "recognize" the Chinese Communist government. But even after that relations were never very cordial, and the Chinese were made to pay heavily for any economic help received from Russia and even for the help given them during their own intervention in the Korean War.

After Stalin's death, when "his successors disbanded the joint-stock companies [profitable to Russia], renounced direct control, and waived the humiliating conditions that Stalin had attached to aid, . . . the time seemed auspicious for the establishment of something like a socialist commonwealth between the Elbe and the seas of China."*

* Deutscher, *The Unfinished Revolution*, p. 91.

For a time, indeed, Russia greatly helped China to build her new industries and even promised her atom bombs; but in the end, according to Deutscher, the interests of the nation state prevailed. Perhaps it was no coincidence that the massive aid to China should have been stopped in 1960, soon after Khrushchev's "peaceful coexistence" visit to the United States.

The Russians, of course, give a different interpretation to the withdrawal of the thousands of Russian engineers and technicians from China. Thus, Suslov, in his famous speech of February 1964, declared not only that the withdrawal had been made necessary because the Chinese had embarked on their disastrous Great Leap Forward experiment, which had made nonsense of all Russian planning, but that as early as the spring of 1960 the Chinese had started brainwashing Soviet specialists, trying to arouse their hostility to the Central Committee of the CPSU and to the Soviet government itself.* At the end of the same year, according to Suslov, both Mikoyan and Khrushchev proposed to the Chinese leadership that the Russian specialists should be sent back to China "provided they were allowed to work in normal conditions," but these proposals met with no response.

But things went from bad to worse; the hopes entertained in Russia that with the fall of Khrushchev, the "archrevisionist," Soviet–Chinese relations would improve did not come true. In 1965 the Chinese "Cultural Revolution" was initiated. For a year after that, the Soviet papers were filled with Chinese atrocity stories—for instance, that of a Chinese pianist who had his hands smashed to pulp because he played "degenerate Western music," or that of the composer Ma Sy-tsung, as told by himself in the Moscow *Literaturnaya Gazeta* in July 1967, about how he had to flee abroad, since his pupils at the Peking Musical Academy, after putting him and his family through a series of the most refined and elaborate humiliations, had threatened to kill them. In the course of his "re-education" he and other "criminals" had to sing every morning and every evening this "Howl of the Black Gangsters" chorus:

> *I am a monster with a cow's head;*
> *I sinned, I sinned, I sinned.*

* M. A. Suslov, *O borbe KPSS za splochennost mezhdunarodnogo kommunisticheskogo dvizheniya* (Moscow, 1964), p. 59.

I must submit to the people's dictatorship,
For I am an enemy of the people.
I must be very candid,
But if I'm not
Then tear me limb from limb.

In a long article in *Pravda* on August 16, 1967, called "Against the Interests of the Chinese People," I. Alexandrov analyzes what he calls the "real nature" and the "deplorable results" of Mao's Cultural Revolution:

> Far from resulting in those great "victories" of which they boast, the Cultural Revolution—which has nothing to do with either socialism or culture—has merely inflicted the most appalling ordeals on the Chinese people and is threatening the socialist achievements of the past, besides isolating China more and more in the international arena.

According to Alexandrov, the real trouble started in the late 1950s, when Mao decided on the Great Leap Forward, which meant nothing less than skipping over several normal stages in the economic development of the country, and creating, in the social sphere, a "barrack-room" regime which would mark an immediate transition to what Mao and his friends thought fit to call Communism—in reality an absurd parody of the latter.

The proclamation of the Great Leap Forward came at the end of eight years in which, with the help of the Soviet Union and the other socialist countries, the Chinese people had successfully carried out their first Five-Year Plan and had thereby laid the foundations for the rapid growth of the economy, the development of culture and a rise in the living standard of the Chinese people.

> But for the voluntarist decisions of Mao and his colleagues, the Chinese People's Republic could have successfully continued along its socialist course after 1957. Instead, ignoring the experience of the other socialist countries, Mao and his friends tried to replace the normal industrialization process by the creation of countless primitive artisan enterprises . . . and the creation of both urban and rural "communes" in which people were to live like soldiers.

. . . All warnings from the Chinese people's foreign friends were ignored.

This introduction of a military-barrack regime, together with the organization of both urban and rural labor on the basis of a primitive kind of egalitarianism, could only lead to "disastrous results":

> The Great Leap Forward wholly disorganized the Chinese economy; industrial production was cut in half, and agriculture found itself in a state of decay. Millions of people died of hunger.* The loudly heralded "quick transition to Communism" had proved a failure. . . . Then, completely contradicting himself, Mao announced that the building of socialism in China was a very long-term affair and might take a hundred or even a few hundred years.

This failure of the Great Leap Forward produced a serious crisis inside China; Mao and his friends retorted to the criticisms by carrying out a purge in the Party, in the National Liberation Army and among the intellectuals.

It was also in 1960, together with the failure of the Great Leap Forward, that the Peking leaders openly opposed the general line of the international Communist movement. Using an ultraleftish phraseology, they demanded a speeding up of the world revolution. Though it was not stated openly, the Peking leaders were striving, in their chauvinist way, to acquire a special and exclusive position for China in the international arena.

> Having met with a strong retort from the true Marxist-Leninist parties, the Chinese Communist leaders then proceeded to set up and finance anti-Party groups in various countries—groups composed of all kinds of adventurers and renegades. To egg these people on, the Peking leaders hurled at the bulk of the working-class parties the slanderous charge of revisionism.

The most violent attacks of all were launched against the CPSU. With the attack by armed bands against the Soviet ship *Svirsk,* and the provocations by bands of young hooligans against the Soviet

* This is flatly denied by Edgar Snow in *The Other Side of the River* (New York, 1962), p. 619.

Embassy in Peking, it was obvious that the Mao Tse-tung group was trying to bring about further complications in Soviet–Chinese relations. Alexandrov continues:

> While trying to provoke grave military incidents outside Chinese territory [an obvious reference to Chinese attempts to bring about a Soviet–American clash] the Maoists started inside China an absurd slanderous campaign about the "encirclement" of China by the combined forces of [American] imperialism and [Soviet] socialism. Before long, the Mao Tse-tung group made it perfectly clear that, despite all its leftist phraseology, the policy it was pursuing was a mixture of petty-bourgeois adventurism and Great-Power chauvinism.

Alexandrov then comes to the opposition which Mao's policy met "amongst numerous members of the Chinese Communist Party and politically educated members of the Chinese working class and peasantry, as well as amongst the Chinese intellectuals." Instead of recognizing his errors, Mao proceeded to take reprisals against these people; and, in launching his so-called Great Proletarian Cultural Revolution, he decided to set up in the country a bureaucratic and military dictatorship. The Cultural Revolution had nothing to do with culture, but assumed the forms of a terrorist movement against the Party, Komsomol and trade-union cadres, and against the intellectuals and the more progressive members of the working class and the peasantry.

The campaign was started in the spring of 1966 in the form of a violent attack by the Army newspaper on the Peking Party Committee. The same paper now glorified Mao and his Great Leap Forward, blaming on others all the misfortunes it had brought about. This persecution of the enemies of Mao Tse-tung spread from Peking to the rest of the country. Before long it was clear that what the Cultural Revolution amounted to was an attempt to concentrate all political and military power in the hands of the Mao group. The executive organs of the Cultural Revolution were now the security police and the Army. To give this conspiracy the appearance of a popular movement, the so-called *hun-weibin* teams were formed, consisting of schoolchildren, students and other youngsters fanaticized in a spirit of chauvinism and practicing the personality cult of Mao.

After describing some of the more revolting methods of these young people, who before long embarked on an "uncontrollable, irrepressible orgy of violence" in which "parading an enemy of Mao's through the streets wearing a fool's cap is mild punishment compared with the beatings-up, tortures and murder," Alexandrov says in effect that it was finally the Army and the secret police who had to direct and control the activities of these fanaticized young people. For his own part, Mao was now setting up "Revolutionary Committees" to take the place of the regular Party organs, the Party having in fact been purged at every level, as had the Chinese government. In the Central Committee of the Chinese Communist Party alone, two thirds of the members had in one way or another been eliminated. But there proved to be some opposition to Mao in the Army too, so this also had undergone a purge.

All this, to older Russian readers, must have had an uncannily familiar ring: personality cult, the Chinese equivalent of Yezhov or Beria, the elimination of two thirds of the Central Committee, finally a purge in the Army. And what difference is there between the description of Mao as "the brightest of all bright suns" and certain "Odes to Stalin," by Djambul, the one-hundred-year-old Kazakh bard, which appeared on the front page of *Pravda* around 1938?

As Alexandrov remarks, the only major difference between China now and Russia then is that in the midst of the chaos created in China by the Cultural Revolution, which had also had a deplorable effect on the people's standard of living, the bourgeoisie was being left in peace. As for a Military Committee having been appointed to supervise the activities of the Chinese Academy of Sciences, this also had, to Russians, a remarkably familiar ring, what with Lysenko, Zhdanov and similar sacred monsters.

So, oddly enough, many Russians found some consolation in *Pravda*'s description of the major absurdities of Mao's Cultural Revolution: "We've had all this kind of thing ourselves, and we survived it. So there's hope for China."

RUSSIAN POPULAR FEELING AGAINST CHINA

There was a time, between 1953 and 1959, when relations between China and the Soviet Union seemed good, and the Soviet leadership had, in the words of M. A. Suslov, "a disinterested and internationalist attitude" to China. Not that this meant that all or most of the Russian aid to China was given free of charge. Suslov described this aid as follows in his speech of February 14, 1964:

> Our Party and our people know of the help we gave to China. . . . We helped her to set up over two hundred large plants, workshops and other economic objectives, all provided with the most modern equipment. With our help, entire new branches of industry, which had never existed before, sprang up in China, among them an aircraft industry, an automobile and tractor industry, industries producing machine tools and electrical equipment, and various new branches of the chemical industry.
>
> All these industries, built or re-equipped with Soviet help, enable China now to produce 8.7 million tons of pig iron, 8.4 million tons of steel, 32.2 million tons of coal and shale. . . .

After giving some further details of all the benefits the Soviet Union had brought to a genuine industrialization of China, Suslov turned to the personal services rendered by the Russians to the Chinese:

> Between 1950 and 1960 over ten thousand Soviet specialists were sent to China for periods of varying length; between 1951 and 1962 about ten thousand Chinese engineers, technicians and skilled workers received scientific and practical training in the Soviet Union. During the same period over eleven thousand Chinese students and postgraduate students graduated from Soviet universities and other higher-education establishments.

And Suslov made a point of saying that Chinese–Soviet relations greatly improved after Stalin's death.

> This cooperation reached its highest point after 1953 when, on the initiative of the Central Committee of the CPSU and of Comrade Khrushchev himself, all elements of inequality were removed in our relations, such elements having arisen from the Stalin "personality cult."

And he even added this startling tribute from Mao Tse-tung himself: "On the Chinese question," Mao Tse-tung said in 1957, "all the credit for the liquidation of all the unpleasantnesses must go to Comrade N. S. Khrushchev personally."*

Suslov went on to say that up to 1959 there had been a constant growth in Soviet–Chinese mutual aid, the Soviet Union also benefiting from it; she had, during those years, "received valuable commodities of Chinese export," had exchanged scientific information with the Chinese and had worked, together with China, to "consolidate peace in their joint struggle against imperialism and colonialism." Suslov also recalled (but we must remember that this speech was made in February 1964) Khrushchev's message to President Eisenhower in the autumn of 1958: "An attack on the People's Republic of China, a great friend, ally and neighbor of our country, will be regarded as an attack on the Soviet Union itself."

The gradual termination of Soviet–Chinese "cooperation" Suslov naturally attributed entirely to the Chinese, who, with their Great Leap Forward, had made complete nonsense of Soviet industrial and technical aid; and the last straw was when the Chinese started "brainwashing" the Soviet specialists and engineers against the Soviet Union.

I remember my visit to the Soviet Union in 1959, when there were still many thousands of Chinese students there. They were not popular with the Russian students; but they were unpopular in a quite different way from, say, African students, who were perhaps the most unpopular of all foreign students in Russia. The Africans— and this was true in both 1959 and 1967—were not only poor workers, they were arrogant and provocative. Any Russian rebuff they hastened to attribute to Russian "anti-black racialism," saying that the Russians were "worse than the Americans in their hatred of Negroes." The Russians, for their part, attributed their dislike of Africans not to any color prejudice but to the fact that most of these Africans claimed to be princes or princelings or tribal chiefs and belonged in reality to the "neocolonialist plutocracy." Whether because of their arrogant social manner or simply because of their skin, the Russians certainly strongly discouraged any "fraternization" between African students and Russian girls. The attitude to other "colored" students was entirely different in this respect; if there was a prejudice against Africans, there was none against Indians, Arabs or Japanese.

* M. A. Suslov, *op. cit.,* pp. 52–53.

The antipathy to the Chinese students was of quite a different order: the Russian students found that *they worked too hard;* they were determined to get top marks in every class and in every subject; they kept apart from the Russian students and ganged together in preparing for exams, swotting collectively. As a result, the Chinese very often proved by far the most brilliant students in Russian universities and technical colleges, and the more easygoing Russian students looked upon them with a mixture of admiration and acute envy. They also took a poor view of such Chinese gestures as asking the university authorities, "in the name of socialism," to cut their student grants by one third or one half, since they "could live on less." Altogether, the Chinese students left in Russia the impression of belonging to a people of immense talent, efficiency, intelligence and an unequaled capacity for work.

There is good reason to suppose that, whatever "provocations" there may have been from the Chinese side, the Russians were glad to have an excuse to stop extensive and intensive economic aid to China in 1960. In other words, it became important for Russia not to turn China, in a very short time, into a vast industrial power; this would also have given China that additional international prestige which would have helped her to claim for Peking the "central" position in the world Communist movement held up till then, however precariously, by Moscow. The Russians, including Stalin, had always been highly sensitive to this question of the "center" of the world Communist movement; as early as 1949 they even ignominiously expelled from Russia their very, very old friend Anna Louise Strong for having dared to suggest that the center of the Communist movement was shifting from Moscow to Peking. (Miss Strong, though in her eighties, is now Mao Tse-tung's top propagandist in China and enjoys Mao's personal friendship more than any other foreigner ever did.)

There is another possible argument why the Russians stopped their aid to China, and that was the danger of having, in the name of socialist solidarity, to pool economic resources with China—which would inevitably have meant a lowering of the Russian standard of living. As Deutscher puts it:

> After Stalin's death . . . the time seemed auspicious for the establishment of something like a socialist commonwealth between

the Elbe and the seas of China. In such a commonwealth one-third of mankind would have jointly planned its economic and social development on the basis of a broad rational division of labour. . . . Socialism might at last have begun to turn into an "international event."

[This] would no doubt have met with a host of difficulties, arising out of the huge discrepancy between the . . . standards of living and the national traditions of the many participating nations. *The cleavage between the haves and the have-nots . . . would have made itself felt in any case. The have-nots, the Chinese in the first place, were bound to press for an equalization of the economic levels and the standards of living . . . and their demands could not but clash with rising consumer expectations in the Soviet Union, Czechoslovakia and East Germany.* [My italics.]*

If, much to Deutscher's disgust, nothing came of it, it was because of the "national self-sufficiency" and the "bureaucratic arrogance" particularly of the Russians. Here, indeed, we come up against the same charity-begins-at-home mood of the Russians, busy as they were, in the 1950s, raising their own standard of living to an unprecedently high level. Even this "unprecedented" standard was not very high compared with, say the Western-European average; to pool Russia's economic resources with China meant raising slightly the have-not standard of 700 or 800 million Chinese, but at the same time lowering very appreciably the standard of living of the 200-odd million Soviet citizens. As Deutscher suggests, such sacrifices for the good of international socialism would have been even less appreciated in countries like Czechoslovakia and East Germany. It was, in fact, a choice between conforming, more or less, with European standards of living and at least partly descending to the Asiatic or, more specifically, Chinese standard.

Russia, in the summer of 1967, was very conscious of China's deep hostility to her. There were many who were saying that not America and not even West Germany (which, if necessary, could be wiped out in no time) was enemy number one, and that China was. If at the high Soviet level the Chinese H-bomb was not—not yet—taken very seriously, ordinary Russians felt that sooner or later

* Deutscher, *op. cit.,* p. 91.

there would inevitably be a showdown with China. Already there was talk about countless frontier incidents which were supposed to be taking place along the infernally long Soviet–Chinese border; there were also some discreet references to them in the press, notably in an article in *Pravda* of July 19 by Konstantin Simonov, writing from Khabarovsk on the Soviet–Manchurian border. I met officers' wives who were extremely worried about their husbands who were somewhere along that border. Fantastic stories were told about one, two or three million Soviet troops being stationed there. Some pessimists went so far as to say that it could end only in a Soviet–American alliance against China. (There was a short story in the *Atlantic Monthly* about an atom bomb having suddenly been dropped on Ryazan, a town about a hundred miles southeast of Moscow. Washington produced evidence to show that it was a Chinese bomb which was intended for Moscow, but had been dropped on Ryazan by mistake. The story ended with the American and Soviet chiefs of staff leaning over a map of China. Russians who heard about this piece of science fiction did not think it funny.)

All sorts of wild rumors and stories were current in Moscow that summer. one was that all provisions had already been made for the decentralization and evacuation of Moscow if necessary. There was also the macabre incident of somebody blowing himself up in the Red Square, outside the Lenin Mausoleum, and several Chinese cameramen happening, by some strange coincidence, to be present. Half jokingly people were also saying that the Chinese were sure to do something spectacular for the Fiftieth Jubilee of the October Revolution—perhaps invade Mongolia, which they regarded as part of China, but which, since the early twenties, had been a sort of Russian protectorate. Or they might even, on November 7, blow up the Kremlin—difficult to arrange, "but then the Chinese are such infernally clever people."

In reality, nothing sensational happened on November 7, except that two junior members of the Chinese Embassy (the only Chinese present) walked out at a great Kremlin celebration in the middle of Brezhnev's speech when he referred to China more in sorrow than in anger.

But the Soviet press was quite amusing to watch during those November days. The Russians claimed to have received numerous messages from "loyal Chinese friends of the Soviet Union," whose names, however, could not be mentioned—it was more than their lives were worth; at the same time the Soviet press spoke indignantly of some "unnamed Russians"—"obviously nonexistent"—who, according to Peking, were telling the Chinese that "countless sane Soviet Russians" were longing desperately for one thing: "that the banner of President Mao's ideas be planted on top of the Kremlin." The same "nonexistent" Russians also claimed that "the brightest sun shining in every Russian's heart"—except for the "revisionist traitors"—was President Mao.

On a much smaller scale this kind of thing has, of course, happened before. In 1948–49 the Russians claimed that all true Yugoslav patriots were pro-Stalin and anti-Tito, while the Yugoslavs claimed that all true Soviet patriots could not but rebel against Stalin's tyranny and feel the deepest sympathy for freedom-loving Yugoslavia. I don't know how many pro-Russians there are in China; I doubt that there are many Maoists in Russia, though, deep down, some ideological Communist purists in Russia may not feel altogether easy about Russian policy with regard to China and about the facility with which all the trouble is attributed to the "Mao group" or even to the "Mao clique," which allegedly has nothing in common with the Great Chinese People.

To the ordinary run of Russians, the trouble is, of course, that the Chinese people are great—far *too* great; soon there will be a thousand million of them, four times more people than in the whole of the Soviet Union. And China today is the only country in the world to have made far-reaching claims on Soviet territory—a dangerous, and possibly literally explosive, situation between a big have country and an even bigger have-not country, both armed with nuclear weapons.

One question, however, to which it is very hard to get a clear answer, despite Khrushchev's warning to Eisenhower in 1958, is: What would Russia do if the United States today attacked China? Would the socialist-solidarity principle come into its own again; or would the nation-state interest prevail over all else, with an additional incentive to sit back—for if an American war against little Vietnam may still be "profitable," one against China might well ruin even America, and Russia's economic and political power would rise in the world accordingly.

However, the whole Soviet–Chinese quarrel is not perhaps nearly as serious as is often assumed. Already, by the end of 1967, much better cooperation than before was developed between the two countries in helping Vietnam. My old friend Julio Álvarez del Vayo, the former Foreign Minister of the Spanish government during the civil war of 1936–39, and the "last optimist," as he had once described himself, had spent two months in China during the previous summer. It was his third visit in the last two years, and each time he had spoken to Mao. What del Vayo now said in effect was that the wild Chinese charges against the Russians were on the whole every bit as absurd as the Russian charges against China. In time it would all blow over. And meantime, he said, there was one thing of which he was certain: among the Chinese people there was no hatred of Russia or the Russians. No doubt, they had been bitterly disappointed when Khrushchev stopped economic aid to China and withdrew the Russian engineers and technicians; and, strangest of all, many of these Russian engineers and technicians literally wept as they were leaving China. And the Chinese H-bomb, del Vayo said, was not dangerous. The Chinese would never use it, unless attacked; but it gave them a greater feeling of security and self-confidence.

I asked him whom he thought the Chinese hated more, the Russians or the Americans. He replied, "They don't hate either; but they have strong grievances aginst both. On the whole, they still dislike the Americans more than they dislike the Russians."

And another thing del Vayo said was this: "If the Russians, looking back on the last fifty years, have reason to be proud, how much more reason have the Chinese for having within less than twenty years turned a completely chaotic country into a country which is orderly, disciplined and, by Chinese standards, more prosperous than ever before? One must understand the Chinese people's love for Mao. Thus, an elderly Chinese worker told me, 'This is an altogether different country from what it was when I was a child. My father died of hunger, and my mother was so poor that she had to sell my twelve-year-old sister to a brothel.' And that was less than fifty years ago. Neither of these things is remotely conceivable today. And if the Russians are proud of *their* achievements, the Chinese have even more reason to be proud of theirs. Today *nobody* in China dies of starvation."

19

Literature in Transition

READERS will have seen that the one aspect of Russia today that I—and not only I, but hundreds of Russian writers and millions of Russian readers—are least happy about is the state of affairs in literature. Everything else seems to be going marvelously well. Economic development since the war has been altogether spectacular. The housing problem has been nearly resolved. The health service is admirable. The Russian people give one the impression of being the best-read, most cultured people in the world. There are no national or racial hatreds to speak of. Nowhere in the world is Russia today waging a war. Science has emancipated itself. There is, of course, a crying need for a little revolution in shopping and the whole distribution system generally. But only in art and literature is the heavy weight of authority making itself felt to an almost unbearable—to some, wholly unbearable—extent.

THE BIRTH OF SOCIALIST REALISM

The golden age of Soviet literature was in the 1920s, a decade which produced writers of talent and even genius—Babel, and Vsevolod Ivanov, and Zamiatin, and Pilnyak, and Paustovsky, and Katayev, and Ilf and Petrov, and Zoshchenko—and when the present "old men" like Fedin and Leonov were young and dynamic writers. Mayakovsky was the great revolutionary poet of those years; other great poets who flourished during that decade were Esenin, Pasternak, Zabolotsky, Bagritsky and many more. Some were later purged or driven to suicide.

When the Writers' Union was formed in 1932, under the chairmanship of Gorki, it seemed that this was a step in the liberal direction. For two years before that, RAPP, the Russian Association of Proletarian Writers, had tried to establish a particularly savage dictatorship over literature. The much more independent LEF (Levyi Front Isskustva), the Left Art Front, had been absorbed into RAPP in 1929–30, a terrible capitulation which may well have contributed to Mayakovsky's suicide in 1930. Zamyatin could not stand the oppressive atmosphere and, with Stalin's permission, emigrated to France. RAPP had reached its most objectionable point in 1932, when writers were almost forced to travel in brigades to industrial plants, and when the proletarian writer reigned supreme. The end of the NEP and the defeat of Trotsky (who of course abhorred the notion of proletarian literature) had obviously made RAPP particularly cocky.

The Writers' Union was really formed to suppress the power of RAPP, and to give another chance to the "fellow travelers," who had been silenced since 1929. Gorki started the Writers' Union with apparently the best of intentions: it was, he said, high time to abolish "the military Communism in the arts." Although this finished the RAPP tyranny, it created something much worse in the long run, though something Gorki had probably not foreseen. With the establishment of the Wrtiers' Union, all writers' groups were brought under one roof, subject to one committee and, for the first time, to a single censorship board. The effect was to incorporate literature effectively into the state machinery. Gorki, anxious to free writers like Pilnyak and Leonov, and others who had flourished in the 1920s, from the tyranny of RAPP, thought he was doing them a great service and was unaware that he had created an even more fearful and more official weapon of literary tyranny.

When the First Writers' Congress met in 1934, the "fellow travelers" were very much in evidence. Pasternak, Babel and Olesha all made modest but intelligent contributions. These writers obviously felt themselves, rather ominously, on show after the "literary amnesty" of 1932, and Babel was particularly sensitive to the situation. He went out of his way to praise Stalin's prose style; Stalin's sentences, he said, were "forged as if of steel." At the same time he made some self-deprecating remarks, announcing himself to be "a master of silence"—meaning that he wrote little and slowly, or perhaps that he did not quite know what to write about now.

Bukharin spoke intelligently on Marxism and aesthetics, and Radek spoke of the importance of the capitalist heritage, saying that the Soviet writer should learn from Joyce and Proust before surpassing them. Zhdanov's speech was one in many and did not arouse any special interest, though it already contained the essentials of the socialist-realist doctrine. He was the main Party spokesman at the congress, and his concepts of a utilitarian literature soon began to be applied in practice, especially from the great purge year of 1936 onward, when writers—among them Babel and Pilnyak—began to be arrested right and left. At the time, however, it did not seem that Zhdanov had gone much further than Gorki himself in his advocacy of socialist realism, under which, in Stalin's phrase, the writer became "the engineer of souls."*

In a recent number of *Novy Mir* a writer recalls the atmosphere of panic that reigned in that journal in 1936–37, when about half its staff and regular contributors had already been arrested and deported, so much so that the December 1936 number did not have the usual annual index of authors—since most of these had vanished in the course of the year.

Gorki himself died mysteriously in 1936, a Professor Levin "confessing" in the 1937 purge trial to having caused his death. Although Gorki was a sick man of sixty-eight, it is conceivable that he was becoming embarrassing for the great disappointment he had latterly been expressing about the activities of that very Writers' Union he had set up four years before, ostensibly with Stalin's blessing.†

What the late 1930s produced by way of literature was mainly utilitarian and industrial novels, and such "soul builders" as Nikolai Ostrovsky's *How the Steel Was Tempered,* with its portrait and life story of the "ideal" Communist, Pavel Korchagin.

But the years of the Stalin terror were not exactly conducive to good writing. Much more satisfactory was some of the poetry and prose produced during and just after the war, which had an inspiring effect on writers like Simonov, Surkov, Leonov, Alexander Beck,

---

* In describing the origins of the Writers' Union I have made full use of a memorandum kindly lent me by its author, my friend David Gallagher of the *Times Literary Supplement.*

† Stalin, in a speech made in March 1929, had advocated a more propagandist approach to the arts than even RAPP was proposing at the time.

Emmanuil Kazakevich and Vasili Grossman, with occasional but significant contributions from poets like Pasternak and Akhmatova, and many other poets and prose writers, such as Margarita Aligher. One of the best novels published just after the war was by a young lieutenant, Victor Nekrasov—*In the Trenches of Stalingrad.* The great Leningrad tragedy inspired such important writers as Vera Ketlinskaya, Olga Bergholz, Vera Inber and many others.

It is not quite true that the last years of Stalin were completely sterile in the literary field; they produced several novels by women writers like Vera Panova and Antonina Koptyayeva. Nevertheless, the terror Zhdanov unleashed among writers in 1946 by attacking Akhmatova, Zoshchenko and Pasternak left its withering mark on literary output.

THE KHRUSHCHEV YEARS

The whole Khrushchev period was very uneven; Ehrenburg's novel *The Thaw,* published in 1954, was a landmark of outstanding importance; the *Den Poezii* annuals, and almanacs like *Literaturnaya Moskva*—published during the next few years without the approval of the Writers' Union—showed that poets had become less tongue-tied than before. Young new talents began to blossom—Yevtushenko, Voznesensky, Bulat Okudjava, Bella Akhmadullina and, among story writers, Vladimir Tendryakov, Yuri Nagibin, Yuri Kazakov, Vasili Aksyonov and many more. V. Dudintsev's *Not by Bread Alone,* though not an outstandingly good novel, was still a *succès de scandale* in showing up the hidebound Stalinist bureaucrat victimizing a young inventor of talent. The "rehabilitation" of writers who had been shot or driven to suicide in the Stalin days was undertaken, particularly by Ehrenburg; among them were Isaac Babel and Marina Tsvetaeva. Emigré writers like Nobel Prize–winner Ivan Bunin were at last being reprinted in the Soviet Union. The years from 1954 to the end of 1956 were the "thaw" years; things seemed to have changed drastically for the better. Poems written by Nikolai Tikhonov, Semyon Kirsanov and others during the war but unpublishable then were printed now. But soon after the De-Stalinization Congress of February 1956 came the "October Revolution" in Poland and the more violent anti-Russian uprising in Hungary.

For a time, a sharp brake was put on liberalization in literature and the arts. The freeze lasted from 1957 to 1960. The Second Writers' Congress, at which a few "dangerous" thoughts were expressed, had taken place in 1954; then there was another one in May 1959; here its president, Alexei Surkov, proudly announced that the membership of the Writers' Union had increased in four years from 3,695 to 4,801. Khrushchev, who also made a speech at the Writers' Congress, seemed less sure that such literary inflation was a good thing. He described, from his own experience, the case of a newly baked peasant poetess in the Ukraine whom the local Writers' Union insisted on giving a flat in Kiev, whereupon her "talent" ran completely dry and she merely became a burden to the Litfond, the financial fund taking care of writers. Ever since the events in Poland and Hungary in the autumn of 1956, Khrushchev had considered many Russian writers the dangerous accomplices of the Polish and Hungarian enemies of the Soviet Union.

Already in 1957 he had made some angry speeches on art and literature:

> What our people need is works of literature, art and music properly rendering the pathos of labor, and understandable to the people. The method of socialist realism provides unlimited possibilities for supplying such works. The Party is waging a relentless struggle against the penetration of alien ideologies into our art and literature. . . . We have to defend ourselves not only against attacks from abroad, but also from those writers and artists in our midst who are trying to divert our literature . . . onto wrong roads.

Whereupon he sharply attacked Dudintsev's *Not by Bread Alone,* which, "though containing some truthful pages," was still "a slanderous book." Many writers, he said, had misinterpreted the resolutions of the Twentieth Congress and had been guilty of revisionism; in particular, he took to task the *Literaturnaya Moskva* almanacs and Margarita Aligher; his attack on her was so violent that she fainted. Among other things, Khrushchev said that "certain writers" had played straight into the hands of the Hungarian counterrevolutionaries.

However, by 1959 he was satisfied that revisionism had been defeated, and he even gave Dudintsev a pat on the back, saying that he had never considered him an enemy; all the same, in trying to help the Party he had badly "overdone it." The "rather violent battle" of 1955–56, he said, was now over; the "revisionists" had been defeated; but writers now should, without embellishing Soviet reality, still preferably dwell on its "positive" sides:

> I want to take the side of those who, for some reason, have been given the unflattering title of "varnishers"—that is, of those who make it their aim to demonstrate positive heroes in their books. . . . It is important that our people be brought up on good examples. . . . Comrades, the power of the example is a great example!*

On the face of it, there was really little to choose between this 1959 Khrushchev line and the Stalin-Zhdanov line of 1946. Surkov, president of the Writers' Union, praised as great literary achievements such books as Sholokhov's *A Man's Destiny* and Polevoi's *In the Deep Rear* (both dealing with the war), Kochetov's *The Yershov Brothers,* books by Ovechkin, Panova, Galina Nikolaeva's *Battle on the Road,* Granin's *After the Wedding* and others; not all of them, it is true, were in the best socialist-realist tradition, though he carefully omitted mention of such "dubious" writers as Vladimir Tendryakov. Also—it was a few months after the "Pasternak scandal"—he referred to Pasternak's "treasonable activities" and said he was "unworthy of being called a Soviet writer." Pasternak had, indeed, recently been expelled from the Writers' Union.

Could Surkov take any other line, after Pasternak had been officially condemned by the Party? Some of my best friends—wartime friends, like Surkov himself, Simonov and Polevoi—felt at that time that they had to take an anti-Pasternak line, though all three have, in fact, a decent and unconventional side to them. Surkov, after all, as editor of *Ogonyok,* published some of Anna Akhmatova's latest poems in 1949, three years after she had been expelled from the Writers' Union and branded by the unspeakable Zhdanov as "half nun, half whore," and at a time when she was in the depths

* Speech at Third Writers' Congress, May 22, 1959. This was reprinted under the title *The Soviet Writers' Vocation to Serve the People* (200,000 copies were printed). His 1957 speeches (500,000 copies) were printed under the title *For Close Bonds Between Literature and Art and the Life of the People.*

of disgrace and poverty. Polevoi, though a socialist realist, wrote in some of his more recent books, like *Doctor Anna,* some pungent anti-Stalin pages, while Simonov unearthed his 1941 *Diaries,* which in 1966–67 were too strong meat to be published even in *Novy Mir,* and which he refused to publish in an expurgated form.

Novy Mir was not able to publish anything outstanding in 1957–59, though its courageous editor, Alexander Tvardovsky, wrote at the time about the Stalin personality cult as much as could conveniently be written. Thus, *Pravda* published a long poem by him containing these lines:

> *And so he reigned, and so he ruled,*
> *Clasping the reins in his ruthless hand.*
> *Find a man who did not praise him and glorify him!* . . .
> *Not in vain did this son of the East*
> *Reveal to the end his ruthless and cruel*
> *Rightness and unrightness.* . . .
> *Many of us saw him, and before he even spoke*
> *We would rise to our feet, crying "Hurray!"*
> *And saying "He will be right again."*
> *We made a god of him, and why deny it?*
> *We called him the father of our land.*
> *There's nothing to add, and nothing to subtract.*
> *For so it was on earth.*
> *For a quarter of a century this man's name,*
> *Coupled with the name of our country,*
> *Was like a clarion call summoning our people*
> *To go to work and to go into battle.*
> *We owed him victory,*
> *And he owed victory to us.* . . .

Perhaps the three most important writers to emerge even during the bleak post-Budapest period of 1957–59 were Yuri Kazakov, Yuri Nagibin and Vladimir Tendryakov (whose admirable "Three-Seven-Ace" was published in *Novy Mir* in March 1960). As I wrote at the time:

> All three have . . . been described as Chekhovian. Kazakov has been sharply attacked by *Literary Gazette* . . . for being

decadent, aestheticist and pessimistic. . . . He, and others, have been attacked along the following lines: "They imagine they are in the Chekhov tradition; they assume that Chekhov took a detached pessimistic, shoulder-shrugging attitude to the world around him, whereas he was, in reality, a revolutionary writer . . . , a harbinger of the Revolution. See *The Cherry Orchard.* . . . Chekhov was not tolerant toward evil."

This was a very one-sided interpretation of Chekhov; it could, at a stretch, be applied to stories like "The Grasshopper," but not to others, like "The Fit, or A Dull Story." Thus, in "The Fit," a young student in the presence of his doctor throws a fit over the horrors of brothels and prostitution which he has observed the previous night. The doctor merely shrugs his shoulders, implying, "Well, that's life, and what can you do about it?"

In the same article, I reported a conversation with one of the younger writers in 1960:

> "Our country is making tremendous progress, and we are now equal to America in many ways. . . . But our literature is lagging behind our technical and economic progress. . . . Writers are *beginning* to look for new formulae, for new solutions. The quality of our writing is improving: there is more variety, more imagination, more *style* than there was a few years ago. . . . We can write pretty well what we like about foreign countries, kick the Nazis in the teeth, be rude about American imperialism. . . . But when we write about Russia, many of us are in a bit of a quandary. We are supposed to write 'in the tradition' of Tolstoy, Turgenev and Chekhov; but all these were 'critical realists.' . . . They had a skeptical, ironical, sometimes downright satirical attitude to Russian reality. But *we've got to believe* all the time; and we can't be ironical about Soviet reality, and satirical in only a very limited way."

And he continued:

> "In the Stalin days, our literature began to develop a peculiar kind of pathos; it was becoming positively 'classical'—like Derzhavin's *Odes to Catherine the Great.* . . . Our cult of the heroic, 'positive' character went so far that, in all seriousness, Communist journals started boosting—hold tight—whom do you think? Cor-

neille! Yes, the Cid, though admittedly a little archaic, was treated as a kind of ancestor of the Soviet positive hero with his infallible sense of honor and duty!

"At that rate, Corneille *should* be much nearer to us than Shakespeare; you may remember that, during the last years of Stalin, a revival of *Hamlet,* with its dithering hero, was put off time and again at the Moscow Art Theater; somebody high up must have decided *Hamlet* wasn't good for us!"

My friend went on to say that life was really easier for the writer under Stalin; you knew exactly what to say, and in dealing with the truly heroic material of the Second World War you could hardly go wrong.

"But the war has become a thing of the past, and now a certain amount of debunking of the war heroics is going on—take, for instance, Simonov's *The Living and the Dead.* The 'Chekhovian' shoulder-shrugging approach is becoming fashionable with writers like Nagibin, Kazakov, Tendryakov. Only it isn't enough. There are some young writers who are *anti*-Chekhov. I don't mean the didactic, dogmatist writers. I mean young, original writers to whom Chekhov is too anemic, flat, water-colory, lacking the blaring, glaring revolutionary rhetoric of Mayakovsky, but also the verbal pungency of Leskov, Dostoevsky, Gogol, Saltykov-Shchedrin. I mean, for instance, the Gogol of *The Nose.* In short, back to the eccentric, the fantastic, back to neologisms and verbal jugglery. Back to Zamyatin, Pilnyak, Babel, back to the 1920s, to all the fun and nonsense; back also to *funny* books, like Katayev's *Embezzlers* and Ilf and Petrov's *Little Golden Calf!*"*

In 1960 there seemed three possible escapes from the more rigid canons of socialist realism—which had, on the whole, produced little except a vast bulk of essentially provincial literature. They were (1) "Chekhovianism," the treatment of Soviet reality in a slightly ironical, undidactic manner; (2) satire, which had, however, only very limited possibilities; and (3) a reaction, as my friend put it, to "anemic Chekhov and relatively flat Tolstoy (*the* wholly approved model), to bumpy Leskov, to bumpy Saltykov-Shchedrin,

* See *The Khrushchev Phase* (London, 1961), pp. 198–217; the quotations from this are supplemented by some additional notes taken in 1959–60 and not included in the book.

to verbal virtuosity, to Gogol's *Nose,* to the *fantastica* of the 1920s. Only," he added, "verbal bumpiness often leads to dangerously bumpy thoughts!"*

Such was the situation as I assessed it after a lengthy stay in Moscow during the winter of 1959–60. The Stalinites were vigilant, but uneasy. Nagibin, Tendryakov, Kazakov, Aksyonov were beginning to make names for themselves. It was *new* writing, different from almost anything seen in the last thirty years except for outcasts like Akhmatova and Pasternak. Those who had taken part in the hounding of Pasternak, now a sick and deeply discouraged man, were feeling uneasy about it, too. They blamed not so much Pasternak as the Nobel Prize Committee, for trying to stage an "anti-Soviet provocation" by awarding the prize to him. As for him, he was "a pigheaded old man" who had rejected even the slightest cuts and changes in the manuscript of *Doctor Zhivago.* "Of course, of course we would have published it"; and some even said, "It was a mistake we didn't print a small edition of even the full text; there would have been a few nasty notices in the press, and that would have been the end of it." And it was said that Khrushchev, "who had never read a line of Pasternak in his life," thought it had all been rather a stupid mistake to make such a fuss. For all that, Pasternak was sad and embittered:

> *Chto zhe sdelal ya za pakost*
> *Ya, ubiitsa i zlodei?*
> *Ya ves' mir zastavil plakat'*
> *Nad krasoi zemli moyei. . . .*†

He died in the following summer, in 1960. Many of the young poets and writers went to his church funeral at Peredelkino; so did Ehrenburg's wife, Ehrenburg himself being abroad at the time. The pundits of the Writers' Union did not go. Akhmatova, herself in her seventies, wrote one of her most beautiful poems, "The Poet's Death." The coffin was carried out of the church by Siniavsky and Daniel.

---

* *Ibid.,* p. 217.

† What swinishness have I done, I, the murderer and villain? I have made the whole world weep over the beauty of my country.

Liberalization in literature was making headway throughout 1961 and 1962. Thousands of young people flocked to the Luzhniki Stadium to hear those new young idols of Soviet poetry, Yevtushenko and Voznesensky. At the end of 1961 the Twenty-second Party Congress took place; it was much more outspokenly anti-Stalinite than the Twentieth had been; not only was Stalin denounced, but even some others, such as Zhdanov. At the end of it, it was decided to remove Stalin's embalmed body from the Lenin Mausoleum and rebury him discreetly somewhere below the Kremlin wall.

It was in October 1962 that Yevtushenko wrote one of his most famous poems, *The Heirs of Stalin,* which, with Khrushchev's approval, was published in *Pravda.* The theme was simply this: Stalin was merely pretending to be dead. As he was being taken out of the Lenin Mausoleum clouds of breath were coming out through the cracks of the coffin. He looked to see who these silly young soldiers were who were carrying him out of the mausoleum; he was making mental notes; one day they would have to pay heavily for it. In the coffin was a phone, and he phoned to Enver Hodja of Albania and to many others, perhaps also to that old man now peacefully living on a pension and clipping his rosebushes—an allusion to Poskrebyshev, his *éminence grise,* who knew more about the purges, shootings and arrests than anyone else. (Poskrebyshev was not to die till 1966.) In short, the "heirs of Stalin" were still around, and the poet appealed to the government to double and treble the guards watching Stalin's grave, so that he did not rise from the dead.

The year following the De-Stalinization Congress of 1961 was the most exciting one in literature. In November 1962 *Novy Mir* published (again with Khrushchev's approval) Alexander Solzhenitsyn's *One Day in the Life of Ivan Denisovich,* which describes an "ordinary day" in a Siberian labor camp. The book is too well known to need describing. There are no particular horrors of the Auschwitz or Maidanek kind; what is so striking is just the kind of people one finds here: Ivan Denisovich himself, who was taken prisoner by the Germans and is therefore suspect; Latvians and Estonians, there just because they *are* that and "may" have collaborated with the Germans; a naval officer who had something to do with the British Arctic convoys during the war and who, in the end, received a souvenir from a British admiral; Baptists and members of

other religious sects. For some minor offense the naval officer is sent
to the inner circle of that hell the detention block:

> The walls there are of stone, the floor of cement. There is no
> window. They heat the stove just enough so that the ice on the
> walls should melt and lie on the floor in puddles. You sleep on
> naked planks. Daily bread ration three hundred grams, and soup
> only on the third, sixth and ninth day. . . . Ten days! If you sit
> them out . . . you lose your health till the end of your life.
> Tuberculosis, and you'll never get out of hospital. . . . And
> anybody who's done fifteen days is already under the damp earth.

November 1962—an exciting month! The "slave-camp" story
was no longer taboo; *Novy Mir* continued to publish Ehrenburg's
Memoirs, in which he talked freely of Western art, enormously
"widening the cultural horizons" of the young generation, who came
to regard Ehrenburg as one of the great liberal leaders of Soviet
literature. More startling still was Victor Nekrasov's article "On
Both Sides of the Ocean," describing his visits to the United States
and Italy. It was soon to be denounced as a plea for ideological
coexistence, for he freely talked about finding good things as well as
bad in Italy and America. He reported that the Italian Communists
he had talked to were quite incredibly broad-minded and saw no
harm in the Italian workers reading both *Unità* and the *Osservatore
Romano*. They now freely talked about Stalin, wondering why they
had assumed in the past that what he did was always right. He gave
a balanced account of both America and Italy. He reported plenty
of poverty in the Italian south, but said that the country was boom-
ing; much building was going on, and the standard of living was
sharply rising. In America he saw two Negroes having dinner in an
ordinary restaurant, and nobody came to throw them out—much to
the disappointment of a Soviet correspondent who happened to be
with him. I was to see Nekrasov in Paris soon after his American
trip. "They talk," he said, "of France being a fascist country under
de Gaulle. Doesn't feel like fascist to me at all!"

Yevtushenko and Voznesensky also came to Paris that winter.
Both were lionized by the French. Voznesensky visited both Chagall
and Picasso, and each gave him a precious souvenir. Yevtushenko
wrote his *Precocious Autobiography* for a French magazine, without

letting it first go through the Soviet censorship. Voznesensky was full of stories of the great overflow meeting at Luzhniki, where fourteen thousand people had come to listen to his new poems from his newly published book with the extravagant title *The Triangular Pear*.

Voznesensky was at the top of his form that winter in Paris, not yet knowing what was coming to him. In a London *Times* interview he attributed his great popularity with the young generation to the simple fact that these young people were sophisticated. This technical intelligentsia, he said, which now ran into millions, worked on highly complicated industrial processes, and that was why they liked poetry too to be "complicated" and not childishly obvious. "I consider Pasternak my master, not people like Surkov. Surkov may have been all right for the peasant recruits in the Red Army during the war; but our Russian intelligentsia want something different, not glimpses into the obvious."

Nothing, indeed, is less obvious than Voznesensky's poetry. It is rich in unexpected sound-images (a favorite trick of his is to build them on alliterations, as in his *Goya* poem); his rhythms range from the rock 'n' roll and Negro-jazz rhythms of his American poems, with their beatnik themes, to the exquisitely elegiac pianissimo of *Autumn in Sigulda*,* or to this strange little poem dedicated to Jean-Paul Sartre:

> *I am a family and, as in a spectrum,*
> *There are in me seven "I's,"*
> *Unbearable like seven beasts.*
> *But the luest of them plays a pipe,*
> *And in springtime I dream*
> *That I am*
> *An eighth one.*

* But in the midst of this pianissimo there suddenly blare out these lines:
  Andrei Voznesensky, genius
  Has broken in between your shoulderblades
  Like a big red male fist
  Entering a rubber glove.
One day in Paris, with boyish bravado and feeling very pleased with himself, he said to me, "Look, Alex, this is a very subtle piece of symbolism: it means my standing *hui* getting into a French letter. Do you think our anti-heads will see the point?"

"To a socialist realist," the *Times Literary Supplement* wrote at the time, "this may sound like pure gibberish; but is it? The old guard . . . have attacked him for the poem, and for much else, and have even accused him of 'double-think,' and of writing beatnik poems under the guise of antibeatnik poems, such as his *Beatnik Monologue:*

> *"Roaring from its rocket-sites,*
> *Sprinkling the world with atomic dust,*
> *Time spits at me,*
> *Just as I spit at Time. . . .*
> *We are beatniks, and amidst all their insults*
> *We are like little wolves and beasts*
> *Dragging clanging scandal with us like convict chains. . . .*

"Some," the article continues, "have even accused him of 'atomic catastrophism'; only, as he himself has said, 'I am no pessimist. But even when, lying on the grass, I kiss a girl, I still remember at the back of my mind that the grass is poisonous with atomic fall-out.' "

This catastrophism of Voznesensky's was perhaps typical of his mood in 1962. "At the height of the Cuban crisis," he said, "many of us thought it was the End. Many young girls who had never made love before now wanted to because it was perhaps their last chance." And in his later poem *Marilyn Monroe* we have the same theme: Marilyn commits suicide because, with a nuclear war threatening the world, life has become unbearable.

Voznesensky loves Russia in his own way, but he is nonconformist, and even rebellious at times; thus, in 1960 he wrote:

> *You try to frighten me with formalism;*
> *How divorced you are from life,*
> *You experts stinking of mothballs and incense!*

Formalism, the dangerous, explosive word, the most heinous sin the artist could commit, according to Zhdanov, Stalin's art dictator back in 1946–48, but a sin which still remains a sin. In *The Triangular Pear,* the book of poems published at the end of 1962 ("the triangle," he has explained, "is the geometrical essence of the pear, and also the shape of the New York subway lamps"), he simply sticks out his tongue:

How I love my critics!
Perched on the neck of one of them
I see there shining a fragrant naked anti-head.

Voznesensky, Nekrasov, Yevtushenko threw their weight about in Paris during that winter. Old Paustovsky behaved with great tact and discretion. But he also got it in the neck from Khrushchev for good measure. Trouble started while they were still in Paris. In December Khrushchev visited the Manège exhibition of modern painting and sculpture, and his comments on what he called "abstract" art were, to say the least, lavatorial and scatological. There followed a particularly vile speech from L. F. Ilyichev, Khrushchev's propaganda chief, which singled out Ehrenburg for abuse, condemned formalism and "ideological coexistence," and was marked by a great number of anti-Semitic innuendoes.

But worse was to come. On March 8, 1963, Khrushchev himself delivered a twenty-thousand-word speech in which he not only defended Stalin from complete condemnation ("those were bright, happy years") but launched ferocious attacks on Ehrenburg, Nekrasov, Yevtushenko, Voznesensky and even Paustovsky; on a film like *The Ilyich Suburb* (which dealt with the conflict of the generations in Russia, and about which Nekrasov had been particularly enthusiastic when speaking of it to me in Paris); on a sculptor like Neizvestnyi, and "abstractionism and formalism" in art and literature generally, as well as dodecaphonic music, adding, "When I listen to Glinka, tears of joy always come into my eyes." This endless speech was delivered at the Kremlin at a meeting of Party and government leaders with writers and artists.

It was, as it were, the all-out Stalino-Zhdanovite offensive against all that was fresh and modern in Russian art and literature. Anything that interested the West, Khrushchev said in effect, was *ipso facto* suspect, if not downright rotten. Thus he said to Yevtushenko, "If the enemies of our cause start to praise you, our people will justly criticize you; so choose which suits you best." What was a defense of Marxism-Leninism was, in effect, a defense of a sort of spiritual isolationism and provincialism. If Khrushchev and Ilyichev had been taken at their word and their virtual ultimatum had been obeyed, Soviet literature in 1963–64 would have sunk to its drab 1948–49 level. Nevertheless, the warning against ideological co-existence with the West could not be entirely overlooked. Khrushchev began to be as deeply detested by the younger and more independent writers as Zhdanov had been.

HIGH HOPES AFTER KHRUSHCHEV'S FALL

When Khrushchev was thrown out in October 1964, there was rejoicing among these younger writers. Not that there had been no open resistance to this return to *simplisme*. In Moscow, the liberal opposition was symbolized by *Novy Mir,* whose editor, Alexander Tvardovsky, refused to be bullied beyond certain limits. Despite Khrushchev's and Ilyichev's attacks on Ehrenburg, *Novy Mir* continued to publish his *Memoirs,* though it seems that before every new installment, there had to be a fierce battle with Glavlit. There was also the publication in *Znamya* of Simonov's *Men Are Not Born Soldiers,* which was an essentially anti-Stalin novel and so ignored Khrushchev's semi-defense of Stalin. But the theme of Yevtushenko's *The Heirs of Stalin* had now become virtually taboo; Khrushchev had shown that he himself somehow qualified for the title, since in the winter of 1962–63 he had obviously reached the conclusion that art and literature were getting out of hand. Concessions had to be made to public taste—within narrow limits, it is true. Pasternak's poetry was now being reprinted; so were selections of Akhmatova; she was also included in annual almanacs like the *Den Poezii. Novy Mir,* though warned against publishing any more concentration-camp stories, continued to publish short stories by Solzhenitsyn which, though not dealing directly with camps, spoke of other injustices that were possible under Stalinism, such as denouncing an innocent man to the NKVD. Why was Khrushchev, the de-Stalinizer, so dead against the publication of more concentration-camp stories—which were now arriving at *Novy Mir* and in other editorial offices by the hundred? No doubt because it was better to forget about that discreditable period of the Soviet regime, and perhaps because, after the Cuba fiasco, he felt his position weakening in the Party hierarchy.*

By the beginning of 1965, after Khrushchev's fall, it seemed that the deep freeze of the previous two years had come to an end. *Novy Mir*, in its January 1965 number, which was also the number marking the journal's fortieth anniversary, contained further installments of Ehrenburg, and this time that part of his memoirs relating to the ugly days of Zhdanovism; several exquisite new poems by Akhmatova; some newly published works of Pasternak; and, most important of all perhaps, the long "jubilee" introduction by Tvardovsky himself, and the history of the journal written by Dementiev and Dikushina. People were eagerly awaiting Tvardovsky's manifesto three months after Khrushchev's fall. Would there be, in his view, a new thaw?

Tvardovsky had to be cautious, though what he said was significant enough:

> The ideological and political position of our journal is, of course, determined by the policy of our Party. . . . Our attention goes preferably to works giving a truthful and accurate reflection of reality, simple in form, though not tradition. At the same time, they need not shun new forms of expression when these are justified by the content.

Many dangerous thoughts could, in fact, be read into this; but Tvardovsky was not frightened. His defense was straightforward: after all, he said, *Novy Mir* had published writers of such different styles and manners as Sholokhov and Pasternak, Alexei Tolstoy and Solzhenitsyn, Simonov and Tendryakov, and he intended to give the journal the same variety. He did not use the phrase "socialist realism," but, rather, suggested that this phrase had covered too great a multitude of sins.

As the *Times Literary Supplement* summed up this Tvardovsky manifesto:

> What he says, in fact, is that Soviet literature should strengthen its "denunciatory" role; it was one of the great achievements of a writer like Ovechkin to have shown up as early as 1953 the real

* See Michel Tatu's *Le Pouvoir en URSS* on this point.

state of affairs on certain collective farms, even before a new
official line had been laid down; similar services had been rendered
by Yefim Dorosh's *Village Diary* and some of Tendryakov's
stories. . . . Some *kolkhoz* chairmen had been particularly in-
censed by Dorosh's book. What Tvardovsky says in effect is that
the writer should be a pioneer, just as Turgeniev was, for instance,
before the Emancipation of 1861.

And it quotes the following admirable passage from Tvardovsky's
manifesto:

> It is not the task of literature to supply with "artistic illustra-
> tions" decisions already taken at the top. . . . The author should
> study life honestly and boldly below the surface, and he can be of
> real help if he reveals something new and important which has
> perhaps never yet been mentioned in the daily press, or in any
> official documents or decrees.

After arguing that there was still much "falsity," "faking" and
"makeup" in what was supposed to be realistic Russian literature,
Tvardovsky said that there was also too great a tendency to write
only about "good" kolkhozes and not about "bad" kolkhozes; and
to give most of the credit for their goodness not to the peasant
masses but to the "good chairman"—usually a good urban Party
man! The buildup of such "heroes" should not be overdone. In
Soviet literature the little man tends to be neglected, as are also the
peasant masses and particularly *their* reactions to "the tragic collectivization process."

Touching on even more dangerous ground, Tvardovsky then
spoke of those "bogus historical memoirs" with their omission of
"unmentionable names"—a genre which flourished not only under
Stalin but also (though to a lesser extent) under Khrushchev.
(Thus, in the official six-volume history of the war much is made of
Khrushchev's presence at Stalingrad during the great battle, and
Malenkov's presence is omitted altogether.)

There follows a passage which is particularly ominous in the light
of what happened later: speaking of Solzhenitsyn, he referred to the
attempt to "silence him," an attempt perhaps still continuing (*certainly* continuing, as we learned in 1967). Although Solzhenitsyn
had enough material for many more books of camp literature,

Tvardovsky, to reassure those who disliked the subject, asserted in 1965 that Solzhenitsyn was a man of an "enormous and many-sided talent"; it was like a desperate plea that Solzhenitsyn be allowed to go on writing—a plea to the Party to give writers the greatest possible freedom, now that the "bad" 1963–64 period was over. Tvardovsky also spoke of the enormous number of letters received by the journal, showing the extraordinary maturity of Russian readers today; many of the letters were denunciations of the crypto-Stalinism of other journals, such as *Oktyabr;* occasionally some reader also defended this crypto-Stalinism. In the jubilee issue of the journal there was a violent denunciation of Lysenkoism, with its pseudo-scientific "incantations"—another curious manifestation of the *Novy Mir* spirit.

In 1965, soon after the fall of Khrushchev, Tvardovsky hoped that things would improve under Kosygin and Brezhnev. It was perhaps with the hope that there would be something like a return to the 1920s that he published the history of *Novy Mir,* in which the glorious 1920s were contrasted with the hideous 1930s.

Clearly, the great days of the journal had been in the 1920s, when, under the editorship of Skvortsov-Stepanov and Polonsky (assisted by Lunacharsky, the then Commissar for Education), it was the least cliquey of Soviet journals and published such very different writers as Gorki, Alexei Tolstoy, Babel, Bagritsky, Pilnyak, Pasternak, Esenin, Mayakovsky, Leonov, etc.—almost all the major writers of that brilliant decade, so many of whom were later to perish in the purges. In 1928, with 28,000 copies, it had the highest circulation among the fat journals.

But then, after 1932, when socialist realism was proclaimed the official dogma, things went from bad to worse.

By 1936, every issue opened with a portrait of Stalin, a *skaz* [folklore epic] on Stalin, "folk songs" about Stalin. Nothing is more depressing than to read today the account, published in *Novy Mir* of September 1936, of a meeting held in the editorial office at which members of the staff made confessions and admitted not having been vigilant enough to notice the "enemy activities" of Serebryakova, Pilnyak* and other contributors. Soon

* Serebryakova was to be released after Stalin's death; Pilnyak was to perish in the purges.

afterward the editor, Gronsky, was arrested, along with several other members of the staff and contributors. . . . The December 1936 issue did not have the usual annual index—too many of the contributors had become unmentionable.

This hideous meeting in the editorial office of *Novy Mir* took place in 1936, with the Stalin purges getting into their stride. But were all the editorial meetings of *Novy Mir* in recent years all that different? Tvardovsky had fought like mad to keep his journal *the* great liberal journal of Soviet literature, both under Khrushchev and after Khrushchev. He had had his moments of triumph, for instance when Khrushchev personally allowed him to publish Solzhenitsyn's *Ivan Denisovich,* and later when, after almost endless resistance, he was still able to publish the two Katayev stories. But he had his bad moments too—for instance, when he was told that one of his foremost critics, Andrei Siniavsky, had been arrested for "publishing anti-Soviet propaganda abroad," and when he was pretty well forced to publish the dreary and interminable sub-Gorki *Bonfire,* which took up a good part of each issue, merely because its author, Konstantin Fedin, had become president of the Writers' Union. No doubt Fedin had been a reasonably good writer in the 1920s, though not one of the truly great names of that decade. Then, getting on in years—he was now over seventy—he took the easy line of becoming a bureaucrat of the Writers' Union; his was a respectable presidential name with which to cover up the tricks of the more unscrupulous bureaucrats nominally under him.

This, and much else that happened in 1965–66, badly upset Tvardovsky. When I got to Moscow in June 1967, it was said that there wasn't much fight left in him; he was tired and exhausted. Another blow to him, shortly before, had been Glavlit's refusal to pass for publication in *Novy Mir* Konstantin Simonov's 1941 *War Diaries;* Glavlit proposed an expurgated version, but this Simonov himself rejected.

SINIAVSKY AND DANIEL

The Siniavsky-Daniel trial had taken place over a year before; but people were still talking about it, and even more so about Mikhail

Sholokhov's "incredible" speech at the Twenty-third Party Congress of the previous spring. Now, Sholokhov had, in recent years, become a highly controversial name in Russia. Although he had written *Quiet Flows the Don* nearly forty years before, and several versions of *Virgin Soil Upturned* from fifteen to twenty-five years before, he seemed to have run dry, except for one or two short stories. *The Don* had been an anarchist kind of book, rather unsympathetic to both Reds and Whites, and there were some who still believed the (highly improbable) legend that he had not written it himself. The point is that this wild Cossack of the 1920s had become the supreme Party boss as far as literature was concerned. Some of his criticisms were, of course, not unjustified; he had, time and again, made fun of the Writers' Union with its thousands of members only very few of whom were really worthwhile writers. But, at the same time, he demanded that all the great books, of which he said there weren't nearly enough, should be proper Communist and socialist-realist books; the trouble, however, was that young Soviet people seemed to take an inordinate interest in the wrong kind of books, and especially in the "hysterical" poetry of people like Voznesensky and Yevtushenko. He had attacked these at the Twenty-second Party Congress in 1961. Now, in 1966, he went one better: he regretted that Siniavsky and Daniel, who, he said, were traitors to their country, should have been let off so lightly; under Lenin, under revolutionary justice unhampered by such-and-such an article of the criminal code, they would simply have been shot.

This was the extreme point of view, but was meant to represent the view of the Party, in whose name Sholokhov claimed to speak; and he was, indeed, the only Russian writer to be allowed to speak at that Twenty-third Party Congress.

The two writers had been arrested in September 1965; their trial was in February 1966, the first of its kind since the death of Stalin. Shortly *before* the trial, Z. Kedrina in *Literaturnaya Gazeta* and D. Yeremin in *Izvestia* wrote the kind of denunciatory articles against the accused men that the late David Zaslavsky used to write in the days of the great Stalin purge trials or on the eve of the trial of the Polish underground leaders in June 1945. The trial took place, but it was "open" only to a carefully selected public. Both Siniavsky and Daniel pleaded not guilty (which was more than ever happened in trials under Stalin, when "confessions" were extracted in advance by torture and threats concerning the accused's family). But it did not help much: they were sentenced to seven and five years in a labor camp. Siniavsky and Daniel were charged with having conducted anti-Soviet propaganda abroad, and, the relevant Soviet law being what it is, it was not difficult to interpret their actions in that way. Both Siniavsky's *Lubimov* and Daniel's stories like "Moscow Calling" and "The Man from MINAP" poke fun at the Soviet Establishment and the press. What is, however, particularly odious is that in his labor camp Daniel was to be subjected to great physical suffering; thus, according to well-substantiated reports, he was refused anti-mosquito ointment in the mosquito-infested camp. This was clearly the work of one of the more sadistic Stalin jailers still in business.

The reactions to the verdict were what was to be expected: the Stalinites, like those of *Oktyabr*—Kochetov and company—welcomed the verdict; the liberals were outraged. Sixty-two of these, headed by Kornei Chukovsky and Ilya Ehrenburg, wrote to the presidium of the Twenty-third Party Congress offering to "go bail" for Siniavsky and Daniel if they were released, as the signatories hoped they would be.

The letter said that, "even though we do not approve of the methods used for getting these books published abroad," the trial had failed to prove that the books had been published for an anti-Soviet purpose.

> Besides, sentencing a writer for publishing satirical works creates a very dangerous precedent, and one liable to slow down the development of Soviet culture. Neither art nor science can exist without the possibility of expressing paradoxical ideas or of creating hyperbolical characters. The complex atmosphere in which we live calls for an extension (and not a limitation) of artistic and intellectual experiments. From this point of view, the trial of Siniavsky and Daniel has done more harm than all the errors they themselves have committed.

In short, the signatories asked that Siniavsky and Daniel be given a chance to correct their errors; the signatories, among them V. Shklovsky, Pavel Antokolsky, V. Kaverin, Yefim Dorosh, Bella

Akhmadullina, Yuna Moritz, Yuri Nagibin, Bulat Okudjava, Lydia Chukovskaya and several younger and lesser-known writers, would vouch for them. It took courage to sign this letter; Ehrenburg and Chukovsky had, obviously, initiated it. If many obvious signatures were missing, such as Tvardovsky's, Voznesensky's and Yevtushenko's, it was, I gather, because they believed that their signing the appeal would do more harm than good. Others, like Simonov, always at daggers drawn with Ehrenburg, refused to sign it. Many, while fully in sympathy with the appeal, preferred not to stick their necks out. Nearly all writers I saw in both 1966 and 1967 deplored the trial; many said that Kosygin had been "definitely against it" but had been outvoted on the Politburo. No one knew for certain whether this was really true. The signatories were not let off lightly by Sholokhov; not only was he "ashamed" of Siniavsky and Daniel, but he was "doubly ashamed" of those who had offered to vouch for them.

The most devastating reply to Sholokhov's Party congress speech came from Lydia Chukovskaya, Chukovsky's old, half-blind daughter, whose husband had perished in the purges, and whom we shall meet again later. No national or international prizes in the world, she said, alluding to Sholokhov's Nobel Prize, would make him live down the ignominy of his Party congress speech, which was a betrayal of all that Russian literature at its noblest had ever stood for. She quoted Pushkin and Tolstoy and Chekhov to show how they would have acted vis-à-vis the Siniavsky-Daniel affair. Her letter was not published in any paper in Russia, but everybody somehow read it or came to hear of it. It was like the voice of the old Russian intelligentsia speaking to the Party Inquisitor.

Aragon's statement deploring the trial and disassociating the French Communist Party from it was published in *L'Humanité* on February 16, 1966. It took a week before copies of the paper were allowed to be sold in Moscow. Sholokhov had said that only Siniavsky's and Daniel's "bourgeois defenders" had spoken against the trial; Chukovskaya pointed out that the French, Italian and several other Communist parties in the West had condemned it.

Whether Kosygin had originally approved of the trial or not, there is good reason to believe that he realized, especially after Aragon's statement, that it had all been a very bad mistake. Soviet correspondents abroad were particularly angry about it; it put them in a highly embarrassing position even vis-à-vis their Communist friends in France and other countries. When I arrived in Moscow in June 1967, an official of the Writers' Union tried to explain that it had "unfortunately had to be done, since otherwise hundreds of writers would have started sending their works abroad"; he also said that if they had published their works under their own names, and not under pseudonyms, no one could have objected—a rather dubious assertion, for what law provided for this kind of distinction?

THE 1967 WRITERS' CONGRESS

By the middle of 1967, there were already other worries.

The Fourth Writers' Congress, which had been put off and off and off, finally met on May 22. There had been a kind of gentlemen's agreement between the liberals and the Stalinites not to attack each other; but the semblance of Fiftieth-Jubilee unity somehow could not be maintained. The agreement was first broken by Sholokhov, who, still annoyed by the liberals' reactions to his Party congress speech a year before, now attacked the initiator of the appeal to the Party congress, Ilya Ehrenburg. He did not mention the Siniavsky-Daniel affair, but complained, unjustly, as we have seen, that his "dear old friend Ilya Grigorievich" had dissociated himself from the Writers' Congress and had preferred to lie in the sun in sunny Italy.

More serious than this ill-mannered and uncalled-for attack on Ehrenburg was the letter that Solzhenitsyn sent to the congress. Moreover, Solzhenitsyn had 250 copies of this letter typed; these were sent to numerous political and literary personalities, and one copy found its way to Paris and was published only a few days later in Le Monde and after that in several other papers.

It was a terrifying document. It was written not by a hack but by a true master of Russian literature. For several years his name had not appeared in the press. After saying that there is no provision in the constitution for the censorship,* he makes the terrifying (and

* This is, of course, the most arguable of the points he makes. Censorships of various kinds exist in most countries—e.g., for films and plays in Britain, for erotic and pornographic books in nearly all countries, etc. But ordinary

perfectly true) assertion that "this censorship gives to uncultured persons the possibility of taking arbitrary measures against writers."
And he continues:

> There is no suggestion, and no recognition, of the right of our writers to state publicly their opinions about the moral life of men and of society, to elucidate in their own way the social problems or the historical experiences which have so profoundly affected our country.
> Works which could have expressed the thoughts matured among the people, which might in time have exercised a valuable influence in the spiritual domain or on the evolution of the social conscience, are prohibited or distorted by the censorship out of considerations which, from the point of view of the people, are pettifogging, egotistic and shortsighted.

And then he explains why, with very rare exceptions, practically no books of lasting value, or with a worldwide appeal, have been published in the land of Tolstoy and Dostoevsky in the last thirty-five years:

> Excellent manuscripts by young authors still completely unknown are today rejected by editors on the sole ground that they will not pass the censor. Many members of the Writers' Union, and even delegates at this congress, know how they themselves have had to bow to the pressures of the censorship, to capitulate on matters concerning the structure and orientation of their works. They have rewritten chapters, pages, paragraphs, phrases; they have sweetened them, only because they wanted to have them published; and, in so doing, they have damaged them irreparably. What is best in our literature is mutilated when it appears.

---

literary censorship, where it exists, can vary enormously. In Franco Spain, for instance, it affects only extreme political hostility to the regime or anything that can be construed as Communist or anarchist propaganda; in the Spanish version of my *Russia at War*, only about half a dozen sentences were deleted. The tsarist censorship, as we have seen, was reasonably mild and seldom arbitrary. There is a much tougher censorship, in comparison, in the people's democracies (except latterly in Czechoslovakia, where it was entirely abolished), but undoubtedly the worst censorship in the world is to be found today in the Soviet Union.

In fact, there *is* no literature in Russia today worthy of the name.

> Literature cannot develop between the categories "permitted" and "not permitted." Literature which does not breathe the same air as contemporary society, which cannot communicate to society its pains and fears, which cannot give warning in time against moral and social dangers, does not deserve the name of literature. It deserves only the name of literary makeshift. Such a literature loses the confidence of the people. Its books do not deserve to be read. They are nothing but wastepaper.

And then comes the most damning charge of all: one of the richest literatures in the world till about 1930 has been reduced to the most abject spiritual and intellectual poverty and debility.

> Our literature has lost the leading position which it occupied in the world at the end of the last century and at the beginning of this; it has also lost the passion for experimentation which distinguished it during the 1920s. The literature of our country appears today to all the world as infinitely poorer, more flat and worthless than it is in reality, than it would look if it were not being restricted, if it were not being prevented from developing. The loser is our country . . . and world literature is also the loser. If it had before it all the fruits of our literature, without restrictions, if it could gain a deeper insight as a result of our spiritual experience, the artistic evolution of the entire world would be different; it could find a new vigor and reach a new artistic level.
>
> I propose that the congress should demand and obtain the abolition of all censorship, open or concealed, of artistic works, that it should liberate the publishing houses of their obligation to obtain permission from the authorities before publishing any work.

About a quarter of the delegates (so I was told) asked that the letter be publicly read and then discussed by the congress. The Writers' Union officials, and the rest of the delegates, horrified by such bold and damning words, were absolutely opposed.

For here is something worse than the censorship itself. The censorship would not and could not be what it is if it did not have the full weight of the Writers' Union behind it—that is, of its hundreds of bureaucrats and of the thousands of hacks who could not get a line of their "prose" published but for the Writers' Union.

In other socialist countries—in Poland, in Czechoslovakia, in Hungary, Rumania and Yugoslavia—the writers' unions and similar organizations are strongholds of liberal, radical and progressive thought; in Russia alone is the Writers' Union the stronghold of all that is most reactionary, obscurantist and Stalinist. The liberals in the Writers' Union are in a small minority—cowed, intimidated and, when necessary, plainly terrorized, as in the case of Solzhenitsyn. Yet to belong to the Writers' Union is almost a matter of physical survival; except for the very young, who have not yet been admitted, every writer must in practice belong to the Writers' Union if he wants to be published at all. After Zoshchenko and Akhmatova were expelled from the union in 1946, they would have almost died of starvation but for the help of a few personal friends.

And, in fact, the Writers' Union and the censorship are a pair of Siamese twins. I mentioned before the tragic fate of an outstanding writer, Andrei Platonov, who died in 1951, at the age of fifty, of tuberculosis and undernourishment. Technically, it was not the censorship which prohibited his books; as he put it to me a few years before his death, "Fadeyev [president of the Writers' Union] has now been sitting on my manuscripts for years"; in short, they did not even reach the censorship. Andrei Platonov, now one of the most popular Soviet writers, was not "rehabilitated" until ten or twelve years after his death; even now most of his books have remained unpublished.

The Soviet Writers' Union is one of the world's greatest anomalies. And this is recognized by Sholokhov himself. Though, politically, the man most hated by the progressive writers, the Grand Literary Inquisitor at all recent Party congresses, he himself talks, at these very congresses, of the utter absurbidity of the Writers' Union, with its five thousand or six thousand members, all bearing the proud title of "Soviet author." I recall his pungent joke about the Tula section of the Writers' Union, with its 2,000 per cent increase —"Superb progress: today there are in Tula twenty-three writers; in 1910 there was only one! He was called Lev Tolstoy."

How, then, does one become a member of the Writers' Union? It is incredibly simple. The criterion here, as in so much else concerning Soviet literature today, is purely quantitative, not qualitative. Anyone who has published *two books* qualifies for membership in the Writers' Union. It does not matter what these books are; they may be two 1,000-page novels, or two thirty-page books of doggerel or third-rate lyrics, or two fifty-page books containing a few short stories, no matter how bad. Young authors have no difficulty in getting themselves published, provided they are strictly conformist in what they write. No one is more ferocious than Sholokhov (though himself the most extremist member of the Establishment) about the vast quantity of junk published, in this way, in the Soviet Union. The result of this system is altogether lamentable: the small minority of writers of quality are completely swamped by the great majority of writers of quantity, most of them hacks (*halturshchiki*) of the worst sort. The fearful weight of this overwhelming mass of hacks is bound to have a considerable influence on the bureaucrats of the Writers' Union, and it is the hacks, much more than the good writers, who have an influence on the choice and election of these bureaucrats.

Once you are a member of the Writers' Union and well-behaved in the eyes of the authorities, you never have to worry about your bread and butter. Besides being the only central literary institution in the country (with a variety of local branches, which occasionally try to show some independence), it is also a sort of charity and welfare institution. The Writers' Union takes care of finding flats for its members when necessary, arranges for their holidays, and plans and pays for their "creative trips" (such as to remote corners of the farflung Soviet Union), though such trips seldom produce anything in the least worthwhile. Having produced, say, two little books of doggerel, the writer tends to regard himself as a "Soviet author" for the rest of his life. Obviously such writers fear the return of liberalism and the weakening of the Writers' Union's power.

So long as the Writers' Union exists in its present form, dominated as it is by the great quantitative superiority of the *halturshchiki* over the real writers, it is hard to see things in Soviet literature greatly improving—*even if the government and the Party themselves were to adopt a much more liberal literary policy than they pursue today. The thousands of hacks have a vested interest in the perpetuation of the Writers' Union, with its "creative trips", its Litfond and all the other material benefits accruing from it.* Nothing is more terrifying to them than the thought of a return to the 1920s, when there was no centralized organization for writers and nobody practically guaranteed them a life pension if they did not feel like working except very occasionally. Then, to make a living, a writer had to work hard and use great talent and ingenuity to make his works acceptable at all.

A drastic transformation of the Writers' Union would help enormously to create good, and even great, literature. True, there would probably still be the censorship, but it is my deep conviction that the censorship would, as in the 1920s, be far more liberal than it is today, if only because it would in the main have to deal with original writers and have no allies among the bureaucrats. If Stalin set up the writers under one roof in 1932, it was in order to exercise on them the strictest control and to subject them to perpetual pressure of one kind or another; that is why I think the Writers' Union today is a particularly dangerous survival of Stalinism in Russia.

Several writers attending the 1967 Writers' Congress wanted Solzhenitsyn's letter discussed; but the "organizers" of the congress, the top bureaucrats of the Writers' Union, were against it; the matter was more or less hushed up, though it was, in a way, the most important thing to have happened at the congress. Among those who asked for a discussion of some of the points raised by Solzhenitsyn—particularly what he said about censorship—were Konstantin Simonov and the Leningrad writer Vera Ketlinskaya; but when I saw her at her *datcha* near Leningrad a few months later and asked her for the text of her speech, as distinct from the anodyne version published in *Literaturnaya Gazeta,* she evaded the issue.

Of special interest to the West was the short speech made by M. Armand Lanoux, a leading authority on Maupassant, on behalf of the four-man French delegation, composed of two Communists and two non-Communists (the latter including Lanoux). He spoke on behalf of all the four delegates, thus stressing the fact that French Communists and "bourgeois liberals" saw completely eye to eye when it came to Soviet literary and arts policy. Both the Communists and the non-Communists of the French delegation enormously admired the Soviet Union, but they could not swallow this policy, still less the Siniavsky-Daniel affair; and, according to Lanoux, they warned their hosts that they would raise the question at the congress; not to do so would be to condone the imprisonment of the two writers.

So, in the course of an extremely friendly and cautiously worded speech, Lanoux uttered these words, which had the effect of a bombshell: "There are certain measures you have taken in recent years that have filled your worst enemies with glee and have caused nothing but grief and consternation to your best friends."

The effect was immediate: half the hall, in Lanoux' own words, burst into frantic cheering, while the other half observed an icy silence. And then he went on to make an appeal to the Russians to accept ideological coexistence:

> Dear Soviet friends! It is your country which launched its famous appeal for peaceful coexistence amongst all nations. Well, peaceful coexistence in literature and art means a plurality of tendencies, of different ways of feeling and expressing oneself, and opposite currents; in short, the admirable and complete diversity of man. Life is plurality itself. *The framework of your humanism is, surely, large enough for you to permit and welcome all such differences with the generous smile of your strength.* [My italics.]

At the end of his speech, once again half the hall cheered and the other half was silent. And then, as he later wrote:

> The answer to my speech came like a flash. Somebody had mounted the rostrum—somebody called Evgeni Surkov. I could scarcely believe my ears. He was doing me the honor of answering me immediately, of improvising his answer—a very unusual thing at Soviet congresses. This representative of the powers that be informed me, very politely but also very firmly, that he disagreed with me, and that *there could be no such thing as ideological coexistence with the West* [my italics]. There was some vague little clapping here and there. The incident was closed. There was not a single allusion, right to the end of the congress, to the question I had raised.

In the Soviet press there was a brief account of Lanoux's speech, but not a word was printed of his plea for greater intellectual freedom, still less for Siniavsky and Daniel. This was only too typical of the official line, first clearly defined by *Pravda* early in 1967, and repeated almost word for word by A. Chakovsky, editor of *Literaturnaya Gazeta,* the official organ of the Writers' Union, a year later. This position might be described as very right of center:

two-thirds hostile to *Novy Mir*, with its "modernism," its "formalism" and its hankering for ideological coexistence with the West, including the French and Italian Communist parties, and one-third hostile to *Oktyabr*—not on political grounds, but only because of the appallingly low standard of its writing. Thus the official line is most fully represented by the third Moscow monthly, *Znamya*, on the whole a rather dreary production.

It is not true that there are no good writers in Russia, though there are virtually no great ones. The last truly great poets, now both dead, were Pasternak and Akhmatova, and we know how *they* were treated; their example shows that, to the hack-ridden Writers' Union, nothing is more alarming than the existence of great writers or the emergence of great original talents. When one comes to think of it, it is never the hacks but only exclusively writers of real talent and originality who have been in serious trouble in recent years: Pasternak, Victor Nekrasov, Yevtushenko, Ehrenburg, Voznesensky, Paustovsky, Margarita Aligher and, above all, Solzhenitsyn, whose troubles are not momentary but permanent, as it were.

The question of government policy changing in regard to literature is another matter; but there cannot be the slightest doubt that the bureaucracy of the Writers' Union, largely representing the hacks, exercises a powerful influence on the Party's and the government's literary policy; these top rulers (most of them with little time to spare for literature) take the advice of the Writers' Union bureaucrats; and though a man like Suslov might know better (or else is—which is quite probable—one of the literary ultras himself), who is Madame Furtseva, the Minister of Culture, to have a policy of her own to oppose to that of the literary bureaucrats? She has remarkably little culture herself to know any better. "Back to the twenties," which is all that the better Soviet writers are asking for, would mean enormously widening the range and possibilities of Soviet literature. For its range is appallingly limited now.

The writers suffering least from the present system are the poets. There is never much difficulty about writing lyrical verse of the more or less traditional kind; even verse that is fairly obscure is tolerated, for it can do no harm. And several, like Akhmadullina, *can* be regarded as major poets. It is when poets start writing in a highly original language of their own, or in a manner reminiscent of

Khlebnikov or Tsvetaeva (like Voznesensky), or start making little digs at the "anti-heads" (another favorite amusement of Voznesensky's) that trouble becomes almost inevitable. But, on the whole, the poets are having far less trouble under the present system than the prose writers. Here again, of course, apart from the hacks who can be trusted a hundred per cent, every line is examined through a microscope by the Writers' Union bureaucrats and by the censorship. An *avis défavorable* by the former is quite sufficient to bring about the killing of a book by the censorship; at best, it leads to that bargaining between the author and the censorship which almost invariably ends in partial or complete mutilation of the book, unless the author refuses to have it published at all in a mutilated form. In the vast majority of cases, the author would rather be published in such a form than not at all, keeping an unexpurgated copy for his friends or publishing it separately in *samizdat*.

The range of subjects for present-day novelists in the country of Tolstoy, Gogol and Dostoevsky is lamentably limited. The last war is, of course, the eminently approved subject, though it too might lead writers into trouble if they dwell too much on its "untypical" sides—such as collaboration with the Germans in the occupied areas (except when this is treated as plain villainy and treason), or cowardice, or treasonable tendencies shown by such-and-such Russian soldiers. The psychology of Russians who either were forcibly enlisted into the Vlasov (Russian quisling) army or joined it voluntarily is not an approved subject for psychological analysis in the Russian novel today; altogether, introspective novels are very badly looked upon; sex is almost a taboo subject; the industrial novel, whose functional value in the 1930s was unquestionable, is no longer of much interest, now that industry is in perfectly good working order and has no problems to speak of. After Stalin's death more attention began to be paid by novelists to the Russian countryside, and some, like Yefim Dorosh, played an important role in showing up the lamentable deficiencies of Soviet agriculture and of village life. On the other hand, "historical novels" about Lenin and the early years of the Revolution are encouraged, though, as Tvardovsky openly said in *Novy Mir,* most of these are completely phony. In fact, except possibly *Zhivago* and one or two more, no great novel in the real sense has emerged from Russia in the last thirty-five years.* It is lamentable to think that during this period Russia should have produced not only nothing to equal the great Russian classics, but practically nothing to equal the twentieth-century literature of the West. There is no Soviet equivalent of Marcel Proust, Joyce, Kafka, Malraux, Mauriac, Steinbeck, Hemingway, Norman Mailer or even relatively minor figures such as Isherwood, Virginia Woolf or Evelyn Waugh.

Any kind of sophisticated prose writing is almost invariably prohibited, so much so that the enormously colorful and expressive novels of the 1920s, with their verbal virtuosity, such as Leonid Leonov's *The Thief* or Vsevolod Ivanov's Russian Civil War stories, have for many years now been available only in "translations" into socialist-realist prose.

For satire there is practically no room at all. At a pinch, a satirist can be funny about Germans or Americans, or even about the kolkhoz chairman or the *upravdom*, the house manager, but that is about all that the heirs of Gogol and Saltykov-Shchedrin are allowed to do. I defy anybody to produce even a faint smile, let alone a chuckle, reading *Krokodil* or the "Page of Humor" in *Literaturnaya Gazeta*. The only kind of literature that can still produce a smile is children's books, such as Kornei Chukovsky's or the late Samuel Marshak's. Altogether exceptional among books for adults in recent years is Katayev's hilarious nightmare *The Holy Well*.

Other exceptional works include novels and short stories by Yuri Bondarev, Vasili Bykov, Grigori Baklanov; novels or novellas on the 1941–45 war by Simonov, Anatoli Kuznetzov (*Babi Yar,* a novel on the German occupation of Kiev available in English), and a few more; other novels by men like Vasili Belov (who first appeared in an obscure Petrozavodsk monthly with a circulation of ten thousand); short stories, novellas or diaries by Nina Kosterina (*Diary*), Mark Shcheglov (*Student Notebooks*), Vladimir Tendryakov, Yuri Kazakov, Sergei Zalygin, Alexander Yashin, Yuri Nagibin, Yevgeni Nosov, Vasili Aksyonov, Georgi Vladimirov; Boris Mozhayev's novella *From the Life of Fyodor Kuzkin;* and books on rural conditions in Russia like Yefim Dorosh's and Fyodor Abramov's books Solzhenitsyn's three or four (now virtually prohibited) stories, and Yuri Dombrovsky's *The Keeper of Antiquities,* an

* Most of Sholokhov's *Quiet Flows the Don* was written in the 1920s.

autobiographical novel by a man deported during the Stalin purge.*

Some outstanding books of both prose and verse have lately been contributed by non-Russians: novellas by Chingiz Aimatov (Kirghizia), the prose writer Fazil Iskander (Abkhazia, on the Black Sea coast), the Daghestan (Caspian coast) poet Rasul Gamzatov, the Bashkir poet Mustai Karin, the Belorussian poet Arkadi Kuleshov and the Ukrainian poet Ivan Drech. Among the "grandfathers" who are first-rate writers are Katayev, Ehrenburg and Paustovsky; among the "fathers" (in their late forties or fifties) are Daniel Granin, Victor Astafyev, Vera Panova and Victor Nekrasov.

There are perhaps half a dozen more names I have forgotten to add of good or very good writers of today. But what is so profoundly significant is that, with a very few exceptions, all these writers should be *Novy Mir* authors, and the publication of any of their works in the liberal monthly is usually preceded by a long struggle between the journal on the one hand and the Writers' Union bureaucrats and the censorship on the other. Finally most appear in an "expurgated" form.

As we have seen, the poets have a much easier time than the novelists. Poetry writing is almost a national sport in Russia, probably the only country (at least in Europe) where poetry is read by "the people" and where books of poetry can be sold in hundreds of thousands and even millions of copies. There must literally be tens or even hundreds of thousands of poets in the Soviet Union, and of these several thousand are published—if not in book form, at least in the daily or weekly press. At least a hundred poets can be ranked as good, and perhaps twenty or thirty as very good; one has only to look at annual poetry almanacs such as *Den Poezii* to realize that much of this poetry is not only technically excellent but inventive and original. But there is, all the same, a limit in poetry beyond which it is inadvisable for poets to go, as we have seen in the cases of Yevtushenko and Voznesensky—the former with his extremely controversial and "dangerous" political subjects, such as the heirs of Stalin, anti-Semitism (as in *Babi Yar*) and the like, the latter a genuine modernist in Soviet poetry, a juggler with words, a disciple as it were of two of the *poètes damnés,* Tsvetaeva and Pasternak,

---

* It is available in an excellent French translation by my old friend Jean Cathala, the top French translator of the best Russian fiction; living permanently in Moscow, he "discovers" the books himself.

and, moreover, a believer in ideological coexistence with the West, with a special fascination for America and particularly for beatnik poets like Allen Ginsberg and Ferlinghetti.

And what of the Russian reader? People in their fifties, remembering the exciting twenties or even a good deal of inspiring literature written during the war, are disgusted with the literature of the last few years—with a few rare, very rare exceptions, such as Simonov's war novels or a few young or youngish short-story writers like Tendryakov, Nagibin, Aksyonov and half a dozen others. People of the very young generation are simply puzzled: why did Russia have Tolstoy and Dostoevsky and Chekhov; and why hasn't she got anything even remotely like them? And to the young the great favorites continue to be the "eternal companions," the Russian nineteenth-century classics, together with a few writers of the 1920s (provided they have been reprinted, which they seldom are), the very few "unconventional" writers of both prose and poetry, and a few (relatively rare) fairly recent foreign novels available in Russian by Hemingway, Thomas Mann, Erich Maria Remarque and a few more. But no Malraux or Evelyn Waugh, for instance, In the 1920s hundreds of foreign books were translated into Russian. The ordinary people may be quite happy to read the nineteenth-century classics, but they wonder why there are so few new novels that are really worth reading.

No, *everybody* feels that there is something wrong about Soviet literature today; and everybody (except the profiteers of the Writers' Union) prays for some miracle: for a truly cultured Minister of Culture, for instance, or, better still, for a Politburo which will make up its mind to appoint at last another Lunacharsky—one of Lenin's closest companions—as ideological and cultural chief, who would demolish or at least rebuild the Writers' Union and return to the 1920s.

OLD AND NEW FRIENDS

In spite of my reservations about the Soviet literary Establishment, I was still happy to see some of my old writer friends, mostly people I had first met during the war: the exuberant, ever happy Boris Polevoi, editor of *Yunost;* Alexei Surkov, whom I could not help associating in my mind with our first meeting in the tragic autumn of 1941; Margarita Aligher; my old friend Savva Dangulov; and then some of the younger people—Vasili Aksynov and Yuri Trifonov and the exquisite poet Evgeni Vinokurov. And, of course, Valentin Katayev, who was like a breeze of warm fragrant wind from the Black Sea, from his native Odessa.

Alexei Surkov, now seventy, though chubby and gay, could now be considered a back number. The subscription to the multivolume set of his poems had not been a success; people were, it seems, no longer interested in simple and (at the time) inspiring wartime verses, which had been very popular in the Army twenty-five years ago; but he had not made himself popular with the left intellectuals (this also applied to Polevoi and Simonov) for the hostile stand he had taken in the Pasternak affair; but then he was president of the Writers' Union at the time, a top bureaucrat. Anyway, he now thought, a bit insensitively, that it had all proved a storm in a teacup; Pasternak was now being reprinted in a big way—yes, even with a preface by Siniavsky!

Surkov had two sides to him: that of the hard bureaucrat and that of the man not free of all sensibility; it was he who, as editor of *Ogonyok,* first started printing Akhmatova's new poems, three years after she had been damned "forever" by Zhdanov as half nun, half whore. As for Ivinskaya, Pasternak's friend, I was to hear about her not from Surkov but from old Chukovsky, a man with absolutely no ax to grind, and a man of the greatest charity and kindness. And about Ivinskaya he said the same as Surkov had said a few years ago.

Boris Polevoi, though now nearly sixty, was as bright as ever. We talked about our wartime meetings, especially in the Ukraine, where we spent a week together in March 1944 during Konev's famous blitzkrieg through the mud. He was editor of *Yunost,* which he proposed to make as liberal a paper—Yevtushenko and all—as *Novy Mir,* and which had a two-million circulation. But lately pressures had been applied by somebody (one could never quite make out by whom exactly), and it had had to follow a more conformist line. Meantime Polevoi was turning out wartime novels (with little anti-Stalin side kicks; this was permissible) and also his book of wartime reminiscences, in which I figured largely though, to me totally unrecognizably—complete with a nonexistent wife and two children trapped in Prague under the German occupation! And, of course, he made me ask all the silly-ass questions foreign correspondents would normally ask in a Soviet description of them, like "You aren't too cross with us for not having opened the Second Front yet?" and so on. However, we had a good laugh, and he agreed that, on the whole, I had described him in *Russia at War* more accurately than he had described me.

Evgeni Vinokurov was one of the finest of the younger poets, though a quiet poet, who liked to call himself an Acmeist—the school to which Gumilev and Akhmatova had once belonged. I spent a whole day at his *datcha* at Vnukovo. Not only was he a good poet, he was also a subtle and sensitive essayist whose essays on Fet, Blok and other poets are among the finest produced in Russia today. He was keeping clear of politics and so was having a fairly quiet life. He said that after nearly fifty years of hardships, wars, famines, police terror and all kinds of misfortunes, Russia was at last settling down to a peaceful, contented, well-fed life, and long may it continue. He felt fairly confident that nobody would dare attack her. He liked to speak of his own poetry and contrast it with all the noise and thunder of Yevtushenko and Voznesensky. "I never get onto a platform to scream and bellow. I don't want a Luzhniki audience of fifteen thousand." Yes, I felt, he was a good poet—but was it not important for poets to scream and bellow and be provocative, as Voznesensky was with his *Anti-Heads,* and Yevtushenko with his *Heirs of Stalin?* It was not necessarily great poetry, but politically it was enormously important.

I had known Yuri Trifonov only from his novel *The Students,* written in the last years of Stalin. Now he had written a strange book, *The Reflections of the Bonfire,* in which he described the life of his own father, a Rostov revolutionary who took part in the 1905 Revolution, the October Revolution and the Russian Civil War, only to be destroyed, in the end, in the Stalin purges.

Everybody, or nearly everybody, among Russian intellectuals had some trouble at one time or another. Vasili Aksyonov was one of the most brilliant younger writers, author of *Morocco Oranges* and so on—unusual writing for the Soviet Union, jerky, allusive, without the monotonous flow of the socialist-realist novel. I told Aksyonov he was one of the most popular young writers abroad, especially in France. "Not here," he said rather gloomily; he was having difficulty lately in getting his new books published. He had a tragic family history. His brother had died of hunger and cold at the age of sixteen, while being evacuated from Leningrad in 1942 across the ice of Lake Ladoga. He was young and handsome, and with nothing of the rakishness and thuggishness which appeared in the photograph on the jacket of one of his books I possessed. He also spoke of his mother, Evgenia Ginsburg, author of *Into the Whirlwind*, which tells the lurid story of her first three years as a deportee of the Stalin purges. "Yes," he said, "she lives in Moscow, is not having any trouble, and even writes for *Literaturnaya Gazeta*. The book was issued as a *samizdat* production, and somebody got hold of a copy, took it abroad and sold it for huge sums of money to an Italian publisher. My mother knew nothing about it and was very angry."

The same thing happened, of course, to two other famous books in the Stalin purges—Akhmatova's *Requiem* and Lydia Chukovskaya's *The Deserted House*. The authorities were somehow turning a blind eye to anti-Stalin literature of this kind being published abroad. But Siniavsky and Daniel were a different case.

Chukovskaya, Anna Akhmatova—yes, they had both done their months of queuing in Leningrad outside prisons and prosecutors' offices in 1937–38. One had written one of her greatest poems, *Requiem*—not published till 1963, and abroad at that; the other had written the intensely human, moving and harrowing short novel *The Deserted House*, showing how a perfectly loyal family was destroyed in the Stalin purges, those purges which often turned even the finest and noblest people into cowards or vindictive creatures ready to betray anyone to save their own skin. Lydia had queued in vain during all those days and nights; her husband, an eminent Leningrad scientist, was shot as an "enemy of the people" (as she learned only much later). Akhmatova's (and Gumilev's) son was to spend many years in a camp.

Of all the many writers I met in Moscow that summer, I remember only two or three who approved of the trial of Siniavsky and Daniel; some felt that, at a pinch, they should have been given some kind of vote of censure, that they should even have been ostracized for a time, but five and seven years in a camp—surely that was absurd. It was really not *their* fault if foreign anti-Soviet organizations were making such a song and dance about them. If it hadn't been for these heavy sentences, nobody would have bothered much about either them or their books.

But the Solzhenitsyn letter to the Writers' Union was taken much, much more seriously. First, there was the almost general conviction that here was a really major writer, perhaps a great writer, who was being victimized by the police; and second, he had raised *the* fundamental of all fundamental questions: censorship. It was censorship which was preventing Russia from producing great writers —and there were several who were potentially great. Most felt they could have written better than they did if it weren't for the mysterious hand of Glavlit, which not only was doing the censorship but was also creating in every writer—except for a few incorrigible rebels like Pasternak—*self-censorship.*

"Surely," one of my writer friends reflected, "we are sufficiently responsible citizens not to write scurrilous anti-Soviet books. Most of us like and admire our regime. Short of damning and challenging the Soviet regime, why can't we write anything we like?" And he added, "Yes, let there be a law against treasonable, seditious and pornographic literature, but let the terms be clearly defined in every case. Let's do away with a system in which a good book's fate depends on the whim of some anonymous and usually stupid and malevolent bureaucrat." Another argument often heard among writers was something like this: "With those 1932 canons—socialist realism and educational value and engineers-of-human-souls stuff— we have reached a dead end. Our people are now sufficiently educated not to need all this "improving" literature. All that sort of thing may have had some purpose in the 1930s, when our people were still scarcely literate. The war is still a subject, and the Stalin era is a subject; neither has been entirely exhausted. But let's write also about present-day Russia, in human, psychological terms; let's write satire; above all, let's get back to the experimentalism, the new writing, the fantasy—yes, above all, the fantasy—of the 1920s. Let satire be allowed to aim a little higher than the chairman of the kolkhoz or the *upravdom.* Isn't the whole Khrushchev ménage, for instance, a glorious subject for satire? Yet in the last few years there is only one man who has done it, and done it brilliantly, and that's Valentin Katayev, in his *Holy Well.* But we could have dozens of books on the same lines; instead, we keep on being reminded of the fact that we are "the heirs of Maxim Gorki," and the worse a hack is, the more passionately will be invoked the supreme authority of Gorki."

One day, on a visit to Peredelkino, I went to see Katayev; though seventy-one, he was full of youth and vigor, the last of the great pleiad of the "fellow travelers" of the 1920s. (Fedin and Leonov had become little more than hacks after years and years of Stalinite discipline.) Katayev was the exuberant Odessite, a worthy brother of Eugene Petrov—the Petrov of the immortal Ilf and Petrov tandem, who, with their *Twelve Chairs* and *Little Golden Calf,* had written the two funniest satirical books produced since the Revolution (apart from some Zoshchenko stories). They had appeared round 1930, but had been reprinted only after Stalin's death. Katayev was in the same Odessa tradition—southern, exuberant, witty, funny. Back in the 1920s he had written another very funny book, *The Embezzlers,* and his *Time, Forward* was the only truly readable Five-Year-Plan novel; in it he conveyed all the excitement of the Revolution, but without allowing his writing to be stifled by doctrinaire single-mindedness. Now he had had prostate trouble; and, as he said, "it was awful to have to go and pee every ten minutes, so I decided to have an operation, and under the anesthetic I had such strange dreams that they gave me the idea for my *Holy Well.*" This exuberant kind of comic-Kafka story is full of the weirdest symbols: Stalinism is a talking cat which says *"Máma"* in Russian and *"Maman"* in French but which dies when they try to make it say "neocolonialism." Katayev flits from one mood to another. He flies to America, where he is obsessed by everyone in New York noticing a speck of dust on one of his shoes, and a nightmarish kind of *marchandage* goes on between him and the shoeshine man, whose surrealist mathematics finally deprives Katayev of his last half dollar. In New York he meets a traveling Russian "intellectual," the post-thaw version of the talking cat, who warns him not to show his admiration for America too openly; Katayev has, however, a sly, snobbish laugh-back at this bureaucrat, the sort of Russian who travels the world in delegations, delivering platitudes about cultural exchanges. At a banquet in the Waldorf-Astoria the "intellectual" dips his fingers into what he takes to be a fingerbowl, only to find, to the capitalists' amusement, that the bowl contains a pineapple dessert. Whereupon "Alfred Parasyuk, Intellectual," as his visiting card describes him, concludes that the Americans are always up to some kind of provocation, while his bosses decide he had better be sent to a less difficult continent to pursue his cultural activities.

This succession of surrealist scenes is one of the very best things to have appeared in Russia in recent years, and it delighted Yevtushenko so much that he called it a work of genius. It is, especially in the rather drab context of Soviet literature in 1966–67. Almost as exciting, though in a different way, is *The Grass of Oblivion*, Katayev's reminiscences of two literary figures so entirely different from each other as Ivan Bunin and Mayakovsky. Katayev was only a lyric-writing schoolboy when he went to see the Master, then living in a seaside villa near Odessa. Bunin was then very much the *barin*. When, after the Revolution, Bunin and Katayev met again in Odessa, the *barin* had fled from the Revolution, which he found too cruel, and Katayev was now a former tsarist officer who had been decorated for bravery with the St. George's Cross. One left Russia and became an emigré in Paris, in due course winning the Nobel Prize; the other stayed in Russia. Visiting Bunin's widow in the drab emigré world of Paris some forty years later, Katayev argues that Bunin would have done better to stay in Russia. But would he have survived? Would he have shown the same cynical opportunism as "Count" Alexei Tolstoy, who was prepared to do anything Stalin demanded of him? Maybe Katayev had some doubts. Bunin, with his contempt for modernism, would not have fitted into the uproarious twenties any more than he would have fitted into the Stalin era. Katayev survived, though, like Ehrenburg, he did not find life comfortable or easy under Stalin.

There is something in common between the memoirs of Ehrenburg, the Kiev-born cosmopolitan, and *The Grass of Oblivion* by the Odessite First World War officer—the same kind of pre-Revolutionary intellectual refinement. But Katayev, I think, has even better visual observation, more humor and a finer turn of phrase. Almost as good as the unforgettable Bunin portrait is that of Mayakovsky, a gargantuan exhibitionist who buys caviar by the kilo and yet feels a hunted and unhappy man; and it so happens that he spends the last evening before his suicide in Katayev's house. A strange phenomenon indeed: for these two Katayev books form a kind of link between pre-Revolutionary culture and these late 1960s, in which the young people, bored with thirty-five years of socialist realism, welcome the near-surrealist fantasy of this author in his seventies. There was also something symbolic in this choice of Bunin and Mayakovsky—of the last of the "Turgenev" classics and the great romantic of the Revolution—one fleeing from the Revolution, the other driven to suicide by it. But Katayev, with his happy Odessa temper, lived through it all without ever losing his own identity, though secretly loathing Stalinism and all it stood for.

The great question is: Were these two extraordinary books of 1966 and 1967 just a lucky fluke, or do they provide a promise for the Soviet literature of the second fifty years?

Another visit I paid in Peredelkino was to that grand old man of Russian literature, Kornei Chukovsky, writer of the best-loved children's books, great literary scholar, author of books on children's speech and Russian usage, translator of Walt Whitman. A young lady told me Kornei Ivanovich could not see me the morning I called, because he had tummyache, having eaten too many apricots. However, I was allowed to see him in the afternoon. He was a real youngster of eighty-six, and his favorite toys were his Oxford gown and mortarboard, which he promptly put on in my honor.

I reminded him of how I first saw him in 1915 in a concert hall in the Mokhovaya in Petrograd, where he was then giving a lecture on Oscar Wilde, of all people. We recalled our meetings during the war, here in Peredelkino. He gave me a volume of his essays, including one on Oscar Wilde, with a particularly touching dedication, "To my adored Alexander Werth—Kornei Chukovsky." It moved me deeply.

"Dear Kornei Ivanovich," I said, "I promise you your book will be in good company—between an inscribed copy of Akhmatova's little volume published in Tashkent in 1943 and the tiny book of poems, *On Early Trains,* which Pasternak gave me here at Peredelkino in 1945 with the leg-pulling inscription 'To my dear Alexander Werth, eloquent Soviet agitator, with best wishes, Boris Pasternak.' "

There were tears in Chukovsky's eyes. "Pasternak, Akhmatova," he said, "our two greatest poets, and look how they were treated!" He then paid me wonderful compliments on my last big book on the war in Russia, the English paperback edition of which was lying on his table. And then he spoke of the last two years of Pasternak's life. "Yes, it was tragic. He would burst out sobbing. He felt like a hounded animal. He didn't think people could be so vicious, so malevolent." Then Chukovsky spoke of Olga Ivinskaya. "There," he said, "all your various Crankshaws got hold of quite the wrong end of the stick. She *was* a bad woman, she made him sign any old thing to get hold of his foreign royalties, and she went in for currency speculation in a big way. They had every reason to lock both her and her daughter up. But there was something even worse. Ivinskaya played on his senile eroticism—he was nearly seventy then. Pasternak's wife, Zinaida, would nurse him when he was ill, give him enemas, carry bedpans. But the moment he was better, he would rush off to Ivinskaya. No, Zinaida—she died only a few months ago—was a very wonderful woman, but she got a very, very raw deal. She was a true companion to Boris; but Ivinskaya played a very evil part in the last years of Boris Leonidovich's life. Your 'Russian experts' should have shown a little more sympathy for Zinaida, and much, much less for Ivinskaya, who strictly deserved none."

"So what Surkov said about Ivinskaya was substantially true?"

"Yes," said Kornei Ivanovich, "I'm afraid so. There's much about Surkov I don't like—you remember *his* foul attacks on Pasternak? But where Ivinskaya is concerned, he's perfectly right. I can say so with greater authority because to me Pasternak and Zinaida were very dear friends and I knew about all the harm Ivinskaya was doing to both of them." If this had come from anyone else, I might have had some doubts; but Kornei Chukovsky had always been a man of the greatest intellectual honesty and integrity.

He was not a very happy man at heart during that summer. His son, Nikolai Chukovsky, an outstanding novelist, had recently died, and, as we have seen, his daughter Lydia, now over sixty, was in poor health, half blind and generally embittered.

I was allowed to see Lydia for just a moment. She was a tragic figure: one of those Russians whose lives had been wrecked by the Stalin purges, and who still felt very bitter about it. What she had described in *The Deserted House* was based on her own experiences during the purges, in which her husband had died. It was scarcely surprising that she should have reacted as sharply as she did to Sholokhov's advocacy of shooting people without trial.

"Yes," she said, "that loathsome hunchback in my book, the

public prosecutor, was a real person. There *was* such a hunchback in Leningrad. But then, like other NKVD men, he himself was shot during the purge of the purgers following the disgrace of Yezhov." She had written the book soon after the events; then, after the publication of *Ivan Denisovich* in *Novy Mir* in 1962, she had hoped to get it published there. But Khrushchev suddenly decided there were to be no more purge or camp books. Then somebody must have taken one of the numerous *samizdat* copies out of the country; for it appeared, with minor differences, in both Paris and New York. "Oh, what does it matter?" she said, "Everybody here has read it in typescript anyway."* And she briefly mentioned her great friendship with Anna Akhmatova, with whom she had shared the agonies of 1937–38. She was now working on a book on Akhmatova.

I felt that many a life had been broken or crippled, as Lydia Chukovskaya's was, by the Stalin purges. I recalled my young eighteen-year-old friend who had never suffered from anything, and to whom Stalin's funeral was nothing but a dim childhood memory. . . .

I left Moscow for Leningrad with a somewhat confused feeling. I recalled what Togliatti wrote shortly before his death: "You are still very slow in liquidating the consequences of the Stalin cult." Were they slow or weren't they? They were the young, to whom Stalin meant little or nothing; there were those whose lives had been crippled by the purges. There were some who still saw in Stalinism a source of strength and power. Was the great de-Stalinization debate that Khrushchev had opened in 1956 still going on? Or, as has been suggested, had Khrushchev foolishly thought he had opened nothing, but merely closed the debate? There are some, like my friend Professor Boltin, who now say that Stalinism has stopped being a vital issue in Russia; that people are trying to forget it, and that young people are being given the haziest possible view of the Stalin epoch—in short, that Stalinism now belongs to the past. But does it? It still lives on in many fields, and perhaps most tangibly in the realm of art and literature.

So those "heirs of Stalin" of whom Yevtushenko spoke in 1962

---

* An English translation by my wife, Aline B. Werth, was published in England by Barrie & Rockliff and by Pan Books (paperback) and in the United States by E. P. Dutton.

are still active. People die off; but can one say for certain that the grandchildren and great-grandchildren of the Revolution will not inherit some Stalinist characteristics? For the Stalinites have at least one thing *always* to fall back on: the international situation. What, they say, is the ban on Solzhenitsyn's books, or the arrest of a few writers here and there, compared with the massacres which have been going on for years, day after day, in Vietnam? The Stalinite bureaucracy, the supercentralizers, have always made rearmament and the international tensions of these last years their chief excuse for not giving way to the liberals; and this, absurd as it may seem, applies to literature too. These Stalinites have one argument which it is not always easy to dispose of. There was total disregard for the human person under Stalin; innocent people were accused and shot and deported by the million; but, as Yevtushenko himself said in *The Heirs of Stalin,* there were also Turksib and Magnitka (representing the industrialization of Russia) and "the flag over Berlin"— Russia's victory over Nazi Germany. So on balance, the Stalinites claim, Stalinism had justified itself. *Only, is it necessary now?*

They also claim that great concessions have been made to the young people wanting to read sophisticated books. All sorts of writers who were taboo only a few years ago are being published now in large editions: Tsvetaeva, and Andrei Belyi, and Pasternak, Zabolotsky, Bagritsky, Akhmatova. (A confirmation, by the way, of the Solzhenitsyn argument that "they'll publish you, but only after you've been dead for years.")

No doubt the pressure of the young intellectuals in favor of a freer, more varied literature cannot be ignored; but it is hard to say whether Ehrenburg's optimistic prophecy that Russia will begin to have a great literature in twenty years' time, or Katayev's even more optimistic view of the future, can be taken literally.

MUSIC: A HOPEFUL PRECEDENT

There is not, at the moment, much ground for optimism about the immediate prospects of Soviet literature. Yet one reason for hope, which I have not yet mentioned, is what has been happening to Russian music in the last few years.

Literature was the first, and music the last, of the victims of Zhdanov's cultural and ideological purge in the late 1940s. Literature was the most obvious victim, and Zhdanov started with it in 1946; there followed the cinema, painting, history, sculpture, philosophy, science; and then—but not until two years after the beginning of the cultural purge in 1948—came music. Music being by its very nature almost entirely an abstract form of art, the very notion of trying to apply to it socialist-realist canons seemed the height of absurdity. And yet Zhdanov demanded, in the most threatening manner, that music conform to the strictest socialist-realist canons, too.

I described this incredible episode in great detail in a book I wrote shortly afterward.* Even under Stalin it would be difficult to find anything to equal the odious absurdity of Zhdanov's victimization of the composers. How absurd it was they all knew, but, while some "agreed" with the arts dictator only halfheartedly, others found it expedient to cringe to Zhdanov and to proclaim his cretinous statement on music to be the greatest and most profound masterpiece, which had, "thanks to the wisdom and genius in all things of the Party and our beloved Stalin," opened their eyes to the evil they had done in allowing themselves for years to write meaningless, formalist and antipopular music. It is shocking to think that among those who cringed most was one of the two greatest Russian composers of the time, Dimitri Shostakovich. The other one, and the greater of the two in my opinion, Sergei Prokofiev, either refused to attend the three-day conference Zhdanov had convened at the Central Committee (there is no mention of his presence in the shorthand record of the conference) or else, as rumor had it in Moscow at the time, behaved with the greatest truculence, saying nothing, but merely sitting on a piano stool with his back turned to Zhdanov. Miaskovsky, heartbroken, also apparently was absent. Khachaturian paid lip service to Zhdanov's wisdom, but expressed, all the same, important reservations.

Until only a few weeks before, the Soviet press had treated the "Big Four"—Shostakovich, Prokofiev, Khachaturian and Miaskovsky—as "the supreme and worldwide glory of all contemporary music." Now all these and many others were singled out as "the

* *Musical Uproar in Moscow* (London, 1949).

most pernicious influence" in Soviet music. What had been their greatest crime? Under corrupt Western influence, they had for years been writing music which was unintelligible to the people, with their healthy instincts; they went in for sophisticated, cacophonous gibberish, instead of writing beautiful, melodious music, which the people loved and demanded. Zhdanov's central argument was that there could be no good or great music which was not based on folk song and could thus be "instantly understood and remembered." He reached the height of cretinism when he said that if, say, Bach, Mozart and Beethoven were great geniuses, it was only because their immortal works were the direct outcome of the folk songs they had heard in their childhood and youth.

Even more shocking than Shostakovich's acceptance of this "fundamental truth" was the instant profiteering that took place at the Zhdanov conference. Second- and third-rate composers, such as Tikhon Khrennikov, and various hacks—mostly writers of more or less popular hits, such as Zakharov—supported Zhdanov with almost unequaled viciousness, denouncing Prokofiev and Shostakovich as a pair of charlatans, and Khachaturian and Miaskovsky as not much better.

The consequence of this could have been foreseen: the Composers' Union was purged from top to bottom. Shostakovich, Khachaturian and other distinguished composers were ignominiously thrown out of their "commanding posts" and replaced by Khrennikov, Zakharov, etc. For several months the works of Shostakovich, Prokofiev, Miaskovsky and Khachaturian were banned from the concert halls, and so were all Prokofiev's ballets, including the immensely popular *Romeo and Juliet* and *Cinderella,* from the Bolshoi and all other theaters. Miaskovsky was totally discouraged, and he died a broken man three years later. The others tried to mend their ways—Shostakovich apparently genuinely, by writing "tuneful" cantatas and other works; Prokofiev, with his tongue in his cheek, wrote his Seventh Symphony, a sort of conscious *pastiche* of Glière or Glazunov at their worst, whereupon the Soviet press, going into raptures, said that this was by far the finest work Prokofiev had ever written, and exalted the immense and salutary service the Party and "our beloved Stalin" had rendered Soviet music!

But it was all too absurd. A few months later, and especially after

Zhdanov's sudden death in August 1948, the formalists were gradually readmitted to the theaters and concert halls; nevertheless, the new bosses of the Composers' Union kept an eagle eye on what Prokofiev, Shostakovich and the rest were going to do next. Prokofiev's opera *The Story of a Real Man,* though much more "tuneful" than his earlier works, was damned outright by the Composers' Union as "deplorably formalist." It was not retrieved from the wastepaper basket until many years after Stalin's and Prokofiev's deaths. (By an extraordinary coincidence, they had died on the same day. There were no flowers at Prokofiev's funeral; all the existing supplies of flowers in the whole of the Soviet Union had gone to Stalin!)

The incredible absurdity of Zhdanov's attempt to enforce on music the most rigid canons of socialist realism was, of course, even more patently absurd than in even the other forms of creative activity. All the same, the music hacks clung to their "commanding heights" at the Composers' Union and in the principal music journals, such as *Soviet Music,* and nothing much changed for some time after Stalin's death. It was not until 1958, ten years after the infamous Zhdanov decree on music of February 10, 1948, that the Central Committee of the Party issued a new decree, agreeing with the "general principles" of the 1948 decree but declaring much in it to have been erroneous, above all the sweeping condemnation of "eminent composers" like Prokofiev and Shostakovich.

When I returned to Russia in 1959, after an eleven-year "exile," one of my most pleasant surprises was to find that music had been almost fully restored to health. New names which I had scarcely heard, if at all, in 1948 had now become prominent in Soviet music: Sviridov, Sidelnikov, Artemiev, Shchedrin, Volkonsky, Galynin, Kara-Karayev, Arapov, Chervinsky and many others. Since Stalin's death or, at any rate, since 1955 or 1956, composers had been left to do almost what they liked. Here was a brilliant new generation of Soviet composers, many of them not Russian, but Caucasian or Central Asian; they were masters in all kinds of genres—oratorios in the grand Russian style (by Artemiev, Sidelnikov), ballet music (by Shchedrin), symphonies and piano and violin concertos, chamber music (notably by Volkonsky, Galynin, Kara-Karayev, etc.).

Old Shaporin, whom I met several times in Moscow in 1959, was particularly enthusiastic about Volkonsky—in reality, Prince

Andrei Volkonsky, who had been born into an emigré family in Paris, and whose first teacher had been Rachmaninov himself. He had only recently "returned" to his native country, which he had never seen before. Of Volkonsky, Shaporin said, "He is an exceptionally brilliant and original composer—the author of *Eluard Cantata*, with a quite heavenly aria, of incidental music for Shaw's *Saint Joan*, and of some admirable chamber music, including a trio, a quintet, and much else: polyphonic, lapidary, classical and chromatic music." When I asked what he remembered of that famous Zhdanov conference with the composers in 1948, he made a grimace and said, "Let's not talk about it; it was *horrible*."

Ten years after, Shostakovich had again become "our greatest living composer" and was now writing precisely what he liked; Prokofiev had now become "the Great Ancestor"—nearly all new Soviet music had been inspired and influenced by Prokofiev more than by any other composer. All this new music was progressive, experimental, full of new and brilliant ideas; if it did not try to imitate the most extremist, truly cacophonous experiments in Western Europe, it was simply because none of the Russian composers had any genuine use for them. As for dodecaphonic music, practically every young Russian composer agreed with Shostakovich (himself the very opposite of a "traditionalist" or "conservative") that there was absolutely no future in it:

> I know that in music, as in everything else, new ways should be sought. But . . . dodecaphonic music can get us nowhere. Its narrow dogmatism is purely artificial. . . . Not a single work by Schoenberg has yet gained general recognition. The same is true of Webern. We [recently] heard a very early (1910) work of his, and it made a bigger impression than anything he has written since; his talent, I feel, was dried up by the dodecaphonic dogma. The means of expression in this kind of music are, indeed, extremely limited. At its best, it can only express depression, prostration and deadly fear. . . . It belongs to the old world; it has been invented by people who are afraid of the present and do not believe in the future. . . . It is nothing but a passing fashion. The even newer tendencies to which it has given rise, such as *pointillisme*, are altogether contrary to what we mean by music.*

* Shostakovich, quoted in the author's *The Khrushchev Phase* (London, 1961), p. 222.

Another peculiarity of 1959, as compared with 1948, was that much *real* modern Western music was played in Russia; the most popular of new Western composers was Benjamin Britten.

I speak here, of course, of the Soviet "musical public." As in all other countries, there is in Russia a fairly clear distinction between this "musical public" and the ordinary run of concertgoers and record collectors. The latter still vastly prefer classical music—all the way from Bach* to Rachmaninov—plus a few Prokofiev and Khachaturian "favorites," to anything modern. The general public in Russia, as elsewhere, takes ten, twenty, even fifty years to catch up with the musical public. It is funny to think, but perfectly true, that the general public (in Russia, at any rate) discovered Brahms about 1910 and Mahler not till the 1920s! But the same is broadly true of all countries.

Since 1959, nearly ten more years have passed; and if in 1959 there was still a little official "supervision" over music, this has now—I speak of 1967—practically completely disappeared. Virtually entirely free rein had been given to composers; and the results have been little short of remarkable. Still many more new names have appeared, most of them wholly unknown in 1959. These are men in their twenties, thirties or early forties. The new composers' names I heard most frequently mentioned in 1967 are Tishchenko (about thirty), Karavaichuk and Slonimsky (both about forty), all three of them from Leningrad; among the most famous of the young Moscow composers are one with the startling name of Edison Denisov (in reality, "Edison" is merely—except for the *v*—an anagram of his surname, Denisov!), Schnittke and Karetnikov (both about thirty-five) and a few others. Tishchenko, like most last-generation composers, is described as being "left of Prokofiev"; but, to Tishchenko, Prokofiev was merely a starting point, and he has developed an original and many-sided talent of his own, his output including a piano concerto and several piano sonatas, some of them "ultramodernist" and others in the "tradition" of Monteverdi—something entirely new in Russian music.

Karavaichuk (of whom, oddly enough, I *had* heard during the

* It is only since quite recently that a growing number of people in Russia are becoming genuinely interested in pre-Bachian music, notably Monteverdi. But so far there are practically no Soviet gramophone records of this music in existence.

war, when he was an infant-prodigy pianist in Tashkent) has written in a great variety of genres; his most famous work is *The Bedbug,* an opera based on Mayakovsky's satirical extravaganza. He lives in Leningrad and is one of its best-loved and most famous composers. He is also a superb pianist, but highly eccentric: he can stop at any moment and declare, "I don't like the way I play this. I'll start all over again." Or else he stops and begins to comment on the piece he is playing. His programs usually consist of such odd mixtures as Bach, Debussy and himself. In one recital, in which he was wearing a hired tailcoat, he suddenly stopped in the middle of a tricky prestissimo passage and said, "This damned coat is too tight under the arms." He disappeared for half a minute and then reappeared on the platform clad in a sort of bright-green football singlet and resumed his prestissimo amidst loud laughter. One of his greatest achievements is that of improvisation, the audience shouting out themes—jazz, Mozart, Stravinsky, anything. He ranks as probably the most stupendous improviser in the world.

Like the scientists, like most historians, the composers today are amongst the happiest people in the Soviet Union. And I come to this obvious conclusion: If in the last fifteen, and especially the last ten, years there has been a fantastic liberalization and, almost literally, liberation of music, is there not reason to believe that the same will happen to literature, though no doubt much more slowly? The reasons for the slower progress are obvious, too; literature, much more than music, is a "political object," and, more important still, the musical world suffers incomparably less than the literary world from bureaucratic interference or from the *de facto* majority rule of the hacks and mediocrities. Zhdanov, it is true, tried to bureaucratize music—but somehow it didn't work.

20

The Dangerous Farce of the NTS

VERY little was known when I was in Moscow in the summer of 1967 about the trial of a young poet, Bukovsky, or about a number of similar trials in Leningrad; and the Bukovsky case would have passed almost unnoticed but for the very severe allegations made in December by Pavel Litvinov, a lecturer in physics and grandson of Maxim Litvinov, the famous Commissar for Foreign Affairs in the 1930s—the man of "collective security" and "indivisible peace." It is totally inconceivable that Pavel would have risked his job (which he immediately lost) or his freedom if he had had insufficient grounds for making his allegations, including the fact that Bukovsky had been beaten up by the police to make him "confess" anything the police required.

However, I take a rather different view of the trial of Alexander Ginsburg, Yuri Galanskov and two others in January 1968, and so, clearly, does not only Soviet public opinion generally but even those very intellectuals who fought desperately to get Siniavsky and Daniel released or at least amnestied. Whether scared or, more likely, impressed by the allegations that Ginsburg and Galanskov *were* in direct contact with the anti-Soviet NTS (National Labor Federation) organization in Germany, those relatively few intellectuals who did protest did not assume that the accused men were innocent; they simply protested against the trial not being public.

The prosecution at the trial in January 1968 alleged that Galanskov and his colleagues had received from somewhere some two thousand dollars, which they had disposed of in the black market in Moscow, and also that they had been "in direct contact with the NTS."

In this connection there appeared in the *Times Literary Supple-*

ment of February 8, 1968, an article by a correspondent who recalled a press conference held in February 1967 by the French publishers La Table Ronde. The occasion of the press conference had been the publication in French of *Le Livre blanc de l'Affaire Siniavsky-Daniel,* compiled by Alexander Ginsburg—that very Ginsburg who, with the poet Galanskov, editor of the clandestine magazine *Phoenix 66,* had now been sentenced to imprisonment in a labor camp (for terms of five and seven years respectively). As this *TLS* correspondent wrote:

> After some introductory remarks by a representative of La Table Ronde the floor was taken by a young Russian who flourished at the audience a fat typewritten copy of *Phoenix 66* which, he said, had just been received from Moscow. About a week before, he said, it was learnt that Ginsburg and Galanskov had been arrested by the Soviet police in the course of a street demonstration demanding the release of Daniel and Siniavsky. He spoke at some length of SMOG, a clandestine group of writers in Moscow. The word SMOG meant *Smelost', Mysl', Obraz, Glubina* (boldness, thought, image, depth).
>
> After the press conference, I got into conversation with the young Russian, and asked whether I could be lent the copy of *Phoenix 66.* He replied that since this was the only copy he had and as, moreover, he was leaving with it for Frankfurt the next day, where the magazine *Grani** was published, he could not let me have it. Then, after some hesitation, he said I could go to their Paris office, near the Vaugirard métro, and spend an hour or two looking through the typescript. The office turned out to be a strange, narrow, old house, with four floors but without any plate or inscription on the door. I was admitted by a young lady with a distrustful look on her face. There were several offices on the various floors, with at least a dozen people busy writing and typing furiously. However, I was given a quiet office where I was able, for a couple of hours, to peruse *Phoenix 66.* It was an untidy volume, about a dozen sections of which, typed on different machines, were loosely held together by a bit of string. It is hard to imagine that there can be many copies of this unwieldy affair in existence.

* A small-circulation magazine appearing at irregular intervals (two or three times a year), part of a much bigger publishing organization, Possev, specializing in anti-Soviet propaganda along NTS lines.

At the press conference, the young Russian had said that this and other clandestine reviews had now been published in Moscow for five or six years; until recently, they had been mainly literary, with poetry which the authorities considered "too modernist"; but latterly some of these reviews, and particularly *Phoenix*, had become "predominantly political magazines," and these pointed *to the existence of "a genuine political Opposition" in the Soviet Union—one with whom, he implied, the émigrés were in close contact.*

The *TLS* correspondent then gave an account of the contents of *Phoenix 66*, which, he said, "proved disappointing and amateurish." There was an editorial by Galanskov himself, and the final section was made up of poems by a number of unknown or little-known poets. Some of this verse was of reasonable quality but no more. But the large part of *Phoenix 66* was made up of documents which had already been published in the West before, and he concluded that as the "organ" of a "genuine political opposition" in Russia, *Phoenix 66* was "little short of ridiculous."*

The question arises whether there *was* a contact between Galanskov and the NTS. It seems possible that there may be something in the Soviet charge. On the other hand, it is also possible that Galanskov and his colleagues were genuine protesters and had no real connection with the NTS (apart from Ginsburg's sending his book on Siniavsky to La Table Ronde). It would certainly pay the NTS to claim a connection with Galanskov to show that its backers' money was having some effect.

What, then, is the NTS? Some very detailed information on it was provided in a long article by Mr. Viv Broughton in the February 2, 1968, issue of *Peace News,* a little weekly published in London. For reasons unknown to me, its editor sent me a copy of this particular issue. I found Mr. Broughton's two-page article on the NTS of considerable interest, as I also did his second article, in the February 9 issue, on Gerald Brooke, who had been arrested in Moscow for having smuggled NTS material into the Soviet Union.†

* For a full account of the contents of *Phoenix 66* and some examples of the poems it contains, see the *Times Literary Supplement* of February 8, 1968.

† Mr. Broughton quotes Mr. Harold Wilson during his visit to Moscow as describing Brooke as "a silly young man used by a disreputable organization." Mr. Broughton thinks the description "callous," but believes Mr. Wilson used it merely to ingratiate himself with the Kremlin.

In the first article, Mr. Broughton described the organization and activities of the NTS. Their purpose was nothing less than "overthrowing the Soviet system" and replacing it, not by a fascist regime, but by some kind of parliamentary democracy!

Where, then, did the NTS money come from? According to Mr. Broughton it used to come from the CIA and the British Intelligence Service, but now it came from secret sources the identity of which it would not disclose; the amount "ran into six figures." The NTS, Mr. Broughton said, had a secret bank account in Switzerland and "flooded" Russia with its leaflets. "Somewhere outside the Soviet Union" it had a wireless station called Radio Free Russia (there was even a photograph of a wagon which was supposed to be Radio Free Russia, standing on a snow-covered field); moreover, there was a huge network of a "very secret" NTS underground in Russia.

Now, there is one thing I found rather odd about this. I had spent several months in the Soviet Union in the last few years, among them the two months of 1967. I talked to every variety of people, among them some "old-regime" people, and others only lukewarm, if that, toward the Soviet system; not once did I hear anybody say anything about an NTS underground or even about having heard Radio Free Russia—though everybody talked openly about listening regularly to the BBC and the Voice of America. Nor did I ever see a single NTS leaflet or hear anybody say he had seen one. (The leaflets do apparently exist, but no doubt in only tiny quantities, mostly sent from abroad by ordinary post to anybody in, say, the Moscow phone book, on the off chance that the postal authorities would let at least a few of them through. As elsewhere, the postal censorship opens only "samples"—it could not conceivably open every letter.)

So I have come to the conclusion that once again the Americans are suckers. Senator Robert F. Kennedy, in criticizing American policy in South Vietnam, said that "hundreds of millions of dollars intended for setting up the 'American way of life' in South Vietnam scarcely ever got any farther than the pockets of thousands of South Vietnamese ministers, officials and other crooks." The same, on a smaller scale, obviously also applies to the NTS, these promoters of "the counterrevolution in Russia." The Russians today are the most intensely patriotic people in the world, and this includes those who do not much care for the Soviet system. I am convinced that the NTS are wasting their time, and that they know this perfectly well.

But they have to pretend to the Americans that the "anti-Bolshevik revolution" is, thanks to them, making wonderful progress, or else there would be no more subsidies of several hundred thousand pounds a year—and what then would the NTS live on, and how could they pay for their sumptuous offices in Paris, Frankfurt, Munich, etc.?

Quite recently an old White-Russian emigré friend of mine living in Paris told me of an extraordinary encounter he had had during a recent visit to Munich. At the most expensive Russian restaurant there he saw someone he knew eating a large helping of fresh caviar.

"Hullo!" my friend exclaimed. "It can't be you!"

But it was. My friend had known this fellow in Paris just after the war; he had arrived there as a post–Second World War emigré and had lived in Paris for a long time, making a meager living as a waiter. Now he was in Munich, obviously living in the lap of luxury.

"Well, my dear fellow, you seem to be getting on fine. What are you doing in Munich?"

"What am I doing? I'm working to overthrow the Soviet regime! Well, you see, it's like this. I am now director general of one of the great NTS organizations here, and the Yanks pay me twenty thousand dollars a year. I've never known such riches before! So I hope I'll go on overthrowing the Soviet regime for the rest of my life. Here, have a glass of our good Soviet *stolichnaya!* Here's to the health of the Soviet government; may it last forever, or at least as long as I'm alive!"

All this, in fact, is no more than a rather bad joke. But there is one potentially very grim side to it. The real basis of the Stalin-Yezhov terror was the supposition that the Soviet Union was crawling with German, British, Japanese and other foreign "spies and diversionists." With all the song and dance by the NTS about the tremendous subversive activities they are carrying on in Russia, a Soviet ruler of the Stalin type might indeed get it into his head that Russia is once again crawling with spies and that not a single Soviet citizen can be absolutely trusted not to belong to or have connections with the NTS. It might be merely a pretext for starting a new wave of police terror, or it might be a mania that some top Communist leader could genuinely develop, just as Stalin did. Thus, there is in reality only one thing that the NTS can (at least theoretically, but perhaps also in practice) achieve, and that is to unleash a wave of terror in Russia in which millions of Russians would be shot or deported. This is no joke, and I trust that those subsidizing the army of NTS parasites will think about this aspect of the problem very seriously indeed.

21

Leningrad Finale

THE most pleasant way, I found, of going from Moscow to Leningrad was by the fairly slow and leisurely train that leaves at noon. The carriage, very like an American coach, is cheerful and matey, especially in August, with nearly everybody going on holiday—civilians, and soldiers, and children. Traveling in Russia has become civilized and "European," with the added advantage that there is a camaraderie amongst all, something you wouldn't find in, say, a Paris–Bordeaux or London–Edinburgh train, where you could spend hours with people in a compartment without exchanging a word.

From time to time, there would come through the coach a young man with bright-yellow hair and a squeaky voice selling sandwiches and lemonade and ice cream. The scenery is monotonous, mostly wooded country, sparsely inhabited. There is only one big city on the way, and that one close to Moscow—Kalinin, the old Tver. Then, of course, that classical stop halfway between the two capitals, Bologoye. It figures in Chekhov stories, in *Anna Karenina,* in lots of other books. Here is a bit of the old rustic Russia which has not changed very much: the same peasant women selling little paper bags of particularly fragrant raspberries at fifteen kopecks.

It was with a touch of sadness that I was returning to Leningrad this time. In 1964 I had seen Anna Akhmatova at her tiny tumbledown *datcha* at Komarovo, and in her queenly way she had spoken to me graciously for nearly two hours. Now there was no Anna Akhmatova any more; she had died in March 1966. And I knew I would miss even more Yuri German, the Leningrad novelist, who had been a very dear friend and who had also died, in January 1967 after a long illness. I knew it would be uncanny to visit his wife,

Tatiana, in their flat overlooking the Marsovo Pole and the Summer Garden and not to find him there. His novels, many of them wartime novels with good plots and full of adventure, were unusual in Russia and, therefore, enormously popular. I never thought Yuri German a truly great writer. But he was a man of great moral courage and infinite goodness. To show what kind of man he was I need relate only this seemingly small episode: After the horrible meeting in 1946 at which the unspeakable Andrei Zhdanov demanded Zoshchenko's and Akhmatova's expulsion from the Writers' Union (Akhmatova was absent), Zoshchenko, a broken man, stood alone on the steps outside the building. All the writers walked past, pretending not to notice him. Alone Yuri German went up to the "leper" and put a hand on his shoulder. "Thank you, Yuri," said Zoshchenko, and he burst into tears. More recently Yuri German moved heaven and earth to get the poet Joseph Brodsky released after his odious "trial" and his deportation to the Far North.

I had never learned to love Moscow, which had always been to me a strange city in a strange country. The Kremlin and Red Square were to me like the stage setting for operas such as *Boris Godunov* and *Khovanshchina,* full of brutal and barbarous people. But St. Petersburg, Petrograd, Leningrad, was my native city. I had childhood friends here, and my cousin Olga, and, as it turned out, even one surviving schoolmate, who turned up after I had written an article in *Leningradskaya Pravda* a week or two after arriving there this time. Olga, now sixty-seven, thin, tall, with close-set little eyes and a mop of untidy gray hair, I had already seen in 1964 and then during a brief flying visit in 1966. Someday, when both Olga and I are dead, I may have a book published about her; although she has several war decorations, she "loathes publicity" so much that I had to promise not to write anything about her now. I can, however, say that she is a genuine heroine of the Leningrad blockade. Half dead with hunger herself, day after day she would accompany first-aid teams as a doctor, picking up the dead and the wounded, many of them children, during the shelling of Leningrad; and at the height of the famine she would also search frozen houses for any children dying of hunger and cold with no one to help. In this way she had saved dozens, perhaps hundreds. Not everyone she had rescued could be saved; some were too far gone, and, with the desperate food shortage, there was little in those days that hospitals could do even for half-dead children.

Olga, in poor health ever since the blockade, was living in the same large "communal flat" right in the heart of Leningrad, on the Moika River, a few minutes' walk from St. Isaac's Cathedral and the Bronze Horseman. Soviet patriot though she was, this was the part of Leningrad where she wanted to live to the end of her days; and she would not dream of moving to a "modern comfortable" new flat on the outskirts. Here, moreover, living next door to her, were very old friends, who also turned out to be childhood friends of mine—Nina, whom I remembered as a little girl on the beach at Kuokkala, back in 1916 and 1917, and her mother, now an old lady of eighty-six. Nina's husband, Boris, one of the great Leningrad masters of cut glass and ceramics, was charming. Olga and these three had lived and nearly died together in the blockade. Nina's father, Vasili Petrovich, who was an outstanding cellist much more than an official of the tsarist War Ministry, had died in 1938, and her brother Volodya, the exuberant young pianist, had died in the blockade—not of hunger but when a bomb destroyed the house on which he was fire-watching. He was one of the greatest of my childhood friends, and I was often asked to their house when they played chamber music. The great Siloti would sometimes be there and play Chopin or Liszt, or else (a great treat for us youngsters) reminisce about Liszt, whose pupil he had been at Weimar during the last two years of the Master's life; but usually Olga Vladimirovna, the mother, played the piano in the trios, and Vasili Petrovich the cello; the violinist was Mikhail Nikolaevich, a second fiddle from the Mariinsky. He had one son, and in 1939 this boy of nineteen or twenty was arrested suddenly and shot. He had told an "anecdote" about Stalin, and, as was later learned, it was Volodya's and my piano teacher, a Tamara Lvovna, a somber brunette, who had for some obscure reason denounced him to the NKVD.

The Stalin purges had not spared Leningrad. On the contrary, they seemed to have been particularly savage here, as though there was something about Leningrad that Stalin specially distrusted. The big purges had started here, with the mysterious murder of Kirov, a man genuinely popular in Leningrad. And there followed the period described by Anna Akhmatova and Lydia Chukovskaya, when, "like an unnecessary appendix, Leningrad dangled from its prisons."

During the blockade the people of Leningrad again showed a spirit that was, in some curious way, different from any other. In Moscow there had been a "great skedaddle" of October 1941; in Leningrad people would not leave, and their determination that the city would never be surrendered hypnotized the soldiers into stopping the Germans, who were only a mile or two outside the city boundary. Moscow was saved by the Army, not by its population, most of which panicked; in Leningrad it was the other way round: without the tremendous moral example of the Leningrad people— their determination to die rather than let the Germans in—Leningrad would not have been saved. Here was a mixture of everything: the revolutionary tradition of the Leningrad proletariat; the people's unequaled love and pride in their city; the spirit of the intelligentsia, to whom every stone of Leningrad was sacred with literary associations—Pushkin, Gogol, Dostoevsky, Blok . . .

This was a spirit that was too independent for Stalin's Russia. As we know, Stalin was prepared at one stage to surrender Leningrad. But the people of the city would not hear of it. I do not believe in the theory that Stalin allowed Leningrad to be trapped and starved out as a kind of punishment, but some believe that there may be something in it.

Strange, too, that the literary freeze was started by Zhdanov in Leningrad, of all places; in 1946 he denounced two Leningrad journals, and two Leningrad writers—Akhmatova and Zoshchenko. And the Museum of the Heroic Defense of the City was disbanded on Stalin's instructions; there was too much here about the mass sacrifice of the people, too little about Stalin. And the old museum was not allowed to be reassembled again, even after Stalin's death. Four years before he died, he staged the Leningrad Affair, in which practically all the Party leaders associated with the defense of the city were liquidated. They had become too particularist and had even had the effrontery to say that Leningrad deserved a special reward—why not make it the capital of the Russian Republic, leaving Moscow the capital of the U.S.S.R.? When I was in Leningrad during the blockade in 1943, Popkov, head of the Gorsoviet, spoke openly of this proposal. He was to be among those shot in 1949.

Perhaps Stalin's supreme insult was to give Leningrad University its new name, Zhdanov University. It was like calling an arts academy in Florence the Savonarola Art Academy. Zhdanov, the archobscurantist in art and science and literature!

There was no doubt about Stalin's malignant dislike of Leningrad. He had had the Academy of Sciences moved from there to Moscow before the war; he did not like its independent *frondeur* spirit. When Stalin died, Leningrad must have heaved a sigh of relief, though it had no great illusions about his successors—except possibly Kosygin, a Leningrad man himself. But he did not come to the forefront until much later, and Khrushchev, the central-Russian Fat-Snout, was not liked in Leningrad. They were quite openly offensive about him when I saw the people of *Leningradskaya Pravda* in 1964, two months before he was thrown out. For one thing, Moscow was now flooding Leningrad with its own papers, and the Leningrad *Pravda* had become just a little provincial sheet.

In 1964 the Leningrad writers seemed to be like the last of the Mohicans—people who had been associated all their lives with Leningrad, like Akhmatova, or, more specifically, associated with the blockade, like Olga Bergholz and Vera Ketlinskaya; the others seemed gradually to be moving to Moscow, "the center of everything." Now in 1967 I had quite a different impression: not only had the exodus to Moscow stopped, but many were coming to Leningrad; many non-native Leningraders were becoming so enamored with and so proud of their city that they were going to give it a unique place in Soviet literature. They would not allow Leningrad, the city of Pushkin, and Gogol, and Dostoevsky, and Blok and Annensky and Akhmatova, the most musical city in Russia—for this was the city of Glinka, Mussorgsky and Rimsky-Korsakov*—to become a provincial backwater, as it had nearly become when Stalin unleased Zhdanov against the martyred city.

There cannot be more than ten per cent of the four million population of Leningrad who are of truly Leningrad origin. Many native Leningraders perished in the blockade; some remained in the east together with their evacuated industries. But the newcomers soon became real Leningraders. They loved to belong to a Russian city which was different from any other, with the historical beauty of eighteenth- and nineteenty-century St. Petersburg merging with

---

* Paradoxically, the most "Western" of the famous Russian composers— Tchaikovsky, Rachmaninov and Skriabin—are Muskovites.

the romantic associations of the October Revolution and the heroic terrors of the blockade. Moscow was architecturally increasingly modern and historically insignificant; in Leningrad the old city was the same as it had been under Pushkin and Dostoevsky; the new Soviet suburbs, looking like the suburbs of any other Soviet city, were built strictly outside the old city.

Olga was very determined to remain in the old city, in the house on the Moika. One day we talked about the strange differences in our destinies. "As you know," she said, "I was determined not to go abroad. When, in 1919, my mother and two brothers emigrated, I said to them, 'Look, you can do as you like; but you'll regret it. I know we're hungry, terribly hungry, here, but this is *my* country, and this is *my* city, and I'm staying here.' And you, I suppose," she said to me, "couldn't help leaving in 1918 with your father. He would have been bumped off if he'd stayed any longer—and quite rightly, too."

I had been very reluctant to go, but my father, as a big capitalist, had subsidized the strike of Vikzhel, the railwaymen's trade union, at the beginning of the Bolshevik Revolution; and then, by hook or by crook, on some flimsy pretext, he got himself (and me) a *laissez-passer* with a German eagle stamped on it from the German Consulate General that had been opened in Petrograd after the Treaty of Brest-Litovsk. However, it was touch and go; the Cheka was on the point of arresting him. So we fled to the "freedom" of German-occupied Kiev, which was ruled by a German puppet, Hetman Skoropadsky.

"It was all rather shameful," I said, "but then lots of other members of our patriotic anti-German bourgeoisie did precisely the same; they weren't squeamish. The trouble is that national sentiment was thrown to the winds once you had to choose between the Bolsheviks and even the Kaiser's protection."

"Well, I can hardly blame you," said Olga. "You were very young then, and your father seemed to know what he was doing. And then my mother, and my brothers, and all our blessed aunts got away abroad. You're the only one in our whole family I am glad to see; I wouldn't see any of the others. You at least were with us during the war, and even—for a short time, it's true—in Leningrad during the blockade."

"But, Olga," I said, "you can't have had such an easy life these last fifty years. Didn't you ever 'sit'?"*

"Let's not talk about it; even if I did, it was for only a short time and long ago. But I can tell you this: with my bourgeois origins, I doubt whether I would have pulled through if I hadn't made a clean break with my family."

"What do you think would have happened to me if I'd stayed?" I asked.

"Well, my own father died long before the Revolution, and my mother was harmless enough from the Soviet point of view; but your father *was* an active counterrevolutionary. I don't know what would have happened to you, but I imagine nothing very good. If it hadn't been at the beginning, you would have got trapped by the Stalin purges, or you would have died of hunger in Leningrad. I suppose it *was* lucky for you to have got that filthy German pass in 1918. . . . No, it wasn't an easy time we Soviet people had, least of all we Leningraders. That blockade was really something. But I'm proud to have justified my existence even in that small way."

She was not only a Soviet patriot, but above all a Leningrad patriot. If she disliked Paris, where she had never been but where her emigré mother and two brothers (now all dead) had lived, she did not like Moscow much better. It was barbarous, provincial, vulgar. Her reaction was typical: "In Leningrad we live in the midst of beauty, but what's beautiful about Moscow?" And I think she loathed the Germans more than anyone in Moscow did by now. There were lots of tourists in Leningrad that summer; she was indifferent to the British and the Americans, rather liked the French ("for we all respect de Gaulle"), but thought it indecent of the Germans—whether West or East—to come to Leningrad "after all they had done to us."

"Toward the end of the war," she said, "when the blockade was over, I was sent to a hospital for German war prisoners not far from Leningrad. I couldn't stand it for more than a day. I kept on thinking and thinking and thinking of my starved and murdered Leningrad children. So, in the end, I said to the colonel in charge, 'Look, I can't stand it. I did the whole Leningrad blockade, and I can't, I can't, I can't behave like a normal doctor toward these

---

* "Sitting" is the all-too-familiar colloquialism for "being in jail."

people.' The colonel said this was quite irregular from a professional point of view. However, he said he understood. And he let me return to Leningrad that same night."

She was living on an undeservedly small pension of only sixty rubles a month, but was quite happy. The blockade had wrecked her digestion, and she ate hardly anything except bread and butter and tea and boiled vegetables or kasha, and her room cost her only five rubles a month. It was crammed with books, and she had a record-player and hundreds of records. She wore any old thing, but spent nearly all her money on books and records—Bach and Beethoven at a pinch, but above all Tchaikovsky and Rachmaninov, and Italian opera. Shostakovich she loathed, and she barely tolerated Prokofiev, making an exception only for his Third Piano Concerto.

I need not describe here the Neva Embankments, the Summer Garden, the Winter Palace and the other places that millions of tourists have seen, scarcely any of them realizing that twenty-five years ago they were littered with the dead bodies of those who had collapsed and died of hunger. It was a kind of *radeau du Méduse* multiplied thousands of times. People were driven insane by hunger; some ate pieces of dead bodies lying in the street and would then often die of ptomaine poisoning. But those who survived now formed a kind of Leningrad aristocracy, as proud of what they had done as were the survivors of the defense of Stalingrad or Sebastopol.

I visited my old friend Mikhail Stepanovich Kurtynin, editor of *Leningradskaya Pravda,* and his deputy, Boris Abramovich Feld, in a new building on the Fontanka, behind the old Alexandrinka Theater, where in my schooldays I used to see the great Davydov playing in Ostrovsky plays, and Yuriev in *Gore ot Uma,* and Gorin-Goriainov in Gogol's *Inspector General.* He asked me to write him an article on my impressions of Leningrad during the Fiftieth Jubilee year. I wrote it in Russian, resisting as much as I could the temptation to fall into Soviet newspaper jargon and newspaper clichés. The next day after publication I received several astonishing phone calls. One was from the secretary of the boys' school in Tambov Street, on the southern outskirts of Leningrad, which I had visited during the blockade. She explained that the headmaster, Comrade Kamenetsky, could not speak on the phone himself, as he had been deaf since the blockade, but he remembered my visit in 1943 and would be glad if I came to see them again, though because of the summer holidays all the children were at *datchas* or in holiday camps.

I had described that visit at great length in the book I wrote at the time and published in London in 1944 under the title *Leningrad*. The school was then only some three miles from the German lines, and this part of the city was shelled more than most, but the boys were cheerful all the same, full of optimism that the war would soon be won and that the German *svolochi* would be driven from Leningrad in a few months. Oh, they were glad to get American chocolate, but they'd rather have the Second Front. I had talked to the boys (those were the days when coeducation had temporarily been stopped on Stalin's instructions), and also to the headmaster, Comrade Tikhomirov, an elderly man who had been a teacher since 1907. He had died in 1965, and had been replaced by his deputy, Y. M. Kamenetsky. The latter was a remarkable man. Although stone deaf since the blockade—hunger affected people in a variety of ways—he ran the school with the greatest authority, lip-reading and using a little notebook in which people scribbled their answers if he could not understand by watching their mouths. He showed me all the workshops and labs—these had been enormously enlarged since the war—and said he remembered how I had quoted that extraordinary Famine Diary composed of essays written by schoolchildren during the famine months and ending with the headmaster's obituaries of the teachers who had died in the famine. He was glad I had reproduced those extracts in *Russia at War,* which I now presented to him in Russian.

Before I left, I quoted to him a passage from *Leningrad* concerning the Tambov Street school in September 1943:

We [I and Savva Dangulov] were seen to the car by the headmaster and the Pioneers' Guide, the lovely girl with the dark hair, lively dark eyes and fresh red cheeks. Pointing across the courtyard, she said, "That's the place where one of our women teachers was killed by a shell on the first of May." And as we went out into the street, with its eyeless houses, she said, giving me a friendly feminine smile and a warm manly handshake, "You will come and see us again next time you are in Leningrad?" And as we drove down toward the Obvodny Canal, with its cabbagetapestried slopes, I felt that here was one of those Russian girls who in no time can set a man daydreaming, and suddenly make him think of his life in terms of "ifs" and "if onlys."*

I asked the headmaster about this girl; did he remember her? Probably a mother of several children by now, I suggested. The headmaster shook his head sadly. "No. About ten days after your visit a shell hit our school, and she was killed. Yes, just like that woman teacher she told you about that day."

As I have said before, I had still had the impression in 1964 that Leningrad was gradually dying off as a great cultural center; but now, on the contrary, even despite the deaths of Akhmatova and Yuri German, those fanatical Leningraders, the city was determined to be its own individual self. It had an immense literary tradition which Moscow hadn't got: the serene, harmonious, sunny St. Petersburg of Pushkin, to whom this was Peter's "window to the West"; and the crazy, surrealist St. Petersburg of Gogol's *Nose,* and the sinister St. Petersburg of Dostoevsky's *Crime and Punishment* and *The Idiot* and his *Notes from the Underworld,* not to mention all the other St. Petersburgs—the mystical, poetic St. Petersburg of Blok; the more than surrealist St. Petersburg of Belyi; the doomed St. Petersburg of Innokenti Annensky; and that of Osip Mandelstam and Anna Akhmatova. Moscow had never inspired writers as St. Petersburg had, except very, very rarely, as in a few Pasternak verses, like *On Early Trains.* The only truly great literature on Moscow was really that of two superb satirists, Griboyedov and Ostrovsky.

The blockade and Stalin had very nearly killed Leningrad; and now—now there *seemed* to be a revival. I was sorry not to see my old friend Olga Bergholz, the great poet of the blockade, but she had gone south. But I met the admirable Vera Ketlinskaya at her *datcha* at Komarovo on the Gulf of Finland, quite near the place where I had visited Akhmatova three years before. Ketlinskaya was writing new—and more original—books on Leningrad and was the editor of a remarkable new annual, *Molodoi Leningrad,* full of fresh and specifically Leningrad talent, where there was much that was

---

* The slopes of the canal, like any other cultivable piece of ground, were used for growing vegetables during the blockade. (See *Leningrad,* p. 89.)

fantastic and mildly surrealist, and above all new. Much of it smelled of wet ropes and ships and the pale Baltic and was wrapped in a Leningrad mist or glittered with the wet pavements of the Nevsky Prospekt. Leonid Borich, author of a sixty-page short novella characteristically called "Welcome, Sea!," was one of the thirty-three contributors. There was Andrei Bitov's other novella, equally unconventional in its writing, "Journey to a Childhood Friend"; and Olga Larionova's "Lost in the Future: A Fantastic Tale"; and poets—many of them genuine poets, like Alexander Kushner, Alexander Morev, Vladimir Trifonov, Joseph Brodsky, Yuri Burygin, Anatoli Berger and so on. It is unfair to quote half a dozen names almost at random out of more than thirty. Most of them are young and talented and had something specifically Leningrad in their manner. One evening I had looked through a copy of the Moscow *Znamya*—two short stories, both flat and obvious and undistinguished, and literary essays, all equally trite, reflecting the orthodox views of its socialist-realist editor, Vadim Kozhevnikov; and here was this *Young Leningrad*—full of surprises, and practically none of it obvious. In Moscow, Vasili Aksyonov's writing came nearest to this kind of thing.

I wish I had room to examine all these pieces of prose and poetry one by one. Of course one name stands out, not because he is necessarily the greatest Leningrad poet, but because of the "Brodsky scandal," which the Western press wrote about a lot at the time. One of the bosses of the Leningrad Writers' Union, the Establishment poet Alexander Prokofiev, took a violent dislike to him, and young Brodsky was tried as a "parasite" and a "vagrant." He was sentenced to several years in a labor camp, but in fact was sent to a kolkhoz near Archangel and was made to carry dung from one place to another. This went on for a year or more, and then he was suddenly released. Anna Akhmatova thought him one of Russia's best poets, and Kornei Chukovsky and Shostakovich, and Samuel Marshak and, in Leningrad, Yuri German and lots of other people thought the trial the height of absurdity. Finally the authorities had to release him.

Unlike Akhmatova, Ketlinskaya did not think him all that outstanding, but thought him a first-rate translator, especially of English seventeenth-century verse. What had annoyed some of the pundits of the Writers' Union was that he threw his weight about too much, fancied himself the Leningrad version of Voznesensky and Yevtushenko, loved to bellow his poems at all kinds of meetings; so they decided to teach him a lesson. It was all both odious and ridiculous.

I went to see Brodsky. There was something childishly and Jewishly arrogant about him; and he did bellow his poetry—some of it a little mystical, mildly religious, obscure in spots, but enormously effective in its rhythms, rhymes, images and rhetorical sweep. He had on his desk *The Oxford Book of Seventeenth Century Verse*; and besides translating John Donne and other seventeenth-century poets, he used them as inspiration for his own work and even wrote a long *Elegy to John Donne,* which, together with other poems of his, was recently published in English.* Another Western poet he deeply admired, translated and imitated was T. S. Eliot.

I wish I could quote the title poem, but it is too long, and this extract will do to show Brodsky's Van Gogh–like sense of shape and color:

> *I clasped those shoulders and I snatched a glance*
> *At what lay half revealed behind that back,*
> *And saw the chair moved out into the room,*
> *Merged with the illumination and the wall.*
> *A raised, extended glare lurked in the bulb,*
> *Unwise for furnishings so worn and thready,*
> *Which made the sofa and the corner shine*
> *From brown and chestnut leather, too bright-yellow.*
> *The table empty, parquet floor ablaze,*
> *The stove all dark, inside a dusty frame*
> *A landscape froze, the sideboard standing bare*
> *Appeared to be the only living thing.*
> *But then a moth went circling round the room*
> *And moved my glance from trantic immobility.*
> *And if some ghost had ever settled here,*
> *It soon forsook this dwelling, twice forsaken.†*

---

* Joseph Brodsky, *Elegy to John Donne and Other Poems,* selected and translated by Nicholas Bethell (Longmans, 1967).

† Quoted with Nicholas Bethell's kind permission. I have substituted "clasped" for Bethell's "kissed" in the first line and have inserted line 13, which is omitted in Bethell's version.

Brodsky's poems are scattered through a variety of magazines and almanacs, but he hopes that, with the publication of his translations from seventeenth-century English verse in book form (and perhaps another book), he will be admitted to the Leningrad Writers' Union. For the rest, he said, "Of course I am a vagrant, of course I am a parasite." He seems to write a lot, but mostly for the bottom drawer. Nevertheless, he already had a big reputation among Leningrad writers, the liberals loving him and the conservatives loathing him. No doubt he had a bumptious, disagreeably aggressive side to him; but was not this natural? Anna Akhmatova had thought him a major poet, but they had made him go through an odious trial and had sent him for a year or more to cart dung in a kolkhoz near icy Archangel; and he couldn't get his poems published in book form.

Compared with the Moscow Writers' Union, that of Leningrad is clearly less conservative. Alexander Prokofiev, the archconservative, though still on the forty-eight-member board of the Leningrad Writers' Union and held responsible for the "Brodsky scandal," was recently eliminated from the more select secretariat of nine members, which now includes such liberal names as Daniel Granin (whose admirable travel books and novels, including a recent travel book on Australia, are well known in the West, and who is now head of the union's secretariat); it also includes Ketlinskaya, excellent novelist and editor of *Molodoi Leningrad,* Vera Panova and several other well-known names. There are altogether about four hundred members in the Leningrad Writers' Union, including fifty-four playwrights, fifty-four writers of children's books, twenty-two who call themselves "phantasts," and twenty-two "satirists."

Perhaps my most interesting talk was with Alexander Rosen, who had recently written an exciting historical novel, *The Last Fortnight,* dealing with the moods among a group of people a fortnight before the German invasion. He was a typical Leningrader; it was he who spoke at length of the unique psychological process whereby the Leningrad people's determination not to abandon the city had communicated itself to the hitherto wholly demoralized Army during the most critical days of August and September 1941. There had never been anything quite like it anywhere during the war: civilian morale restoring the very low morale of the troops. No doubt Zhukov's taking over on September 11 from the utterly incompetent

Voroshilov had also helped to save Leningrad; but without the spirit of the Leningrad people, even Zhukov would have been helpless.

Leningrad had also great cultural achievements to its credit outside literature proper. There was Lenfilm, the Leningrad film studios which were producing some of the finest Soviet films—several famous ones by Vengenov, Heifetz's *Lady with the Dog* (after the Chekhov story), Ivanov's *Pervorossiane,* Shapiro's *Katerina Izmailova* (after the Leskov story), and, last but not least, Kozintsev's superb and highly original *Hamlet,* with I. Smoktunovsky in the title role and Vertinskaya (daughter of Alexander Vertinsky, the famous cabaret singer) playing an unforgettable Ophelia. My two favorites of recent Soviet films, *Once There Lived an Old Man and an Old Woman* and *The Ballad of a Soldier,* were not made in Leningrad, but many of the finest recent Soviet films do come from Lenfilm studios. What I think distinguishes the best Soviet films from "approved" Soviet novels is a kind of warm humanity (as, for instance, in the two just mentioned)—something very akin to classical Russian literature, and something very unusual in Western films today, with their frequent cruelty and cynicism. Leningrad also has some of the finest theatrical producers, such as G. Tovstovsky and N. Akimov; probably the greatest of Russian conductors, E. Mravinsky; and several highly distinguished composers, as we have seen.

We must not assume that the heavy hand of the "heirs of Stalin" will always spare Leningrad; the trial of Brodsky showed that it existed here too; but Leningrad opinion—assisted, it is true, by ex-Leningraders like Chukovsky and Shostakovich—still somehow managed to have him brought back from his Archangel dungheap within a fairly short time.

The fact remains, however, that Stalin made a point of persecuting Leningrad on every possible occasion, and stamping out its individuality; is the danger of a new anti-Leningrad offensive completely past? There undoubtedly exists a certain anti-Moscow polycentrism in Leningrad. But is Leningrad a freer city than Moscow today? Yes, of the two cities Leningrad assuredly feels freer. In the local Writers' Union the liberals predominate, whereas the Moscow union is dominated by the ultras, and the Leningrad climate may even have had a mellowing effect on the censorship there. All the same, one comes across a few anomalies pointing to the presence in

Leningrad too of some ultras in the top Party organizations. Thus, a number of avante-garde Moscow theatrical productions have been prohibited in Leningrad, and the famous Italian film *Divorce Italian Style,* which was shown not only all over Moscow but even in the small town of Oranienbaum some twenty-five miles from Leningrad, was banned in Leningrad itself!

My *Leningradskaya Pravda* article produced two other unexpected phone calls. One was from a former schoolmate of mine, now a venerable professor of English. The son of a well-known St. Petersburg doctor, he was one of the comparatively rare Soviet citizens I met who had somehow sailed through the fifty years of the Soviet regime without ever having had any trouble, not even during the purges. He had stuck to his job of teaching English, was now a full-fledged professor and the author of several textbooks, and he still lived in the same flat where I had visited him about fifty years ago; his father had only recently died, aged ninety-five. He himself had had only one uncomfortable period—when he was in the Army as an interpreter on the Leningrad front and "felt so hungry that, for the first time in my life, I took to smoking, just to keep my hunger down." He was married, but had no children. When I went to see him, he showed me a photo taken of our whole class, back in 1912, when we were each eleven. And this was a grim sight. Our brilliant Polish-born history master, Viktorin Strzeszkovski, had died in the Leningrad famine, and so had one or two others in the photograph; two had been killed in the war; several others had died since the war. It had been an odd school; it was one of the three great German schools where the upper bourgeoisie and some of the top bureaucracy liked to send their children to "get a European culture." The teaching language was German, but in 1914 it had promptly to be changed over to Russian, which some of the teachers, though Russian subjects, scarcely knew. Of the thirty boys in the photo, we knew for certain that only four were alive—the two of us, a Swiss *grand bourgeois* with whom I had recently spent a weekend at Zurich, and another man who was a White emigré in Stockholm

We had several long talks. In the course of one of them I said, "But, Boris, you surely knew I was in Moscow during the war, and especially after my famous interview with Stalin in 1946. Why didn't you write?"

"Oh," he said, "be your age! To write to a foreigner in the Stalin days—why, it was more than your life was worth."

"But now?" I said.

"Oh, now—now it's quite, *quite* different."

This was one of the best things I heard throughout that 1967 visit to the Soviet Union. If this very cautious professor, who had steered his life so carefully through these fifty years, said so, then it must be true, I felt. Were we not seeing Stalinist ghosts even where there were none?

However, my other phone call resulted in a story which, though it had a relatively happy ending, was a grim one for all that.

"This is Maria Pavlenko speaking. Does the name—my maiden name—mean anything to you?"

I thought for a moment. "Well, yes, I did have some second cousins of that name."

"Well, I *am* a second cousin of yours."

She came to see me—a woman of sixty-eight, in reasonably good health, and even quite elegantly dressed. She had had a first husband, rather a boring little man, when I last saw her. But then, in 1923, she married again, this time a Pole, though a Soviet citizen. They had a son. Then in 1937 her husband was arrested and shot as "an enemy of the people." Her three brothers were killed in the war. Her son, though only sixteen then and a son of an "enemy of the people," had volunteered in 1941 for the Red Army and had been killed soon after.

"But then," I said, "when we visited you at Sheshaki in the German-occupied Ukraine in 1918,* you had a very handsome Georgian lieutenant with whom you seemed to be much in love."

"Yes," she said, "it was a great love affair. Yes, poor Irakli. He also was killed in the war."

And she herself? After the arrest of her husband, she was deported to the Far North, and she remained in exile (though not in a camp) for *twenty-five years*. It was not till 1962 that both she and her dead husband were finally rehabilitated (that is, declared not

---

* The occupation of the Ukraine by Wilhelm II was very mild and correct compared with the inhuman Nazi occupation of the Second World War.

guilty); and it was only then that she was allowed to return to her native Leningrad, where she was now living on a small old-age pension of forty rubles a month.

Here was an all-too-typical story of a Russian family—more typical than that of my English professor. A whole family destroyed, except this one woman. All she now had was a cousin and the latter's son. I did not meet either of them, but she brought along the young man's charming young wife. This one was of that new generation—like my friend Sasha—who scarcely remembered Stalin, knew nothing of wars, of hunger, of purges, or camps, and thought the Soviet Union the most wonderful country in the world.

22

Why They Invaded Czechoslovakia

I WISH I could conclude on this note. Of course, in saying that the Soviet Union was the most wonderful country in the world, the sweet young thing had really no standards of comparison. She had never been abroad, not even to Helsinki; but *her* Russia was truly wonderful compared with the Russia of which her parents and grandparents had told her. And, like most young Russians today, she was not starry-eyed about foreign countries, as they were ten years ago. Maybe, they now argued, things were still much better in Stockholm than in Leningrad; but then Sweden had not been involved in any real war for over two hundred years; and for Russia to catch up with Sweden was now only a matter of perhaps ten or twenty years.

And what does this young Soviet generation really think of the outer world? There is only a small part of Europe for which there is really wholehearted admiration: Scandinavia, France and Italy. There are greater doubts about England, what with devaluation, inflation, a race problem of her own, and a "Socialist" prime minister who was, whatever the reasons, the only Western-European statesman to have staunchly supported the American war in Vietnam throughout. West Germany presents to the Russians a special psychological problem, and it is hard for any Russian to be happy about her, whatever her economic achievements and her unquestionable technical efficiency. The Eastern-European socialist countries are "friends," but in varying degrees. Until recently Czechoslovakia was thought to be the best friend, and her revolt in 1968 came as a shock; the non-Slav Hungarians and Rumanians are not believed to be real friends, less even than the East Germans;

Poland, without being a real friend (the centuries of antagonism between Poland and Russia have not been entirely overcome), is, however, the Soviet Union's most important military ally; what unites Russia and Poland (and Czechoslovakia, for that matter) above all else is their common distrust of Germany, and their constant awareness of the "German menace." I have talked before of the Russian attitude to the "developing" countries and need say no more.

And America? Here there is clearly, at least on the Russian side, a kind of love-hate attitude. On the one hand, Russians have an immense respect for America's might and stupendous industrial efficiency, as well as a profound interest, especially among the intellectuals, in American culture, literature and art; on the other hand, she is felt to be by far the most dangerous "imperialist power," one with aggression in her blood, as the war in Vietnam shows. America will also be increasingly troubled by its Negro and other racial problems.

Yet, at heart, no Russian really believes in a Soviet–American war; for this, as we have seen, would mean the end of everything, for both Russia and America—and most probably for the rest of the world. There is a strong feeling in Russia that there is a sort of unwritten agreement between the Soviet Union and the United States never to start a nuclear war, and, what is more, that there is a similar tacit agreement between these two and China. This may sound completely cynical in the case of Russia and China; but the truth is that, in a sense, the war in Vietnam suits them both, if only because it discredits America in the eyes of the whole world. Both give help to Vietnam—Russia with enormous quantities of military equipment and (probably) a large number of military instructors and advisers, China also with armaments and with many thousands of men repairing, almost overnight, the roads, railways and bridges damaged or destroyed by the American Air Force.

However, 1968 was not to prove a comfortable year for the Soviet government. True, it derived, at least for a time, some satisfaction from America's growing recognition of the ruinous futility of the war in Vietnam, and from President Johnson's reluctant decision to start peace talks with the North Vietnamese in Paris in May. It was gratifying for the Russians to feel that in the name of socialist solidarity they had helped North Vietnam and the Vietcong to hold out as long as they did. But by the autumn of 1968 the Paris peace talks had still produced no results, even though the United States was finding the thirty billion dollars a year the war was costing her increasingly burdensome; in comparison, the two billion dollars the Soviet Union was spending on Vietnam was a tolerable, though unpleasant, expense. Though nothing was said about this in the Soviet press, China too was helping with small arms and with thousands of men rapidly mending the roads and bridges smashed by the American bombers. But although there was better coordination than before between Russia and China in helping Vietnam, relations between the two countries were showing no signs of improvement; both the Western and the Soviet press spoke of increasingly chaotic conditions in China, and the attacks on "the Mao Tse-tung clique" were becoming more and more violent in the Russian press.

But there was something that worried the Soviet government far more than China or Vietnam, and that was Czechoslovakia. Ever since February 1948, when the Communists in Prague seized control of Czechoslovakia, the Czechs had been the least troublesome of all Russia's satellites. After Yugoslavia's rebellion against Stalinism in the summer of 1948, Czechoslovakia was—or at least seemed—the most wholehearted in her condemnation of Titoism. The Stalinist terror, it is true, was fiercer in Czechoslovakia than almost anywhere else, and arrests were far more numerous than in the other satellite countries, notably Poland; but, on the other hand, a large part of the population, either out of conviction or for safety's sake, jumped on the Stalinist bandwagon. This state of affairs continued under Klement Gottwald, Antonín Zapotocky and Antonín Novotny. During the major troubles in Poland and Hungary in 1956, Czechoslovakia did not budge. It was not till 1962 that the giant Stalin monument dominating Prague was pulled down.

The trouble, from the Russian point of view, did not start in Czechoslovakia until 1966, and, significantly, it started among the students and writers. With the Kremlin's blessing, Novotny dealt ruthlessly with the "disorders."

When Novotny was ousted from his position as secretary of the Czech Communist Party on January 5, 1968, and his successor, Alexander Dubček, embarked on a course of liberalization, most of this book had already been completed. I have explained in the preface how grave a view I took of the Czechoslovak situation from January, when Dubček took over, and especially from the moment he and his friends in the Party and the government abolished the censorship—thus fulfilling that "incredible" demand Alexander Solzhenitsyn had made, in the case of the Soviet Union, in his famous letter to the Writers' Congress in May 1967. To the Kremlin bureaucrats and those of the Moscow Writers' Union, Dubček was simply the international equivalent of Solzhenitsyn—a man who for years had been under constant police persecution, complete with the confiscation of most of his manuscripts.

By May 1968 it seemed to me that an invasion of Czechoslovakia was a possibility, since Dubček and, with him, the entire Czechoslovak people were obviously extremely reluctant to yield to Russian economic pressure, threats and blackmail. But I still thought that the price Russia would have to pay in international terms for this invasion would make her hesitate. In July, after the orgy of love and kisses at Bratislava between the Czechs on the one hand and the Russians, the East Germans, the Bulgarians and the Poles on the other, the situation seemed better again.

But the Kremlin leaders, or, rather, those whose invasion plan was finally adopted, completely miscalculated their chances.* They assumed that the Czechs would accept the occupation with the same Good-Soldier-Schweik shrug of the shoulders as they had accepted Hitler's invasion of Bohemia and Moravia in March 1939, and that the establishment of a puppet government would be a matter of a few hours. But the Nazi invasion of 1939 and the Russian invasion of 1968 had entirely different contexts.

The Czechs did not prove fatalistic this time, and although President Ludvik Svoboda and Alexander Dubček did not have the physical means of fighting the Russian armed forces, they knew that the overwhelming majority of Czechoslovaks were absolutely hostile to the Russian invaders. The Russians, in making their fateful decision, imagined that a substantial part of the country would show, if not joy, at least a relative indifference and resignation toward Russia's "brotherly help," and that a quisling would turn up

---

* Some of what follows is taken from an article, "The Censorship War," which was published in *The Nation* September 16, 1968, but which I wrote on August 28, a week after the invasion.

without much difficulty. There is no denying the existence of potential quislings in Czechoslovakia—in any country ambitious scoundrels can be found in such circumstances—but the reason nobody volunteered to set up a puppet government lay precisely in the fact that the whole of Czechoslovak public opinion would have regarded any such government as utterly odious and unacceptable.

But one must ask the determining reason for the Russian invasion. The existence of a "bourgeoisie" inside Czechoslovakia was not the real reason for the invasion. Nor was the "German menace" and the alleged Czech collusion with "the militarists and *revanchards* of West Germany." This is one of the silliest of all the Russian arguments used. Even the fact that some Czech leaders may have seriously thought of establishing diplomatic relations with West Germany was no reason for the invasion. Rumania has had diplomatic relations with West Germany for a long time and the Russians did nothing about it; moreover, for many years the Soviet Union herself has had both trade and diplomatic relations with Bonn.

The real, indeed the only, reason for the invasion of Czechoslovakia was the liberalization of the regime and (to the Russians) the unholy alliance of socialism and intellectual freedom. The timing was significant: it was essential to occupy the country before the opening of the Czech Communist Party congress, scheduled for September 9, which would have produced a virtually all-liberal Central Committee, eliminating from it the last remnants of the Stalinite-Novotnyite element. And the greatest crime of the liberals, in the Russian view, was their championing of a free press, free speech, and uncensored radio and TV. This plague might have spread to Moscow!

One of the biggest phobias of the Russian government is its fear of the kind of intellectual polycentrism which, as I found last year (and as this book shows), manifested itself in the non-Russian parts of the Soviet Union (Georgia, Armenia, the Ukraine) and also in a city like Leningrad, which, though Russian, has a long pro-Western and anti-Muscovite tradition of its own. This terror of independent thinking *inside* the Soviet Union (which Moscow hastens to brand "bourgeois nationalism" in the case of the non-Russian areas and "tsarist nostalgia" in the case of Leningrad) helps to explain the extreme exasperation caused in Moscow by the fantastically independent way of thinking that has developed in Czechoslovakia. In its famous *Survey* of the first fifty years of the Soviet regime the Central Committee of the CPSU pays lip service to polycentrism— to every foreign Communist party's right to follow its own course, in accordance with the local conditions—and to the sacrosanct principles of national sovereignty and noninterference in the internal affairs of other countries. We have now witnessed how all these lofty principles have been respected in the case of Czechoslovakia.

The Prague coup, more than anything the Russians have done since the Second World War, has made the Soviet Union hateful in the eyes of the world. Rumania, Yugoslavia and Czechoslovakia have become violently anti-Soviet; the Italian and French Communist parties now detest Brezhnev; numerous reports show that Poland and Hungary are in a state of extreme nervousness bordering on Russophobia. The great reputation the Russians have tried for years to build up as the number-one peace factor in the world—as the nation which is helping North Vietnam in the name of socialist solidarity and in the name of peace, and which has behaved with commendable restraint in the case of the Arab–Israeli war—has now been blown to the winds.

Why was this done? Primarily because of the maniacal desire of the Moscow bureaucrats to silence the free Czech press. Inside Russia, censorship is the pillar on which the Stalinist conformism of the Soviet Union rests. In the other socialist countries there is also a censorship of varying severity, which may be one reason why, despite much else the Russians dislike about Rumania, they have left that country alone (at least up until now). And when one considers it, Stalin behaved infinitely more cautiously and intelligently over Yugoslovia than Brezhnev did over Czechoslovakia. Stalin denounced Titoism as a heresy, took economic sanctions against Yugoslavia, isolated her as a leper, but did nothing more about it; no tanks were sent to Belgrade. And the context of Budapest was also different: it could be argued that there *was* a counterrevolution there, encouraged both by Radio Free Europe and by the powerful Catholic hierarchy.

What puzzled me most of all during the weeks following the invasion was how the Russian people were reacting to it. For years they had been told about the sanctity of national sovereignty and about noninterference in the internal affairs of foreign countries and foreign CP's as two of the golden rules of the Soviet Union's "peace-loving" foreign policy. And now? The reactions were very slow in coming. One of the reasons for this may have been that the Russian government had resumed, for the first time in many years, the jamming of the Voice of America, the BBC and other foreign radio stations with a Russian-language news service. This certainly must have had a deadening effect on many of the less sophisticated Russians I had met. But I still found it hard to believe that even they would lap up as gospel truth the incredible Yuri Zhukov editorials in *Pravda* and the even more incredible stories by the Soviet correspondents writing from Prague (or at least claiming to write from Prague) of the deep friendliness and gratitude shown to the Soviet soldiers, their "liberators," by the Czech people; these correspondents added, however, that some Czechs were very unpleasant and unfriendly—which just showed how wise the Soviet government had been to send troops into Czechoslovakia, with its by no means negligible number of counterrevolutionaries.

I wrote to several Russian friends in September and October. Simply personal friends (with the one exception whose letter is quoted on the title page) did not answer; clearly, they were scared to write to anyone living abroad. Of the three Stalinites to whom I wrote, only one replied. His letter was friendly; he deplored my misunderstanding of the situation; but what his letter amounted to was nothing that I had not already read in *Pravda* or *Izvestia*, except for one highly significant phrase: "Perhaps in the end you will agree with me or I may agree with you. Time will show."

But I was certain that the numerous liberals whom the reader has already met in this book must feel about Czechoslovakia as we did. The proof came with the trial of Pavel Litvinov and Larissa Daniel—the wife of Daniel the writer—who, with a few others, had had the almost incredible courage to stage a "Hands off Czechoslovakia" demonstration in the Red Square. They were, of course, almost immediately picked up by the MVD.

But something more important transpired a few days later, and the best report of it, to my knowledge, appeared in the Paris *Le Monde,* under the byline of Henri Pierre, the paper's Moscow correspondent. What Pierre said was, briefly, this:

Since the invasion of Czechoslovakia, the bureaucrats of the Writers' Union, as well as other Soviet officials, had been pestering both writers and scientists to sign a declaration heartily applauding the sending of Soviet troops into Czechoslovakia to help the brotherly Czechoslovak people against both the counterrevolutionaries and the West-German *revanchards* threatening the independence of that admirable socialist country. Naturally, Alexander Chakovsky, the editor of *Literaturnaya Gazeta,* and the like signed the declaration; so also (for reasons best known to himself) did Professor Nesmeyanov, the president of the Academy of Sciences. But, apart from the inevitable Sholokhov, not a single writer of any standing signed it, and not even any of the second- and third-rate writers (except one hack poet); nor did a single even mildly prominent scientist, technician or engineer. In fact, the vast majority of all writers, technicians and scientists of all levels throughout the Soviet Union refused to sign the declaration, some bluntly—among them Leonov, Tvardovsky and Yevtushenko, who said he could never again look into the eyes of a Czech friend without feeling the deepest shame. Even such very conformist writers as Konstantin Fedin, president of the Writers' Union, made some excuse for not signing.

So Henri Pierre's report showed that the Soviet intellectuals—including the technicians—almost unanimously said no. And yet what, in reality, can they do, apart from silently protesting? Not all are heroes like Pavel Litvinov and Larissa Daniel. They are perpetually conscious of an invisible police pressure surrounding them, which makes them feel utterly helpless.

The hopes and the fears are much as before. The fears continue to center on the Russian leaders' repression and horror of freedom of expression and ideas. The Czechoslovak censorship, which Dubček tried for a long time to restore as only a limited kind of censorship, is by now probably not very different from what has existed for nearly forty years in the Soviet Union. A Stalinlike police terror, or even a Soviet-type police oppression, has not yet, as I write this in November 1968, reappeared in Czechoslovakia; but I fear there may be something in the gloomy prophecies made at a press conference in Vienna a few days ago by L. Mnacko, the well-known Czech novelist. The day may not be far off, he said, when the first arrests will be made by the Soviet police or their stooges in the Czech police, after which President Svoboda, Dubček, Josef Smrkovsky and Premier Oldřich Černik will have to resign as a sign of protest.

The harsh cynicism I found when I inquired into the treatment of writers and intellectuals in Russia has been revealed for all to see in Czechoslovakia. But hopes for a steady liberalization are not dead. The aspirations I heard voiced by so many Russians are still alive in the actions of radicals like Litvinov and Mrs. Daniel, and in the resistance of the Writers' Union.

Between the two forces, the Russian man in the street probably remains almost untouched. All that really concerns him is the question of when he and his family will move into a new flat or where they will go for their holidays next year. To him, Czechoslovakia, and its "counterrevolution" are no more a piece of exciting news than what *Pravda* says, for instance, about that wicked man Mao Tse-tung, or about the errors of the French Communist Party, or about the new President of the United States. All this, to many Russians, is infinitely less interesting than next Saturday's football match.

Index